WJEC/Eduqas

Media Studies

Revised Edition

for A Level Year 1 & AS

Christine Bell • Lucas Johnson

Illuminate Publishing

Published in 2022 by Illuminate Publishing Limited, an imprint of Hodder Education, an Hachette UK Company, Carmelite House, 50 Victoria Embankment, London EC4Y 0DZ

Orders: Please visit www.illuminatepublishing.com
or email sales@illuminatepublishing.com

British Library Cataloguing-in-Publication Data

A catalogue record for this book is available from the British Library
ISBN 978-1-913963-28-6

Produced by DZS Grafik, Printed in Slovenia

Editor: Dawn Booth
Design and layout: Kamae Design
Cover design: Nigel Harriss
Cover image: iStock / dem10

Authors' acknowledgements
Huge thanks to Eve and Dawn for their endless support, advice and patience and also to Jo Johnson at WJEC.

Thanks also to the following former students of Heaton Manor School, Newcastle who allowed their work to be used: Azura Alwi, Hannah Phipps, Olivia Cullen, Joe Lunec and Simba Makuvatsine.

Contents

9 Examination Preparation and Tips 244

10 Quick Guide to Theoretical Approaches 262

How to Use this Book

Introduction

The content of this student book is designed for those learners following the linear Eduqas Media Studies specification in England and Northern Ireland. However, some of the content is also relevant to those following the modular WJEC specification in Wales and Northern Ireland. For the WJEC specification there is an overview at the end of this section and there are helpful indicators throughout this book showing you the sections of the Eduqas content that are relevant to the WJEC specification. Look out for the information in orange WJEC boxes, as seen on the right.

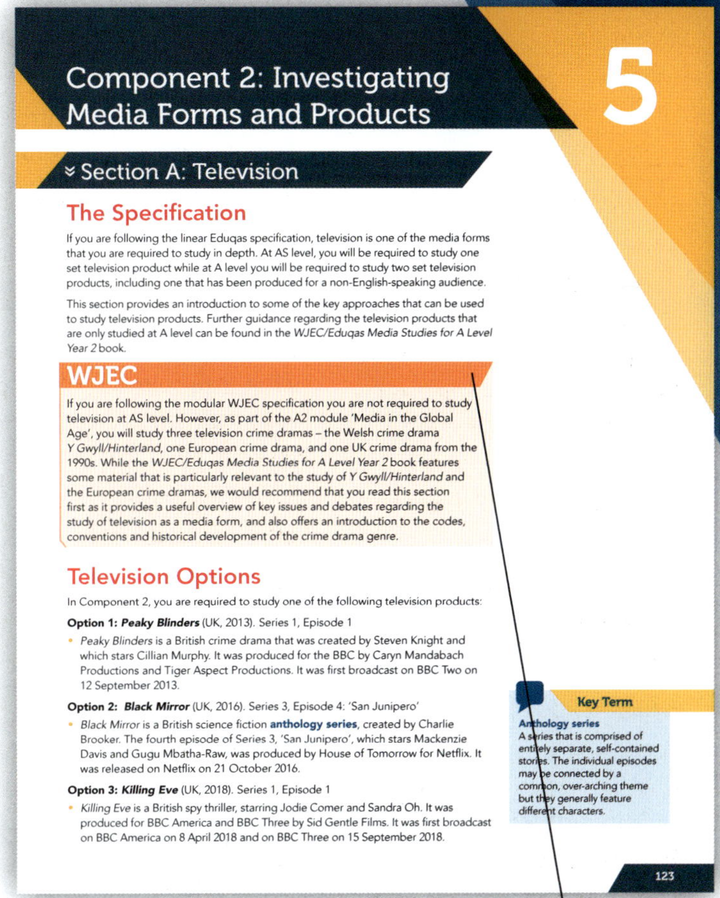
Component 2: Investigating Media Forms and Products

5

Section A: Television

The Specification

If you are following the linear Eduqas specification, television is one of the media forms that you are required to study in depth. At AS level, you will be required to study one set television product while at A level you will be required to study two set television products, including one that has been produced for a non-English-speaking audience.

This section provides an introduction to some of the key approaches that can be used to study television products. Further guidance regarding the television products that are only studied at A level can be found in the *WJEC/Eduqas Media Studies for A Level Year 2* book.

WJEC

If you are following the modular WJEC specification you are not required to study television at AS level. However, as part of the A2 module 'Media in the Global Age', you will study three television crime dramas – the Welsh crime drama *Y Gwyll/Hinterland*, one European crime drama, and one UK crime drama from the 1990s. While the *WJEC/Eduqas Media Studies for A Level Year 2* book features some material that is particularly relevant to the study of *Y Gwyll/Hinterland* and the European crime dramas, we would recommend that you read this section first as it provides a useful overview of key issues and debates regarding the study of television as a media form, and also offers an introduction to the codes, conventions and historical development of the crime drama genre.

Television Options

In Component 2, you are required to study one of the following television products:

Option 1: ***Peaky Blinders*** (UK, 2013). Series 1, Episode 1

- *Peaky Blinders* is a British crime drama that was created by Steven Knight and which stars Cillian Murphy. It was produced for the BBC by Caryn Mandabach Productions and Tiger Aspect Productions. It was first broadcast on BBC Two on 12 September 2013.

Option 2: ***Black Mirror*** (UK, 2016). Series 3, Episode 4: 'San Junipero'

- *Black Mirror* is a British science fiction **anthology series**, created by Charlie Brooker. The fourth episode of Series 3, 'San Junipero', which stars Mackenzie Davis and Gugu Mbatha-Raw, was produced by House of Tomorrow for Netflix. It was released on Netflix on 21 October 2016.

Option 3: ***Killing Eve*** (UK, 2018). Series 1, Episode 1

- *Killing Eve* is a British spy thriller, starring Jodie Comer and Sandra Oh. It was produced for BBC America and BBC Three by Sid Gentle Films. It was first broadcast on BBC America on 8 April 2018 and on BBC Three on 15 September 2018.

Key Term

Anthology series
A series that is comprised of entirely separate, self-contained stories. The individual episodes may be connected by a common, over-arching theme but they generally feature different characters.

123

WJEC specification

This book has been written for the Eduqas AS course you are taking and includes useful information to help you perform well in the examination and the internally assessed unit.

While the focus of this student book is the AS assessment, many of you may be following the linear A level. This book will introduce you to the theoretical framework and some of the set forms and products you will need to study for the A level. It will also give you information regarding the additional set products required for the A level assessment. More detailed analysis of these is included in the Year 2 book.

This book is split into chapters related to aspects of the specification. Each chapter includes the following elements:

- Examples of how to analyse a range of media forms and products including relevant terminology. These include approaches to the set products and related wider examples that are required for the examination.
- Definitions of key terms and their application to help you in your study and revision.
- Quickfire questions designed to test your knowledge and understanding of the media forms, set products and the theoretical framework.
- Tips to help you broaden your understanding and improve your examination technique.
- Stretch and Challenge tasks to encourage your independent learning, and to broaden your knowledge and understanding.
- Named Theorists that are listed in the specification, related to the subject, are included to broaden your knowledge and make you aware of the theorists and the key theories you must know in each component. Key Figures are also shown, giving you additional examples.
- At the end of each chapter there is a summary page to help you structure your revision.

Chapters 1 and 2

These are introductory sections. They introduce you to the theoretical framework that underpins all that will follow. This includes:

- media language
- representation
- media industries
- audiences.

These chapters will introduce you to the specific language required for the subject. This is particularly useful for those of you who did not study Media Studies at GCSE. You will also be provided with an overview of the requirements of this specification so that you are aware of what you are studying and how you will be assessed.

Chapters 3 and 4

These chapters focus on Component 1: Investigating the Media. They will cover what is required for Sections A and B of the examination paper. In Component 1 you will study set products and forms in breadth. These chapters prepare you for this by looking at the set forms and products, but they also consider wider examples to prepare you for the unseen element of the assessment.

Chapters 5 and 6

The focus here is on Component 2: Investigating Media Forms and Products – the set forms and products you will study and how you will be assessed. These forms are Television, Magazines and Online Media. There will be detailed examples introducing you to each of these media forms, as well as suggestions regarding how to apply the relevant elements of the theoretical framework to the set products.

Chapters 7 and 8

These chapters deal with the non-exam assessment and guide you through the production briefs, and the preparatory research and planning required. There are also tips on how to produce a successful production and complete your Statement of Aims and Intentions. Here you also will find examples of work from 'real' students to give you an idea of what is expected of you at this level.

Chapter 9

Chapter 9 of the book covers the key skills for examination success, including the important skill of essay writing and how to structure different kinds of examination responses. There are also some ideas for what to include in answers to possible types of questions that may appear in the examination. They offer a guide as to the approach that is required and key points you may include. You will be offered advice on how to structure your writing to produce an effective examination response.

Tip

The theories are outlined in Chapter 10 of this book.

Chapter 10 and Glossary

Finally, at the end of the book you will find some supplementary material to aid your learning. This includes a quick guide to the theories and theoretical perspectives required for the examination (Chapter 10) and a Glossary of media terminology.

What is Expected from You

Remember that, although there are examples of annotated products throughout this book to help you, it is more important that, for some areas of the specification, you gain the knowledge and understanding to allow you to analyse any media products, including your own independently researched examples. The introduction to the theoretical framework will help you do this. It is not the intention that you just use the wider examples in this book in your examination responses. They are here to illustrate how knowledge and understanding can be applied effectively.

Those of you following the Eduqas specification need to be very familiar with the set forms and products, and need to also engage in independent research of wider examples to prepare for the unseen element of Component 1.

For both the WJEC and Eduqas specification, you should use the overview of theories and theoretical perspectives in Chapter 10 as a starting point to familiarise yourself with this challenging element of the course.

In order to support your study of AS Media Studies you can look at the Eduqas website www.eduqas.co.uk. Make sure you access the correct part of the website for the specification you are studying. Look for sample assessment materials, past papers and mark schemes, which will help to familiarise you with the assessment.

Tip

Importantly, take responsibility for your own learning and do not rely on your teachers to give you notes or tell you how to gain the grades that you require. Using the 'Stretch and Challenge' activities in this book will help you to be a more independent learner.

WJEC

This book is aimed at those of you following the Eduqas specification in England and some centres in Northern Ireland. Centres in Wales will follow the WJEC specification. This means that some, but not all, parts of this book will be relevant to the WJEC specification.

The main differences in the WJEC specification are:

- The AS and A2 remain coupled. This means that you will sit an examination and complete an internally assessed production at the end of Year 12 and those marks will then be carried into Year 13. The AS counts for 40% of the final mark.
- There is only one examination in each year. Learners following the WJEC specification will take one AS examination at the end of Year 1 and one A level examination at the end of Year 2.
- Section A has set forms but not set products. Section B has a range of set products including options.
- Many of the elements of the existing specification remain unchanged.
- The specification has a Welsh perspective. For example, some of the options for the set products are in the Welsh language.

AS	A2
Unit 1: Investigating the Media 100 marks One written examination of 2 hours 30 minutes	Unit 3: Media in the Global Age 90 marks One written examination of 2 hours 30 minutes
Unit 2: Creating a Media Production 80 marks Non-exam assessment	Unit 4: Creating a Cross-Media Production 80 marks Non-exam assessment

Tip

Chapter 1, which covers the theoretical framework, will cover the analytical skills required for both WJEC and Eduqas.

Tip

In Chapter 3 Section A, other examples of adverts and music videos are explored as well as the set products for Eduqas. This will be very useful for WJEC students as the codes and conventions of the forms are analysed in detail.

The main similarities between the Eduqas and WJEC specifications are:

- The focus on the theoretical framework, which is comprised of media language, representation, media industries and audiences.
- Some of the set products are the same, for example the historical magazines.
- Some of the forms are the same, for example music videos.
- The theories and theoretical perspectives named in the WJEC specification are also in the Eduqas specification and are therefore covered in this book.

In Unit 1 Section A of the WJEC specification, the products to be studied are chosen by the teacher. The set products included in the Eduqas specification could be used for the WJEC examples. In Chapter 3 on Component 1: Section A, other examples are also included to broaden knowledge of the form, these could also be used as examples for the WJEC specification.

The tables on pages 12 and 13 show the overlap between the two specifications, this allows you to see which Eduqas set products covered in the book will be relevant to you if you're following the WJEC specification.

WJEC

Overview

Table showing overlap between the WJEC and Eduqas AS Level specifications

Media Forms Common to WJEC and Eduqas	Media Products Common to WJEC and Eduqas	Media Theories Common to WJEC and Eduqas	Relevant Unit or Component	Relevant Sections of the Book
Advertising	*Tide* print advertisement *Super. Human.* Tokyo 2020 Parlympic Games audio-visual advertisement	Semiotics (Barthes) Representation (Hall) Theories of identity (Gauntlett) Reception theory (Hall) Cultivation theory (Gerbner)	**WJEC:** Unit 1 Section A: Selling Images **Eduqas:** Component 1: Sections A and B	See Chapter 3: pages 59–65 (Section A) and pages 107–114 (Section B)
Music videos	*Formation*, Beyoncé *Underdog*, Alicia Keys	Semiotics (Barthes) Representation (Hall)	**WJEC:** Unit 1 Section A: Selling Images **Eduqas:** Component 1: Section A	See Chapter 3: pages 72–77
Newspapers (Print and Online News)	*Daily Mirror* Print edition (set edition for Section A) Print edition and selected pages from the website (centre's choice for Section B)	Semiotics (Barthes) Representation (Hall) Theories of identity (Gauntlett) Reception theory (Hall) Cultivation theory (Gerbner)	**WJEC:** Unit 1 Section B: News in an Online Age **Eduqas:** Component 1: Sections A and B	See Chapter 3: pages 77–81 (Section A) and pages 99–106 (Section B)

Table showing overlap between the WJEC and Eduqas A Level specifications

Media Forms Common to WJEC and Eduqas	Media Products Common to WJEC and Eduqas	Media Theories Common to WJEC and Eduqas	Relevant Unit or Component	Relevant Sections of the Book
Television	*The Bridge*	Narratology (Todorov) Genre (Neale) Structuralism (Lévi-Strauss) Postmodernism (Baudrillard) Feminist theories (bell hooks and van Zoonen) Representation (Hall) Reception theory (Hall)	**WJEC:** Unit 3 Section A: Television in the Global Age **Eduqas:** Component 2: Section A: Television in the Global Age	See Chapter 5, Section A: pages 123–158 See also the *Media Studies for A Level/Year 2* book
Magazines	*Vogue* *Woman* *Woman's Realm* *Huck* *Adbusters*	Semiotics (Barthes) Structuralism (Lévi-Strauss) Feminist theories (bell hooks and van Zoonen) Theories of identity (Gauntlett) Reception theory (Hall)	**WJEC:** Unit 3 Section B: Magazines: Changing Representations **Eduqas:** Component 2: Section B: Magazines: Mainstream and Alternative Media	See Chapter 5, Section B: pages 159–179 See also the *Media Studies for A Level/Year 2* book
Online Media	*Attitude* website	Semiotics (Barthes) Structuralism (Lévi-Strauss) Theories of identity (Gauntlett)	**WJEC:** Unit 3 Section B: Magazines: Changing Representations **Eduqas:** Component 2: Section C: Media in the Online Age	See Chapter 5, Section C: pages 180–195 See also the *Media Studies for A Level/Year 2* book
Video Games	*Assassin's Creed III: Liberation*	Media effects (Bandura) Fandom (Jenkins)	**WJEC:** Unit 3 Section C: Media in the Digital Age – Video Games **Eduqas:** Component 1: Section B	Chapter 3: pages 115–119

1 Introducing the Media Studies Framework

What is the Framework?

The AS Media Studies specification is based on a framework that provides you with the tools to help you develop a critical understanding of the media.

The framework underpins the study of the media in all three components of the specification and is made up of four inter-related areas:

- **media language**: how the media communicate meaning through their **forms**, codes and conventions, and techniques
- **representation**: how the media portray events, issues, individuals and social groups
- **media industries**: how production, distribution and circulation are linked to and affect media forms and **platforms**
- **audiences**: how media forms target, reach and address audiences. How audiences might interpret and respond to different media forms and how audiences may themselves become producers.

Key Terms

Forms
Different types of media, for example music, newspapers and radio.

Platforms
A range of different ways of communicating to an audience, for example television, social media, etc.

Products
What is produced by media organisations, for example films, video games, television programmes and music videos.

Encode
Communicate ideas and messages through a system of signs.

Decode
The process through which an audience interprets a message.

Codes
These are signs contained within a media product that give clues to the product's meaning.

Effect
The impact a code may have upon the audience.

Media Language

Textual Analysis Toolkit

The creators of media **products encode** messages and meanings within the products through media language, the audience then **decode** these messages and respond to them in different ways. All media products are constructed and the messages of the creators will be contained within the product.

You must study the following aspects of media language and be able to apply your understanding to the forms set for each component.

Technical Codes

In preparation for the examination it is important that you are able to confidently discuss the technical **codes** of a range of products, and that you are then able to apply that knowledge and understanding across different products. Some of the media products will be chosen by your teacher and some will be set by the awarding body. In order to do this you need a 'Toolkit for Analysis'.

This is a set of key points that you know you must refer to when analysing a particular media product. It is also very important that you discuss and analyse the purpose and **effect** of the particular technique employed by the text.

Technical codes are one of the ways in which a media product is constructed. With regard to moving images, including music videos and television programmes, this is the way in which camera shots, angles and movements are edited together to communicate messages to an audience. In print texts this refers to the design, layout and key features of the text.

Tip

Analysing technical codes is relevant to all areas of this specification, so remember to transfer your knowledge across all the components.

Technical Codes in Moving Image Products

Tip

When you are analysing technical codes consider how they reflect the product's genre.

Camera Shots

There is a range of shots that are used to create specific effects.

- **Close-ups** can be used to convey emotion or tension or to draw attention to particular objects within the frame. A close-up of a character's face can make the audience feel more involved with the character.
- **Extreme close-ups**, for example a hand on a door handle, where information is withheld from the audience, create suspense or draw attention to something important that will be used later in the narrative, for example a tattoo.
- **Medium close-ups** are also called 'newsreader shots'. The head and shoulders shot is how the audience would expect a news anchor to be within the frame, this shot is therefore related to a specific genre.
- **Long shots** are used to provide more information about the context or location in which the action is taking place. Here, the audience may be shown the characters and part of their surroundings, as in this crime scene example on the right.
- **Establishing shots** are rapid ways of advancing the narrative by showing the audience where the action is about to take place. Audiences may then have expectations of what will happen next and this enhances their pleasure. For example, the establishing shot used in the BBC crime drama *Shetland* (below) illustrates the remoteness of the location and foreshadows the bleak narrative.

Extreme close-up

Long shot

Establishing shot

Medium close-up

Quickfire 1.1

What other camera shots are there and what are their purposes and effects? Refer to specific examples of media products to illustrate your points.

Camera Angles

- A high-angle shot with a character as its subject will have the effect of making the character appear vulnerable and insignificant. An aerial or bird's-eye view is often used in action films to film sequences such as car chases to allow the audience to see fully what is happening. This type of shot also suggests the high **production values** of the product.

- A low-angle shot of a character or object will create a sense of power and dominance. The low-angle shot used in the marketing campaign for the 2020 Paralympics (left) makes the subjects appear strong and powerful, and challenges misconceptions of disability. It reinforces the campaign's slogan '*Meet the Super. Humans.*'

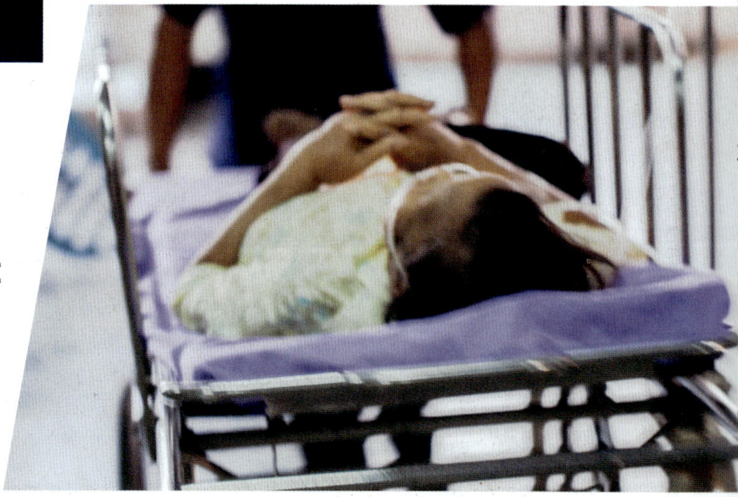

Key Terms

Production values
The features of a media product that illustrate how much it cost to make. A high-budget film is recognisable by its settings, use of stars and more complex editing, for example. The reverse is true of low-budget films.

Hand-held camera
A style of filming whereby a decision has been made not to use the steadicam on the camera or a tripod but to allow the camera to move freely during filming. This gives a jerky style of filming that suggests realism and makes the audience feel involved in the action.

Camera Movement

- **A tracking shot** is when the camera follows the character or the action. The effect is to make the audience feel involved in the action. If the tracking shot is filmed using a **hand-held camera**, then the effect is further enhanced. In a reverse track, the camera moves back as the subjects come towards the camera. Again, this involves the audience. This shot is used often in hospital dramas where the camera follows the hospital trolley in an emergency or the doors open and the trolley comes towards us. The audience is then caught up in the panic and action.
- **A zoom** is when the camera moves from a long shot towards the subject or out to a long shot exposing more detail. A zoom shot is usually virtually unnoticeable; it should not be intrusive unless that is the desired effect. The zoom to a close-up allows the audience to be involved in the emotion of the character and to more clearly see facial expressions.
- **A panning shot** is when the camera moves across the scene, imparting information to the audience. It is often used to show location, for example the London skyline. In a whip pan, the camera rotates at high speed, causing a blurring effect and suggesting pace and action.
- **In a tilt shot** the camera rotates vertically from top to bottom, or vice versa. It can be used to imply mystery when introducing a character by focusing first on the feet and then gradually tilting upwards to the face. The audience then makes assumptions about the character in different ways.

Tip

In your examination responses don't just name the technical code, always explain why and how it has been used.

Quickfire 1.2

Give another example of when and how a zoom may be used.

Editing

The process of selecting, ordering and **editing** shots in order to convey meanings to the audience, can be complex. The editing of a media product also changes according to the genre. In an action scene the expectation is that the editing will be fast paced and the **transitions** will be cuts to convey action and speed. However, in a horror sequence the editing may be slower, along with the transitions, in order to build suspense and create enigmas. It is also through editing that the narrative is created.

Technical Codes in Print Products

Print products, for example magazines, film posters and advertisements, also use technical codes to transmit meaning. These products are constructed by employing a range of techniques designed to appeal to and attract an audience. These include:

- **Layout and design**: the way in which the print text is constructed is partly through the technical codes of the text. The use of colour, font and text positioning all contribute to the overall style of the publication. Magazines have a house style and readers recognise this and expect it to be consistent. This may be established through, for example, the font used for the masthead and the colour codes.
- **Camera shots**: the choice of shot on a print product helps to communicate meaning. A screenshot from a film used on a film poster suggests the narrative and genre of the film. A close-up of the creator on a vlog contributes to their star persona and attracts their fan base.
- **Lighting**: the way in which the image is lit helps in the construction of messages.
- **Use of colour**: the colours chosen to be incorporated into print products convey messages about each product's genre and often about the audience who will consume it. Pastel colours employed on a film poster suggest a specific film genre. Print-based adverts for fragrances convey messages quickly to their audience by the digitally applied colour washes.
- **Graphics**: logos and graphical representations appear in many forms on print products. The graphics included in a film trailer will communicate messages about the film's genre.
- **Post-production techniques**: in the media today, still images are manipulated and enhanced digitally to create a special effect. In advertising, eyelashes are extended and skin is made to appear flawless through airbrushing (as in the image below right). Film posters manipulate images to communicate the film's genre and attract audiences.

Key Terms

Editing
The way in which the shots are put together to create a particular effect. Editing can be described in terms of pace and the transitions that are employed.

Transitions
The way in which the shots move from one into the other, producing a particular effect. Different transitions include cuts that produce a faster-paced sequence. Fades and wipes suggest a more controlled and slower section.

Graphics
A precise type of design. For example, in media terms, the titles and credits in a film or for a television programme, or the seemingly hand-drawn but usually computer-generated images in a video game.

Tip

The 'Toolkit' will help you to analyse media products in all components of the specification. It is essential when analysing media language, for example genre and narrative. It is equally important when researching products for your own production work.

Tip

Often, when students are analysing print products the tendency is to pay less attention to the technical codes. Remember that the product has been constructed and the technical codes convey meanings to an audience.

Quickfire 1.3

How do technical codes construct meanings in print products? Use specific examples to support your points

Key Terms

Diegetic sound
Sound that is part of the mise-en-scène and can be heard by characters in the scene. For example, a gunshot as we see it being fired in a crime drama.

Non-diegetic sound
Essentially, sound the characters within the frame cannot hear. It is sound that may have been added post-production or has been used to suggest mood and atmosphere.

Lexis
The specific type of language or vocabulary that is used.

Suspension of disbelief
Where the audience are involved in the action and do not question impossible aspects of it; for example, the sound of dramatic music in a crime drama confrontation scene.

Contrapuntal
Sound that does not match what is happening on screen. For example, the introduction of ominous music in a seemingly peaceful scene.

Audio Codes

Audio codes are an important way in which the creators of media products communicate messages. No audio codes are there by chance, they are part of the construction of the text. However, it is invariably the case that students spend less time analysing the audio in favour of the visual elements of the product. It is important that you learn to discuss audio codes, their purpose and effect, and to use the correct media terminology to ensure that your analysis is informed and coherent.

Sound in a media text is either **diegetic** or **non-diegetic** and can take the following forms:

- **Dialogue** is an important audio code that has the purpose of imparting information to the audience and establishing characters and relationships. The mode of address of the speaker and the specific **lexis** used can also anchor the product in a particular genre. For example, the way in which the presenters on *The Today Programme* on Radio 4 converse is formal and suggests their expertise in the topic and their role as the news anchors interpreting the news for the listener.
- **Sound effects** add to the realism of the product and are also an indication of genre, and they support action codes. In some genres they are enhanced in order to create an effect. For example, in a horror film trailer the sound effects are stereotypical and recognisable – the wind howling and doors creaking. They often made louder post-production in order to build tension and suspense.
- **Music** is obviously an important audio code. The choice of music or the specific song used will convey narrative information to the audience. Music, as with other audio codes, suggests genre. There is an expectation that, at a tense moment in a television crime drama, appropriate non-diegetic music may be heard. The audience will **suspend disbelief** as the music adds to the atmosphere. It is often the case that **contrapuntal** music acts as an action code.
- **Voice-overs** are examples of non-diegetic sound that serve to give information to the audience. For example, the voice-over accompanying a film trailer fills in missing pieces of the narrative for the audience and often establishes the genre through the use of lexis.

Tip

Make sure that you know how to analyse audio by referring to pace, types of instruments, choice of song to match the narrative, purpose and effect. Avoid simplistic descriptions such as 'the music was loud'. Consider what made the music loud and why it was important at that point in the product. What effect did it have on the audience?

Theoretical Framework: Semiotics

Roland Barthes

Barthes was a French writer who studied **semiotics**. He argued that all texts communicate their meaning through a set of signs that need to be decoded by the audience. He was particularly interested in the way in which signs take on the ideology of a specific society, and their meanings become accepted and appear natural through repetition over time. He also argued that the way in which the audience interprets the image is influenced by other forces, for example culture and context.

Media producers encode meanings in their products, which audiences need to learn to decipher. However, not all audiences will decode the meanings in the product in the same way – this will change according to cultural experience and context. For example, the Union Flag is a sign that may be interpreted in different ways according to whether it is seen at a royal wedding or as a symbol of the British National Party (BNP). Similarly, a red rose as a sign may have a different **connotation** according to the context in which it appears. It may signify love or the Labour Party, for instance. Both these 'signs' take on a symbolic quality above and beyond their basic image.

Barthes introduced the idea that signs can function at the level of **denotation**, the literal meaning of the sign, and connotation (the meanings associated with it). In your examination response you must discuss the connotation and not just the denotation of the visual codes within the product.

Visual Codes

One of the means by which media products convey messages to audience is through visual codes. Messages are encoded by the creators of the product and audiences decode these messages. In the section dealing with audience you will see what affects the way in which different audiences interpret and respond to media products – not all audiences take away the same messages. Media products may be **polysemic** and are open to a range of interpretations. Everything we see in a product will contain meanings and has been constructed with a purpose.

The main visual codes are:

Clothing: what is worn in a media product communicates messages about the person, for example a uniform or a football shirt. Within a media context, clothing can communicate messages quickly to an audience and may advance the narrative without the need for complex explanations. When a new character enters the frame in, for example, a forensics crime drama and is wearing a white suit and plastic gloves (see right), the audience understands the role of this character and has expectations of their behaviour.

Key Terms

Semiotics
The language of codes and signs; it deals with the way in which media texts are encoded and the way in which audiences decode them.

Connotation
Refers to a meaning we associate with the sign, for example a red rose may connote love or the hoot of an owl may connote night-time.

Denotation
The literal or common-sense meaning of a sign rather than the associated meaning of the sign.

Polysemic
A sign that has more than one meaning.

Tip

Roland Barthes is one of the theorists you will study in relation to semiotics; you may also study others.

Quickfire 1.4

What are the different connotations of a red rose according to where it appears?

Tip

In this section there is a general introduction to aspects of the theoretical framework. In the examination you will be expected to be able to apply your understanding of theories to the products you study.

Stretch and Challenge 1.1

Research Roland Barthes' theories of semiotics in more detail to develop a more sophisticated understanding.

Facial expressions quickly communicate messages.

Colours are non-verbal communicators.

Key Terms

Mise-en-scène
Everything that appears within the frame in, for example, a television programme. This includes characters, iconography and graphics.

Symbol
A sign that suggests another idea beyond the simple denotation, the meaning of which has been culturally agreed. A woman wearing a red dress in a music video may symbolise that she is passionate or dangerous.

Tip

When analysing media products, avoid simplistic descriptions of visual codes. Always use the appropriate media terminology, and consider the impact, purpose and effect of the visual codes upon the audience.

Quickfire 1.5

Suggest another media product that uses colour to transmit messages.

- **Expression**: facial expressions are also ways in which messages are communicated rapidly. Combined with close-up shots, emotions can be clearly represented in a product and easily interpreted by an audience.
- **Gestures**: are non-verbal communicators and, as such, cross language barriers. Characters can convey emotion easily through the code of gesture, for example a shrug, a wave or something more aggressive or offensive. In, for example, music videos, the gesture and body language of the featured performer may also convey messages about their self-representation and the genre of music.
- **Technique**: the way in which a product is constructed and presented conveys meaning. For example, the use of black and white photography in an advertising campaign may suggest sophistication, and the use of soft focus may carry connotations of romance or emotion.
- **Colours**: can transmit messages and in some cases are key parts of the product's construction. For example, in fragrance advertisements they can suggest the type of fragrance being marketed even though the audiences cannot smell them. Pastel colours may suggest a light, daytime fragrance, while dark, rich colours, such as purples and reds, will convey the sense of a heavier evening perfume. Advertisements do not have time to convey meaning so they use colour codes that are easily understood by the audience.
- **Images**: consider the selection of images within the product. They have been placed in the **mise-en-scène** for a purpose to communicate messages. For example, the choice of model or celebrity on the front cover of a magazine will give clues to the target audience of the product. Add to this their code of clothing, gesture and expression, and the meaning may become more complex.
- **Iconography**: objects, settings and backgrounds within a media product that contain meanings. Some objects take on significance beyond their literal meaning. The denotation of Big Ben is a clock in London. However, when it appears at the start of *The News at Ten*, it signifies tradition, reliability and the capital city at the centre of the news. In this sense it becomes a **symbol**. Certain media products are recognisable by their iconography, which places them in a specific genre, for example the setting of the lab and the instruments in a forensics crime drama.
- **Graphics**: do not ignore the graphics contained within the product as they too are significant and establish meaning. The graphics contained within a television credit sequence, for example the typography, will give a clue to the programme's genre and target audience.

Language and Mode of Address

The ways in which media products 'speak' to an audience and the language used give clues to who that audience may be and to the genre and purpose of the product. This may refer to the written language of print products or the spoken word in audio-visual products. The language and the way it is used are encoded to convey meaning.

Language

- The lexis – the actual words – used in the product may pertain to the genre of the product and be recognisable to audiences. Some products employ subject-specific lexis, for example the front covers of gaming magazines may include lexis that is specific to the world of gaming. Television crime dramas will create a sense of realism by employing specific terminology related to the story world. Audiences become familiar with the vocabulary used for specific police or forensic procedures. The purpose and effect of this is that the audience who understand the terminology will feel part of the programme's community.
- **Language features**: certain styles of language are used by media products for a specific purpose. For example, the use of puns and alliteration on the front pages of **tabloid** newspapers.
- **Advertisements** often use **hyperbole** to make whatever they are selling appear new and exciting.
- **Magazines** often employ the imperative to suggest a sense of urgency and importance about what they are suggesting, for example: 'Lose six pounds in six days! Get that beach body now!'
- An **ellipsis** is used in magazines and other print products as an enigma code to encourage an audience to buy the product in order to find the answer.
- The use of slang and **colloquialisms** in, for example, websites and blogs aimed at teenagers, creates an informal relationship with the user.
- Direct quotations anchor points and suggest realism. They are often used in print and digital versions of magazines and newspapers related to 'real-life' stories.

Key Terms

Tabloid
Refers historically to the dimensions of the newspaper: a tabloid was traditionally smaller and more compact in size than a broadsheet. The term now more commonly refers to a popular newspaper whose content tends to focus on lighter news, for example celebrity gossip, sport and television, such as *The Sun*.

Hyperbole
Exaggerated language used to create a dramatic effect.

Ellipsis
Where sentences are incomplete and instead are finished with a set of three dots creating an enigma; the words need to be filled in by the reader.

Colloquialism
An informal expression that is often used in casual conversation rather than in writing. However, it is used in some media products to establish an informal communication with the audience.

Tip

Words or phrases that contain a command or an order are known as the imperative. They usually start with a verb.

Quickfire 1.6

Think of another example of a media product that uses subject-specific lexis. What is the intended effect upon the audience?

Key Terms

Register
The spoken or written register of a media product is the range and variety of language used within the product. This will change according to the purpose and the target audience.

Hybrid genres
These are media products that incorporate features of more than one genre. *Strictly Come Dancing* includes features of reality television, game shows and entertainment programmes, for example.

Sub-genres
A smaller category or subdivision within a larger genre.

Story arc
The way in which the narrative progresses from the beginning to the end of the product. A story arc may also cross episodes.

Formulaic structure
Where the product has a clear structure that is recognisable and rarely changes. For example, the front cover of a lifestyle magazine has key conventions and the audience has expectations of what will appear throughout the publication.

Mode of Address

This is the tone and the written or spoken style of the media product that establishes communication with an audience. When analysing the mode of address of any product, consider:

- **Informal mode of address**: some products, for example print and online magazines aimed at young people, adopt an informal **register**. They use slang, colloquial vocabulary and personal pronouns to engage their target audience and make them feel as if they are addressing them directly. The reader then feels as if they are part of the seemingly exclusive world of the magazine.

- **Formal mode of address**: other media products, for example quality newspapers, will adopt a more formal tone with more complex vocabulary and writing styles. This suggests that the target audience are more serious and sophisticated, and want more detailed information. News anchors combine a formal mode of address with a serious code of expression; this encourages the audience to trust what they are saying.
- **Direct mode of address**: where the product communicates directly with the audience. An example would be television presenters, for example Tess Daly and Claudia Winkleman in *Strictly Come Dancing*. The effect is to make the audience feel involved in the programme; it is as if they are talking directly to us at home. The anchors of news programmes engage in direct mode of address as they are dealing with serious and important matters. The models and celebrities on the front covers of lifestyle magazines often look directly out of the magazine, engaging in seemingly direct eye contact with the reader. The effect is to draw the audience into the magazine, persuading them to purchase the product.
- **Indirect mode of address**: in many products the audience do not expect a direct mode of address. In most television programmes and films it would be unusual for the characters to step out of the film world and speak directly to the audience.

Genre

Another key element of media language that helps in analysing products is genre. A genre is the type or category of a media product. Each genre has its own set of conventions or repertoire of elements that are recognisable to audiences. They are what place the text in that particular genre. These key conventions are recognised and understood by audiences by being repeated over a period of time. However, some media products are **hybrid genres** or **sub-genres**.

The repertoire of elements for any genre can be broken down into key areas:

- **Narrative**: the plot/**story arc** is how the story is told. All media products convey information through a **formulaic structure**. This may be a linear structure comprising a beginning, middle and end, or a non-linear or circular structure. Certain genres have predictable narratives and plot situations within the narrative. For example, the story arc of a soap opera may have several interweaving narrative strands that run from episode to episode and are focused on the lives and relationships of a community. A specific plot situation for any programme belonging to this genre may be a confrontation between a husband and wife over an affair or an argument in the pub.

Tip

When analysing media products remember to pay close attention to the language and mode of address used, and consider how this contributes to the impact and appeal of the product.

Quickfire 1.7

What effect does the mode of address used have upon the audience?

- **Characters**: most genres have a set of recognisable characters, known as stock characters, that help to establish the genre, for example a rebellious teenager in a soap opera. Audiences become used to the character types that appear in certain genres and can predict their behaviour in any given situation; they may be disappointed if they do not conform to type. An audience expects James Bond to deal with situations in predictable ways: his character belongs to the action genre. Stars are also often associated with particular genres and therefore audiences will have an expectation of the role they will play. For example, Cameron Diaz tends to play similar roles in romantic comedies.
- **Iconography and setting**: the locations, backgrounds, props and costumes used in a media product communicate messages about genre, narrative and character. The clothing and objects used in *Peaky Blinders*, for example, signify the time period in which the programme is set. The entrance of a police officer wearing a suit in a crime drama tells the audience that they are a detective and of a superior rank. The audience then will have expectations of how that character will behave. This is also true of print texts: the front covers of video games may include specific, recognisable iconography that will appeal to a certain audience. In music videos the iconography may suggest the genre of music, for example the objects and clothing of a rap artist.
- **Technical codes**: these are very important in establishing genre. Some genres have a particular style of filming and will use certain camera shots and editing. Fast-paced editing with rapid cuts is a convention of action dramas, whereas slower editing with fades is more conventional of tense dramas. Music videos will often feature a range of shots of the performer and related iconography in order to establish the music genre. For print products, audiences have expectations about the generic codes and conventions of the front cover of a lifestyle magazine, which may include airbrushing and high-key lighting.
- **Audio codes**: the technical codes may be combined with conventional audio codes, for example the soundtrack that introduces the news and traffic slots in radio programmes. Particular sound effects are typical of certain genres and specific programmes, for example the sound effect that heralds the arrival of Doctor Who's Tardis, which has remained constant throughout the life of the series. Typical dialogue may be expected in a genre incorporating specific lexis. For example, in a forensics crime drama the audience expect to hear scientific language.

Quickfire 1.8

Look at Drake's video *Energy* on YouTube. How does it suggest the genre through iconography?

Quickfire 1.9

Give an example of the repertoire of elements for a genre of your choice.

Theoretical Framework: Steve Neale

Steve Neale investigated genre; specifically in relation to film, but his findings can be applied to other media forms. He stated that:

- '*Genres are instances of repetition and difference*' (Stephen Neale, *Genre*, 1980). This may mean familiar elements presented in an unfamiliar way or completely new elements are introduced.
- Difference is essential to sustain a genre, to simply repeat the codes and conventions of the form would not appeal to an audience. However, audiences also like to anticipate what is familiar about a genre.
- Genres change, develop and vary as they borrow from and overlap with one another.
- Audiences also derive pleasure from seeing how the genre has been manipulated to produce something recognisable but 'different', for example *Killing Eve* repeats many of the typical conventions of the assassin/action genre but introduces a 'difference' with the complex and enigmatic character Villanelle.
- Genres with set codes and conventions are an advantage to the media institutions that produce them as they have a predetermined audience, are easy to market and success can be predicted, thus reducing the economic risk to the producer. This can also be applied to other media platforms.

Narrative

All media products have a structure or narrative. The producers of media products use a variety of techniques to convey the narrative. There are three types of narrative structures: linear, non-linear and **circular**.

Theoretical Framework: Tzvetan Todorov

Linear narrative was studied by the theorist **Tzvetan Todorov**, his research into stories suggested that the narrative is conveyed using a chronological structure:

1. The initial state of equilibrium at the beginning of a narrative.

↓

2. A breakdown or disruption of equilibrium.

↓

3. A recognition that the equilibrium has been disrupted.

↓

4. An attempt to restore or re-establish equilibrium.

↓

5. The restoration of equilibrium at the end of the narrative.

Named Theorist

Steve Neale
Steve Neale was a Professor at the University of Exeter. Much of his research focused on genre in Hollywood cinema but can be transferred to other media forms.

Stretch and Challenge 1.2

Research Steve Neale's work on genre in more detail, considering how you can apply it to the products you are studying.

Key Term

Circular narrative
When the narrative starts at the end and then explores the action up to that point. It is sometimes only at the very end of the film or television programme that the narrative makes sense.

Quickfire 1.10

Give an example of a media product that demonstrates 'repetition with difference'.

Named Theorist

Tzvetan Todorov
Tzvetan Todorov was a theorist who researched narrative structures. He suggested that narratives were linear with key points of progression and that narratives involved characters solving a problem ending in a resolution.

Quickfire 1.11

Give another specific example of how media texts manipulate time and space.

Non-linear narrative manipulates time and space, and is more challenging for an audience as the narrative moves backwards and forwards. A good example is a crime drama where the beginning of the story arc may be the discovery of the body and then the audience may be shown the events up to the murder – this becomes the middle sequence – and the narrative then moves on to the end when the crime is solved.

Narrative Techniques in Audio-Visual Products

- **Manipulation of time and space**: narrative shapes a media product in terms of space and time. We, as an audience, may be visually transported to America, for example, to watch a live tennis match. In programmes such as *Match of the Day* we are shown action replays and slow motion shots to give us a better view of the action. In dramas we are shown long reaction shots to build tension and create empathy with a character.
- **Split-screen narratives**: this technique is sometimes used in television dramas whereby the screen is split into sections with different narratives going on in each screen. For example, in a crime drama this may be: the shot of the body, the killer escaping and the arrival of the police. In the television drama *The Queen's Gambit* (Netflix, 2020) the technique was used to build the tension in the chess match, withholding information about the winner from the audience.
- **Three-strand narratives**: this is a common narrative structure used by television dramas, for example *Casualty*. At the beginning of the episode three narrative strands will be introduced, for example a continuing problematic relationship between regular characters, an accident outside of the hospital setting and an incident in the casualty department. These strands then interweave through the episode and some of them may carry on to the next week.
- **Flexi-narrative**: this is a more complex narrative structure often with layers of interweaving narratives. This challenges the audience and keeps them intrigued. The narrative will be full of enigmas and characters will develop in their complexity. In *Baptiste* (BBC, 2021) the narrative moved between two different time periods, the only clue being the changed appearance of the protagonist. Each episode ended with a **cliff-hanger** to ensure that the audience watched the next one.

Key Term

Cliff-hanger
A narrative device that creates suspense. It is typically used at the end of an episode or, in some cases, before an advert break, as its main function is to persuade the viewer to watch the following instalment of the programme in order to find out what happens next.

Key Terms

Positioning
When audio, visual, technical or narrative codes place the audience in a particular position. For example, emotional or from the point of view of a character.

Restricted narrative
When the audience only sees the narrative from the point of view of one character so only knows as much as they do.

Tip

Ensure that when you are discussing the narrative of a product you extend your analysis beyond a simple discussion of storyline. Demonstrate your understanding of a range of techniques using the appropriate terminology.

Narrative Conventions in Audio-Visual Products

- **Flashbacks**: these are used to give the audience additional information. They may also involve the audience with a character by seeing inside their mind. They are also a way to manipulate time and space within the narrative.
- **Point-of-view shots**: allow the audience to see the action from different perspectives. The camera may **position** the audience as the eyes of the murderer or the victim, or may move between the two in order to build tension.
- **Apparently impossible positions**: where the camera gives the audience a view of the action from an unusual position, for example in the air or from behind a barrier of some kind. Audiences tend to accept this view if the narrative itself is believable, as this enhances their involvement. A famous example is when the audience is positioned behind the shower curtain in *Psycho*. They can see the unsuspecting victim and the shadow of her killer. This clearly enhances the tension of the scene.
- **Privileged spectator position**: when the camera places the audience in a superior position within the narrative. They are shown aspects of the narrative that other characters cannot see. For example, a close-up showing a character taking a knife out of her pocket. The audience can then anticipate the action that will follow later in the drama.
- **Voice-over**: used to move the action on or to fill in missing information. In documentaries a voice-over provides the audience with contextual information and establishes a link between the audience and what is on screen.
- **Enigma codes**: used in both audio-visual and print products. In films and television programmes the camera may only show a **restricted narrative**, leaving the audience with unanswered questions. The editing of a film trailer will also use enigmas in the selection of scenes included and voice-overs.

The shower scene from *Psycho* (Hitchcock 1960, Paramount Pictures)

Narrative Conventions in Print Products

It is not only moving image products that have narratives. The narrative of any product also refers to its structure and the codes and conventions that are recognisable to audiences. The audience has an expectation of how the narrative of a media product will develop and be conveyed. The narrative of a newspaper involves the front page, which tends to be a conventional structure for that particular newspaper, followed by the regular placing of other pages, including the sport on the back page. Film posters convey their narrative through features including a central image, **taglines** and the name of the film. The narrative techniques used in print texts include:

- **Headlines**: can convey a detailed and informative narrative in quality papers and may be more dramatic and enigmatic in popular papers where the aim is to attract the attention of the reader.
- **Cover lines**: in magazines will give the audience clues to what will appear in the magazine. They may give the start of a story but we need to buy the magazine to get the whole picture. The **jump line** indicates that we need to 'read on'.
- **Images and captions**: the image that appears on the print product can develop the narrative. This may be through the technical codes, the mode of address, the code of clothing or the way in which the audience is positioned by the look of the subject. An image without a caption is open and the interpretation is up to the audience. Once there is text with the image then the audience will interpret the narrative in a different way and this closes down the meaning. Photographs often capture moments in time and the narrative can be deconstructed to establish meaning.
- **The language** used on a print media product will convey messages about the genre of the product and its narrative features. The blurb on the back of a video game cover is constructed in order to give a taste of the narrative. This may include hyperbole and enigma in order to attract a potential audience.
- **Enigma codes** are a way of holding the interest of the audience. The creator of the product will withhold information and 'tease' the audience so that they will access the whole product in order to find the narrative in its entirety. In print products enigmas are created through, for example, headlines, taglines and cover lines.

Key Terms

Taglines
A short, memorable phrase that sums up the print product and conveys a sense of its brand identity.

Jump line
Used in magazines at the end of a cover line. Usually tells the audience which page to turn to in order to read the full story.

Quickfire 1.12

What techniques are used on the front pages of newspapers to convey the narrative of an event? Give examples from newspapers covering an event on the same day.

Quickfire 1.13

How has a narrative been constructed in the image below of Syrian refugees arriving in Greece?

Quickfire 1.14

How can the meaning of an image change depending on the words that accompany it?

Key Terms

Contexts
The aspects of the environment that surround a product at the time of its creation, distribution, circulation or reception and that may affect its meaning.

Representation
The ways in which the media represents the world and aspects of it, for example social groups, issues and events.

Stereotypes
A construction whereby characters' traits are over-exaggerated to make them easily recognisable. Stereotypes can be positive or negative and are quick ways for the creators of products to convey messages to an audience.

Encode
Communicate ideas and messages through a system of signs.

Decode
The process through which an audience interprets a message.

The Media Studies Framework: Representation

What is Representation?

In the context of Media Studies as a subject, representation means the way in which aspects of society and social identity, including gender, age and ethnicity, are presented to an audience in specific media products through media language. It is also relevant to consider how issues and events are represented in the media, and what effect this might have upon how an audience may respond. The way in which these aspects are represented will change according to the **context** of the product. It is important to consider the following questions when addressing the concept of **representation** across the products you will study:

- What kind of world is represented by the media product? How do the media construct versions of 'reality' through representation?
- How and why may particular social groups be under-represented or misrepresented?
- How and why are **stereotypes** used both positively and negatively in media products?
- Who is in control of the representation contained within the media product? How are ideas and values apparent in the representations?
- How are representations encoded through media language and how do they reinforce particular values, attitudes and beliefs?
- How may representations position audiences and in what different ways might audiences respond to and interpret those representations?

All media products, both factual and fictional, are constructed. They offer versions of reality that have gone through a process of mediation. The constructions contain messages that will be interpreted differently by different audiences. The values, attitudes and beliefs of the product's creators will often be encoded in the constructed representations. You need to be able to effectively discuss representation as a concept by referring to the following.

Tip

Demonstrate your understanding of the links between the product, the representations contained within it and the audience that consumes it.

Encoding and Decoding

The media is very powerful and the way in which it represents aspects of society, issues and events links directly to the way in which audiences interpret, understand and respond to these areas. Repetition by a media product of a particular representation over time has the effect of making that representation appear 'normal'. For example, the front covers of some women's magazines and pages of online magazines continually offer unrealistic representations of perfect women. The producers of a media product use media language to **encode** ideas and messages through the representations constructed within the product. The audience then **decode** these messages and respond to them in a range of different ways. The way in which women are represented in magazines may be accepted by some audiences who will 'buy into' the messages regarding body size. Other readers may challenge or ignore the message and will decode the product differently, extracting from it only what matters to them.

Quickfire 1.15

What effect may the repetition of particular representations within a media product have upon an audience?

Stereotypes

The creation of stereotypes by media products is a quick way of categorising groups of people according to their shared, recognisable but exaggerated characteristics. **Tessa Perkins** conducted research into stereotypes and concluded that a stereotype:

- is a group concept that categorises a group, not an individual
- works by exaggerating certain shared features of the group
- has features that are recognised and understood, as they tend to be repeated across media forms
- where stereotypes are negative they may block the capacity of the audience to be objective and analytical
- not all stereotypes are negative; 'all Italians are romantic' is a positive stereotype
- communicates messages quickly
- can convey the ideas and beliefs of society, for example 'teenagers today are a problem'.

Construction

The elements that make up any media product will have been constructed to achieve an effect. This finished construction, particularly in factual products, gives an illusion of reality that becomes accepted by an audience as the truth. The **fly-on-the-wall** filming style of a television documentary constructs a narrative that positions the audience through the editing of film footage. The hours of film have been edited to present a particular view of a character or situation in order to manipulate the emotions of the audience. For the programme *Educating Essex*, the hidden cameras were placed in the school for several weeks and the final episodes of the programme were constructed from that footage. Characters were focused upon and narratives were created, but we were not seeing real life in that school, we were seeing a selected representation.

Mediation

This relates to construction and **selection** and is the process that a product may go through before it is consumed by an audience. For example, coverage of the government's post-pandemic recovery plans in 2021 were regularly covered on newspaper front pages. With stories like this, audiences have to rely on how the issues are represented and mediated by the newspaper. This will reflect the values and attitudes of the newspaper and the expectations of their readers. The processes used by the *Daily Mirror* (see right) were:

- The main image selected by the producers reflects the message the newspaper wants to convey, in this case a negative image of Boris Johnson.
- The main image is also anchored by a headline and sub-headings that reinforce the uncaring attitude of the PM, mediated by the newspaper, '*Struggling workers to be hit hardest …*'.

Key Figure

Tessa Perkins

Perkins was a lecturer and researcher who, in an important paper entitled 'Rethinking Stereotypes' (1978), explored and challenged the misconceptions regarding how the media constructs and uses stereotypes to communicate messages.

Key Terms

Fly-on-the-wall
A form of documentary filmmaking in which the camera is an invisible presence, positioning the viewer voyeuristically as an unseen observer – hence the term 'fly-on-the-wall'.

Selection
What is chosen to be included by the creators of the product. This selection may reflect the values, attitudes and beliefs of the product, as decisions have been made about what to include and what to leave out.

Quickfire 1.16

How does mediation manipulate the way an audience may respond?

- The image chosen of Sir Keir Starmer, leader of the Labour Party, is more caring and sympathetic.
- Within the newspaper the **editorial** may offer further opinion, offering a representation of the event.
- The way in which the event was mediated through the images, text and representations affects the way in which an audience may respond.

Theoretical Framework: Stuart Hall

Stuart Hall is a cultural theorist whose research encompasses several media concepts, including how representations are constructed and the ways in which audiences may respond to these constructions. He put forward the idea that:

- representation is the way in which meanings are produced through the signs and codes that are a part of media language
- stereotyping reduces people to a few simple, recognisable characteristics
- stereotyping tends to occur where there are inequalities of power, for example minority groups in society may often be represented as 'other' and 'different'.

Context and Purpose

It is important that you demonstrate an understanding of representation in terms of context and purpose. The representation in any particular media product, according to the type of product it is, i.e. the context, will have a different purpose. It will also be interpreted differently by audiences. For example, the representation of young people in *The Young Offenders* (BBC Three, 2018) is different from that of *Show Trial* (BBC One, 2021), as the purpose of one is comedy and the second is crime drama. In *The Young Offenders*, stereotypes are used in order to rapidly transmit messages about characters, in order that the audience will recognise the stereotypical character traits. It is from these stereotypes that the comedy evolves and the audience have expectations of how the characters will behave. They accept that they are not realistic representations but are created for a purpose.

Self-representation

The rise of new digital media platforms offers a range of opportunities for self-representation. Websites, **blogs**, YouTube, Instagram, TikTok and **vlogs** allow users to represent themselves and regularly update this representation. The choices made about which images to upload, what to wear and how to construct the self-representation communicate messages about how we want others to see us. Unlike in real life, we can control this version of ourselves we show to others.

'Selfies' are also used in modern society to construct a narrative for our lives, as we select what we want the image to reflect about where we are and who we are with. Instagram stories enable users to create and post a narrative of their day through photos, videos, doodles and stickers.

Vloggers, bloggers and YouTubers such as JJ Olatunji/KSI and Zoe Sugg are very aware of how they present themselves to their millions of followers and carefully construct their social media persona. These media platforms have also given an opportunity for under-represented and misrepresented social groups to construct representations that reflect their identity. The increasingly easy access to digital platforms can also allow minority groups and individuals to air their points of view to a wide audience.

Stretch and Challenge 1.3

In order to prepare for the unseen element of Component 1, research how other newspapers represent issues and events.

Stretch and Challenge 1.4

Conduct some independent research to further your knowledge and understanding of Stuart Hall's theoretical perspective.

Key Terms

Editorial
The part of the newspaper written, supposedly, by the editor who comments on the day's stories. It offers an opportunity for the paper to express its views and to demonstrate its values, attitudes and beliefs.

Blog
A regularly updated website or web page, usually posted by an individual or small group, written in an informal or conversational style.

Vlog
A blog in video form. Short for video blog.

Quickfire 1.17

What is the disadvantage of self-representation on digital platforms?

Theoretical Framework: David Gauntlett

David Gauntlett's theoretical perspective revolves around the idea of the autonomy of the audience, and how they use and respond to different media products. He asserts that:

- the media provide audiences and users with the resources to allow them to construct their own identities
- while, in the past, media products tended to convey straightforward messages about ideal types of male and female identities, contemporary media products offer audiences a more diverse range of icons and characters, allowing them to 'pick and mix' different ideas.

Named Theorist

David Gauntlett

David Gauntlett is Canada Research Chair in Creative Innovation and Leadership in the Faculty of Communication and Design, Ryerson University, Toronto. He writes about the ways in which digital media give people new opportunities to create and connect.

Stretch and Challenge 1.5

Visit David Gauntlett's website to further your understanding of his theoretical perspective: www.davidgauntlett.com

Representations of Gender in the Media Today

Women

The representation of women in the media has developed and adapted to reflect cultural and sociological changes. As women's roles in society have undergone a transformation, this has been reflected in some areas of the media where there is evidence of representations of strong, independent women. However, there are still some stereotypical representations of women where they are defined by how men see them and how society expects them to look and behave. Women still tend to be judged on their looks and appearance foremost, and many media products offer **aspirational** images of women. Representations tend to concentrate also on their sexuality and emotions, and narratives tend to be based around relationships. The way in which the representation of women is constructed in products such as lifestyle magazines remains largely unrealistic and instils unattainable aspiration in the audience.

Interestingly, while the representation of men has become more complex and rounded, the criteria for whether the representation of women is positive tend to be how strong they are. A more effective judgement may be whether they have a central and effective role within the narrative. Tasha Robinson, writer and film critic, introduced the term 'Trinity Syndrome' which is related to the character of Trinity in *The Matrix*. She uses this to describe those female characters in certain media products, particularly films, who start strongly, and then end weak and vulnerable, either dead or defined by their romantic relationships.

In an examination response it is important that you explore the representation of gender within the set products at a sophisticated level and go beyond a basic discussion of positive and negative, as gender representation is much more complex than that.

Key Term

Aspirational

Aimed at or appealing to people who want to improve how they look, attain a higher social position or have a better standard of living.

Quickfire 1.18

How does the 1960s advertisement on the left reflect the representation of women at the time?

Stretch and Challenge 1.6

Read Tasha Robinson's article, which explores her theory of the 'Trinity Syndrome' in more detail: https://thedissolve.com/features/exposition/618-were-losing-all-our-strong-female-characters-to-tr/.

Quickfire 1.19

Give an example of a representation of women in the media that challenges outdated stereotypes.

Older media products reflect outdated attitudes to the representation of gender.

While there remain many stereotypical representations of women in the media, there are also products that are constructed to challenge these representations in order to meet the demands and expectations of a contemporary audience and to more accurately reflect the contemporary role of women in society.

These examples hold messages that offer a more realistic or refreshing representation of women in the media today. In film and television we see more women who have key roles and who are active rather than passive. They are defined by what they do, rather than what they have done to them. They are less the victim and more the hero.

Since the #metoo movement and other high profile cases about the treatment of women, some media producers have become more aware of how women are represented in their products.

Men

Stereotypically, men in media products are represented differently from women, but their representation, like that of women, has changed in order to address changes in society. There have been many cries that **masculinity** is in crisis and that men no longer have a traditional role to play in society as they once did. However, it is the case that men, just like women, have had to change their roles and this has been reflected in their representation across a range of media products. With the advent of the **new man** there appeared different representations of masculinity.

However, even when disguised as a new man, representations of men in the media tend to often still focus on:

- body image and physique
- physical strength
- sexual attractiveness and relationships with women
- power and independence.

There still exist in the media the more stereotypical representations of men in strong roles, defined by their power, independence and ability to survive against all the odds. These representations tend to be associated with particular genres, for example crime dramas and advertising.

Music video as a media form reflects the diverse representations of gender in the media today. Artists such as Sam Fender present representations of anguished masculinity in their videos, which contain themes such as a regretted past, relationships and the pressures of modern-day society. In *Seventeen Going Under* he sings about his younger self and the regrets he has about his life then and the decisions he made. This representation contrasts with music videos from the rap genre, which often offer the notion of men as having the power in society and relationships with women as their accessories.

Key Terms

Masculinity
The state of 'being a man', which can change as society changes. It is essentially what being a man means to a particular generation. This is then reflected in media products of the time.

New man
A term that was introduced to describe a new era of masculinity. These men rejected sexist attitudes; they were in touch with their feminine side and were therefore not afraid to be sensitive and caring, and could sometimes be seen in a domestic role.

Quickfire 1.20

How does the poster for *From Russia with Love* (top) reflect the time in which it was made?

Quickfire 1.21

What types of representation of masculinity can we expect to see in music videos from the rap genre?

Ethnicity

Consider the following general points about how **ethnicity** is represented in the media today:

- Just like representations of other aspects of social identity such as gender, representations of **race** and ethnicity matter as they can shape and influence the way in which we see ourselves and those around us.
- However, while representations of race and ethnicity have started to change in recent years, people from minority ethnic groups still tend to be defined in terms of their differences and their perceived 'otherness'. This can be used to offer both positive and negative representations of ethnicity in the media.
- Just like other groups within the media, there are stereotypical representations of ethnicity defined generally by **racial** characteristics.
- Stereotypes, misrepresentation and under-representation are even more dangerous when dealing with ethnicity compared to gender, as the representation that is constructed through the media is often the only experience of these cultures that some audiences will encounter.
- Black and Asian people are often represented as being exotic in some media texts, for example magazines. Beyoncé, in her music videos, regularly manipulates her own ethnic representation using visual codes including clothing and iconography.
- Young black people have been demonised by some areas of the media and at times are presented as linked to violence and gang culture in news programmes and the press.
- **Tokenism** can also be an issue with regard to the representation of ethnic minorities. For example, black, Asian or minority ethnic characters have often been relegated to the status of secondary characters in mainstream films and television programmes, denied a meaningful role or voice within the narrative. However, there are signs that this is beginning to change. For example, the BBC has used predominantly black casts in recent primetime dramas such as *You Don't Know Me* and *The Pact*.
- There has been criticism of some media products for the stereotypical representation of ethnic groups. However, ethnic minorities are presented more positively in some areas of the music industry, where there is more scope to celebrate their cultural roots. Rap music's increasing popularity has changed the perceptions of young white people to black and Asian culture. Beyoncé is an aspirational figure for many black audiences as her music videos often convey empowering messages of black pride.

Tip

In preparation for Component 1 you will need to analyse other products that challenge the representations evident in your set products.

Key Terms

Ethnicity
Many people confuse ethnicity and race. Your ethnicity is defined by your cultural identity, which may demonstrate itself through customs, dress or food, for example. Ethnicity suggests an identity that is based on a sense of place, ideology or religion. You can be British but of Jewish ethnicity, for instance.

Race
Your race is defined by the fact that you descend from a common ancestor giving you a particular set of racial characteristics. These may be related to the colour of your skin and facial features, for example.

Tokenism
Providing a cursory or superficial representation of those groups in society who are often underrepresented in order to convey an impression of equality and inclusivity.

Stretch and Challenge 1.7

Watch the music video for *Brown Skin Girl* by Beyonce: www.youtube.com/watch?v=vRFS0MYTC1I.

How are race and ethnicity represented?

Stretch and Challenge 1.8

Visit the ethnicity resource on the WJEC Eduqas website to access more information and examples.

Key Terms

Issue
An important matter or topic that is of public concern.

Event
Something that occurs or is about to occur and is of interest to an audience. Events come in a range of shapes and forms and can be local, national or international, for example a royal wedding or birth, the Olympic Games or a pop festival. International events may include wars and global recession. A local event may be the local football team being promoted.

Dominant ideology
A set of values and beliefs that have broader social or cultural currency. This may be implicit or explicit as is evident in media products such as tabloid newspapers.

Opinion leaders
Those in positions of power who aim to persuade an audience of their point of view. Within the media these may be newspaper editors, programme producers or bloggers.

Quickfire 1.22

How might the way in which the producers of a documentary choose to represent an event affect how the audience may respond?

Issues and Events

The representation of **issues** and **events** in different media products is one of the areas of the specification you will cover during your course. When studying the representation of issues and events you need to consider:

- The values and attitudes of the product in which the issue/event features. Is it clear what the product you are analysing thinks about the issue/event? Is there any evidence of opinion or bias in the way in which the issue/event is represented?
- How the issue/event has been represented, referring to, for example, aspects of media language, including terminology and mode of address, anchorage, technical, visual and audio codes, and the use of images.
- The construction of the representation. The elements that go to make up the final product will have been constructed in a way that real life is not. For example, when we witness an event in real life we do not see it from several different perspectives. However, this is often the way we are shown an event as it is presented to us in the media. It is a selected construction and has been edited often to show a particular viewpoint.
- True crime documentaries are a popular genre but receive both praise and criticism. While these programmes are a totally immersive experience for the binge-watching generation, they are also criticised for being one sided and selective in the information they include. The Netflix mini series *Inventing Anna* starts each episode with the statement: '*This whole story is completely true. Except for the parts that are completely made up.*'
- With regard to issues, the media construct a representation of the specific issue, for example the migrant crisis, and may in fact create the issue itself.
- The process of selection. For whatever ends up in print or in a television documentary, a lot more will have been left out. Someone will have made the decision about what will be included and what to omit. Consider how this might affect the way the audience feels about the issue or event.
- That mediation has occurred. During the construction of the representation there will have been opportunities for the creators of the product to encode messages and meanings, for example through the caption that accompanies an image that anchors the meaning. This will reflect the **dominant ideology** of that particular media product.
- The product, for example the newspaper, becomes the **opinion leader** and offers a constructed view of the issue/event.
- The focus of the representation, the way in which a media product is mediated, encourages the audience to focus upon a particular aspect of the product to encourage us into making assumptions and draw conclusions. For example, our eyes are drawn to the headlines or the central image in newspapers.
- The audience and their different responses to the representations encoded within the product.

Stretch and Challenge 1.9

Explore how a newspaper front page you have studied has represented an issue or event.

The Media Studies Framework: Audience

An understanding of audiences and how they respond to media products is an essential aspect of the Media Studies course.

Understanding Audiences

- The relationship between the media product and the audience is fluid and changing.
- Unlike in the past, there is no longer assumed to be only one way of interpreting a product and only one audience response.
- Audiences are not mass; their responses are complex and sophisticated, and are influenced by a range of factors.
- Audiences are made up of individuals whose social and cultural experiences may affect how they respond to any media text.
- Media products and the industries that produce them are acutely aware of their audience and the strategies needed to attract them.
- There is a range of theories that explain the different ways in which audiences respond to media texts and the reasons for this.

In studying audiences in relation to the set products you will explore in breadth and those you will study in depth, you will need to consider:

- how audiences are grouped and categorised by media industries including by age, gender, social class and lifestyle
- how media producers target, attract, reach, address and possibly construct audiences
- how media industries target audiences through the content and appeal of the media products and through the ways in which they are marketed, distributed and circulated
- the relationship between media technologies and how audiences **consume** and respond to different media products
- the different ways in which audiences may interpret and respond to the same media products according to how media language creates meanings
- how audiences are positioned by media products
- how audiences interact with the media and can be actively involved in media production.

Key Term

Consume
Another way of saying how an audience uses a media product. We consume media products for different reasons.

Quickfire 1.23

Why is it important that media industries are aware of their audience?

Different forms and platforms allow audiences to interact with media products.

Key Terms

Demographic profiling
A way of categorising audiences by dividing consumers into groups based on age, sex, income, education, occupation, household size, marital status, home ownership or other factors. This information is of use to some media industries, for example it can help advertisers determine their target audience for particular products and develop adverts that focus on a specific demographic.

Psychographic profiling
A way of categorising audiences based on personality, values, opinions, attitudes and lifestyles.

Silver surfer
An older person who is computer literate and uses the net to purchase goods and find out information.

Tip

Consider how useful demographic and psychographic profiling is when analysing examples of historic advertisements and magazines.

Key Figure

Young and Rubicam
Young and Rubicam is a New York advertising agency that developed a method of categorising people into recognisable stereotypes that reflect their motivational needs.

Audience Categories

Audiences can be categorised by media industries in a number of ways in order to define them more easily and to consider how they can be targeted. These include by age, gender and class. The magazine and advertising industries, in particular, still tend to categorise audiences in terms of income, lifestyle and needs, although this is seen to be an outdated method of classifying. It may still be used because these industries are focusing on selling a clearly defined product and they must therefore be accurate about the target audience. Audiences can be defined through their **demographic profile** or through their **psychographic profile**.

Stretch and Challenge 1.10

Many companies collect audience data. One of the most reliable is Statista, www.statista.com. Visit its site and engage in research into media audiences for the different set forms.

A demographic audience profile categorises an audience from A to E according to their class, occupation and income, where categories A and B are the wealthiest and most influential members of society, and are therefore assumed to have the most disposable income. It is often used by advertisers to determine where advertisements should be placed according to the demographic profile of the audience. Some media products will use the demographic profiling to inform advertisers of the target audience.

- Interestingly, retired people used to be in category E to reflect their loss of income, but with the rise of early retirement with a lucrative pension and the **silver surfer**, this group has moved to a higher category to reflect their disposable income and their obvious appeal to advertisers.
- Age and gender are also aspects of demographic profiling and some media products will publish details of their target audience in order to provide broad information for the advertisers.

A psychographic audience profile defines an audience by their values, attitudes and lifestyles (VALs). As the concept of class and income became a less appropriate way of defining an audience, advertisers considered different ways of categorising audiences. One of the most useful to consider when discussing how advertisers define audiences is **Young and Rubicam**'s Four Consumers (four Cs). This advertising agency considered how cross-cultural consumer characteristics can group people into seven recognisable stereotypes reflected through motivational needs and VALs, including security, control, status, individuality, freedom, survival and escape. The main groups are:

- **Mainstreamers**: these make up 40% of the population. They like security, tried and trusted brands, and like to think they belong to a group of like-minded people. They are persuaded by value for money and are less likely to take risks.
- **Aspirers**: this group want status and prefer brands that show their place in society. They are happy to live on credit and will buy designer label items. They are stylish and dynamic and may be persuaded by celebrity endorsement.

- **Explorers**: like to discover new things. They are attracted by brands that offer new experiences and instant results.
- **Succeeders**: people who already have status and control, and have nothing to prove. They prefer brands that are serious and reliable and believe that they deserve the best.
- **Reformers**: this group are defined by their self-esteem and self-fulfilment. They tend to be innovative and are less impressed by status. They are not materialistic and are socially aware. They may be more inclined to buy brands that are environmentally friendly or those that are considered healthy.

At Channel 4, the producers felt they did not know enough about one of their target markets, 16- to 24-year-olds, so they decided to conduct their own research called *UK Tribes*. The channel wanted more than a demographic segmentation of their youth audience but wanted to find out from the young people themselves how they arranged themselves in society. They asked lots of young people a range of questions, including what brands they liked, how they spend their time and money, and what they thought about the future. From their findings the researchers came up with five 'Tribes': Mainstream, Alternative, Urban, Aspirant and Leading Edge. What is interesting about this research is that it is based on how young people see themselves: on **self-identification**. This research is ongoing and is constantly updated, identifying new tribes and changing behaviour. This research has had an impact on Channel 4's commissioning and marketing. The recent research has expanded into audio-visual identities (AV:ID) considering how young people consume media.

Channel 4 make their research findings available to other media organisations to help them more effectively and accurately target the needs of young people.

Key Term

Self-identification
How you see yourself and how you may categorise yourself as belonging to a particular group or class, for example a skater, a member of the Green Party, etc.

Quickfire 1.24

How might Channel 4's research be useful to other media industries?

Stretch and Challenge 1.11

Visit Channel 4's *UK Tribes* website and look in more detail at their research and how it has been used: www.uktribes.com.

How Do Media Products Target/Attract/Reach and Address Audiences?

In the examination, you may be asked a 'product out' rather that an 'audience in' question. This means that you will have to consider how the different media products you have studied attempt to attract their audience. Firstly, it may be useful to consider the **target audience** of the media product. This will differ according to the type of product; for example, some media products operate narrow casting and are targeting a **niche audience**. Other products will attempt to attract as wide an audience as possible through a range of methods. You will then need to consider how the products attract, reach and address their target audience. Methods may include:

- **Technical and audio codes**: the product may employ these to target an audience. The fast-paced editing and dramatic music of a trailer for a television drama serves to attract audiences, likewise the large dramatic headlines of a tabloid newspaper.
- **The language and mode of address** may target a specific audience and alienate another. For example, the images and text on the *Call of Duty* game's cover may use lexis and a tone specific to an audience of young men: only they will understand the language and references as they are the intended audience. The voice-over of a television documentary may attract fans of the sub-genre by the tone of voice and the narrative enigmas.
- **The construction** of the product and the audience within the product. The way in which, for example, the opening sequence of a television drama is edited and constructed will be designed to target an audience. This may involve enigmas, multi-stranded narratives and the use of stars and their roles.
- An audience can also be targeted through the ways in which the product is marketed and distributed. For example, viral, online and social media teaser campaigns for television dramas are used to target a younger audience. WitcherCon in 2021 was a global virtual marketing campaign created to launch the new series of *The Witcher* and streamed across social media platforms.
- **The positioning of the audience**: this may be through the camera shots and angles, the use of music and other audio codes, the language and mode of address or through empathy with the characters.

How are Audiences Constructed by Media Products?

- Audiences are constructed by products. The producers will spend a lot of time researching their target audience and constructing an idea of who they are, what they like, their opinions, etc. Some products, for example newspapers, will produce **media or press packs** for advertisers, containing information about their audience. Some of this will be from audience research but some will be an idea of who that audience is and who the creators of the product would like them to be. There is often a difference between the product's construction of the audience and the actual consumer of the product; this is particularly the case with lifestyle magazines.
- A newspaper, for example, may, using the image, headlines and plugs on its front cover, construct a clear idea of who the reader of the newspaper should be. It will create assumptions about the lifestyle of the audience and establish what is 'normal' within the world of the newspaper.

Key Terms

Target audience
The specific group at whom the product is aimed.

Niche audience
A relatively small audience with specialised interests, tastes and backgrounds.

Media/press pack
Put together by the owners of products, for example magazines and newspapers, and intended to give information to advertisers. It informs them about the details of the assumed target audience, including income, marital status and age. It usually gives a pen portrait of the audience. The pack also includes the rates to place an advertisement in the print publication. However, they are also a useful resource for media students and can be downloaded or requested from the magazine.

Quickfire 1.25

Give an example of a media product that targets a niche audience.

Tip

When constructing your examination response, make sure that you have picked out the key word related to audience in the question, for example 'target'. This will help you to focus your answer.

Quickfire 1.26

Give another example of how a product constructs its audience.

Stretch and Challenge 1.12

Look at the press pack or marketing materials for one of the set products you are studying and consider how they construct their audience.

- **YouGov** engages in a range of audience research, for example data related to newspapers and their readers is collected at regular intervals tracking changes over time.

Is the British press a force for good?

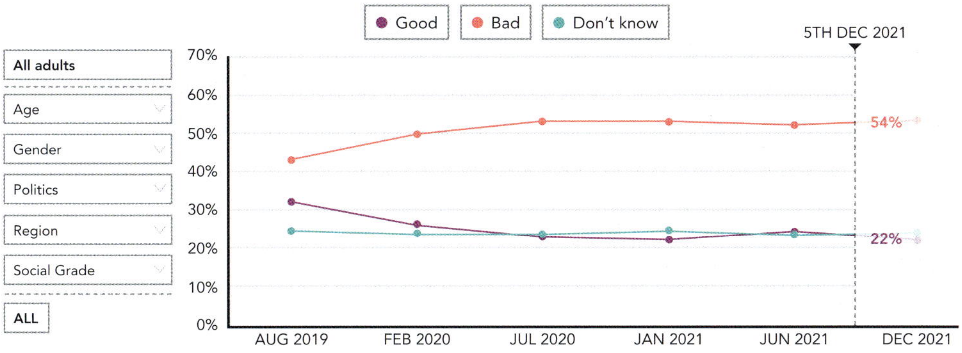

Audience Positioning

Media products are constructed in order to place audiences in a particular position in relation to the product. Audience positioning concerns the relationship between the specific product and the responses an audience may have to that product. The producers encode the product with meanings and messages through media language, and the audience decode these messages. Different audiences will decode the same products in different ways and will therefore have a different response.

How Do Media Products Position Audiences?

- **Through the technical codes employed by the product**. In an audio-visual product the camera shots and angles used place the audience in a particular position. For example, the use of a close-up shot at an emotional time in the narrative may encourage the audience to be sympathetic to the character. A point-of-view shot positions the audience as a character and allows them to experience events from that perspective. This may enhance the audience pleasure in the text. However, the positioning may be an uncomfortable one. For example, the use of an extreme close-up of a character's face in a tense moment may make the audience feel uncomfortable. The camera may take the audience where they do not want to go, for example in a horror film trailer.
- **Through the language and mode of address**. The use of chatty and colloquial language in vlogs and blogs positions the intended audience as part of the world of the vlogger/blogger. This makes the audience feel involved through the use of a direct and informal mode of address and the use of a specific lexis. In contrast, the formal language and mode of address used by quality **broadsheet** newspapers positions the audience differently. It makes them feel superior and valued as a reader and the expectation is that they will understand and want to be informed.
- **Through the construction of the product** and of the audience within the product, media products can be said to construct an idea of their audience or user. The audience for a vlog, for example, is 'told' by the creator what is important and how they should live their lives.

Audience Responses

The positioning of audiences by the creators of media products suggests that they should accept the messages contained within the product and decode the text in the way expected. However, as we have stated previously, audiences do not all respond to the same product in the same way. They may accept or challenge the messages encoded within the product.

Key Figure

YouGov
YouGov conducts research on the internet about politics, public affairs, products, brands and other topics of general interest. YouGov surveys are taken by people, from all over the nation, who have agreed to share their thoughts on a wide variety of important issues. The data collected are used by, for example, the news media and marketing agencies to broaden their understanding of their audience.

Quickfire 1.27

Why is the YouGov research useful for newspaper producers?

Stretch and Challenge 1.13

Visit the YouGov website to look at the available research into newspapers and their readers: https://yougov.co.uk.

Quickfire 1.28

What is the usual mode of address of a vlog aimed at a youth audience?

Key Term

Broadsheet
Describes a quality newspaper that publishes more serious news, for example the *Daily Telegraph*.

In this shot the audience is positioned as a character in the narrative.

Named Theorist

Stuart Hall

Stuart Hall was a cultural theorist who explored the issue of how people make sense of media products. He was a proponent of the reception theory and suggested that products are encoded by the creators of the product and decoded differently by different audiences.

Key Terms

Active audience
This describes an audience who responds to and interprets the media products in different ways and who actively engages with the messages encoded in the products.

Passive audience
This describes an audience that does not engage actively with the product. They are more likely to accept the preferred meaning of the text without challenge. This also suggests that passive audiences are more likely to be directly affected by the messages contained within the product.

Desensitisation
This is a psychological process which suggests that audiences who are exposed regularly to acts of violence through films and video games, for example, are increasingly less likely to feel empathy or concern when exposed to violence, bad language or other forms of aggressive behaviour.

Quickfire 1.29

Using the set products you have studied in class, explain how gender or age may affect responses. Be specific in your response.

Theoretical Framework: Stuart Hall

Stuart Hall accepted that **audiences** were **active**, not **passive**, and suggested that there were three main ways in which an audience may respond to a media product:

- **The preferred reading**: where the audience accepts the dominant reading and interprets the messages contained within the product in the way that the producer intended. This is usually the case if the product reflects the ideas and beliefs of the audience. For example, the readers of the *Daily Mail* will broadly agree with the paper's stance on issues such as immigration and young people, or they would not read the newspaper. There is, therefore, little for the audience to challenge.
- **The negotiated reading**: where the audience accepts some of the product's messages and disagrees with others, therefore negotiating over their acceptance of what is presented to them. For example, an audience may agree with sections of the press that something must be done about the numbers of migrants but feels that they are being represented badly and that we have a moral duty to help.
- **Oppositional readings**: where the audience does not agree with the values, attitudes and beliefs of the product or its content. This may be related to the culture, age, gender or other factors affecting audience response. For example, an older person watching *Bridgerton* may have an oppositional reading of the product because of the narrative content.

What Affects the Way in which an Audience Responds to a Media Text?

As said earlier, an audience is not generally thought to be a mass all behaving in the same way; it is made up of individuals who, according to a range of factors, will respond to the same media product in different ways. This may be related to:

- **Gender**: different genders respond to different media products differently. It has been suggested, for example, that women enjoy the themes and narratives of television programmes such as soap operas more than men. This may be because soap operas deal with relationships and domestic narratives that are in the experiences of most women, who can therefore empathise with the characters and their situation. However, it is important to avoid simple generalisations; many men also watch these genres of programmes.
- **Age**: again, we need to be careful of making generalisations, but different ages will respond differently to media texts. Older audiences may be less comfortable with sexually explicit media products with a high level of bad language. However, a younger audience, who have been more **desensitised** to this sort of content, may be more comfortable consuming this type of text.
- **Culture and cultural experience**: the culture, upbringing and experiences of the audience will often shape their view of and response to media products. Media products also shape our experience and manipulate our responses to other products. For example, we may have never been in hospital but our experience of hospitals has been formed from television programmes. Audiences then feel in a position to challenge or comment on procedures in one media product from their experience of viewing a different product. The experience will not be actual.

- **Ethnicity**: ethnic groups from different cultural backgrounds may respond to texts differently because of their ideas, beliefs and upbringing. Different ethnic groups may also have strong responses to how they themselves are represented in media products. For example, the Channel 4 comedy *We Are Lady Parts* was welcomed by Muslim women as it offered refreshing representations, but some audiences were concerned about the irreverent dialogue.
- **Cultural competence**: this may also relate to age and gender but is developed over time. Some audiences have different **cultural competences** to others, this is particularly true with regard to users of the internet and video games, where understanding is shared among those who 'use' the products. The playing of video games tends to be within the cultural competence of younger people. Older audiences are not digital natives and may not be as familiar with these products, they are therefore alienated as this experience is outside of their cultural competence.
- **Situated culture**: concerns the 'situation' of the audience and how that may affect how they respond to a media product. This may mean literally where the audience is. The communal viewing of a film in a cinema, in the dark, produces a very different response and pleasure compared to watching the same film in a well-lit sitting room, where you may be interrupted and distracted. Who you watch the product with will also affect response. For example, watching a comedy programme with bad language and sexual references with an older person in the room may produce a more uncomfortable viewing experience for a younger person.

Theoretical Framework: Albert Bandura

There are several theories that have been written about audiences, how products appeal to them, and how and why they respond in different ways. It is essential when answering some of the questions that may be set in the examination, that you refer to and use theories and theoretical perspectives and demonstrate your understanding of them in relation to your set products.

Albert Bandura conducted research into media effects. His 'social learning theory' suggested that children may learn aggressive behaviour from viewing others. He also asserted that:

- the media can implant ideas in the mind of the audience directly
- audiences acquire attitudes, emotional responses and new ways of behaving through modelling those they observe
- media representations of violent behaviour, for example in video games, can encourage audiences to imitate that behaviour.

This theoretical perspective is also known as the **hypodermic syringe model** and is criticised by some, including David Gauntlett, as being outdated and unhelpful when analysing audience responses.

Named Theorist

Albert Bandura
Albert Bandura was an American psychologist who conducted research into observational learning, which has been used to discuss the effect of some media products on audience behaviour.

Key Terms

Cultural competences
Within a media context, this concept suggests that the cultural competence of an audience is the shared knowledge, related to their cultural understanding, of that audience, which means that they will take a particular pleasure from a media product. For example, the audience who understand and engage with the rules of *Call of Duty*, and have a certain computer literacy, will enjoy the control aspect of the game and the online sharing of techniques.

Hypodermic syringe model
Also known as the hypodermic needle model. Now largely viewed as an outdated effects theory, which suggests that audiences are a mass that behave the same way in response to a media product. The media product injects ideas into the minds of the assumed passive audience who will respond as one.

Quickfire 1.30

Can Bandura's theory be applied to contemporary media products and audiences?

Tip

It is acceptable in some questions that as well as using theories to help understand products, you can also challenge their validity.

Key Terms

Participatory culture
A culture where individuals are not only the consumers of media products but also contribute to existing products or produce their own.

Event television
Describes programmes such as, for example, the final of *The Great British Bake Off* that attract a large, live audience and as such become an 'event'.

Prosumer
Derives from a marketing term 'production by consumers' and is used to describe those individuals who comment on, create and adapt existing content, and then distribute it through the internet and social media. These people can be very valuable to the success of a product.

Buzz marketing
Can also be simply termed 'buzz' and refers to word-of-mouth advertising whereby the interaction of consumers creates a positive association, excitement and anticipation about a new product.

Quickfire 1.31

What enjoyment can an audience get out of interacting directly with a media product?

Quickfire 1.32

Why are bloggers and vloggers important in the marketing of a product?

Interactive Audiences

In contemporary society there are more opportunities than ever before for audiences to interact with products. The ease of access to the internet, and social media in particular, gives audiences a platform from which to immediately interact with others about media products. This **participatory culture** enables audiences to access, comment on and represent media content. This can be done immediately and across multimedia channels.

At another level, despite media commentators heralding the death of **event television**, audiences are actively engaging with programmes that allow them to participate in voting, blogging and using Twitter to comment on a programme's content while they are watching. As well as giving its viewers opportunities to engage with the programme through voting, *Strictly Come Dancing* actively encourages its audiences to interact with the programme through social media platforms. It also posts positive Twitter messages on its website and promotes the *Strictly Come Dancing* podcast, presented in 2021 by Joe Sugg and Kim Winston, each week in the programme.

Newspapers and their websites, when unexpected events happen, now often rely upon the images and audio-visual footage taken on a mobile phone from a member of the public who happened to witness the event. This citizen journalism provides a narrative structure for what is taking place, which also provides immediacy through their involvement. There is now a very obvious relationship between the producers of the media and their audiences.

Online fan communities and forums are examples of ways in which audience members come together with shared interests and emotional links to create virtual communities producing original content. New digital technologies have also allowed audiences to become media producers themselves. Fans can create their own unofficial sites, including blogs, images and interactive content. An individual can also create their own original media product; Zoe Sugg is an example of an individual who has created her own popular media products. In the modern internet-dominated world the consumers have become **prosumers**.

These fan sites also allow producers in-depth knowledge of the fan community, which may help in marketing media products.

In 2021, Dove launched its 'Reverse Selfie' campaign which then went viral and generated a 'buzz' around the product and its ideology. The advert showed the reverse process of a teenage girl taking and uploading a selfie to social media. It also encouraged the audience to take the #NoDigitalDistortion pledge to promote unedited, natural beauty. Dove's use of **buzz marketing** via social media proved successful for the product and the related campaign. This use of word-of-mouth buzz marketing via social media proved very successful.

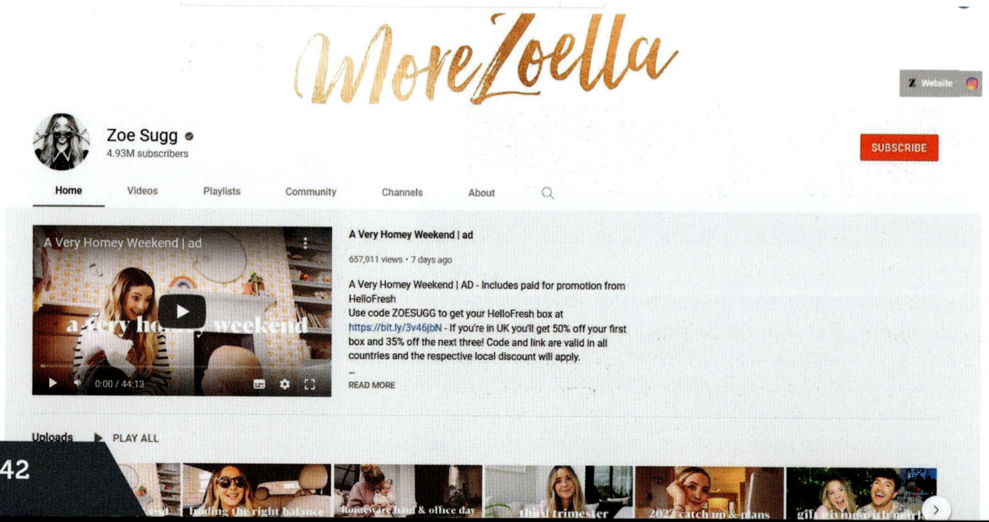

The Media Studies Framework: Industry

It is important when you are studying the set products that you gain an understanding of the industry that produced them and the impact that has upon the products and the audience. You will need to demonstrate knowledge and understanding of industry in the examination. This will include:

- How media organisations, groups and individuals produce, distribute and circulate products nationally and globally. A broadsheet newspaper, for example, has a national circulation, but the online version of the newspaper or an online magazine has a much wider global reach. Individuals as prosumers now have the means to easily distribute content through, for example, social media.
- The relationship between recent technological change and media production, **distribution** and **circulation**. Due to the increased range of digital platforms it is now much easier for distributors to get products to an audience. Relatively new distributors of audio-visual content, for example Netflix and Amazon Prime, have introduced a different way for audiences to access the products they create. As they do not have a specific identity they have the creative flexibility to offer a range of diverse programmes that are not dependent on schedules. Digital streaming, access to all episodes of a series and DVD box sets allow audiences to engage in **binge watching**.
- How media organisations use marketing to maintain national and global audiences. All media organisations will ensure that they market their products across a range of platforms to ensure audiences are reached. **Cross-platform marketing** allows organisations to access a wider audience.
- How different media products are regulated. For example, the new press regulatory body, the **Independent Press Standards Organisation (IPSO)**, is responsible for newspapers and magazines while the Office of Communications (Ofcom) regulates television and radio. However, new digital technologies have proved very hard to regulate, particularly when the content is often created by individuals. This is especially true of the internet where content is easily uploaded without censorship. There is continued discussion about ways in which the internet and social media may be regulated to protect audiences but as yet there is no definitive solution to this problem.
- Some media organisations are very powerful and they have the means to control the distribution and circulation of their products. Large conglomerates with mass ownership of media companies can operate **vertical integration** to maintain control.

Some audiences like to immerse themselves in a product by watching several episodes in one sitting.

Paramount Pictures Corporation is an American film studio that is a subsidiary of American media conglomerate Viacom.

Key Figure

Independent Press Standards Organisation (IPSO)
IPSO is the independent regulator for the newspaper and magazine industry in the UK. It states: '*We hold newspapers and magazines to account for their actions, protect individual rights, uphold high standards of journalism and help to maintain freedom of expression for the press.*'

Key Terms

Distribution
The link between the producer and the audience; refers to all the strategies used in the release, marketing and promotion of the product.

Circulation
A count of how many copies of a particular publication are distributed, including subscriptions. Circulation audits are provided by the Audit Bureau of Circulations (ABC).

Binge watching
Watching multiple episodes of a television programme in succession. On its website, Netflix has a section entitled 'Binge-worthy TV Programmes', which in January 2022 included, *Squid Game*, *The Witcher* and *Emily in Paris*. Netflix states: '*When it comes to great TV, portion control is for suckers. Here are the best programmes – from sitcoms to dramas to reality – to devour all at once*' (www.netflix.com/gb/browse/genre/1191605), tapping into the new ways in which audiences access programmes.

Cross-platform marketing
When one form is advertised on another media platform. For example, BBC One will broadcast promotional advertisements for its radio stations; these will also be on the BBC website.

Vertical integration
A process through which a company develops control over different levels of the value chain. An example of a vertically integrated business would be a production company that is also able to distribute its products or a magazine publisher that owns a printing company.

Quickfire 1.33

What advantages does vertical integration give a company such as Viacom?

Media Contexts

When you are studying your set products, it is very important that you develop your knowledge and understanding of the relevant **contexts** in which the products were created. You will be required to analyse how individual products may reflect their respective social, cultural, historical, political and economic contexts. You will also be required to show your understanding of how specific contexts influence representations and audience responses. These contexts are as follows.

Key Term

Contexts
The aspects of the environment that surround a product at the time of its creation, distribution, circulation or reception and that may affect its meaning.

Historical Context

- How the themes, attitudes, beliefs, values and representations that are encoded in a media product relate to and reflect the time in which it was made. Individual products, for example film posters, will reflect the representations of the time, which may be very different from the representations evident today. Historical media products document social change and as such are important to our understanding of specific time periods.
- How the representations encoded in the media product are affected by the historical context. For example, many of the advertisements from the 1950s and 1960s reflect the domestic role of women at the time and represent men as dominant, in control and as the main wage earners.

Quickfire 1.34

How does the advertisement below for the Kenwood Chef reflect the ideas and beliefs of the time in which it was made?

In the 1960s a woman's place was in the kitchen.

Social and Cultural Context

- The effect on media products of the values and attitudes related to the society in which people live at different times.
- How the values and attitudes related to how different people live may influence their responses to media products.
- How the representations, themes, values, attitudes and beliefs contained within the media product relate to the social and cultural context in which it was made.
- How media products are shaped and informed by particular cultural influences such as genres and styles. For example, how different genres may become popular at different times to reflect sociological changes. For example, the explanation for the rise in popularity of programmes such as *The Great British Bake Off* (*GBBO*) and the falling ratings for the *X Factor*, is that in times of austerity and hardship the *GBBO* offered a warm, nostalgic view of Britain, and baking is relatively cheap and accessible to all. This is a contrast to the celebrity culture of the *X Factor*, which is out of the reach of most people.

Tip

You will be advised which context is relevant for the different set products you will study during your course. Make sure that you can show your knowledge and understanding of these contexts in an examination response. Not all of the contexts will need to be applied to all of the products.

***GBBO* offers a warm nostalgia.**

Economic and Political Contexts

- The importance and relevance of ownership and control, for example the influence of certain media organisations. This can relate to public service broadcasting, **conglomerate** ownership and political viewpoints. For example, the BBC is required to be impartial in its news broadcasts, whereas a newspaper can demonstrate its political allegiance, which will be influenced by the owner of the paper.
- The importance of economic factors such as funding, circulation, sales or audience ratings figures. For example, the constraints upon the producer of a low budget, independent film compared to that of a high-budget Hollywood production.
- The impact of regulation on media industries and their products. For example, the British Board of Film Classification (BBFC), which is responsible for regulating the British film industry.
- How the representations, attitudes and beliefs in the media product relate to the economic and political production context.

Key

Conglomerate
A large organisati interests spanning number of different businesses or industries. For example, the Walt Disney Company is a media and entertainment conglomerate as it has business interests in several different industries, including film, television, music and radio as well as the theme park industry.

Quickfire 1.35

What are the advantages of a media conglomerate?

bbfc

Age Ratings You Trust

U PG 12 15 18 R18

™The letters BBFC and the category symbols are registered trademarks of the British Board of Film Classification. (Numbers 2234547-2234552)

Quickfire 1.36

How is the industry context reflected in the front pages of national newspapers?

2 The Media Studies Specification

OVERVIEW

The aim of the Eduqas Media Studies specification is to provide an integrated approach to studying media in all forms. You will:

- Develop your understanding of the media by analysing media products set by the awarding body using the **theoretical framework** outlined in Chapter 1 of this book.
- Be encouraged to make connections between different media forms and products, between products and their contexts, and between theory and practical work.
- Demonstrate your understanding by creating your own media products for a specified audience.

Key Term

Theoretical framework
This is discussed in detail in Chapter 1. It provides you with the tools to develop a critical understanding of the media and consists of the following inter-related areas: media language, representation, media industries and audiences.

You will be expected to engage with not only recognisable products with which you are familiar, but you will also extend your knowledge and understanding through the study of less familiar products from different historical periods and global settings. You will also study relevant social, cultural, political, economic and historical contexts in relation to relevant products, thus broadening your understanding of the media.

You will also engage with key theoretical approaches and theories related to specific areas of the specification. These will inform and support your analysis of the set products and the industry that produced them.

You will study a range of different media forms, some in breadth (Component 1) and some in depth (Component 2). These forms are:

- advertising and marketing
- music video
- newspapers
- radio
- film
- video games
- magazines
- online media
- television.

Products to be studied will be set by the awarding body and will together:

- have social, cultural and historical significance
- represent different historical periods and global settings
- demonstrate different industry contexts
- be constructed for different audiences
- reflect contemporary and emerging developments in the media
- allow you the opportunity to analyse rich products and apply the theoretical framework.

Theories

During your course you will be required to understand and apply the following theoretical approaches and theories related to the theoretical framework. You may also use others you have studied in class:

Media Language

- Semiotics, including Roland Barthes
- **Narratology**, including Tzvetan Todorov
- Genre theory, including Steve Neale

Representation

- Theories of representation, including Stuart Hall
- Theories of identity, including David Gauntlett

Media Industries

- Power and media industries, including James Curran and Jean Seaton

Audiences

- Media effects, including Albert Bandura
- Cultivation theory, including George Gerbner
- Reception theory, including Stuart Hall

You will be guided as to which aspects of the theoretical approaches and theories you need to study. There is a summary of the main points of these theories and theorists in Chapter 10.

Contexts of Media

In order to broaden your understanding of the media you will also explore the relationship between media products and relevant contexts. These are:

- historical contexts
- social and cultural contexts
- economic contexts
- political contexts.

These are explored in more detail in Chapter 1 of this book.

Stretch and Challenge 2.1

Although the awarding body will provide guidance as to the aspects of the theories that you need to study, in order to broaden your understanding you may want to explore some of the theorists in more detail yourself by reading one of their books, for example David Gauntlett's *Media, Gender and Identity: An Introduction* (2008, Routledge) or some more recent research.

Key Term

Narratology
Refers to the study of narrative structure and how this communicates meaning through, for example, common conventions and signs.

Quickfire 2.1

How can theories and theoretical perspectives help you to analyse media products?

Key Term

Subject-specific terminology
Media Studies as a subject has a range of specific terminology that you must be able to use when analysing products. This may be vocabulary specific to the form or terminology that enhances your analysis, for example the language of semiotics.

Stretch and Challenge 2.2

Reading around the subject and broadening your media consumption will help to develop your knowledge of the media. This may include reading a range of newspapers, watching television programmes you would not normally engage with or being aware of how your favourite band or artist is marketed.

Quickfire 2.2

Why is it important to gain an understanding of the theoretical framework before you create your own products?

Skills

This specification also enables you to develop a range of skills that you will need for analysing existing media products and for creating your own.

In analysing media products you will:

- Analyse and compare how media products use media language to construct and communicate meanings. For example, consider how the front page of a women's fashion magazine communicates messages about how the reader should look and behave.
- Develop your analysis through the application of key theories related to media studies.
- Use relevant **subject-specific terminology** appropriately. Each form you study will have specific vocabulary that you need to know if you are to analyse the set products effectively. There is also key analytical terminology that will help you to express yourself in a more sophisticated way.
- Use discursive and analytical writing to debate key questions about the role of the media.

In creating media products you will:

- Apply what you have learned about media language, representation, media industries and audiences to the creation of your own media product.
- Use what you have learned about media language to communicate meanings to an audience.
- Be able to clearly set out your aims in creating your product and how you intend to fulfil them.

You will also be given opportunities in all the components to pull together your knowledge and understanding from across the full course. This includes the theoretical framework, analytical skills, and the application of practical knowledge and understanding through the production.

The Components

The Media Studies specification is made up of three components that will cover the entire theoretical framework.

Component 1: Investigating the Media

This component is 35% of the qualification and is worth 60 marks. It allows you to study a breadth of media forms and products.

OVERVIEW

This component introduces you to:

- Key aspects of the theoretical framework – media language and representation.
- Media products from specific media industries, for example the newspaper industry, and for specific audiences, to develop your understanding of these areas of the theoretical framework.
- Contexts and how media products relate to these.
- Relevant theoretical approaches and theories.
- Subject-specific terminology.

Component 1 is divided into two sections: Section A and Section B.

Section A: Investigating Media Language and Representation

In studying the set media products for Component 1 and the extended examples you study in class you will develop the ability to:

- Analyse aspects of media language, including genre, and compare how media products communicate meanings.
- Use theoretical perspectives and specific theories to help you explore how the products construct meanings and how audiences interpret these.
- Explore representations of events, issues, social groups and individuals.
- Explore how representations relate to relevant media contexts, including social, cultural, historical, political and economic.
- Discuss how audiences may respond to media products.
- Use key theories and subject-specific terminology appropriately when analysing media products to demonstrate your ability to construct a coherent examination response.
- Discuss key questions relating to media contexts.

Tip

As well as the media products that are set by Eduqas you will also study other examples from the Component 1 forms in order to prepare you for the unseen element of the examination paper.

Tip

An explanation of the different media contexts you will need to study is included in Chapter 1 of this book.

Quickfire 2.3

Why is it important to be able to discuss contexts in relation to media products?

Stretch and Challenge 2.3

Choose a form you are less familiar with, for example newspapers, and expand your knowledge by looking at a range of different examples from this form.

Set Products: Section A

For this component you will be required to study products from the following media forms, some will be specific to Section A or Section B and some will appear in both sections for assessment from 2024 but the specific focus of study will change. These products will be set by Eduqas and for Section A they are:

Advertising and marketing (print and audio-visual advertisements)	Music video	Newspapers
Tide print advertisement (1950s) and *Super. Human.* Tokyo Paralympic Games audio-visual advertisement (2020) Film poster: *Kiss of the Vampire* (1963)	*Formation*, Beyoncé (2016) or *Underdog*, Alicia Keys (2020)	*Daily Mirror* (1 February 2022) front page and article on 'Partygate'

The products set will be reviewed at key points and may be changed when necessary during the life of the specification, but the forms will stay the same. In addition to the set products you will also need to study a range of related media products in order to broaden your understanding of the media framework and to prepare you for the unseen element of the assessment.

Section B: Investigating Media Industries and Audiences

As you can see, the focus of this section is different from Section A. Here you will develop your knowledge and understanding of the key aspects of media industries including:

- ownership and funding and its importance in the creation, production and distribution of media products
- regulation
- the impact of technology
- global production and distribution.

In addition, you will study aspects of media audiences including:

- How audiences are targeted by the creators of media products.
- How audiences are categorised and constructed by producers.
- How audiences consume media products.
- How audiences interact with and respond to the media.

Set Products: Section B

You must study the following media forms and products, which will be set by Eduqas and assessed from 2024:

Advertising and marketing	Film (cross-media study)	Newspapers	Radio	Video games
Tide print advertisement (1950s) and *Super. Human.* Tokyo 2020 Paralympic Games audio-visual advertisement (2020)	*Black Panther* (2018)	*Daily Mirror*	*Woman's Hour* or *Have You Heard George's Podcast?*	Assassin's Creed franchise

Radio is a set form in Section B.

Advertising is only studied in relation to audiences.
Film is only studied in relation to media industries.
The focus of Section B is on the set products as examples of the related media industries and audiences. You should not engage in analysis of the products in relation to media language and representation.

How Will I Be Assessed for Component 1?

This component assesses:

- media language
- representation
- media industries
- audiences
- media contexts.

You will also be assessed on your use of relevant theories or theoretical approaches and relevant subject-specific terminology.

You could be asked about any of the set forms in the examination. One of the questions will require you to produce an extended response that is well structured and coherent.

Section A will assess media language and representation, in relation to two of the media forms studied for this section. You also will be required to analyse unseen media products.

There will be two questions:

- **One question** will focus on media language. You will be required to analyse an unseen audio-visual or print source from any of the forms you have studied for Section A, for example newspapers. You will use what you have learned from analysing the set products and the extended examples in class to enable you to analyse the unseen product.
- **One question** will assess representation. You will be required to compare one of your set products with an unseen audio-visual or print resource from any of the forms you have studied for Section A. The products may be from the same or different media forms. In this question you will be expected to be able to refer to media contexts and to produce an extended response. Across Section A as a whole, there will always be one unseen audio-visual resource and one unseen print-based resource; Question 1 will relate to an audio-visual resource and Question 2 will relate to a print-based resource.

Tip

An extended response is one that is an essay-style response that needs thought. It is a response in which you demonstrate your ability to analyse in detail, showing your understanding of the question. It should be well structured and coherent, including an introduction and a conclusion.

Tip

Completing a brief plan before you start to write an extended response will help to focus your thoughts and ideas.

Section B will assess your knowledge and understanding of:

- media industries
- audiences
- media contexts.

You may be asked about any of the forms you have studied for this section: advertising and marketing, film, newspapers, radio and video games.

There will be two questions:

- **Question 3** will be a stepped question that will assess your knowledge and understanding of media industries in relation to at least one of the forms you have studied.
- **Question 4** will be a stepped question assessing your knowledge and understanding of audiences. This will focus on a different media form in relation to at least one different form from that assessed in Question 3.

Tip

A stepped question is split up into different stages or 'steps', the marks for each step usually increase, with more information being required. Stepped questions allow you to accumulate marks as you move through the question.

Quickfire 2.4

What is meant by breadth and depth of study in relation to the forms set for Components 1 and 2?

Component 2: Investigating Media Forms and Products

This component is 35% of the qualification and is worth 60 marks. It allows you to study media forms and products in depth.

OVERVIEW

In this component you will study three media forms in depth, covering all areas of the theoretical framework – media language, representation, industries and audiences – in relation to audio-visual, print and online media products set by Eduqas. The forms you will study in depth will be:

- television
- magazines
- online media.

You will explore these set forms through the close analysis of set products. There are options of media products in each form. Your teacher will choose one option from each form that you will study in depth. For each form and set product you will develop your knowledge and understanding of the aspects of the theoretical framework, theories and theoretical perspectives detailed in the specification.

You will investigate:

- How the forms and products use media language to communicate messages.
- How the representations they offer reflect social, cultural, economic, and historical contexts.
- The relationship between the products and their industry.
- How audiences are targeted by media producers.
- How audiences interpret and interact with the media.

You will also use relevant theories to develop your understanding.

Section A: Television

Through the in-depth study of one set television product you will explore:

- The importance of genre in the production, distribution and consumption of the media product.
- The **dynamic** nature of genre and how it reflects the historical context of the product.
- The appeal of the product for audiences.
- How audiences may interpret and respond to the media product.
- The significance of the economic and industry contexts in which television programmes are produced.
- How the television industry is regulated.
- How the set product is marketed.
- How the representations contained within the product reflect the values, attitudes and beliefs of the product's creators.

Key Term

Dynamic
Constantly changing, evolving and progressing.

Tip

The three media forms covered in Component 2 are discussed in Chapter 5 of this book.

Options for Television Set Products

Option 1 **Crime drama**	**Option 2** **Science fiction**	**Option 3** **Spy thrillers**
Peaky Blinders (UK) Series 1, Episode 1 (2013)	*Black Mirror (UK)* Series 3, Episode 4: 'San Junipero' (2016)	*Killing Eve (US/UK)* Series 1, Episode 1 (2018)

Tip

The Media Studies subject content requires that you study products that cover different historical periods. In Component 2 this is addressed through the study of a magazine produced before 1970.

Section B: Magazines

The magazine industry in the UK has always been a very competitive industry with thousands of titles competing for readers and sales. In this option you will study a magazine produced before 1970. In studying your set magazine product you will:

- Develop an understanding of the ways in which publishers target, attract, reach and address particular audiences.
- Explore the effect of social, cultural and historical contexts on the representations that appear in magazines.
- Consider how media language and representations convey values, attitudes and beliefs related to the time in which the magazine was produced.

Options for Magazine Set Products

Option 1	**Option 2**	**Option 3**
Woman (23–29 August 1964)	*Woman's Realm* (7–13 February 1965)	*Vogue* (July 1965)

Key Term

Participatory media
This term explains the way in which audiences today are increasingly seen to play an active role in finding, reporting, creating and disseminating media content. This has been made easier by the rise of social media and online platforms.

Quickfire 2.5

Why do bloggers, vloggers and YouTubers such as Zoe Sugg and JJ Olatunji/KSI appeal to young audiences?

Tip

Ensure that you are demonstrating your knowledge of the theoretical framework, including relevant theories and theoretical perspectives, when you analyse these online products.

Stretch and Challenge 2.4

To develop your knowledge and understanding fully, ensure that you regularly access the set online products to see how they change and develop and how they appeal to their audience.

Section C: Online Media

The modern world is increasingly dominated by digital technology, and online, social and **participatory media** have become an important part of the contemporary media landscape. The rise in popularity of online bloggers and YouTubers is a particularly significant development, as this can be seen to reflect important cultural changes in media use and consumption, especially within younger demographics.

Through an in-depth study of one online product you will investigate:

- The role played by vlogs and blogs in the media today.
- The relationship between media technologies and the changing ways in which audiences consume and respond to media products.
- How online products make it easier for an audience to participate and interact.
- The opportunities that online platforms offer for self-representation.
- The impact of media technology on media language.

Options for Online Media Products

Option 1	Option 2
JJ Olatunji/KSI www.youtube.com/user/KSIOlajidebtHD	Zoe Sugg www.youtube.com/channel/UCrUbqTCagwsaP2Fmr0p1TsA https://zoella.co.uk/

Studying online platforms is different from the study of the other media forms in this component as they are, by their very nature, constantly updated to respond to the demands of the audiences and the industry. You are required to explore the following elements of the products you have been instructed to study the codes and conventions of the online product, including aspects of layout and design:

- Examples of posts, such as specific blogs, vlogs or articles from the online products.
- Interactive links, including to social and participatory media.

Anyone can now create and distribute their own content online.

How Will I Be Assessed for Component 2?

This component assesses:

- media language
- representation
- media industries
- audiences
- media contexts.

You will also be assessed on your use of relevant theories or theoretical approaches and relevant subject-specific terminology. Just as with Component 1, you will be required to produce an extended response that is well structured and coherent.

The paper for Component 2 consists of three sections:

- Section A: Television
- Section B: Magazines
- Section C: Online media.

There will be **one two-part question** or **one extended response question** based on the set products you have studied. You will answer one question on each of your set products. Each question is worth 20 marks.

Component 3: Media Production

This component is 30% of the qualification and is worth 60 marks. This is a non-exam assessment; it is internally assessed by your teachers and moderated by Eduqas.

OVERVIEW

This component requires you to:

- Apply the knowledge and understanding of the theoretical framework you have gained over the course to a practical production.
- Apply your knowledge and understanding of media language, representation, media industries and audiences in an individual media production for an intended audience.

Tip

You will need to carefully consider which production brief you will choose. Your teacher will guide you in this decision, which will be influenced by, for example, the equipment available in your centre.

How Does it Work?

You will be given a choice of production briefs by Eduqas. These will be released on 1 September in the year prior to assessment and will be published on the Eduqas website.

The production briefs will give you the intended target audience and the industry context as well as other key requirements to guide you.

You will select the genre/style of your production and demonstrate that you can appeal to the stated audience and show the industry context.

The production should be completed within an eight-week time span.

You will be expected to set out your aims, conduct research and planning, and create a production.

Your teacher will advise you on the best production options.

The Production Briefs

The set production briefs will change every year but the following forms will always be set:

Tip

It is important to remember that the precise requirements of the set production briefs will change every year. You must therefore ensure that you respond to the correct briefs when you create your production.

Television	Create a sequence from a new television programme or a website to promote a new television programme.
Advertising and marketing: music	Create a music video or a website to promote a new artist or band.
Advertising and marketing: film	Create a print marketing campaign or a website to promote a new film.
Magazines	Create a new print or online magazine.

Taking original photographs is important for the print production briefs.

What do I Need to Submit for Component 3?

- A Statement of Aims and Intentions for the production, showing how you have applied the media framework and targeted the intended audience.
- A media production chosen from the list above. Your teacher may offer you all or some of the options.
- A completed cover sheet that will be available on the Eduqas website. This will ask you for additional information about the production, for example the equipment you used.

This component is covered in more detail in Chapter 7 of this book.

How Will I Be Assessed?

This component assesses your ability to:

- Create media products for an intended audience.
- Apply your knowledge and understanding of the theoretical framework in the construction of your production to communicate meaning.
- Respond to the requirements set out by the production brief you have chosen.
- Complete all tasks detailed in the brief you have chosen.
- Create an appropriate production for the industry context specified in the brief, for example a music video for a band signed to an independent record label.
- Appeal to and engage the intended audience by, for example, using appropriate genre conventions that an audience will recognise.
- Apply your knowledge and understanding of media language through, for example, your use of appropriate technical codes for your chosen product. For example, a music video for an independent band will use lots of close-ups of the band members and their instruments.
- Construct representations appropriate to the product you have chosen. For example, a marketing campaign for an action film featuring a female protagonist will require you to use a range of techniques to create a strong female character.

Consider how this strong female character has been constructed.

The total number of marks available is 60:

- **10 marks** for the Statement of Aims and Intentions.
- **30 marks** for creating a media product that uses media language to communicate meaning and construct representations.
- **20 marks** for creating a media product that meets the requirements of the set brief including suitability for the chosen form, genre, industry context and target audience.

3 Component 1: Investigating the Media

OVERVIEW

The aim of this component is to:

- Introduce you to key aspects of the theoretical framework, specifically media language and representation. This is essential to help you analyse media products from a range of forms.
- Develop your knowledge and understanding of media industries and audiences through set products.
- Develop your ability to use relevant theoretical approaches and theories when analysing your set products.
- Consider how media products relate to key contexts, for example social, cultural and historical.
- Allow you to consider how audiences interpret and respond to media products.
- Develop **subject-specific terminology**.

Key Term

Subject-specific terminology
Media Studies as a subject has a range of specific terminology that you must be able to use when analysing products. This may be vocabulary specific to the form or terminology that enhances your analysis, for example the language of semiotics.

Set Forms and Products

In Component 1 you will study products and forms set by Eduqas. They will be studied in breadth rather than in depth, which will be done in Component 2. Component 1 will introduce you to the Media Studies theoretical framework through the study of a broad range of forms and products. These are outlined in Chapter 2 but here is a reminder:

- advertising and marketing
- music video
- newspapers
- film
- radio
- video games.

The set products are a starting point for developing your theoretical understanding and analytical skills. In addition to the set products you will also study other examples to familiarise yourself with the codes and conventions of the form and to prepare you for the unseen products you will be required to analyse in the examination. The aim of this section of the book is to provide you with tools to analyse these products and forms, applying the theoretical framework.

Section A: Investigating Media Language and Representation

This is the focus for the study of the products you will explore in Section A. The products set by Eduqas are:

Advertising and marketing (print and audio-visual advertisements)	Music video	Newspapers
Tide print advertisement (1950s) *Super. Human.* Tokyo 2020 Paralympic Games audio-visual advertisement (2020) Film poster: *Kiss of the Vampire* (1963)	*Formation*, Beyoncé (2016) or *Underdog*, Alicia Keys (2020)	*Daily Mirror*, 1 February 2022, front page and article on 'Partygate'

Investigating Media Language

In investigating **media language** across the set products and your extended examples you will need to consider:

- How the different elements of language associated with different media forms communicate meanings.
- How developing technologies affect media language.
- The codes and conventions of media forms and products.
- The processes through which meanings are established through intertextuality.
- How audiences interpret and respond to these aspects of media language.

Key Term

Media language
The way in which the meaning of a media product is conveyed to the audience through a range of techniques.

Investigating Representation

Representation is one of the main areas of the theoretical framework you will be required to explore in Section A. You will need to consider:

- The ways in which events, issues, individuals and social groups are represented.
- The way in which the media, through re-presentation, construct a version of reality.
- The processes that lead media producers to make choices about how to represent events, issues and social groups.
- How and why stereotypes can be used positively and negatively.
- How and why particular social groups may be under- or misrepresented.
- How media representations convey values, attitudes and beliefs about the world, which are reinforced across a wide range of media representations.
- How audiences interpret and respond to media representations.

Young people can be misrepresented in the media.

Key Terms

Brand
That which identifies one company's products from those of another. The branding may be clearly identifiable by a name, logo or some other trademark, for example the font style used by Kellogg's or the Nike swoosh.

Brand identity
The image that a brand projects and the associations the audience makes with the brand. The brand Nike suggests good quality sports clothing that is also fashionable as leisure wear. The high-budget advertising campaigns and sponsorship at world events have helped to reinforce this brand image over time.

Consumable products
These are the products that we use regularly and that need to be replaced. Some audiences are loyal to a particular brand, whereas others may be persuaded to change as a result of successful marketing devices.

Advertising campaign
Usually run by an advertising agency, a campaign incorporates all of the ways in which a product, event or service is promoted to the audience, for example the packaging, television, print and online adverts.

Hard sell
This is 'in your face' advertising. These adverts are usually short, loud and employ a direct mode of address. They give clear information about the product, for example the price and where you can get it.

Investigating the Set Forms: Advertising and Marketing

Advertising is one of the most powerful media forms and the advertising industry is one of the most lucrative. It is important to be aware of how advertisers use media language and construct representations in order to communicate meanings and market their products. Advertisers persuade us to buy what we want and desire rather than what we actually need. However, advertising is not solely confined to the selling of consumable products. All sorts of areas of society and companies advertise products – not all of which are for sale. Whatever is being advertised, it is important for the advertisers to establish the **brand** and a **brand identity** that the audience will recognise.

While print advertising is still a popular form, with the progress of digital technology advertisers are able to communicate their messages across a range of media platforms to access audiences. Online and social media are important platforms for advertising as they use buzz marketing to create interest.

The colour pink and the ribbon are part of the breast cancer awareness campaign.

Who Advertises and Why?

- **Makers of consumable products**, for example beauty/grooming products: to encourage an audience to buy. This is a very competitive area of the advertising industry.
- **Charities**: to raise awareness and encourage donations. Charity and health **advertising campaigns** are allowed to use more shocking images in their advertising campaigns in order to get the message home to the audience. They use **hard sell** tactics.
- **Government departments**, for example health: to raise awareness about certain issues, for example smoking.
- **Organisers of events**, for example the 2021 Olympics: to boost ticket sales and promote the event to a broad audience.
- **Educational establishments**: to persuade people to go there for their studies. They produce a prospectus and additional promotional material similar to flyers.
- **The media themselves** promote their products through film posters, show reels for television channels, etc.

This section will cover print and audio-visual adverts and film posters in relation to the theoretical framework.

Media Language

In this section you will investigate how advertisements and film posters use media language to communicate meanings.

How Do Advertisements Use Media Language?

Print and audio-visual adverts only have a limited amount of time to communicate messages. Print adverts have to catch your attention as you flick through a magazine or glance at a billboard. Audio-visual adverts are usually only 30–45 seconds in length and modern audiences are in the habit of skipping them where possible. The job of the advertising agency is to create an advert that arrests our attention.

While, as has been said, there is a range of different types of adverts with different purposes and for different audiences, there are codes and conventions that are common to the form. These include:

- **Establishing the genre.** For example, some of the codes and conventions used in charity adverts will be different from those of beauty adverts as the purpose and effect are different.
- **Visual codes.** Including clothing, gesture, expression and colour, which communicate messages about what is being sold. For example, the sad and desperate codes of expression used in many charity adverts elicit audience sympathy for the plight of the victims.
- **A slogan.** This is a catchy phrase that is memorable and becomes associated with the product.
- **Language of persuasion.** Adverts will often use **hyperbole** and emotive written and spoken language to engage the audience.
- **A narrative.** Many up-market products will be promoted through audio-visual adverts that are very cinematic and are produced in a similar way to short films. Watch the advertisement for the *Miss Dior* fragrance featuring Natalie Portman (www.youtube.com/watch?v=3pbpWAt1Dxs). Consider how high production values are used to construct a romantic single-strand narrative and to effectively market the product.
- **Soft sell technique.** Whereby the audience are sold a lifestyle, the product is often not the main focus of the advert and may only appear briefly as an **iconic representation**.

Stretch and Challenge 3.1

Watch the *Miss Dior* fragrance advertisement at least twice. Select a minimum of five different examples of how media language has been use to communicate meanings in the advertisement.

Key Terms

Hyperbole
Exaggerated language used to create a dramatic effect.

Iconic representation
The actual image of the product.

Quickfire 3.1

What does the choice of colour codes and iconography used in the *Miss Dior* fragrance advert suggest about the product?

Quickfire 3.2

What sorts of products use hard sell advertising techniques?

Stretch and Challenge 3.2

Explore a range of adverts from different genres, investigating how they use media language to communicate messages.

Quickfire 3.3

Give another example of how intertextuality is used in an advert.

- **Hard sell technique.** This is much more aggressive 'in your face' advertising. These adverts are usually short and loud with low production values. They give the audience clear information about the product. This technique is also used in awareness raising campaigns that need to communicate a message.
- **Demonstrative action.** This is where the product is seen to be used in the advertisement. This can be a cleaning product, where we may be convinced of its efficacy, or a perfume, where the suggestion is that the wearing of the product may result in the lifestyle portrayed.
- **Logos.** Many companies include a small, recognisable design on all their products and/or promotional materials. This logo often does not resemble anything about the product itself but has become associated with it through repetition over time, for example the Nike swoosh. Sometimes there is a direct link: Chanel uses the iconic intertwined two letter 'C's in all of its products. establishing a strong brand identity.
- **The mode of address.** This is the way in which the advert communicates its message to the audience. This includes use of informal or formal language, directly looking at the audience or the use of the imperative to create a sense of urgency.
- **The use of intertextuality.** This is when one text appears in another and has meaning for an audience. In the Miss Dior 'What would you do for love?' advert the song is Cry Baby by American singer-songwriter Janis Joplin, originally recorded in 1970. This nostalgic reference will resonate with a specific audience.
- **Product endorsement.** This is the use of celebrities and 'ordinary' people to sell the product or service or to raise awareness. Depending on what is being 'sold', an audience may be convinced by the endorser and so will be persuaded to buy the product or to listen to the message. An audience is more likely to believe an ordinary person selling a domestic product but enjoys the aspiration offered by a celebrity endorser. Sometimes celebrities become **brand ambassadors** and appear in several adverts in the same campaign, for example Chris Hemsworth is the global face of Hugo Boss.
- **Unique selling point.** This is the element that makes the product different from its competitors and will be used in the marketing. It could be a new flavour or a claim about what the product can do, for example 'reduce the signs of ageing' for a beauty product.

Key Term

Brand ambassador
A person, often a celebrity, who is paid to endorse or promote a particular company's products or services. They become the face of the brand and are associated with the product.

The Use of Media Language in Other Advertising Genres

Not all advertisements are selling consumable products, some advertisements may be constructed to raise awareness of an issue, for example charity adverts, or to publicise something, for example an event like the advertising set product which is a trailer for Channel 4's coverage of the Tokyo Paralympics in 2020. These advertisements will employ the recognisable **repertoire of elements** of the advertising form, but will also have a set of conventions specific to their genre. The aim of advertisements designed to raise awareness of issues and events is to have an immediate impact upon the audience to make them take notice and therefore may be more memorable and hard-hitting. The conventions used by this advertising genre include:

- Campaign branding including a name, logo and font style, this can then be used on other marketing material to make it recognisable to audiences. For example, the *This Girl Can campaign*, launched in 2015, aims to persuade women to become more active. It has a recognisable brand identity and since then has produced further audio-visual and print advertisements under the *This Girl Can* banner with similar styles and conventions.
- The use of personalisation. Several examples of this type of advertisement use real people telling their stories either as voice-overs to images from their lives or using direct mode of address. The *Mind* 'Racism and Mental Health' campaign, launched to coincide with Black History Month in 2021 (www.youtube.com/watch?v=crEkQyUDQsw), included people talking directly about their experiences of racism. This advertising genre is different from the aspirational advertising used by the makers of consumable products, where celebrities are used to sell the products, using real people makes adverts about raising awareness more engaging and realistic for audiences.

Audio codes:

- Recognisable songs with pertinent lyrics, for example the set product *Super. Human.* uses as its soundtrack *So You Wanna* Be a Boxer from the musical *Bugsy Malone*, which effectively communicates the athletes' struggles and training regime while also maintaining an upbeat, positive feel to the advertisement.
- The use of a non-diegetic voice-over, often with a tone of authority, explaining the issue or the situation. This may be the voice of a recognisable celebrity, thus broadening the audience reach.
- Alternatively, it can be a personalised narrative in the real voice of the 'victim'. It can also be collection of voices with sound bites giving information.
- A soundtrack, the choice of which reflects the themes of the campaign. The most recent *This Girl Can* advertisement, *This Girl Can, Me Again*, highlighting how a range of different women have stayed active during the pandemic, uses excerpts from Little Simz' song Offence (which can be heard at Little Simz - Offence (Official Video) - YouTube), which is confident with a strong drumbeat. The opening line of the song effectively matches the recuring themes of the campaign.

The upbeat soundtrack plays alongside images of the athletes demonstrating their grit and determination.

Key Term

Repertoire of elements
Key features or conventions that distinguish one genre or sub-genre from another.

Tip

The set product is the Channel 4 advertisement for the Tokyo Paralympic Games 2020. This product both publicises an event and raises awareness about disability, it is therefore important to familiarise yourself with examples of similar advertisements.

Quickfire 3.4

How does the *This Girl Can* campaign reinforce and also subvert the typical codes and conventions of advertisements?

Stretch and Challenge 3.3

Familiarise yourself with what you need to know and understand about media language and apply this to a range of examples of advertisements.

Tip

Consider how technical codes are used to communicate meaning in the set advertising product for the 2020 Tokyo Paralympics.

Quickfire 3.5

How does the advert for Shelter use the conventions of a raising awareness campaign?

Tip

A case study for the Tokyo Paralympics campaign is available on the Eduqas website.

Technical codes:

- A typical convention is the use of close-up shots combined with the code of expression and a direct mode of address. This positions the audience in close proximity to the one they are being asked to help, encouraging them to engage, which can sometimes be uncomfortable but effective. The use of close-ups of children's faces is a common convention in charity advertisements, as they are the most vulnerable. In Shelter's 2021 campaign *Fight for Home* (which can be seen at www.youtube.com/watch?v=iHRLOtFfNQ8) close-up shots of faces and eyes looking directly at the audience highlight the plight of the homeless, or those in temporary accommodation in Britain.
- Establishing shots reinforce the themes of the Shelter campaign. In the advertisement the images of people are projected onto the urban buildings at night to highlight their vulnerability and need for a permanent home.
- Some advertisements, as in the case of the one for Shelter, use black and white images to create a greater impact.

Language and mode of address:

- A typical convention used in adverts whose aim is to impart information, promote an event, give advice or raise awareness of an issue, is a voice-over. The aim of the voice-over is to establish a direct relationship with the audience in the hope that they will respond actively, the tone may be conversational or authoritative, depending on the focus of the advertisement. Recognisable voices are often used, for example celebrities who will provide information and may urge the audience to act.
- In an earlier example from the *This Girl Can* campaign, the soundtrack features Maya Angelou, the civil rights icon, reading her poem 'Phenomenal Woman'. The sound of her voice and the accompanying images reinforces the message of the campaign, to empower women. The Shelter campaign features a track with poignant lyrics written and performed by Wretch 32.
- Some advertisements may employ a personalised narrative making the situation seem more immediate, or use personal pronouns to involve the audience. This use of media language influences meaning and makes the situation more relevant.
- On-screen graphics serve to reinforce a message, for example the thought-provoking words on the screen at the end of the *Super. Human.* advertisement. Some advertisements may show the agency logo and the slogan or campaign name. Social media links and the hashtag may also usually be displayed

Analysing Print Advertising Products

Although the set advertising products at the time of writing are the *Tide* print advertisement and the audio-visual advertisement for the 2020 Tokyo Paralympics, these may change at some point. You also need to be prepared for the unseen element of Section A. It is therefore important that you also study how print advertisements use media language to create meanings for an audience. They obviously share similar conventions to audio-visual adverts, but in addition you will need to consider the following questions:

- **Layout and design**: how is the advert constructed? Consider where the images and text are placed and the effect of this.

- **Central image**: what is it and why has it been chosen? What does it communicate about the product?
- **Typography and graphics**: what can you say about the font styles used or any graphics that appear in the advert? How do they help to persuade the audience?
- **Visual codes**: how has the print advert communicated messages through the use of colour, expression, gesture and **technique**? The use of colour, soft focus and the natural iconography suggests what you get when you buy the beauty product in the advert on the left.
- **Colour**: is there a colour palette and, if so, what does this suggest? Does it link to some element of the product? Is it part of the branding? What messages does it communicate about the product itself?
- **Print technical codes**: What camera angles, shots, lighting, editing techniques, for example airbrushing, are used in the advert? How do they communicate messages?
- **Language and mode of address**: how does the advert 'speak' to its audience? What kinds of words and language devices, for example alliteration, are used and what does that say about the product? Is it a hard sell or a soft sell advert?
- **Attitudes and beliefs**: what attitudes and beliefs are conveyed through the advert? Some adverts suggest that purchasing the product will change your life in some way.
- **Associations**: does the advert use **intertextuality** so that we make associations between the product and other media forms or cultural references?

Key Term

Technique
In advertising this describes what has been done to the advert to create an effect. For example, using soft focus in a fragrance advert or enlarging nails to promote nail varnish..

Intertextuality
When one text is used or referenced within another. For example, the use of memorable scenes from an iconic film in an advert.

Analysing an Example: Maybelline Lipstick Advert

- The colour palette of predominantly black and red has connotations of passion, love and sophistication. Red lips and the code of expression of the model also suggest seduction. Audiences will recognise these signs.
- This is further reinforced by the iconography of the rose, a symbol of love and romance.
- There is use of iconic representation of the lipstick and its case so that the audience will recognise the product should they choose to purchase.
- The use of hyperbole language making the product appear natural and healthy appealing to a young, contemporary audience – 'pure pigments', 'honey nectar' – and suggesting the unique selling point of the product.
- Language is also used to suggest that the product will have an effect on the wearer: 'captivating shades', 'fall in love with colour'.
- The slogan is recognisable and used with other products in the brand, establishing a brand identity and making claims for the product.

- The central image is powerful and the mode of address is direct.
- Techniques have been used to construct the advert; the model has been airbrushed to eradicate any imperfections and the striking blue of her eyes has been enhanced. The lighting and the splash effect on the lipstick draws the eye and makes the product more appealing.
- The typography and font style is bold and dramatic, reflecting the product itself. The font used for 'Maybelline' is iconic of the well-established brand and recognisable to an audience. The use of italics for the word 'sensational' serves to make it stand out, suggesting the effect the product will have upon the wearer.

Quickfire 3.6

What typical conventions of beauty adverts are used in the above Maybelline example?

Key Terms

Hook
The element of a media product that catches the attention of audiences and draws them in. On a film poster it may be the image, the tagline or the copy.

Copy
This is the writing on the media product.

Tip

The knowledge and understanding you gain from analysing film posters in this component will prepare you should you choose the Film Marketing option in Component 3.

Quickfire 3.7

What are the differences between a teaser and a theatrical film poster?

Quickfire 3.8

What codes and conventions are used in *The Lost Boys* film poster on the right?

Media Language: Analysing Film Posters

Another aspect of advertising and marketing is the promotion of films through film posters. This is an established form of marketing that has been used since the start of the film industry. To illustrate this and to broaden your awareness of historical contexts and the development of genre, the set product is a film poster from 1963.

Film posters are one of the marketing techniques used by the film industry to promote a new film to an audience. They are a **hook** and are used to persuade an audience to see the film. Their aim is to present the key elements of the film to a fleeting audience; an audience who may be walking past and will not necessarily stop and look at the poster in detail. The poster must therefore encapsulate the film in the images and words contained within, and communicate messages about the film itself. The posters often contain enigmas to encourage the audience to come and watch the film in order to discover the answers to the questions posed by the poster. Teaser campaigns use this device very effectively. The poster also creates an identity for the film and often includes iconic images that will appear in other marketing material.

The teaser posters for *The Batman* (2022) were the first introduction to the new film with Robert Pattinson in the role. They featured a black and red colour palette including an indistinct image of Batman in the rain with the iconic logo of the bat and the release date scrawled on the bottom corner. Another featured a menacing figure holding up a paper on which was handwritten 'To The Batman'. The aim of these is to encourage the audience who have foreknowledge of the franchise to want to find out more about the film.

Key Conventions of Film Posters

- **Genre indications**: the images and **copy** on the poster will usually give a clue to the genre of the film.

- **Visual codes**: including clothing, colour, gesture and expression that may give clues to the film's genre.
- **Iconography**: this is another clue to the genre of the film. The objects, background, clothing and setting will establish the genre of the film.
- **Promise of pleasure**: these are the words and phrases that tell audiences what they will experience through watching the film, for example fear, laughter, etc.
- **Star billing**: the positioning of the images or the names of the stars on the poster. Sometimes there is a hierarchy of importance.
- **Stars**: the stars can also give a clue to the genre – Jennifer Aniston is associated with romantic comedies and Liam Neeson with action/adventure films.

- **The tagline**: this is the memorable phrase or slogan that becomes associated with the film and appears on the marketing material.
- **The image**: this will have been carefully chosen and may suggest the narrative of the film and the role of the key characters.
- **Language and mode of address**: this will be persuasive and often makes use of hyperbole.
- **Expert criticism**: quotes from newspapers, film magazines and reviews suggesting the quality of the film and making it a 'must see'.
- **Mark of quality**: this is usually the film logo, the director's name or references to other successful films made by this director. These are included to convince the audience that this new film is a quality product.

Analysing an Example: *Roman Holiday* Film Poster

On the right is a poster from 1953 for a film called *Roman Holiday*. As you have been set a historical film poster as a product you must study, it is useful to look at other historical posters from different film genres to explore the conventions used and how they reflect the cultural and historical context of the time in which the film was made.

- The genre of the film is romantic comedy and the two stars, Audrey Hepburn and Gregory Peck, were associated with this genre, so the audience of the time would have expectations of the film.
- The mark of quality is the reference to Paramount Films and William Wyler, who was an eminent American filmmaker of the time.
- The central image reinforces the comedy romance genre and the supplementary images create narrative enigmas for the audience, for example the iconography of the crown in the smaller image and the scooter signifying Rome and excitement.
- The relatively simple layout and design, using hand-drawn illustrations rather than photographs, is similar to other film posters of the time. Here the focus is on the relationship between the central protagonists.
- The typography and choice of font style for the film title is quirky and uneven, suggesting the style of film, and contrasts with the bold font style used in the rest of the poster.
- The visual codes of colour are bright and primary suggesting the fun feeling of the film and giving audiences expectations of the narrative.

Interestingly, shots from this film were recreated in an advertising campaign for *Galaxy* chocolate in 2013. The advertisement can be viewed here: www.dailymotion.com/video/xxulzf

This use of intertextuality suggests the cultural significance of this genre of film, its nostalgia appeal and the iconic nature of Audrey Hepburn as a film star, with her aspirational class and elegance. The ambience and iconography of Italy in the 1950s and the elegance of Hepburn were recreated for a modern audience.

It also illustrates how developing technologies have been used, as the original film footage was deemed too low quality so had to be reconstructed. CGI was employed to recreate the face of Hepburn and a **facial action coding system** was used to construct the star. A face double was used and then Hepburn's features were painstakingly grafted on by computer. It was obviously essential that an audience believed it actually was the, now dead, celebrity, as she was at 19 when she starred in this film.

Quickfire 3.9

What other conventions might we expect to be included on a modern film poster?

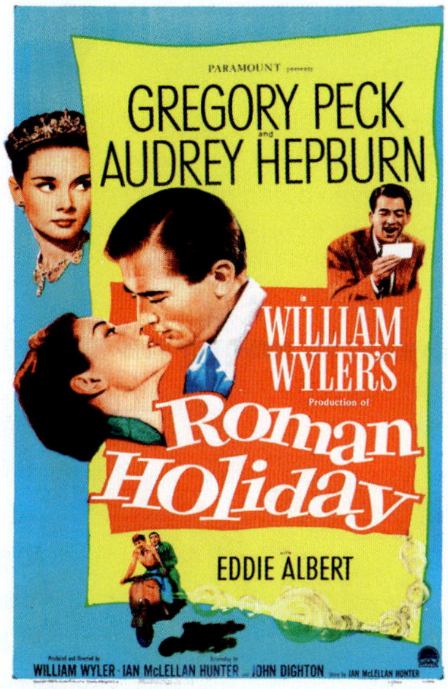

Quickfire 3.10

What does the film poster above tell us about the time in which it was produced?

Key Term

Facial action coding system
A technique whereby computer technology is used to capture a plethora of high-resolution skin textures and different facial expressions. This helped the animators to replicate the computer-generated (CG) Audrey Hepburn and make her look real in the *Galaxy* chocolate advert.

Representation

Representation is one of the key areas of the theoretical framework and must be studied in relation to all of the forms and products in Section A of Component 1. As well as considering the way in which social groups are represented, you will also need to be aware of how the representations constructed by the products convey values, attitudes and beliefs about the world.

Tip

Look back at the chapter on the theoretical framework, this will give you an overview of the concept of representation.

Adverts have a limited amount of time to communicate messages, so will sometimes use stereotypical representations and reinforce common representations. However, not all of the stereotypes used will necessarily be negative.

Representations of Gender in Advertising

The representation of gender in adverts has come a long way since the days of the *Tide* advert on the right, where women were defined by their domestic role as wife and homemaker. Men at this time were seen in a patriarchal role as experts in all things, even the home, which was not their domain. The alternative representation of men in historical adverts was as macho men in beer, cigarette and aftershave adverts, where they were also usually seen to be irresistible to women.

In modern times there are less overtly sexist stereotypes used in adverts as the representation of women has developed and adapted to reflect social and cultural changes. As women's roles in society have undergone a transformation, this has been reflected in some areas of the media. However, there are still many stereotypical representations of women where they are defined by how men see them and how society expects them to look and behave. Advertising is one of the media forms where negative and unreal representations still exist alongside more realistic ones depending on the product.

Women still tend to be judged on their looks and appearance foremost, and this is the case for beauty and fragrance adverts. Representations in this form usually concentrate on the woman's sexuality and emotions, and narratives tend to be based around relationships, as in the *Miss Dior* advert where the perfume is associated with beauty, love and happiness. The way in which the representation of women is constructed in products such as beauty adverts is often unrealistic and instils unattainable aspiration in the audience.

Likewise, make-up adverts such as Maybelline, with its slogan '*Maybe she's born with it. Maybe it's Maybelline*', suggest that natural beauty is not enough. The adverts invariably use close-up shots of the face of a woman that has been technically manipulated to show unattainable perfection, which is linked directly to the product. The woman featured in the advert usually has a direct mode of address and is represented as both powerful and sexual, thus appealing to both genders.

Similarly, men are now also expected to aspire to the unreal images constructed by adverts and are regularly exposed to images of perfect male bodies and successful career men. While beauty products for men have been slow to catch on, fragrance adverts construct idealistic images of the male form.

Representations of Ethnicity in Advertising

Many advertisements, regardless of their sub-genre, are now offering more diverse representations to reflect developments in society and changing expectations of audiences. Charity advertisements are the sub-genre most likely to feature representations of ethnicity, which in the past tended to represent people living in under-developed countries as victims, in order to encourage the empathy of richer, Western audiences who may then donate money. However, critics of this type of advertising focus, calling it 'poverty-porn', suggested that, instead of engaging audiences, it in fact induced apathy and an 'us and them' culture. As a result, some charity adverts have constructed representations of these countries that are more positive, so subverting the more typical stereotype of suffering.

One such advertisement is the *Wateraid* advert, which features a young woman, Claudia as a central protagonist who is in control of her situation and is active. Her independence is established through the camera shots, the close-ups show her singing on her journey, which subverts the stereotype of the helpless, inactive woman. The music in the advert is upbeat, and bright colours and happy facial expressions subvert the common stereotype of suffering. Claudia is represented as part of a community of active women presenting a more contemporary image of women in these situations and countries. This positive representation showed the audience what had been done with their money.

Representations of ethnicity have also progressed in the beauty industry, where more diverse representations are to be found, offering women in particular a more realistic reflection of themselves and products designed for a range of different skin colours. One such company is the Rhianna-backed cosmetics company Fenty, whose campaign included 12 women from different ethnicities and skin tones in an attempt to address the imbalance in this aspect of the advertising industry.

However, it is more common in charity adverts to see negative representations of ethnicity where the characters are defined by their 'otherness', and representations are constructed through emotive images and with the selection of negative language, for example 'famine', 'hunger' and 'disaster'. This is the case in some of the images used in the Oxfam campaign *We Won't Live With Poverty*, where the purpose is to shock the audience into acting and taking responsibility.

Tip

Remember when you are discussing representation in relation to your set products to use the relevant subject-specific terminology. Look back at the chapter on the theoretical framework where the key terminology related to representation is explained.

Quickfire 3.11

How do positive representations in charity adverts work upon the audience?

Tip

You will need to be aware of the key representations constructed in your set products and the extended examples you have studied. It will be helpful to consider examples that are similar to and different from the set products.

Stretch and Challenge 3.4

Although you are required to study and use specific theories and theoretical perspectives, you can broaden your knowledge and understanding by also looking at other relevant theorists. Manuel Alvarado is a useful theorist to consider for representation of ethnicity.

Quickfire 3.12

How may the way in which the representation is constructed communicate meanings to an audience?

Representations of Issues and Events in Adverts

One of the main functions of some advertising campaigns is to raise awareness about an issue or event and by doing so persuade the audience to become active by supporting the event, donating money, volunteering, etc. This may be in response to a particular event, for example the Paralympics, or an earthquake, or for a continuing situation, for example the refugee crisis.

These may include:

- Shocking and emotive images: children are often used in charity campaigns even if they are not the sole focus, as their vulnerability will have an impact on an audience.
- Information about the issue or event, this will be represented in a dramatic way with hyperbolic language to create an impact.
- Celebrities talking directly to the audience: if the celebrity is high profile they may persuade an audience to help.
- Audio codes, including a voice-over and a soundtrack: the use of contrapuntal sound can be effective and challenge audience perceptions; the choice of song may resonate with the audience and be memorable.
- The use of statistics: this is often shocking for the audience and acts as evidence for the severity of the issue or event and the need for help.
- Young, vulnerable people addressing the audience directly: this is a common convention of charities such as Barnardo's and makes the issue more immediate and personal.

Quickfire 3.13

How has the representation in the *Spicebomb* advert been constructed to communicate messages to an audience?

Applying Theory: Semiotics

A key theory you will need to use when you analyse the set products in relation to media language is semiotics. This theory is essential to enable you to analyse how meanings are constructed through signs. All media products have to transmit messages, so they often use signs that are recognisable to an audience. Adverts have a limited amount of time to do this so rely on the audience understanding the signs and codes. Semiotics deals with the way in which media products are encoded and how audiences decode the messages contained within the product. Signs are composed of two elements:

- **The signifier**: the actual form of the signified, for example an image or a sound.
- **The signification**: the meaning we attach to the sign.

When an image is analysed, what is literally in the mise-en-scène is separated from the meanings associated with it. The denotation is simply about identifying the sign, for example the colour red. The connotation is the set of meanings we associate with the sign, which will affect our understanding, for example passion, danger or speed. The connotation will change according to where the sign appears.

For example, looking at the Maybelline advert on page 65, two of the signs encoded are the rose and the colour red. The advert is constructed in such a way that an audience will decode these signs as meaning love, passion and romance. There is an additional significance that reinforces the idea of a cultural myth surrounding the sign; the suggestion that the colour red makes the wearer more sexually attractive and seductive. This connotation is recognisable to an audience as it has been built up over time and appears across media forms, so is accepted.

In the images below, taken from an Oxfam advert, a range of signs appear that will be interpreted by an audience, as they understand the form of a charity advert, for example the image of the cracked land and the face of an innocent child.

Lévi-Strauss' theory of binary opposites is apparent also, as images of poverty are contrasted with images of the Western world and fundraisers who can make a difference. The cultural **binary opposition** is what encourages an audience to be part of the solution.

Tip

Although you will have key theories and theoretical approaches that you must study, you may also refer to other related theories, for example Lévi-Strauss.

Quickfire 3.14

How might the colour red be decoded differently in an advert?

Stretch and Challenge 3.5

Use the theory of semiotics to analyse one of the adverts you have studied as an extended example. Explore how signs have been used in the product to create meanings for the audience.

Key Term

Binary opposition
Occurs when two people, ideas, concepts or values are set up in conflict with one another. In a crime drama there is conventionally a binary opposition between the investigator and the criminal, for example.

Investigating the Set Forms: Music Video

The music video is an important promotional tool used by the music industry to market performers and their music. It also helps to create the 'star image' for a new performer and adapts or develops the image of a more established music artist. The music video is also used to interpret and anchor the meaning of a song and to entertain an audience through a range of strategies. The media language employed in the music video may also give an indication of the style of the performer and the genre of the music. Music videos can differ in style and may be:

- performance
- narrative
- thematic, related to the song lyrics
- a combination of more than one of the above.

The music video as a media form has developed over time and has been influenced by developments in technology. Music videos also often use intertextuality related to other media forms that will resonate with the target audience.

Media Language: How Do Music Videos Use Media Language?

While there is a range of sub-genres and styles of music video, they do share common codes and conventions that establish them as part of the form. The sub-genres of music videos include the following.

Performance Music Videos

Early music videos developed from clips of bands and artists in performance. Today, many music videos include the performance of the artist as part of the video. This can be for different reasons: for a serious band that creates and plays its own music, the performance element of it will demonstrate their musical skill; for an artist such as Beyoncé, her performance skills may be used to develop her **star persona** and to attract a wide audience of both genders.

The codes and conventions of the performance video sub-genre include:

- Clips from live stage performances with shots of the artists performing and of the audience. This gives the audience at home a sense of atmosphere and involvement. Shots of the artists in 'real-life' situations, for example warming up or messing about, give the audience access to a more personal view of the performers, even if it is still constructed for this purpose.

The shots of the band in performance make the audience feel as if they are there.

Key Term

Star persona
Used to refer to those music stars who have an identity beyond their ability to make music, for example Beyoncé. That persona may be demonstrated through character and personality, and be evident in other media products and platforms, for example magazine interviews and advertising campaigns. Some stars are adept at changing their star persona to keep fans interested; this is true of Madonna and Lady Gaga. The producer of the star may be instrumental in creating their persona.

- Several close-ups of the performer who may have a direct mode of address in order to engage the audience. Music videos of this style can also be referred to as 'a spectacle', with direct interaction with the audience.
- The close-ups may also be of iconography, suggesting the music genre or the theme of the song. Sometimes an artist has a particular recognisable **motif** that is echoed throughout videos.
- To add entertainment value, the artists may perform in unusual places and will be lip-synched, for example on roof tops, in fields, etc.

Key Term

Motif
A recurrent thematic element used by an artist and recognised by fans of that artist. It is usually established by the iconography surrounding the artist, including props, costumes and settings.

Tip

As producing a music video is an option for the internally assessed production piece in Component 1, it is important to take note of how different music videos are constructed.

The Narrative Music Video

Another sub-genre of music video is the narrative music video. Music videos can construct narratives to reflect and document the social and cultural context of the time in which they were made. In their content, themes and construction of representations they can also invoke discourses related to contemporary society. In a narrative music video, the performer's aim is to take the audience through the story of their music in some of the following ways:

- Filming and editing that tells the story featured or suggested in the lyrics. In one of the set music video options, *Underdog* by Alicia Keys, the narrative is used to subvert typical assumptions about what it means to be an 'underdog', instead presenting a positive story about those who overcome adversity. The combination of the lyrics and the narrative are used to make a social comment.
- The construction of a narrative that may involve the performer playing themselves or a character they have created. Alternatively, the artist may not appear and the characters in the story may all be actors. In *Proud Family* by Ghetts, directed by Nathan Tettey, the narrative portrays the highs and lows of family life and involves the performer Ghetts and some of his family and acquaintances. This autobiographical music video runs parallel stories and constructs a version of reality, manipulating time and space through the use of a split screen narrative with some images mirroring each other conveying a 'Then' and 'Now 'construction.
- The use of the split screen narrative communicates messages about the central character turning his life around and being part of a 'proud family' who have stuck together through adversity. Ghetts uses the music video to represent the black British experience, the representations constructed are influenced by social and cultural contexts.
- *Proud Family* positions audiences to engage with the narrative and the characters as the notion of a family and its stories has universal appeal. In this narrative music video, the lyrics are interpreted visually and are part of the storytelling, placing of the product within a social and cultural context:
  Nanny was right
  I come from where the mothers are worried
  Sun comes up and the sons aren't coming
- The narrative is also enhanced by the use of CGI effects to highlight aspects of emotion, for example the graphic tears. Realism is established through the use of media language to construct credible representations. Binary opposites are used to illustrate the two different worlds, the warm colour and soft lighting of 'Now' creates a positive aesthetic and the codes of expression are those of comfort and happiness, whilst the 'Then' images are cold and stark and expressions and gestures are sombre and at times desperate.

- The final images show the beginnings of the artist in the young man recently released from jail, set against the successful adult performer he will become.
- Some music videos will use a combination of narrative edited together with shots of the artist performing to enhance the audience experience and to remind them of the various facets of the performer. The shots of the artist singing directly to the audience involve them and the narrative helps them to interpret the lyrics.

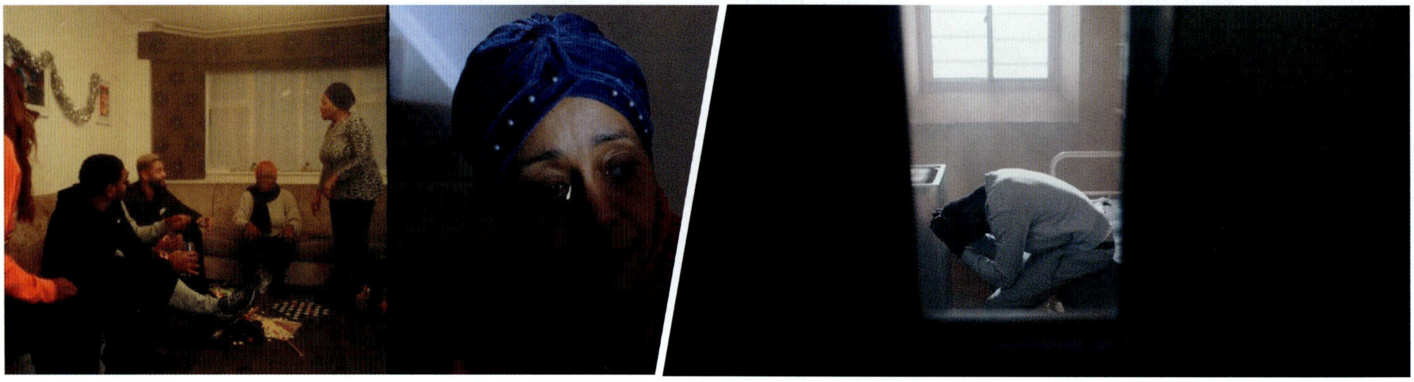

Media Language: Analysing a Music Video

Tip

Analysing examples of music videos that are both similar to and different from your set products will prepare you for the unseen and the comparison question in Section A.

Quickfire 3.15

How does this music video interpret the lyrics for the audience?

Stretch and Challenge 3.6

Consider how semiotics can be applied to this music video.

Taylor Swift's *Bad Blood*

Watch the music video for Taylor Swift's *Bad Blood* here: https://www.youtube.com/watch?=Qcly9NiNbmo. Use the time codes for the examples to consider how media language is used in this product. This music video is an interesting example of the genre and illustrates how creative this form can be. It is a combination of narrative and performance; its construction is similar to the opening sequence of a film. Other marketing devices included posters featuring the key characters in the video, reinforcing the intertextuality with film marketing. These characters are introduced and their names appear on the screen, they are involved in action sequences and there are intertextual references to a range of well-known action films. The opening of the music video shares conventions with *Kill Bill*. The narrative follows Swift's character who, after being betrayed by her friend Arsyn, assembles a gang of *Sin City* characters played by her actual celebrity friends including Ellie Goulding, Cara Delevinge, Jessica Alba and Lena Dunham, all of whom have aliases, Swift's being Catastrophe. They train together before seeking revenge.

The powerful female characters Swift creates in this music video establish for her a star persona that leaves behind the country music girl of her previous albums and illustrates how important the music video form is for creating an image of the artist. Swift plays a central role in the video, which incorporates more traditional conventions, for example singing directly to the audience (1:35).

There are other intertextual references to *The Hunger Games* in the training scene and a classic 'walking away from the fire' scene (3:09). The music video even has its own tagline '*Band-aids don't fix bullet holes*'.

The style of the music video involves the performer in the narrative as the main protagonist but also has shots of her singing, linking her with the character she has created.

Representation: Music Videos

Music videos, like adverts, are relatively short compared with other media products and therefore have to select images that will communicate messages rapidly to audiences. Different music genres will also construct representations of social groups differently.

The representation of women constructed in the *Bad Blood* music video reflects the social and cultural context of the strong, independent female who can take control of her life. It is also interesting that within the narrative the conflict is with another woman, not a male. There is also an absence of a love interest, which has often been the main theme of Swift's earlier songs.

As the narrative was widely reported to be Swift's response to a fall out with Katy Perry, Swift may also have used the video to suggest her own power within the music business and her ability to gather a celebrity gang to support her, so constructing a representation of herself. While the gender representations are strong, many of the celebrities are also sexually objectified through their codes of clothing.

Representations in Beyoncé's Music Videos

Similar to Taylor Swift, Beyoncé is an interesting example to consider when analysing representation in music videos. She is an expert at constructing a representation of herself for her fans. There is often a range of representational themes in her music videos including:

- **Gender**: Beyoncé's body and the way in which it relates to her star persona and her African-American identity is a key element of her music videos.

  Binary opposites exist with regard to representations of gender in her videos, as she is represented as a strong, empowered woman while simultaneously being sexually objectified through codes of clothing, narrative situations and provocative dance moves.

  Therefore, she, at times, challenges stereotypical representations of women in the music industry while also reinforcing a stereotypical representation of women who are defined by their body image.
- **Ethnicity**: Beyoncé has more than once been at the centre of controversy regarding instances of whitewashing, where her racial identity has been erased to make her more marketable to a white audience.

  However, in her music videos she embraces elements of her culture through the inclusion of iconography and clothing related to her cultural heritage. Interestingly, in *Formation* she includes the iconography of the antebellum dress worn by white women in the South of America during the slave trade era. In the video, black women are wearing the dresses, reinforcing the political point regarding the historical treatment of black people in America.
- **Issues**: in *Formation* she refers overtly to the floods in New Orleans in the wake of Hurricane Katrina and suggests the racial tensions following the disaster. She also makes political statements about the treatment of black Americans in *Formation* and references the 'Black Lives Matter' campaign by including a shot of graffiti and a row of white police officers facing a black child in a hoodie.

Key Term

Binary opposites
When products incorporate examples of opposite values, for example poverty and wealth.

Tip

There is a fact sheet on the set product, *Formation*, available on the Eduqas website.

Tip

It will be useful to look at other Beyoncé or Alicia Keys music videos to gain a broader understanding of how these artists use the form to construct representations.

Stretch and Challenge 3.7

Study a historical music video and consider how the representations have changed over time and how the video reflects its historical context.

Tip

At AS level you are required to use key theories in your analysis of the set products and extended examples. At A level you are required to use more advanced theories.

Stretch and Challenge 3.8

While there are named theorists in the specification, you can expand your knowledge and understanding by researching other theorists and theoretical perspectives related to the forms studied.

Consider the following questions for the music videos you have studied:

- What key representations feature in the music video?
- How has this been constructed, for example through visual and technical codes?
- Have stereotypes been used and to what effect?
- How do the representations relate to the lyrics and the genre of music? For example, the rap music genre.
- Has the performer used the music video to construct a representation of themself? Consider how either Beyoncé or Alicia Keys communicates messages about gender and ethnicity in the music video you have studied.
- Is the music video reflecting a historical, social or cultural context?

Applying Theory: David Gauntlett

David Gauntlett's theory of identity is relevant to both the forms of advertising and marketing, and music videos. He asserts that the media provide us with the 'tools' or resources that we use to construct our identities. Both advertising and music videos offer role models for viewers; he suggests that they then 'pick and mix' which aspects of these products they want to use in the construction of their own identities.

He also asserts that the media today, unlike in the past, offer a more diverse range of stars, icons and characters from whom we may pick and mix different ideas. This can be applied to a study of music videos where an audience can find an artist who best resonates with them and their attitudes and beliefs.

Consider the following questions when applying Gauntlett's theory to advertising and music videos:

- To what extent do the representations of gender seen in beauty adverts differ from those in the past?
- Do different sub-genres of advertising offer different types of representation?
- What different representations of gender are apparent in music videos?
- To what extent do the representations of gender and ethnicity in the music videos you have studied offer a range of more diverse types?
- How might an audience respond to the representations they see in advertising and music videos?

Sport England's campaign *This Girl Can* offers a range of more realistic representations of strong, confident women.

Applying Theory: Stuart Hall

Stuart Hall, in his theory of representation, argues that all representations are constructed through a language that is made up of signs and codes that are understood by the audience. In this way it is similar to the theory of semiotics, discussed previously. He also asserts that stereotyping reduces people and social groups to a few simple characteristics that are recognisable to audiences because they are reinforced over time. He also argues that stereotypes tend to occur where there are inequalities of power.

Consider the following questions when applying Hall's theory to advertising and music videos:

- What stereotypes are prevalent in advertising? How are they constructed by the product? What key elements of the stereotype are recognisable to an audience?
- Are the stereotypes constructed by adverts both positive and negative?
- How are subordinate or excluded groups constructed as 'different' or 'other' by some advertisements and music videos?
- How do music videos reinforce and challenge stereotypical representations of gender, age and ethnicity? In Alicia Key's music video *Underdog* (which can be viewed on YouTube), the common stereotype of young people and ethnicity is subverted. While conforming to stereotypical dress codes and urban settings, the sense of a diverse community is celebrated and there are positive representations constructed of usually under-represented social groups, including the homeless and single mothers.
- How are signs and codes used to construct stereotypes in music videos you have studied?

Tip

One of the options for production in Component 3 is music marketing, where you will be required to produce a music video. You will be expected to demonstrate your understanding of aspects of the theoretical framework, for example representation. Analysing how representations are constructed in music videos will prepare you for this element of the course.

Media Language: Analysing Newspaper Front Pages

Although you will be required to study more than just the newspaper front pages, it is a good place to start. The front page will give information about the brand identity and the attitudes, views and beliefs of the paper. The newspaper industry, like other media industries, is very competitive and what the newspaper's **gatekeepers** decide to put on its front page will be essential in attracting an audience. The main conventions of a newspaper front page include:

- **The masthead**: this is the name of the paper, which can signify the paper's ethos and values. For example, the *Daily Mirror* suggests it is giving a true reflection of what is happening in the world. The typography of the masthead also communicates messages. The *Daily Telegraph* has maintained its traditional font style, which has connotations of history and longevity. In contrast, the *Guardian*, in its rebrand, changed its font style to give a more modern feel to the paper.
- **The plug/puff**: this usually runs across the top of the front page and advertises what else is in the newspaper. The focus will often be on lighter aspects of the news or, for quality newspapers, may focus on the arts. The aim of the plug is to broaden the target audience. In the edition of *The Times* on page 78, the focus of the plug is fashion and calorie counting, the aim being to appeal to a wider (perhaps female) audience and to use its *Times2* supplement to demonstrate that there is more in the newspaper than the political stories which take up most of the front page. Here the plug also offers a distraction from the ongoing scandal of 'Partygate'.

Key Term

Gatekeeper
A person or organisation that is involved in filtering content in some way. For example, in the newspaper industry, editors generally perform this gatekeeping function as they determine which stories make it into the paper (through the gate) and which do not.

Tip

Looking at a range of newspaper front pages and articles, considering how they are constructed, will prepare you for the unseen element of Component 1, where you will be required to either compare an unseen newspaper front page with one of your set products, or analyse an unseen newspaper showing your understanding of media language. It is therefore important to familiarise yourself with this form.

Key Terms

Colloquialism
An informal expression that is often used in casual conversation rather than in writing. However, it is used in some media products to establish an informal communication with the audience.

Paparazzi photographer
A freelance photographer who aggressively pursues celebrities and royalty to take pictures to sell to magazines and newspapers for the highest price.

Tip

Using subject-specific terminology is essential when analysing the set products and the extended examples you study.

Stretch and Challenge 3.9

Look back at how the theory of semiotics has been applied to adverts and music videos and consider how it can also be applied to the newspapers you have studied.

- **The headline**: this will be in a larger font than the rest of the front page story, the aim being to attract an audience. Popular/tabloid newspapers have dramatic headlines using devices such as alliteration, hyperbole, **colloquialisms** and puns to target the audience. Quality newspapers are attracting readers who want more serious, detailed news and therefore their headlines tend to be more informative.
- **The strapline**: this is usually placed either above or below the main headline and provides more information or anchors the meaning of the central image. In both the newspaper front pages below, the strap-lines are used to give further detail and, in the case of this story which crossed political divides, to include implicit criticism of the PM and the Chancellor.
- **Subheadings**: these are short headlines, which break up the main text to make it easier to read. They appear throughout the paper but are mainly evident in popular, tabloid papers where they tend to be dramatic, for example 'Tragedy', to encourage the audience to read on.
- **The jump line**: this follows the teaser headline on the front page and encourages the reader to buy the newspaper in order to read on. For example, '*Turn to page 6*'.
- **The central image**: for popular/tabloid newspapers the central image is essential in selling the paper. It may often be of a celebrity or a dramatic image of an event. The image may be indistinct as it has been taken by a **paparazzi photographer**. This often emphasises the exclusivity of the story for the paper.
- **A stand-first**: a block of text that introduces the story, normally in a style different from the body text and headline.
- **A pull quote**: a quote from the story that is enlarged and appears within the text.
- **A standalone**: a picture story that can exist on its own or on a front page, leading to a story inside. They are usually used by broadsheets who want an attractive image on their front cover along with often unrelated news copy.
- **A splash**: a prominent or sensational news story, which is often the front page lead. On all the newspapers featured on this and the following page, the splash is related to the alleged breaking of Covid rules by members of the government.

Andy Warhol
His works sell for more than Picasso's - but does that mean he's better?
The Guardian
Wednesday 13 April 2022
For 200 years
News provider of the year

PM: I broke my own law but I refuse to go

Partygate fines mean Johnson and Sunak are first PM and chancellor to be hit by criminal sanctions while in office

Inside
The PM and chancellor should pay a price beyond their fines *Guardian editorial*
'My husband died of Covid, and we all obeyed the rules No 10 flouted' *Fran Hall*

THE TIMES
White hot!
Why it's the shade of the season
INSIDE TIMES2
Calorie counts on date night? Please no

Johnson refuses to quit over lockdown party fine
● PM is first found to have broken law in office ● Chancellor also penalised for No 10 gathering

Putin bids to outnumber Ukrainians five to one

IN THE NEWS
New York shooting | MP in sex case row | Protests shut Lloyd's | US inflation soaring | Ten Hag for Man Utd

Representation: Issues and Events

Newspapers represent issues and events to readers on a daily basis.

All newspapers have access to the same stories but they will select those that are most appropriate for their audience. They will then make choices about how to represent the events and issues, and the way in which the event and issue is represented will reflect the values, attitudes and beliefs of the newspaper. The construction of the representation will affect the way in which audiences respond to and interpret the issue or event.

When studying the representation of events and issues in newspapers consider:

- The values, attitudes and beliefs of the newspaper in which the event features. Is it clear what the newspaper you are studying thinks about the event? Is there any evidence of opinion or bias in the representation? The *Daily Mirror* is a tabloid newspaper with a **left-wing** bias; this is clearly demonstrated by the front page produced the morning after the then Prime Minister Boris Johnson and the then Chancellor Rishi Sunak had been issued with fixed penalty notices by the Metropolitan Police for breaking lockdown restrictions.
- How the event has been presented, referring to, for example, language and mode of address, anchorage, technical, visual and audio codes, and the use of images. The choice of headline in the *Daily Mirror* is bold and dramatic, using emotive language to express the newspaper's left-wing viewpoint. The caption reinforces this, '*Partners in Crime*', accompanying images of the two ministers, chosen because they are looking relaxed, suggesting their nonchalant attitude. The sub-headings also suggest criticism of the government's behaviour through the use of language – 'flouting' and 'shameful'. The headline from the *Guardian* for the same day (previous page) is less dramatic and more subtly conveys criticism by directly quoting the PM: '*I broke my own law but I refuse to go.*' This newspaper has also made the decision to include links to a more overtly critical editorial and a personal account inside the paper.
- The focus of the representation. The way in which a media product is mediated encourages the audience to focus upon a particular aspect of the product to encourage them to make assumptions and to draw conclusions. For example, our eyes are drawn to the headlines and images in newspapers.
- The process of selection. For whatever ends up on the front pages of newspapers, a lot more will have been left out. Someone will have made the decision about what to include and what to omit. Consider how this might affect how the audience feels about the event.

DAILY Mirror
The Heart of Britain
Wednesday, April 13, 2022 95p
PARTYGATE SCANDAL
Led by liars &
» Johnson, Carrie and Sunak fined by police for flouting OWN Covid rules
» PM & Chancellor refuse to resign as Downing St fines rise to shameful 50
PARTNERS IN CRIME Rishi Sunak and Boris Johnson
lawbreakers
FIRST PM TO BREAK THE LAW IN OFFICE: PAGES 2,3,4,5,6&7

The choice of image anchors the story and can communicate a viewpoint.

How an issue or event is represented in the newspaper will affect how the audience views it.

Key Term

Left wing
A term that refers to people whose view are left of the centre of politics. They believe that existing social inequalities must be addressed and they have more liberal political views.

Stretch and Challenge 3.10

Newspapers are studied in relation to all aspects of the theoretical framework in Component 1, so it is important that you are familiar with a range of examples from this form. Develop your knowledge and understanding by regularly looking at how different newspapers present the news of the day.

- The construction of the representation. The elements that go to make up the final product will have been constructed in a way that real life is not. It is a selected construction and has been edited, often to show a particular viewpoint. Some newspapers will be more explicit than others in the way in which they communicate their opinion.
- The audience who will consume the text and their response to the representations encoded within it.
- The role of **opinion leaders** in influencing the audience about the event.

Key Term

Opinion leaders
Those in positions of power who aim to persuade an audience of their point of view. Within the media these may be newspaper editors, programme producers or bloggers.

How is the Same Story Represented in Two Different Newspapers?

- What choices have the editors of the pages below from 24 March 2022 made about how to represent this event?
- What processes of selection and combination are evident in these front pages?
- How has the central image been used to communicate messages to an audience?
- How does the representation of the event convey the values, attitudes and beliefs of the newspaper?
- How is language used to construct the representation of this event, Rishi Sunak, the then Chancellor of the Exchequer's mini budget in March 2022?
- How may audiences interpret and respond to the representations in these newspapers?

Tip

You can use the questions here to help you analyse the representations contained in the newspapers you have studied.

DAILY Mirror
The Heart of Britain
Thursday, March 24, 2022 95p

SUNAK'S SICKENER

NOTHING to help as energy bills set to soar by £1,300
NOTHING to support struggling pensioners
NOTHING to stop worst fall in living standards since 50s
... and NOTHING much to soften petrol pain

MISERLY Rishi Sunak yesterday

THANKS FOR NOTHING

BY PIPPA CRERAR Political Editor

RISHI Sunak's mini-Budget yesterday did little to help struggling Brits who had begged him to tackle the cost-of-living crisis.

The Chancellor offered no support for families facing energy bill hikes of £1,300, gave out measly benefits rises and snubbed hard-up pensioners.

Even a 5p cut in fuel duty only brings soaring petrol prices back to what they were last week.

It comes as experts warned households face the biggest single-year fall in incomes since 1956.

Labour's Rachel Reeves said: "The Chancellor does not understand the scale of the challenge."

FULL STORY: PAGES 4,5,6&7

THE TIMES
DIEU ET MON DROIT
Thursday March 24 2022 | thetimes.co.uk | No 73739
£2.20 £1.45 to subscribers (based on 7 Day Print Pack)

regular unleaded 166.9
regular diesel 181.9

Best for analysis
Spring statement What it means for you and the economy
News, pages 4-9 Business, pages 39 & 44-45

Quitting at 25 Ash Barty's smart move
Times2

Biggest fall in living standards since 1950s

Rishi Sunak's tax cuts will not offset heaviest burden on the British public in postwar era

Steven Swinford Political Editor
Oliver Wright Policy Editor
Henry Zeffman Associate Political Editor
Chris Smyth Whitehall Editor

Rishi Sunak attempted to assert his credentials as a tax-cutting chancellor yesterday as official forecasts showed Britain facing the biggest fall in living standards since records began in 1956.

The chancellor used his spring statement to cut fuel duty by 5p a litre and announce that the threshold at which people start paying national insurance would rise from £9,568 to £12,750 in July. He pledged to lower the basic rate of income tax from 20p to 19p in 2024.

However, he held back most of a potential £20 billion-a-year war chest for pre-election tax cuts, choosing instead to proceed with plans to raise national insurance next month despite a backlash from Conservative MPs.

The Office for Budget Responsibility (OBR), the government's fiscal watchdog, said the chancellor's tax cuts would offset only about a quarter of the tax rises announced in the budget in October. It said living standards would fall by 2.2 per cent in the next tax year, the largest reduction in a year and twice the size of the falls experienced during the oil shocks of the 1970s and 1980s.

The OBR said the cut to fuel duty and changes to the national insurance threshold would offset a third of the fall in living standards expected in the next year. Despite the tax cuts announced by Sunak, however, it said the overall tax burden would rise to 36.3 per cent in 2026-27, the highest since the 1940s.

This is because of a previous decision to freeze income tax thresholds, which will drag one million workers into paying the higher rate, alongside other tax rises. Inflation could rise by as much as 8.7 per cent by the end of the year.

Tory ministers and MPs are increasingly concerned about the scale of the cost-of-living crisis facing the nation.

At cabinet yesterday, Sunak was told by Kit Malthouse, the policing minister, and Jacob Rees-Mogg, the minister for Brexit opportunities, to cut public spending because of its impact on inflation. Sunak said he understood their concerns but the government was committed to its manifesto pledges. He instead emphasised the need to avoid waste.

The chancellor was last night challenged at a meeting of the 1922 Committee of Tory backbenchers to bring forward income tax cuts and increase defence spending. Sunak said borrowing was too high and that the UK already had the biggest defence budget in Europe. Last night he told broadcasters: "We are facing the same challenges that many countries around the world are facing — that's rising prices and high inflation. I can't protect everyone against the full impact of those global challenges, but where we can make a difference, of course we will, and that's why the policies announced today are a significant intervention. They will put billions of pounds back in the pockets of hard-working British families."

In *The Times*, Paul Johnson, head of the Institute for Fiscal Studies, writes that he has "sympathy" for Sunak given that "we have been hit by world events way outside our control" and warns: "We will be poorer than we expected."

However, he criticises Sunak's decision to raise taxes on workers at the expense of pensioners and investors, and not to help those on benefits to deal with the rising cost of living. "Sunak had difficult choices to make for sure. The choices he made, though, were not the only ones open to him," he writes. The

Continued on page 2, col 5

Rishi Sunak gave his spring statement after Boris Johnson was challenged in prime minister's questions over the cost of living

Extra 6,000 missiles and war funds for Ukraine

Larisa Brown Defence Editor

The prime minister has promised to rush a further 6,000 missiles to Ukraine and provide a significant increase in funding, and today will call on leaders of Nato, the G7 and the European Union to step up support for the country's war against Russia.

Britain's new contribution will include £25 million for Ukraine to pay its troops and for supplies, and £4.1 million for the BBC World Service to tackle disinformation in Russia and Ukraine.

The missiles are in addition to more than 4,000 anti-tank weapons already supplied and include Nlaws and Javelins. Britain is also sending Starstreak anti-aircraft missiles and more body armour, helmets and combat boots.

An extraordinary trio of international meetings will be held in Brussels today designed to concentrate the minds of western allies and encourage them to offer more support to Kyiv.

"Vladimir Putin is already failing in Ukraine," Boris Johnson said. "The Ukrainian people have shown themselves to be extraordinarily brave and tenacious in defending their homeland, in the face of an unprovoked onslaught.

"But we cannot and will not stand by while Russia grinds Ukraine's towns and cities into dust. The United Kingdom will work with our allies to step up military and economic support to Ukraine, strengthening their defences as they turn the tide in this fight."

In his address to the Commons this month President Zelensky praised Britain's response to the invasion. He pleaded: "Please increase the pressure of sanctions against this country [Russia] and please recognise this country as a terrorist country."

The Nlaws are especially prized by Ukrainian soldiers. One senior officer told *The Times* that the shoulder-fired missiles were the weapon of choice for his troops and had been responsible for 30 to 40 per cent of the Russian tanks they had destroyed.

Dominic Raab, the justice secretary, will chair a meeting of justice and foreign ministers in the Hague today to co-ordinate support for the International Criminal Court's war crimes

Continued on page 2, col 3

IN THE NEWS

Losses to public life
Madeleine Albright, the former US secretary of state, and Baroness Howe of Idlicote, the public servant and widow of Lord Howe of Aberavon, have died. Obituaries, pages 57-58

Ferry sackings row
Serious doubts have been cast on Boris Johnson's allegation in the House of Commons that P&O Ferries had "broken the law" over the sacking of 800 crew last week. Page 10

DVLA given warning
The prime minister has told the DVLA to "expedite the supply of driving licences" after a *Times* investigation into the backlog at the government agency. Page 12

Memorial must stay
A memorial to Tobias Rustat, a 17th-century benefactor of Jesus College, Cambridge, with links to slavery, cannot be moved from the chapel there, a judge has said. Page 3

Taliban limits girls
Thousands of girls have been left distraught at school gates across Afghanistan after a last-minute decision by the Taliban regime to ban those over 12 years old. Page 36

Jones falling short
Eddie Jones, the England rugby coach, has failed to meet performance criteria set out by the RFU for two years, it has emerged, as debate over his future continues. Page 76

Applying Theory: Stuart Hall

- Consider how the front pages and articles in the newspapers you have studied use signs and codes to communicate messages. For example, the newspaper examples included here use the codes of gesture and expression to represent the event.
- Consider how newspapers construct recognisable stereotypes to reflect their attitudes and beliefs.
- Consider how these stereotypes reinforce inequalities of power, particularly with reference to excluded groups. For example, some newspapers construct stereotypes of the working class and of refugees through the images and language they use in relation to stories featuring these social groups. They are often constructed as different or 'other' and demonised by some newspapers.

Component 1: Section A Summary

- In Section A you have been introduced to key elements of the theoretical framework – media language and representations.
- The forms to be studied in this component are – advertising and marketing, music video and newspapers.
- You will analyse set products using this theoretical framework.
- The set products will be studied in breadth.
- These will be supported by extended examples to prepare you for the unseen resources in the examination.
- You will also study how the media products relate to key contexts.
- You will develop your ability to use relevant theoretical approaches, theories and subject-specific terminology.

Section B: Investigating Media Industries and Audiences

Production is a key aspect of media industries.

OVERVIEW

In this section you will:

- Develop knowledge and understanding of key aspects of media industries. This will include:
  - ownership and funding
  - regulation
  - the impact of technology
  - global production and distribution.
- Study media audiences including:
  - targeting
  - categorisation
  - construction
  - how audiences consume and interact with the media
  - how audiences respond to the media.

Audiences may respond differently to different products.

Tip

Look back at Chapter 1 where there is an overview of the main aspects of industry and audience that you will be required to know in this component.

You must study the following media forms and products set by Eduqas for assessment from 2024:

Advertising	Film (cross-media study including film marketing)	Newspapers
Tide print advertisement (1950s) and *Super. Human.* Tokyo 2020 Paralympic Games audio-visual advertisement (2020)	*Black Panther* (2018)	*Daily Mirror*

Radio	Video games
Woman's Hour or *Have You Heard George's Podcast?*	Assassin's Creed franchise

You are only required to study Advertising in relation to audience.

Film is only studied in relation to media industries.

In addition to the set products you should also study examples of contemporary and **emerging media** related to these products, for example websites, podcasts and social media.

Tip

You need to remember that in this section you are not engaging in textual analysis of the products themselves, but considering them in relation to their industry and audience contexts.

Key Term

Emerging media
Refers to communication through digital technology and new platforms with interactive elements, for example podcasts, social media, etc.

Investigating Set Forms: The Radio Industry

The radio industry is one of the oldest and most traditional media industries; it has seen many changes, never more so than now with the rapid progress of digital technology. The link between the product, the industry and the audience is still closely related, but the way in which audiences access and respond to radio products has changed dramatically in recent years.

Station Profiles

Each radio station, whether commercial or a **public service broadcaster** such as the BBC, has a distinct **profile** and identity, and appeals to different audiences. This is evident in the programmes they produce, the presenters and the way in which they market themselves to those audiences. Each station also has a logo that is a visual signifier of the station and is used in **cross-platform marketing**. This identity has been built up over time and audiences have expectations of particular stations and their output.

The programmes produced and commissioned by a station are often indicative of the station's identity and its values, attitudes and beliefs. Radio differs from television in that it is available in a range of different formats.

- **BBC radio**: the BBC is a public service broadcaster that is funded by the licence fee and does not air commercials. BBC radio is both national and regional, there are over 40 local/regional stations attracting more than nine million listeners in the quarter up to December 2021 (www.rajar.co.uk/listening/quarterly_listening.php). However, these numbers have been steadily falling due to the competition from commercial broadcasters.

There are over 300 commercial radio stations in the UK and in 2021 commercial radio accounted for 48% of listening time with a total of 36.77 million listeners in the quarter up to December 2021 (https://radiotoday.co.uk/2022/02/uk-radio-listening-remains-static-at-89-of-the-population/). The move to DAB broadcasting has enabled expansion of choice for audiences. Commercial radio incorporates:

- **National commercial radio**: there are three of these stations broadcasting at the time of writing: Classic FM, talkSPORT and Absolute Radio.
- **National brands**: these are regional stations that have been collected into networks, sharing some programmes and **syndicated output**. They are:
  - **Global Radio** – including Heart, Capital XTRA, Smooth and LBC
  - **Bauer Media Group** – became the largest commercial radio network in 2020, including Hits, Magic and Kiss.
  - Guardian Media Group – Real Radio.
- **Independent local radio**: these are regional commercial stations. They are specific to a certain area of the country and are not part of a network group.
- **Community radio**: this is a different format from public service and commercial stations. Community stations serve their local areas and produce content of interest to local people. The stations are non-profit making and are usually funded by the local community.
- **Hospital radio**: there are hundreds of these radio stations based in hospitals and staffed by volunteers, broadcasting in the UK. Many radio presenters started out in hospital or community radio.

Key Terms

Public service broadcaster
A radio or television broadcaster that is seen to offer a public service by catering for a range of tastes and audiences. The main public service broadcasters in the UK are the BBC, ITV, Channel 4, Channel 5 and S4C.

Profile
For radio stations this refers to how they are defined to their target audience through their brand identity, which may be defined by, for example, the presenters or programme style. This includes their aims and their ethos.

Cross-platform marketing
Where one form is advertised on another media platform. For example, BBC One will broadcast promotional advertisements for its radio stations; these will also be on the BBC website.

Syndicated output
When radio stations make and sell a programme to other stations, or buy a programme that may be available to other radio stations.

Tip

When you are analysing technical codes consider how they reflect the product's genre.

Quickfire 3.16

How has the way in which audiences listen to the radio changed over time?

Key Figure

Bauer Media Group
A multinational conglomerate that operates in 16 countries. It owns a range of global magazine titles and part of its organisation is Bauer Radio.

Industry: The BBC

As stated earlier in this section, the BBC is a public service broadcaster with a remit to inform, educate and entertain. Like television, radio has to produce programmes that attract and appeal to a broad audience. BBC radio is funded by the licence fee so there are no advertisements other than those for other BBC television and radio programmes and events organised by the BBC, for example 'Proms in the Park'. As with BBC television, the funding arrangement allows the stations some aspect of freedom to produce programmes that may target less mainstream audiences. All radio stations are obliged to broadcast regular news bulletins, which often will reflect the style of the station and the target audience; for example, the condensed, pacey delivery of Radio 1's *Newsbeat*, which covers issues relating to its younger demographic, or the more traditional mode of address of the *Today* programme on Radio 4. However, it is also important that all stations prove their popularity, as it is a competitive market.

Industry: Marketing

BBC radio engages in the following marketing strategies to promote its stations and programmes:

- Cross-platform marketing. Other radio stations and BBC television will promote radio stations and events related to BBC radio, for example 'T in the Park'.
- Billboard and magazine advertisements for stations and presenters.
- Each station has its own website within the umbrella website for BBC radio. These allow listeners to access live audio streaming and to listen to archive programmes. They also provide interactive opportunities for an audience and can be accessed by a global audience.
- BBC radio produces promotional films focusing on a particular part of its output, for example its presenters or news coverage.
- BBC Taster is an interactive service that enables the BBC to showcase experimental ideas and new talent. It allows audiences to give feedback on what they see and hear. It is also a space for the BBC to develop its ideas for digital content and emerging technology (www.bbc.co.uk/taster/about).

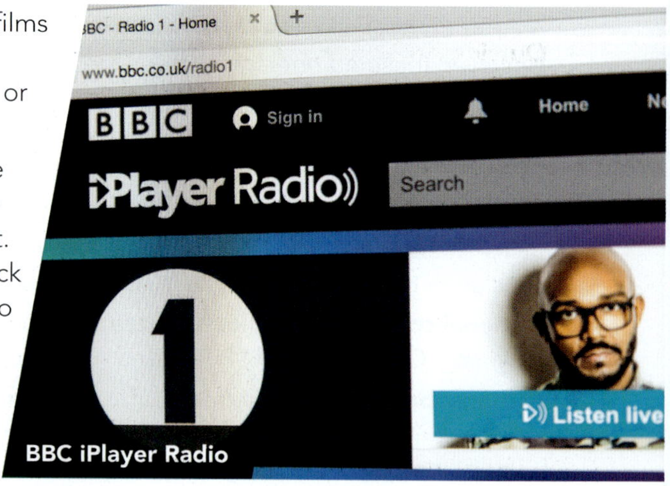

Quickfire 3.17

What marketing strategies are used by commercial radio to promote stations and programmes?

Quickfire 3.18

Why is BBC Taster an important service for the company and its audience?

The Specialised Nature of Radio Stations

Different radio stations will have diverse styles, and their programming will reflect the target audience. This will in turn influence and reinforce the profile of the station. Audiences build up a knowledge based on experience of what each station will offer. Stations tend to be divided stylistically and in terms of content between those that are speech based and those that are music-led. Speech-based stations such as Radio 4 and its individual programmes tend to target an older audience demographic but, recently, as part of its remit, Radio 4 has produced programmes that attempt to reach a younger, more diverse audience. The generic codes and conventions of speech-based radio programmes and podcasts are:

- **A presenter**: although this can also be the case for music-led formats, the presenter in speech-led programmes acts as an anchor to guide the discussion between various guests, for example Emma Barnett on *Woman's Hour*, or as a judge in a quiz programme, for example Sue Perkins in *Just a Minute* on Radio 4. In *Have You Heard George's Podcast?* the presenter, George the Poet, introduces the audience to aspects of inner city life through a combination of storytelling, interviews and music.
- **Discussions**: a group of people discussing a range of topics. This sub-genre of programme is often a key part of Radio 4's schedule.
- **Phone-ins**: these are effective, cheap ways of involving the listeners, who are encouraged to take part in the programme and offer their point of view. For example, Jeremy Vine's lunchtime programme on Radio 2.
- **Contributors**: news magazine programmes such as *Today* and *PM* on Radio 4 invite guests who tend to be experts or knowledgeable in the topic under discussion. The 8.10am slot on the *Today* programme is renowned for being reserved for eminent contributors such as, for example, government ministers. *Woman's Hour* includes a diverse range of female, and sometimes male, guests, including politicians, authors, academics and ordinary women.
- **Drama**: Radio 4 has a regular feature of *The Afternoon Play*. Other dramas include the long-running radio soap *The Archers*.
- **Documentaries**: these may be related to news items or current affairs, or be music themed, for example the life of a particular pop star or musician. Some of the episodes of *Have You Heard George's Podcast?* adopt a documentary style, for example 'George looks at the breakdown of the African American family since the 1970s.
- **Outside broadcasts**: reporters, presenters and mobile studios bring stories and features from different national and global locations. The flexibility of the radio medium means that it does not have to rely on visual images and therefore the reports can be more immediate. The focus is on the human voice and sound effects.

Tip

You need to develop your knowledge and understanding of the output of the station that produces the set product. However, you also need be aware of the profile of the station and its overall output in comparison to other radio stations.

Presenters are associated with particular programmes and become familiar to an audience.

Scheduling

Just like television, each radio station has a schedule and programmes are **stripped** across the schedule. The regular programmes for each station are broadcast at the same time each day. The scheduling of a particular programme will have been researched in order to maximise the target audience. This is still the case even though, with advances in digital technology, listeners can catch up on radio programmes through BBC Sounds and podcasts.

Key Term

Stripping
A technique used in radio and television whereby a certain programme is broadcast at the same time every day. In radio this attracts an audience who associate a particular programme with their daily routine, for example driving home from work.

The radio, more so than television, divides up its day related to what the audience may be doing. Radios 1 and 2 both have breakfast shows, which bring in a large section of audience who are getting ready for, or travelling to, work. These are largely music-led but also incorporate chat, sport, traffic and regular slots specific to the programme. These regular features build up expectations in the audience and give a structure to the programme.

Similarly, a speech-led station such as Radio 4, despite the ability for listeners to access programmes across different digital platforms, still operates stripping as part of its scheduling model. *Woman's Hour*, for example, is broadcast every week day at 10am with a 'best bits' episode on Saturday afternoon. The assumption here is that there is still an audiences who want to listen to the 'live' episode of the programme as part of their daily routine.

Set product: *Woman's Hour* or *Have You Heard George's Podcast?*

These are the set radio products at the time of writing, your centre will choose one for you to study. It is important to study the programme as an evolving media product in terms of its place within the industry and the audience issues that it highlights. While the programme is important as an example of a product that reflects the contemporary radio industry, it is also important to consider the historical significance of the programme in terms of its evolution and how its production and circulation has developed in response to industry and audience demands. In order to develop awareness of the programme and its significance, you should consider extracts from at least two episodes of *Woman's Hour* or *Have You Heard George's Podcast?* chosen by your centre and accessed via the BBC website.

Woman's Hour

- *Woman's Hour* was first broadcast in October 1946 on the then BBC Light Programme, which focused on entertainment and music. In the early days of the programme the focus was on the role of the housewife and tended to concentrate on the domestic sphere.
- The contemporary programme is very different and has evolved to cover more controversial and hard-hitting subjects relevant to women, including abortion, domestic violence and equal pay.
- The programme has had a range of presenters over the years but, most recently there was a significant change when long-running presenters Jenni Murray, who had been with the programme for 33 years, and Jane Garvey left to be replaced by Emma Barnett and Anita Rani.
- Emma Barnett is a journalist and broadcaster who has previously presented the BBC Radio 5 Live morning show and is also known for her incisive interviewing style on BBC's *Newsnight*. She is not afraid of exploring controversial and emotionally sensitive issues. She was named Speech Broadcaster of the Year by the Radio Academy. Anita Rani is a Bradford born television presenter, popular with audiences. She is a regular presenter on BBC's *Countryfile*, was a contestant on *Strictly Come Dancing* and has presented documentaries including My *Family, Partition and ME: India 1947*. Both these presenters reinforce the BBC's aim to reach different and diverse audiences.
- Each episode covers a diverse range of topics through interviews and discussions with invited guests led by the presenters. The topics on *Woman's Hour* are not all serious or focused solely on female experiences, they frequently cover more general subjects, viewing them from a female perspective, for example the war in Ukraine, the arts and cold-water swimming.
- The BBC is a public service broadcaster and *Woman's Hour* reflects the broadcaster's ideology and the ethos of Radio 4. It has been running for over 75 years and continues to focus on issues that are of interest to contemporary women.

Stretch and Challenge 3.11

Develop your understanding of the set product by listening to other *Woman's Hour* episodes and podcasts: www.bbc.co.uk/programmes/b007qlvb.

Emma Barnett is the main presenter of *Woman's Hour*.

Have You Heard George's Podcast?

- Podcasts are an important industry development, changing the way radio programmes are distributed and as a result broadening the audience reach. They suit the listening patterns of a younger audience who may be less likely to listen to a live programme.

- George the Poet is a spoken word performer who was born in London but is from Ugandan heritage. He uses his poetry as social commentary and to celebrate black culture.
- *Have You Heard George's Podcast?* was broadcast weekly on BBC Radio 1Xtra and Radio 4 and is available on BBC Sounds. It addresses the BBC's remit regarding diversity, as the podcast covers a range of issues relating to black culture and communities.
- There are three seasons and 32 episodes. The production format is an interesting one, involving collaboration with Benbrick and the BBC symphony orchestra.
- *Have You Heard George's Podcast?* featured in best podcasts of the year across a range of newspapers, including the *Guardian*, *Financial Times*, *Observer* and *NME*. It was the first podcast outside of the US to win the Peabody Award and has also won a range of other awards.

Both the set products demonstrate the impact podcasting and the ability to listen to podcasts on digitally convergent platforms has had on the radio industry. BBC Sounds has enabled the BBC to distribute its radio content to a wider audience and to offer content that is not available on the traditional schedules. BBC Sounds was created in 2018 to address the developments in technology and the different ways in which audiences consume content. It is a **walled garden** streaming service, featuring live broadcasting, audio-on-demand and podcasts. Its slogan, 'Listen Without Limits', encapsulates the advantages of this BBC service in the digital age.

Key Term

Walled garden
A broadcasting provider that controls access to its services and how content is distributed through, for example, subscription.

Industry: Regulation

The Communications Act of 2003 established Ofcom as the new UK regulator. Previously, the role had been held by a range of different regulatory bodies. The BBC as a public service broadcaster was regulated by the BBC Trust and Ofcom until 2017, but is now solely regulated by Ofcom. Accountable to Parliament, Ofcom is involved in advising and setting some of the more technical aspects of regulation, implementing and enforcing the law. Ofcom is funded by fees from industry for regulating broadcasting and communications networks, and grant-in-aid from the government.

Like television, BBC radio has a public service remit to inform, educate and entertain, which is evident in its range of stations catering for diverse audiences and interests, including the classical output of Radio 3, Radio 1Xtra, which plays contemporary hip hop and RnB aimed at 15- to 24-year-olds, and the BBC Asian Network to cater for the British Asian community. Commercial and community radio stations have to apply for their licences from Ofcom, and have to abide by their rules and regulations regarding output.

The role of Ofcom with regards to broadcasting is:

- To ensure that a wide range of television and radio services of high quality and wide appeal is available.
- To maintain plurality in the provision of broadcasting.
- To adequately protect audiences against offensive or harmful material.
- To protect audiences against unfairness or infringement of privacy.

The BBC is also self-regulatory. The company works with producers to ensure that there will be no need for Ofcom to intervene except in extreme circumstances.

An audience member can complain to Ofcom regarding a particular programme that they may deem offensive or harmful, and audience pressure over certain programmes can often be a successful form of regulation. When Ofcom receives a complaint, it assesses it under the terms of the Broadcasting Code and decides what action to take. Ofcom produces a regular 'Broadcast Bulletin' reporting on the complaints received and decisions taken.

Applying Theory: Curran and Seaton's Power and Media Industries

The main points of **James Curran** and **Jean Seaton**'s theory are:

- The idea that the media are controlled by a small number of companies primarily driven by the logic of profit and power.
- The idea that media concentration generally limits or inhibits variety, creativity and quality.
- The idea that more socially diverse patterns of ownership help to create the conditions for more varied and adventurous media productions.

Consider how you could use this theory to help you to analyse the radio set product, including:

- The importance of the BBC as a major deliverer of radio and television programmes.
- The role of the BBC as a public service broadcaster and its relative freedom from commercial pressures, for example selling advertising. This, in theory, gives it more scope to produce innovative and creative programmes, targeting niche and diverse audiences of which *LNWH* and *Have You Heard George's Podcast?* are good examples.
- The ethos of the BBC and its need to address a range of audiences.
- The flexibility of the BBC, which funds it programmes from the licence fee, not from advertising revenue, to commission new programmes that appeal to minority audiences.
- The organisation of BBC radio, similar to television, means that specific stations have a distinct style and ethos, and therefore appeal to different audiences.
- The podcast format of both set products may also be used to support Curran and Seaton's idea that socially diverse patterns of ownership help create conditions for varied and adventurous productions. These podcasts also illustrate the broadcaster's willingness to produce content in different forms targeting specific social groups.

Named Theorist

James Curran and **Jean Seaton**
Curran is Professor of Communications at Goldsmith's College and Seaton is Professor of the History of Media at the University of Westminster. Their book *Power without Responsibility* was first published in 1981 and has had several reprints. It is a history of media and communications.

Quickfire 3.19

Why is it important to have an independent regulator?

Stretch and Challenge 3.12

Engage in independent research into Ofcom and its role in regulating television and radio.

Audience

In an age when we are dominated by visual images, many will question how radio has managed to survive and indeed develop. The medium of radio has a range of different appeals as it consists of:

- **The blind medium**: it only involves the sense of hearing with no visual images. In this sense the medium can be seen to have advantages in that it allows the audience to use their imagination.
- **The companion medium**: the radio format provides a strong sense of personal communication for the audience. It also offers interactive opportunities – audiences can text and email programmes and get a 'mention' or a 'shout out' on it. Some programmes have phone-ins where listeners can air their views or select music to be played. Podcasts often encourage interactivity by asking audiences to get in touch.
- **The intimate medium**: radio is very personal. It encourages intimacy by the use of the direct mode of address.
- **The undemanding medium**: it allows the audience to do other things while listening. A criticism of television in the early days was that it didn't 'go around corners'; with radio, a listener does not need to devote their time entirely to the platform.

The BBC's Audience Commitment

- To provide impartial news and information to help people understand and engage with the world around them.
- To support learning for people of all ages. To show the most creative,highest quality and distinctive output and services.
- To reflect, represent and serve the diverse communities of all of the United Kingdom's nations and regions and, in doing so, support the creative economy across the United Kingdom.
- To reflect the United Kingdom, its culture and values to the world.

The report also stated:

> *Two years after launch, BBC Sounds continues to grow as more people discover it as the home of music, radio and podcasts from the BBC … reaching record weekly audiences.* (*BBC Annual Report and Accounts 2020/21*, bbc.co.uk)

Quickfire 3.20

How does *Woman's Hour* or *Have You Heard George's Podcast?* go some way to fulfilling one of the strategic objectives of the BBC?

The way in which audiences listen to radio has changed over time.

Radio Audiences and Emerging Media

Recent technological advances have had an impact upon radio in terms of how programmes are broadcast and how listeners receive those programmes. These technological developments have allowed radio to develop and increase in popularity, despite critics heralding the end of the radio format. Although radio is a blind medium, many radio stations now have webcams in their studios, allowing listeners to view the presenters and guests in a radio show. Radio programmes also frequently produce a podcast of the best bits of a particular week. Podcasts can then be downloaded on a range of platforms and make listening to the radio more flexible for audiences.

Most radio stations allow listeners to access the output on the internet through an **audio streaming** facility; this has broadened the global audience. A major development has been digital audio broadcasting (DAB) radio. This has created more wavelengths allowing a greater number of stations. It has also increased the quality of the output, ensuring less interference. BBC Radio 4 had a weekly reach of over 10 million listeners in the quarter up to December 2021: 11% of the listening share. The most popular BBC Radio station is Radio 2.

Key Term

Audio streaming
Where listeners can click on a link to play the radio programme instantly. This has increased the global reach of BBC radio, as listeners abroad can tune in to hear the live programme.

One of the areas of the specification that you will need to address in relation to the radio set products is how they target, reach, address and potentially construct audiences, and how industries like the BBC target audiences through the content and appeal of their products. Consider the following for the set radio product you are studying:

Quickfire 3.21

How do radio programmes construct audiences?

How does *Woman's Hour* Appeal to Audiences?

- The slogan for the programme on the BBC Radio 4 website encapsulates its appeal: '*Women's voices and women's lives – topical conversations to inform, challenge and inspire*' (www.bbc.co.uk/programmes/b007qlvb).
- The programme targets a specific, although not exclusive, audience of women. This is evident through the choice of topics covered on the programme and the mainly female guests that feature as part of the daily content. The programme includes a range of serious and more light-hearted stories to appeal to the female demographic.
- The choice of presenters. Replacing the older female presenters with younger, more diverse women suggests that the BBC is aiming to widen the audience reach of the programme.
- The audience is constructed by the BBC through the choices made about the style and mode of address of the programme, the guests and the topics chosen for discussion.
- The availability of the programme as a live broadcast each day at 10am caters for the loyal listener who includes the programme as part of their daily routine. The additional availability of the programme as a podcast on BBC Sounds appeals to those audiences who want more flexibility about how and when they listen to the programme.
- The BBC website offers a range of ways in which the audiences can access the programme's content, for example there is a print version of some of the interviews, short video clips of two or three minutes featuring extracts from the audio programme, for example Frankie Bridge discussing mental health issues 'I don't need to be fixed', as well as full-length episodes.
- The programme offers a range of ways in which audiences can interact with the programme encouraging listeners to be part of the *Woman's Hour* community and 'have their say'. During the live programme, audience members can email, tweet or text their responses to the programme's content. These are then read out on air, or questions may be put directly to the guest. Other responses are included in the Saturday 'best bits' programme. Some editions of the programme focus entirely on the listener and their experiences, for example the 'phone-in' in April 2022 discussing the change in the law to allow 'no-fault' divorce.

How Does *Have You Heard George's Podcast?* Appeal to Audiences?

- George the Poet uses the medium of the podcast innovatively to engage audiences, the form allows him to 'deep dive' into issues of cultural significance. Dylan Haskins, Commissioning Executive at BBC Sounds says: 'Have You Heard George's Podcast? *is a world-class podcast with the power to tell stories that move, resonate, educate and entertain across borders*' (www.voice-online.co.uk/entertainment/2021/07/16/have-you-heard-georges-podcast).
- The three 'chapters' of his podcast cover a range of topics, both personal and universal, including art, politics and current affairs. The delivery is creative and innovative, changing from episode to episode and including personal memories, reportage, discussion and fiction. The topics include the link between crime and rap music, the modern slave trade, Grenfell and Ugandan politics. This appeals to those who share his interests and those who want to be educated on these topics.

- The podcast offers a voice to the black community who may feel they are under-represented and the appeal will be the topics covered which are of cultural significance to this group.
- His presentational style is unique, *'with a complexly layered sound design, the podcast is mostly but not exclusively spoken by Mpanga, whose voice is gentle, persuasive, and generous, and whose other stylistic innovation is to render the podcast almost entirely in rhyming verse that, like the rapping to which it is indebted, amounts to a naturalistic but heightened form of everyday speech'* (www.newyorker.com/culture/podcast-dept/george-the-poets-undefinably-good-podcast).
- His topics are personal but also universal in appeal, related to finding an identity. They are also often very complex and challenging for audiences, for example one episode he personifies Uganda and Britain as women with whom he is involved in a complex relationship and in another he talks as he travels in a taxi to Grenfell.
- His storytelling is enhanced by the musical collaborations, including with the BBC Concert Orchestra and other musicians, which broaden audience appeal. *For Chapter 3 many parts of the BBC have collaborated to help realise George and Benbrick's creative ambition for the podcast, teaming them up with the BBC Concert Orchestra to record the score* (www.voice-online.co.uk/entertainment/2021/07/16/have-you-heard-georges-podcast/).

Applying Theory: Stuart Hall's Reception Theory

Hall asserted that communication is a process involving encoding by producers and decoding by audiences. He said that there are three ways in which messages and meanings may be decoded by audiences:

- **The dominant position**: the audience accepts the intended meaning encoded in the product.
- **The negotiated position**: the audience acknowledges some of the messages encoded by the producers of the product but may question or adapt the message to be more relatable to their own experiences.
- **The oppositional position**: the encoder's message is understood, but the decoder disagrees with it.

Quickfire 3.22

Consider how could you could apply Hall's theory to *Woman's Hour* or *Have You Heard George's Podcast?*

Stretch and Challenge 3.13

Research the actual responses to *Woman's Hour* or *Have You Heard George's Podcast?*, for example blogs, newspaper reports, etc.

Social and Cultural Context

The inclusion of *Woman's Hour* and *Have You Heard George's Podcast?* in the BBC Radio output demonstrates the BBC's awareness of the need to cater for and reflect all areas of society in their content. The topics included in both products reflect what is of interest and concern to social groups who are often misrepresented or under-represented by more traditional programming.

Investigating Set Forms: The Film Industry

A Cross-Media Study Including Film Marketing

Film must be studied in relation to media industries only. You will study the set film products and their marketing across various media platforms exploring the **convergence** of these media platforms and technologies, and other relevant industry issues.

In order to develop your awareness of the film set product as a contemporary example of the film industry and the marketing strategies used to promote films, you should study:

- at least one trailer from the film
- at least one poster from the film
- online marketing where relevant
- selected extracts from the film to exemplify industry issues, for example the opening credits, which would include the film company logo and the production company, and one other extract.

It is also essential that you develop an understanding of the industry that produced the product including:

- how films are produced and distributed
- how your chosen film is marketed
- regulation issues related to the film
- **global implications**.

Films are defined and categorised by their genre, the stars, the production company and the production values. The production context of the film is also relevant and this will in turn attract different audiences and communicate different messages about the film itself. For example, some films are mainstream, **high-concept films** with a high budget, others may be classified as 'independent' films which are less star-driven and can be seen to have lower production values.

What is Meant by a Mainstream, High-Concept Film?

This is a model for a film and is used to describe the concept of the Hollywood mainstream, 'big budget' film. It originally consisted of a ten-point formula that ensured the film conformed to the high-concept model. The criteria of a high-concept film includes:

- Clearly defined characters, often recognisable in terms of stereotypes and archetypes.
- A simple narrative with universal themes. This can often be summarised in a single sentence or image that makes it easier to market.
- High production values evident in the cinematography, costumes, settings and special effects.
- Elements that are easy to market and promote, for example iconic repeatable images, a recognisable soundtrack and potential for merchandising.
- High-profile stars often related to the film's genre.

Key Term

Convergence
The process through which different media industries and media platforms merge with one another or move closer together. This process is often facilitated by digital technologies. For example, smartphones bring together many different functions in a single device – as well as making phone calls, users can browse the internet, play games, watch video content and listen to music.

Tip

Consider examples of how convergence can be applied to technology, content and industry.

Key Terms

Global implications
The importance of a product in a worldwide context.

High-concept film
A film that can be summed up in a sentence or two. It is recognisable to audiences, easily marketable and high budget.

Tip

Remember that you are not studying the set film in terms of textual analysis, but the industry that produced it. Your teacher will suggest extracts that are suitable for you to view.

Tip

…member: the film you study … an isolated text; it serves …onstrate your awareness …ustry that created it.

- 'Larger than life' protagonists.
- Visual appeal, including lavish sets and expensive action scenes.
- Highly dramatic and hyperbolic plot situations.

All these elements are important in attracting a global audience to ensure the success of the product.

It is important to be aware of the economic context of films and their production. High-concept films are produced by the major film studios that are media **conglomerates** and therefore have the ability to back these films and rely on financial returns. Media ownership is now concentrated in a few multi-national conglomerates, the patterns of ownership and control related to the film industry are important to the success of the film. Many major production companies also have the means for the promotion, exhibition and distribution of the films they make. These companies operate a philosophy of synergy through the practice of **vertical integration** and **horizontal integration**.

What is an Independent Film?

An independent film is one made outside of the financial and artistic control of a large film company. A truly independent film should be privately conceived and funded. However, few films made are really 'independent'. This more commonly refers to a film that is made by a smaller film company on a low budget. An independent film has a set of conventions:

- A distinguishable content and style.
- Evidence of the presence of the filmmaker and their artistic vision.
- It often has a story to tell and therefore there is a focus on the narrative, theme or sub-genre as a selling point rather than star actors.
- It may be aesthetically different, for example the use of black and white or a more grainy, realistic 'look'. Hand-held cameras are also often used to establish realism.
- Clear evidence that it has a lower budget. This may include the lack of known acting stars, the settings and the props.
- May have a limited release and will often be reliant on initial screenings at independent film festivals. The success of the film will then be used in future marketing materials.

The impact of digital technology and the falling costs of equipment have made it much easier to make films on lower budgets than in the past.

The Film Industry

Films can be produced, distributed and exhibited in different ways according to the production context of the film. Some are studio productions and some are examples of independent films.

Distribution is a very important part of the film industry as it is the way in which the film is connected to the audience. The specific distribution strategies will be related to the target audience and how they will view the films. It is the responsibility of the film's distributor to release and sustain interest in the film. This is most effectively supported by vertical integration, where the production, distribution and **exhibition** are controlled by one main company. Distribution also involves the important job of promoting and marketing the film, including global sales of the film. This will involve the production of trailers, posters and online marketing. The distributor is also responsible for deciding the best time to market the films and the logistics, including copying the film and transporting it to the cinemas to be shown.

Key Terms

Conglomerate
A large organisation that owns other companies and has interests spanning across a number of different businesses or industries. For example, the Walt Disney Company is a media and entertainment conglomerate as it has business interests in several different industries, including film, television, music and radio as well as the theme park industry.

Vertical integration
A process through which a company develops control over different levels of the value chain. An example of a vertically integrated business would be a production company that is also able to distribute its products or a magazine publisher that owns a printing company.

Horizontal integration
The process through which different companies that produce or distribute similar products join together through a merger or acquisition. This reduces competition and enables companies to increase their market share.

Quickfire 3.23

Explain the economic context of a mainstream, high-concept film.

Key Terms

Distribution
The link between the producer and the audience; refers to all the strategies used in the release, marketing and promotion of the product.

Exhibition
All the opportunities available to an audience to view a film, including at multiplex and independent art house cinemas, at film festivals and online.

The distributor makes sure the film is ready to be shown in the cinema.

Key Term

Classification
A rating given to a film, informing the audience of its suitability according to criteria that include levels of violence, sexual content and use of inappropriate language.

Stretch and Challenge 3.14

Visit the BBFC website (www.bbfc.co.uk) and look at the criteria for a 15 certificate and at the recent judgements made about the classification of films.

Quickfire 3.24

Why might film trailers be given a different certification to the main film?

Industry: Regulation

In Britain films are regulated by the British Board of Film Classification (BBFC). This was established in 1912 to classify films and has also been responsible for the **classification** of videos and DVDs since the Video Recording Act of 1984. All decisions are made using guidelines produced and regularly updated by the BBFC. The aim of classification is to protect children from harmful content and to give audiences the information they need to guide them before viewing the film.

In some very rare cases, a film will be deemed not appropriate to be given a classification at all. The aim of film producers is to ensure that their film is open to the widest audience to achieve box office success. In recent years the 12A certification was introduced for films that the BBFC considers to be suitable for audiences over the age of 12, with acknowledgement that parents know best as to whether their children younger than 12 can cope with a particular film.

In America, the Motion Picture Association of America (MPAA) operates a voluntary regulation of films. This is a ratings system the aim of which is to distinguish between those films aimed at an adult target audience and those suitable for children. Although voluntary, the expectation is that no film will be rated higher than 'R', which suggests the film is suitable for accompanied children under 17.

However, the MPAA uses different criteria from the BBFC when rating films and tends to be more lenient on violence and less on sexual content. American films for distribution in the UK will be given a rating by the BBFC. It is sometimes the case that the trailers for the films will be given a different classification to that of the main film.

bbfc
Age Ratings You Trust

U PG 12 15 18 R18

™The letters BBFC and the category symbols are registered trademarks of the British Board of Film Classification. (Numbers 2234547-2234552)

Set Film Industry Product: *Black Panther* (2018)

This is the set product for film marketing at the time of writing. It is important to bear in mind that you are not engaging in a textual analysis of the *Black Panther* film, but you are studying it in relation to the industry that produced it. You are therefore expected to study the marketing of this film across various media, exploring the convergence of media platforms and technologies, and other industry issues.

In order to develop an awareness of the film and its marketing strategies you should consider:

- at least one trailer for the film
- at least one poster for the film
- online marketing where relevant
- selected extracts from the film which exemplify industry elements, for example the opening credits and at least one other age-appropriate extract.

Industry Information

You will need to consider the industry elements relating to the film industry set product, including:

- processes of production, distribution and circulation in relation to your set product
- relationship of recent technological change and production, distribution and circulation
- significance of patterns of ownership and control, including conglomerate ownership and vertical integration
- the significance of economic factors to the film.

Black Panther was directed by Ryan Coogler and released in February 2018. It is the 17th film in the **Marvel Cinematic Universe** (MCU) **franchise**, the highest grossing franchise in history. The MCU total worldwide box office revenue in August 2021 was $22.93 billion (www.statista.com). *Black Panther* was a commercial and critical success, its estimated budget was $200,000,000: on the opening weekend in the US and Canada it made $202,003,951 (February 2018) and its gross worldwide was $1,347,597,973 (www.imdb.com).

The MCU is part of the Walt Disney Company, a diversified global entertainment company comprising Disney Media and Entertainment Distribution (DMED) and Disney Parks, Experiences and Products (DPED). The films produced by the MCU and similar high budget films share similarities including:

- they are big screen, spectacle events that are aggressively marketed
- the marketing focuses on the fact the films are part of a recognisable and commercially successful franchise
- they include spectacular imagery
- they appeal to a global market due to the focus on high production values, the straightforward plot and the lack of complex dialogue
- they have the potential for a range of spin-off products, including merchandise, video games and theme park attractions.

Marketing: *Black Panther*

In relation to your film set product you will need to be aware how media organisations maintain, through marketing, varieties of national and global audiences.

How was the Film Marketed?

Consider how Disney and Marvel used marketing strategies to appeal to a broad audience and to maximise profits:

- Marketing focused on the way in which the film celebrated African culture. This ensured that the film became a cultural and political event. This **Afrofuturism** aesthetic appealed to a range of audiences.

Quickfire 3.25

How can film franchises be said to eliminate risk and maximise profits?

Tip

For further information about this set product there is a detailed fact sheet available on the Eduqas website.

Key figure

Marvel Cinematic Universe (MCU)
This is a franchise centred on a series of superhero films produced by Marvel Studios based on characters that originally appeared in Marvel comics. The first film was *Iron Man* (2008) and there are currently 27 films in the franchise. Disney acquired Marvel Studios in 2009. MCU has now expanded into television through the streaming service Disney+, its first series was *Wandavsion*.

Key Terms

Franchise
A series of related media products, for example films, that are recognisable by their common elements, such as the same fictional universe or characters. Franchises are lucrative for film producers as audiences know what to expect and may be fans of the previous films in the franchise.

Afrofuturism
A movement in the arts including film featuring futuristic or science fiction themes and narratives incorporating elements of black culture and history. The aim is to connect audiences from black diaspora with their African heritage.

Stretch and Challenge 3.15

Consider how the set product *Black Panther* conforms to the conventions of a 'spectacle' film. *Black Panther* is part of Phase 4 of MCU products. Research examples of films from the other phases and consider how *Black Panther* is different.

- In June 2017 teaser trailers were released featuring Chadwick Boseman reprising his role as T'Challa and introducing the world of Wakanda. The images were afrofuturistic and the themes of pride and power were designed to appeal to a broad audience. The majority black cast highlighted the film in the early days of marketing as a political and cultural event and distinguishing it from other superhero films.
- The film was released to coincide with Black History Month in the US, a time when there was discourse around black culture.
- The marketing was also conducted at a grassroots level. One example was New York marketing professional Frederic Joseph who raised money through a GoFundMe page to send a Boys and Girls Club from Harlem to see the film. The #BlackPantherChallenge encouraged other people to take part and raise money and also contributed to the film's profile.

Quickfire 3.26

What elements of industry are evident in the trailer for *Black Panther*?

- The theatrical film poster further reinforced the themes of the teaser campaign, establishing the recognisable Marvel brand through the logo and font style while suggesting the unique selling point of the black cast and the focus on the Black Panther character. The iconography of Afrofuturism is also a significant element of this poster. The inclusion of other recognisable stars such as Martin Freeman and the creation of the fictional universe also broadened audience appeal.
- The theatrical trailer launched on 16 October 2018, which can be seen at www.youtube.com/watch?v=xjDjIWPwcPU), had 17 million views. It was carefully constructed to contain something for a range of audiences, both fans of the Marvel franchise and new audiences attracted by the diversity of the cast and the narrative. The trailer focuses on T'Challa's personal and political struggles, introduces the characters. including the antihero Killmonger. and the all-female special forces unit, focusing on their strength and power. In addition, there are also the expected elements of this film genre, including car chases, advanced technology, special effects and battles.
- *Black Panther*'s marketing strategies were wide ranging, designed to reach a diverse audience. They included a 'Welcome to Wakanda' runway show in New York Fashion Week alongside a *Black Panther* Red Carpet event in February 2018. Lexus cars, one of the film's sponsors, launched two new limited edition models with Marvel/*Black Panther* token features including the blue colour of the car featured in the film. Black Panther surfs on the roof of Lexus car and it is also driven by the female warriors in the car chase with the villains.

Stretch and Challenge 3.16

Read 'The Marvellous Marketing Vehicle for the New Lexus', detailing the collaboration between Disney and Lexus in relation to *Black Panther*. Consider how this is mutually beneficial for the film company and the car manufacturer. It can be found at www.forbes.com/sites/csylt/2018/02/26/the-marvellous-marketing-vehicle-for-the-new-lexus/?sh=5ba2236c2717.

- Kendrick Lamar performed songs for the soundtrack appealing to another demographic and fan base. *Pitchfork* online music magazine suggested that Coogler selected Lamar '*because the themes in his music – foremost on that list: blackness as an identity, spirituality, power dynamics, self-doubt and the onus of kingship – align with those in the film*' (https://pitchfork.com/reviews/albums/various-artists-black-panther-the-album/).
- Merchandise was also widely available, including the Black Panther mask and a variety of toys and replica figures from the film.

Tip

Although you are not required to textually analyse the trailer for the film, selecting key examples to illustrate aspects of industry gives you useful specific evidence to use in an examination response.

How the Film Company Used Marketing to Target and Maintain a Range of Audiences

- The marketing strategies were designed to appeal to a broad global demographic. The company employed 360-degree marketing crossing multiple platforms.
- It was a marketing strategy from Disney itself to produce the film at all, in doing so the company broke away from the tried and tested formulas within the franchise.
- The film appealed to mainstream audiences and fans of the Marvel franchise, through ensuring plot continuity with other films in the franchise and easter eggs for hardened fans, but also to arthouse audiences through its inclusion of political and Afrofuturistic themes.
- Cultural marketing was used to target the Afro-American audience by, for example, inviting Kendrick Lamar to produce the soundtrack and showing the trailers as sporting events with an Afro-American following.
- Women and black women in particular, an under-represented demographic in this film genre, were targeted through the inclusion of strong female characters with an active role in the narrative.
- Posters were produced focusing on individual characters in close-up with a tagline reflecting their motivation within the narrative. This encouraged audience members to identify with particular characters. Featurettes were produced where the actors discussed the role of their character and their importance in the film as if they were real people.
- *Time* magazine ran a front cover featuring Chadwick Boseman, this magazine's global readership is well-educated professionals, a different target demographic for the franchise. This can be viewed here: https://api.time.com/wp-content/uploads/2018/02/hk_g1500_blackpanther0219.jpg?quality=85&w=840.

Tip

Look at Chapter 7 in this book where there is additional information about the codes and conventions of film posters.

Contexts

Historical context

Black Panther is set in the fictionalised world of Wakanda and in the modern world, but it does reflect a historical discourse related to exploitation. From the 15th to the early 20th century, European powers colonised African countries forcing their inhabitants into slavery, eroding their culture and exploiting their country's resources. In later years, this mistreatment led to particular groups such as African-Americans attempting to re-establish a black cultural identity, raising awareness of historical inequalities. The film and character take their name from a group of political activists: The Black Panther Party, founded in 1966 and continuing until 1982. It was a political organisation influenced by the speeches of Malcolm X. Its aim was to address racial inequalities and police brutality and murder of black people. It was a controversial organisation due to its advocation of violent tactics and many of its members were arrested or killed in confrontations with the police.

Stretch and Challenge 3.17

Research some of the articles that have been written during the recent protests around slavery and the Black Lives Matter protests. Consider how the decision to make *Black Panther* may have been influenced by these concerns and historical events.

Social and Cultural Context

- The film was released to coincide with Black History Month in the USA, a time when the struggles, achievements and culture of the African-American community are celebrated.
- The narrative, choice of the largely black cast and the themes covered in the film are all socially and culturally relevant. The film was marketed as a cultural event; although Marvel films had regularly featured black characters, these tended not to have central roles and only a limited number of films in the superhero genre have female leads. The #oscarssowhite campaign in 2016 had drawn global attention to the lack of diversity in mainstream films, *Black Panther* addresses this disparity.
- Culturally, the mainstream media tends to portray a negative representation of Africa, presenting the continent through the use of terms such as 'war', 'famine' and 'starvation' as descriptors and putting forward a view of Africa as a developing country with issues.
- *Black Panther* created a cultural footprint with the Afrofuturistic aesthetic and in dealing with issues relevant to the black community. At the film premiere the actors arrived in costumes reflecting their culture.

> *… the very existence of Black Panther feels like resistance. Its themes challenge institutional bias, its characters take unsubtle digs at oppressors, and its narrative includes prismatic perspectives on black life …* (https://time.com/black-panther/)

Economic Context

- The film was a commercial success and made over $1.3 billion at the global box office within eight weeks of its release.
- The fact that the film was made by Disney and is part of the Marvel franchise reduced the financial risk of the film despite the movement away from the more traditional format.
- The narrative, spectacular imagery and majority black cast ensured that this film had global appeal, particularly with regard to African countries who could see positive representations of themselves in a genre where they were usually under-represented.
- The marketing campaign and the launch of the film as a big screen event helped both the financial and cultural success of the film.
- The fact that the film is part of the Marvel franchise meant that spin-off products including merchandise, computer games and theme park rides contributed to the film's profits.

Political Context

- The film is political in that it combines the fictional Marvel world of Wakanda with contemporary politics dealing with issues related to the experiences of Afro-Americans. Wakanda is a representation of Africa which is strong, culturally anchored and free from colonial intervention.
- The film follows in the wake of the Obama presidency, which introduced initiatives to aid minority groups in the US and the Trump presidency which sought to dismantle many of these established schemes, including Obamacare which gave millions of low income Americans access to health insurance.

Stretch and Challenge 3.18

Read the article 'The Passionate Politics of "Black Panther" in which the writer discusses the film's political and social themes: www.newyorker.com/culture/richard-brody/the-passionate-politics-of-black-panther.

- Michelle Obama recognised the political and social importance of the film congratulating the entire team in her Tweet '*Because of you, young people will finally see superheroes that look like them on the big screen. … I know [this film] will inspire people of all backgrounds to dig deep and find the courage to be heroes of their own stories*' (https://twitter.com/michelleobama/status/965641575584935936?lang=en-GB).
- The film, through its name and some of its themes, has links to the group of political activists called the Black Panthers, although Killmonger's political radicalism is rejected.

Stretch and Challenge 3.19

Look back at the key points related to Curran and Seaton's theory of power in the media in the section on radio. Consider how you could apply this theoretical perspective to your study of the film industry.

Investigating Set Forms: The Newspaper Industry

Newspapers as a form are an in-depth study, which means that you will look at it in relation to all areas of the theoretical framework: media language, representation, industry and audience. In Component 1: Section A, the focus is media language and representation. In this component it is industry and audience.

The Newspaper Industry: An Introduction

A range of different newspapers are published every day in the UK, these include national, local and Sunday editions. In the past, newspapers were mainly categorised by their size – **tabloids** and **broadsheets** – however, although these terms are still used, they are no longer accurate, as newspapers over the years have experimented with different sizes and designs in order to attract a diminishing readership and to address audiences' needs. Tabloid newspapers used to be the popular press and broadsheets were quality newspapers – referring to the style of news they carried. Newspapers now can be divided into three groups: the quality newspapers, previously known as broadsheets, for example the *Guardian* and *The Times*, the middle-market tabloids made up of the *Daily Mail* and the *Express*, and the tabloids, or 'red tops' – named such as their mastheads are presented in red – for example, *The Sun* and the *Daily Mirror*.

Key Terms

Tabloid
Refers to the dimensions of the newspaper: a tabloid is smaller and more compact in size than a broadsheet. Also refers to a newspaper the content of which focuses on lighter news, for example celebrity gossip, sport and television.

Broadsheet
Describes a quality newspaper that publishes more serious news, for example the *Daily Telegraph*.

Who Owns the Press?

It is important to be aware of the significance of patterns of ownership and their impact upon the production and distribution of your set newspaper product. By far the biggest player in the newspaper and other media industries is News Corps of which News UK is a subsidiary, owned by Rupert Murdoch. His media empire includes *The Sun*, *The Times*, *The Sunday Times*, and *The Sun on Sunday*. Other main newspapers are owned as follows:

- the *Guardian* and the *Observer*: The Guardian Media Group with one shareholder – The Scott Trust
- the *Daily Mirror*, *Sunday Mirror*, the *Express*, *Daily Star*, *Sunday People* and 240 regional newspapers: Reach plc
- the *Telegraph* and *Sunday Telegraph*: Telegraph Media Group (Frederick Barclay)
- the *Daily Mail*, *Mail on Sunday*, *i* (since 2019), *Metro*: Daily Mail and General Trust (Lord Rothermere).

The newspaper industry is very powerful and, as you can see, is largely in the hands of a few powerful media groups and individuals. Although the sales of print newspapers are falling, the front page of a newspaper is still an important vehicle through which an audience is targeted and messages are communicated.

Key Terms

Right-wing newspapers
Those that tend to support political parties such as the Conservative Party and UKIP, believe in the free market and oppose socialism.

Left-wing newspapers
Those that tend to support political parties such as the Labour party and socialist policies that advocate social equality.

Circulation
A count of how many copies of a particular publication are distributed. Circulation audits are provided by the Audit Bureau of Circulations (ABC).

Quickfire 3.27

Why is it important that newspapers have an online presence?

Quickfire 3.28

How has technological change affected newspapers?

The ways in which newspapers are consumed by audiences is changing to reflect technological developments.

Owen Jones, a journalist and political activist, said the press is:

> *Largely run by a very small group of very right-wing media moguls who defend the status quo of which they are part.* (www.yougov.co.uk)

The political associations of a newspaper will affect how they present particular stories and in turn will influence what their readers think and believe. YouGov conducted a survey into readers' perceptions of the political leaning of specific newspapers. Out of eight newspapers, five were seen to be predominantly **right wing** and two, including the *Daily Mirror*, were perceived to be centre to **left wing**. For the *Daily Mirror*, 76% of those asked thought it was to the left of centre, 11% thought it was 'very left wing', second to the *Guardian* in being the most left wing. The *Daily Mail* was perceived to be the most right-wing newspaper. As this is also the best-selling daily newspaper (www.pressgazette.co.uk), it may be influential in how their readers perceive events and issues.

Newspapers and Technological Change

Newspapers have had to adapt to changes in technology and the needs of their readers. All national and many local newspapers now have an online presence and their news content is also available on other social media platforms and through apps. This allows newspapers to broaden their audience reach in terms of production, distribution and **circulation**. As you can see from the slide below, many audiences are accessing a traditional print form through a digital platform.

Just like the magazine industry, the newspaper industry is facing a drop in circulation figures as the readership diminishes. This reflects sociological changes related to the ways in which readers want to access their news. With the advances in digital technology, news can be more immediate and a new generation of consumers who are used to receiving information in bite-sized chunks, are much less likely to want to pick up a newspaper. Just as, in the past, newspapers themselves have 'downsized' in order to address audience needs for a more compact version, they also had to produce online versions of their papers in order to target a new audience.

The digital revolution has also had an impact on how news is gathered. Frequently, news channels use citizen journalism, information from the general public rather than their own journalists, as the advances in technology mean that ordinary people now have the means to record images and send information immediately. This is particularly true when the story is unexpected or difficult to access by journalists, for example the war in Ukraine where video diaries from people living in the war zone became essential ways for newspapers to get up-to-date news.

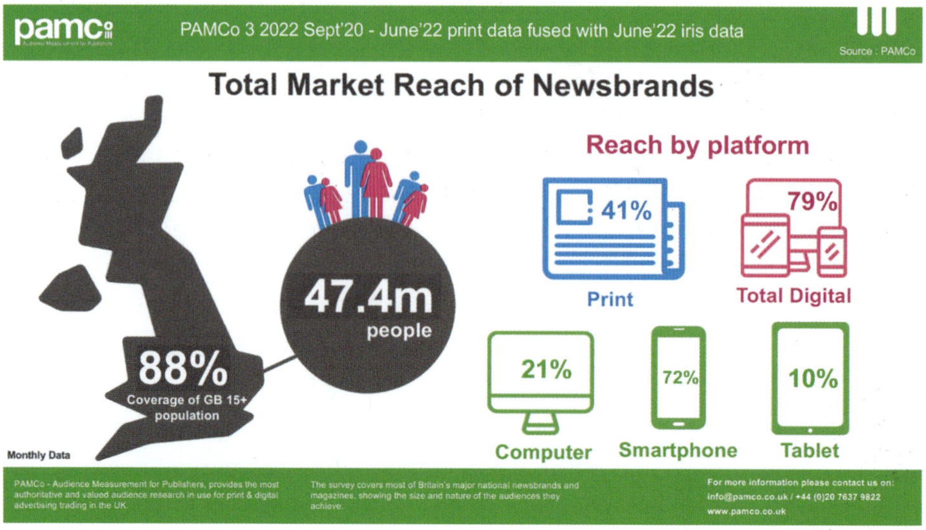

Advantages of Online Newspaper Sites

- They are immediate and up to date. When something happens users can access the news and get regular updates.
- They offer more immediate interactive opportunities, for example there is access to audio-visual clips and opportunities to blog or email opinions. The *Daily Mail*, which has a high percentage of female readers, has had particular success with its online version of *Femail* with its diet of fashion and gossip.
- Apps for several newspapers are available for mobile phones and iPads.
- There is an archive facility so that users can access back issues or features.
- The navigation tool allows users to quickly select the news and features that interest them.

Who Chooses the News and Why?

News values are the criteria that will influence the decisions made by those who run the newspaper industry, including the owners, editors and journalists, about which stories will appear in their newspaper. These decisions are made every day by gatekeepers who decide how the news is selected and constructed for the audience. This will reflect the **news agenda** for the paper. Although not all news values are relevant today, some of the criteria still used are:

- **Threshold**: the bigger the story the more likely it is to get onto the news agenda.
- **Negativity**: bad news is more exciting and interesting than good news.
- **Unexpectedness**: an event that is a shock or out of the ordinary, for example the Russian invasion of Ukraine in 2022. An event like this will push other news stories off the agenda and changes to the front page may be made at the last minute.
- **Unambiguity**: events that are easy to report and are not complex will be higher up the agenda of some newspapers. Modern wars are often difficult to report and are avoided by tabloid newspapers unless they involve personalities or can be graphically represented.
- **Personalisation**: news stories that have a human interest angle are more likely to appear in some newspapers. Readers are interested in celebrities, and stories have more meaning if they are personalised. During the coverage of the war with Ukraine in 2022, the *Daily Mirror* (9 March 2022), on its front page, included the image of a small child with a soldier. This personalises the distant war and makes it more immediate and poignant for readers.
- **Proximity**: the closer to home the story is, the more interested the reader. Tabloid and local newspapers tend to be more **ethnocentric** than quality newspapers.
- **Elite nations/people**: stories about important people and powerful nations, for example the USA, will be higher up the agenda.
- **Continuity/currency**: stories that are already in the news continue to run and are updated as new aspects to the story appear, for example Brexit and the 'Partygate' scandal.

Key Term

News agenda
The list of stories that may be in a particular paper. The items on the news agenda will reflect the style and ethos of the paper.

Key Terms

Ethnocentric
Roger Brown defines ethnocentrism as *'the application of the norms of one's own culture to that of others'* (*Social Psychology*, 1965, page 183). Stuart Hall referred to this definition in his theory of representation as he suggested that ethnocentrism is an example of the way in which stereotypes reinforce the power of certain groups over others.

Key figure

Lord Leveson
Lord Justice Leveson is an English judge who chaired the public inquiry into the culture, practices and ethics of the British press, prompted by the *News of the World* phone hacking scandal. This newspaper subsequently shut down.

Industry: Regulation

The newspaper industry used to be regulated by the Press Complaints Commission (PCC). However, the PCC was severely criticised in the Leveson inquiry conducted by **Lord Leveson**, which in 2012 investigated the culture, practice and ethics of the British press in the light of the phone hacking scandal and other issues related to intrusion of privacy by the press. The PCC was seen to be largely ineffectual in regulating the newspaper industry. Lord Leveson made recommendations for a new regulatory body to replace the PCC.

In his report he says:

> *The press needs to establish a new regulatory body, which is truly independent of industry leaders and of government and politicians. It must promote high standards of journalism …*

He also stated that there would be firmer sanctions for those newspapers that were deemed to have broken the law, including substantial fines. Newspapers at the time were concerned that this would be set up by Royal Charter and therefore the self-regulatory system would be governed by legislation. The press industry was unhappy about these recommendations becoming a legal requirement. Those against the reform wanted newspapers to still have some independence regarding self-regulation in order to protect the freedom of the press.

Tip

Not all newspapers have signed up to the regulator IPSO as they feel it is not independent enough. For example, the *Guardian* and the *Financial Times* have instead established their own independent complaints system.

The new regulatory body is the Independent Press Standards Organisation (IPSO), whose stated aim is to uphold professional standards in journalism. The role of IPSO involves:

- The regulation of over 1,500 print and 1,100 online titles.
- Dealing with complaints about possible breaches of the Editor's Code of Practice.
- Giving help with unwanted press attention or harassment issues.
- Giving advice to editors and journalists.

Set Product: The *Daily Mirror*

In studying this product you should have knowledge and understanding of this newspaper as an evolving media product in terms of the relevant newspaper industry and the audience issues it illustrates, the edition of the *Daily Mirror* you study for this section will be different from the pages studied for Section A. In order to develop this awareness you should consider:

- One complete print edition of the newspaper. This will be chosen by your teacher.
- Selected pages from the newspaper's website including the homepage and one other page.

The *Daily Mirror* is a British national popular newspaper, first produced in1903. It is owned by Reach plc, one of Britain's biggest newspaper groups with a combined digital reach of 48 million per month. It owns over 130 national and local brands including the *Daily Mirror*, *Sunday Mirror*, the *Express*, *Daily Star*, the *Sunday People* and 21 out of 25 top regional titles.

The company states its purpose as:

> *[W]e have a clear core purpose: speaking up and shining a light on the truth. While our titles differ in their political views, they each serve their communities with integrity and passion.* (www.reachplc.com)

The Front Page

Consider what the front page of a newspaper tells us about the industry that produced it. Using the *Daily Mirror's* front page, right, as an example:

- The masthead: this is the name of the paper, which can signify the paper's ethos and ideology. For example, the *Daily Mirror* suggests that the paper reflects and '*holds a mirror up*' to what is going on in society.
- The typography of the masthead also communicates messages, the bold font is strong. This paper is a red-top tabloid along with *The Sun*. However, in recent years the *Mirror* has aimed to distance itself from *The Sun*, and has tried to become less concerned with gossip and celebrity, and more with political issues.
- However, the other main story and the plug both refer to celebrities suggesting that this is still part of the paper's focus.
- The slogan states *'FIGHTING FOR YOU'* suggesting that the reader is part of the community of the newspaper and the newspaper's producers are making the point that the newspaper can be influential within society.
- The paper is one of the only obviously left-wing newspapers. This can be seen in its treatment of the main story, which reinforces the newspaper's anti-government stance in its criticism of the Health Minister, Jeremy Hunt, and the government's policy. The **political bias** of the paper is evident. The caption accompanying the image of Jeremy Hunt is *'HAPLESS Tory Hunt'* further reinforcing the opinion of the paper.

Tip

The work you did on the set inner pages of the *Daily Mirror* for Section A of this component will also be useful for looking at industry and audience in this component.

Key Term

Political bias
When a newspaper may show support for a political party through its choice of stories, style of coverage, cartoons, etc. It may be subtle and implicit or explicit, as in the case of the tabloids on Election Day.

Inside the Newspaper

In Section B you are required to study the newspaper as a whole, its place within the industry and its audience. When analysing the selected pages from your chosen edition it will be useful to consider:

- **Letters pages**: here, the readers have their say; this can give you an insight into the **readership** and values, attitudes and beliefs of the paper. In tabloid newspapers the letters will tend to be more light-hearted and amusing than those of broadsheets, which normally have a more serious tone. However, they will also often reflect the political viewpoints of the readers as this page allows them to comment on the current news. The letters page in the *Daily Mirror* is called 'Your Voice' (below), suggesting that they value the ideas and opinions of their readers. The topic of the parties in Downing Street and the criticism of Michael Gove over the cladding scandal reflect the left-wing ideology of the newspaper and it readership.
- **The editorial**: this is useful to study as it is where the newspaper gives its opinions about the stories it has run that day. This will usually give an insight into the political bias of the newspaper and its attitudes to what is going on in the country at the time.
- **News stories**: the inner pages of a newspaper will often link to the splash on the front page, and will go into more detail. The construction of these pages by the producers of the newspaper and the way in which the news story is represented will reflect the attitudes and beliefs of the paper.

Key Term

Readership
An estimate of how many readers a publication has. As most publications have more than one reader per copy, the readership estimate is very different from the circulation count. These figures were previously produced by the National Readership Survey (NRS), which operated from 1956 until 2018. They are now provided by the Publishers Audience Measurement Company (PAMCo).

Audience

When studying audiences in relation to the newspaper set product you will need to consider a range of points from the specification including:

- How media producers target, attract, reach, address and potentially construct audiences.
- How media industries target audiences through the content and appeal of media products and through the ways in which they are marketed, distributed and circulated.

Who Reads the *Daily Mirror*?

As can be seen from the table on the right, the newspapers produced by Reach appeal to audiences across different platforms illustrating how the newspaper publisher has addressed recent technological change in the way that it distributes its products.

Mirror Total Brand Reach (TBR)
Entities included in these estimates: Print: Daily Mirror, Sunday Mirror & Sunday People Digital: Mirror All numbers are for monthly reach and are in 000's
Total brand reach: 26,349
Print reach: 3,525
Digital reach: 24,419
Mobile reach: 22,925

Source: PAMCo 3 2022 (September 2020–June 2022 print data fused with June 2022 iris data)

Quickfire 3.29

Consider the difference in numbers between the print and digital versions of the newspapers produced by Reach plc.

Quickfire 3.30

How have the producers of the *Daily Mirror* used a range of platforms to reach a broad audience?

How Do Newspapers Target, Attract and Reach Readers?

- **The print version of the newspaper**: uses the front page as the shop window, marketing what the product has to offer its readers. The main headline is usually big, bold and dramatic, and uses devices such alliteration, hyperbole, colloquialisms and puns to target the audience.
- **The central image**: for popular/tabloid newspapers such as the *Daily Mirror*, the central image is essential in selling the paper. It may often be of a celebrity or a dramatic image of an event. The image may be indistinct as it has been taken by a paparazzi photographer. This often emphasises the exclusivity of the story for the paper, this is the case with the image of George Michael's grave (see page 103).
- **The plug/puff**: this usually runs across the top of the front page and advertises what else is in the newspaper. The focus will often be on lighter aspects of the news or, for quality newspapers, may focus on the arts. The aim of the plug is to broaden the target audience and give them teasers of what is in the rest of the paper.
- **The values, attitudes and beliefs of the paper**: shown through the stories and representations. Readers will relate to this and feel part of the community of the newspaper. For example, the readers of the *Daily Mirror* are more likely to be supporters of the Labour Party, or certainly left-wing, and will accept the preferred reading of the stories.

  'The Big Question' section of the *Daily Mirror* asks readers to respond directly to the paper and encourages interactivity.

Quickfire 3.31

What affects the way in which a reader may respond to the stories covered in the newspaper, for example political beliefs?

Quickfire 3.32

What are the advantages of a newspaper website for readers?

The newspaper's website is another platform through which the newspaper reaches readers. This includes a range of features to target and attract readers including:

- **Interactive features**: these are the elements of the website that allow the user to become involved with the site through blogs, forums, surveys, email opportunities, etc. This feature may encourage the audience to return regularly to the site as their involvement develops. The 'Most Commented On' section highlights the stories that are of interest to the readers and encourages other readers to access the comments. Some of the stories on the website have a 'Comment' tab, allowing the reader to feel that their opinion is valued by the paper and other readers.
- **The navigation bar**: this allows the audience to choose which elements of the website they want to visit.
- **Multi-media features**: websites will use a mixture of text, images and sound, and allow the audience to watch videos related to news, current affairs and celebrity stories.
- **External web links**: an image or a key word that will take the user to another page or website, this may enable them to access further information about a news story or related issue.

Applying Theory: Stuart Hall's Reception Theory

Look back at the information about this theory in the 'Radio' section of this component. Consider how this theory could be applied to newspapers. As newspapers, particularly tabloids, tend to be clear about their attitudes to a story, this will invoke a response from readers related to their own ideas and beliefs.

As you can see from the letters page and 'The Big Question' section, the readers of this paper have a diverse range of responses to the political questions posed by it. Different readers will decode the messages encoded by the producers of the newspaper in different ways.

Quickfire 3.33

Consider how different readers may respond to the edition of the *Daily Mirror* you are studying.

Key Term

Opinion leaders
Those in positions of power who aim to persuade an audience of their point of view. For example, these may be the editors of newspapers.

Quickfire 3.34

Give an example of how the *Daily Mirror* could be said to be an opinion leader.

Power and Media Industries: Curran and Seaton

Look back at the information on this theory in the 'Radio' section of this component. Consider how you could apply it to your newspaper set products.

Applying Theory: George Gerbner's Cultivation Theory

The main points of this theory are:

- The idea that exposure to repeated patterns of representation over long periods of time can shape and influence the way in which people perceive the world around them (i.e. cultivating particular views and opinions).
- The idea that cultivation reinforces mainstream values (dominant ideologies).

Consider how you could apply this theory to your newspaper set product. Newspapers often operate as **opinion leaders** mediating the news for the readers. The loyal reader of the *Daily Mirror* will be regularly exposed to the ideas and beliefs of the newspaper and this in turn will influence how they perceive the world around them at both a national and global level.

Contexts

Political Context

The *Daily Mirror* is a left-wing newspaper that has an allegiance to the Labour Party. It is pro the European Union (EU) and anti Brexit, and urged its readers to vote 'remain' in the EU Referendum.

As can be seen in the earlier examples of pages from the paper, the political context is also evident in the letters pages of the newspaper, where the audience consumption and their response is clear. The expectation is that, in this newspaper, political stories will be given a left-wing bias and that the newspaper will be critical of the policies of the current Conservative government and its leader.

Social and Cultural Context

Consider how the *Daily Mirror* reflects the social and cultural contexts of the time in which it was produced. The front page story in the *Daily Mirror* frequently uses the binary opposites of 'us and them', allying with the workers against the bosses or the government and highlighting social inequalities. For example, the newspaper's headline on 9 January 2023 was '*One Rule for the Rishi*' playing on the pun of 'one rule for the rich, another for the poor'. The strapline starts, '*Super-Rich PM ...*' illustrating the social differences between the government and the readers of the newspaper. The use of language illustrates the opinion of the newspaper, constructing a negative representation of those in power.

Quickfire 3.35

Where else in the newspaper may you find evidence of the social and cultural context?

Investigating Set Forms: Advertising

For this component 'Advertising' is only studied in relation to audiences. In Section A you studied media language and representation in the two set advertisements, which at the time of writing were the 1950s *Tide* print advertisement and the audio-visual advertisement for *Super. Human.* Tokyo 2020 Paralympics audio-visual advertisement. In Section B of Component 1 you will study the same two advertisements in terms of the relevant audience issues they illustrate.

Advertising is one of the most powerful media industries. All media products need to market and promote themselves in order to communicate with audiences and achieve success. The aim of all products is to create a brand identity that becomes recognisable to an audience. The advertising industry, like other industries, has adapted in order to reflect sociological and cultural change and consumer demands. The industry has had to examine how it can best access a modern audience. As audiences have changed aspects of their behaviour, for example their television viewing habits, advertisers have been forced to consider new platforms, for example mobile phones and social media, to reach audiences.

Targeting the right audience is essential for the producers of advertisements regardless of whether they want to sell a product, promote an event or raise awareness of an issue. Advertising agencies engage in market research and build databases as part of their preparation for a new advertising campaign in order to ensure that they appeal to the right audience. They are also one of the industries that work particularly hard to place audiences into categories in order to create a more direct appeal.

One of the ways in which audiences for advertising are categorised is through demographics. A **demographic audience profile** categorises an audience according to their class, occupation and income. For other media industries this method is now seen to be outdated, but it is still relevant to advertising and the magazine industry as it clearly illustrates which types of people have the highest **disposable income**.

Key Terms

Demographic profiling
A way of categorising audiences by dividing consumers into groups based on age, sex, income, education, occupation, household size, marital status, home ownership or other factors. This information is of use to some media industries, for example it can help advertisers determine their target audience for particular products and develop adverts that focus on a specific demographic.

Disposable income
The money left when bills, etc. have been paid that can be spent on items such as luxury goods and non-essentials. The people with high disposable incomes can be targeted by advertisers.

Tip

Look back at the information about advertising in Section A of this component, as aspects of this may be useful for Section B, for example establishing a brand identity.

Adverts persuade us to buy what we want, not what we need.

Audiences are categorised in groups from A to E, where A and B are the highest earners in society or the ones with the greatest disposable income. Retired people, for example, may not earn money but sometimes have an income they can and are willing to spend on luxury items.

A different type of profiling used to determine audiences is the psychographic audience profile, where audiences are categorised according to their VALs (values, attitudes and lifestyles). This is clearly very relevant to the advertising industry and this method was first developed by Young and Rubicam, a New York-based advertising agency. They considered how cross-cultural consumer characteristics can group audiences through their motivational needs. The main groups are:

- **Mainstreamers**: these make up 40% of the population. They prefer security, tried and trusted brands, and like to think they belong to a group of like-minded people. They also prefer value for money and are less likely to take risks.
- **Aspirers**: this group want status and prefer brands that show their place in society. They are happy to live on credit and will buy items such as designer labels. They are stylish and dynamic and may be persuaded by celebrity endorsement.
- **Explorers**: like to discover new things. They are attracted by brands that offer new experiences and instant results.
- **Succeeders**: these are people who already have status and control and have nothing to prove. They prefer brands that are serious and reliable and believe that they deserve the best.
- **Reformers**: this group are defined by their self-esteem and self-fulfilment. They tend to be innovative and are less impressed by status. They are not materialistic and are socially aware. They may be more inclined to buy brands that are environmentally friendly or those that are considered healthy.

Quickfire 3.36

How does categorising audiences help in advertising products and services?

Explorers like to discover new things.

Set Product: *Tide* Print Advertisement (1950s)

Tide is a historical advertisement produced in the 1950s. *Tide* is a soap powder produced by Proctor & Gamble. It was initially produced for heavy duty machines but was released into the domestic market in the late 1940s. The company used the advertising agency D'Arcy Masius Benton and Bowles, an American agency that was also responsible for creating the Santa image for *Coca-Cola*. The name of the company is included in the advert as it was seen to be a trusted brand. The print advert was also accompanied by radio and television adverts to build audience familiarity with the brand by using the same housewife characters singing the praises of *Tide*.

Audience: Historical Context

Obviously, this product was not created for a modern audience, and ideas, attitudes and beliefs contained within it may seem outdated, but the advert itself does tell us about the audience of the time. In the post-war boom of the 1950s, particularly in America, new technologies developed rapidly, especially those in the domestic sphere, including vacuum cleaners, fridge-freezers and washing machines. These became desirable products and a symbol of status related to the **American Dream**. Alongside these technological developments came new products, including soap powder. Interestingly, these products tended to be advertised in slots in American domestic melodramas watched by women. These dramas later came to be known as 'soap operas'.

Key Term

American Dream
The idea that every American can have equal chances to achieve their aspirations.

How Was the Audience of the Time Targeted by this Advert?

- The target audience is clearly women who at the time would have sole responsibility for the home. They would be relatively affluent lower-middle class women who were attracted by time-saving devices. Many adverts of the time offered women representations of domestic perfection with the whitest wash and the cleanest floors. Their role at the time was to look after their men and children.
- This product is made to seem new and exciting by the use of strong primary colours and large fonts.
- The use of hyperbole and exclamation marks make the product seem an essential buy. *'NO OTHER WASHING PRODUCT KNOWN – WILL GET YOUR WASH AS CLEAN AS TIDE.'*
- The endorsement of *Good Housekeeping* magazine would have related to the target audience and further convinced them of the effectiveness of the product.
- The advert appeals to the aspirer. Judging by the washing on the line the woman is married with children and would want the ideal home pictured in magazines such as *Good Housekeeping*. The front cover of an edition of the magazine, on the next page, includes the cover line '*Living Electrically in 1956*', reinforcing the importance of the changes in the domestic sphere for women.

Stretch and Challenge 3.20

Look at the television adverts for *Tide*: www.youtube.com/watch?v=BJ5EjNkHeU0. Consider how the audience is targeted in them.

- The use in the *Tide* advertisement of the two women talking to each other was a common convention of washing powder adverts of this time. It is an effective technique, as it is women advertising to women. The advert uses women, from the same demographic as the target audience, hanging out their washing; this makes the claims for the product seem more credible. They use informal language while the more factual information is included in numbered points. The aim is to distinguish *Tide* from 'sudsy' soap powders and so promote its unique selling points.
- There is a lot more copy on this advert than we would expect to see on more modern ones. This is because at the time a lot of new brands were appearing on the market, combined with the technological developments in domestic appliances, so the consumer needed more information about the product and its purpose. This is also reinforced by the images, which include the iconic representation of the packaging and the image of the old-fashioned washing machine with suds pouring out if it, suggesting those days are gone with the purchase of *Tide*.

Quickfire 3.37

What conventions of modern advertisements are evident in the historical advert for *Tide*?

Stretch and Challenge 3.21

Engage in independent research into other 1950s adverts to gain an understanding of how the audience of the time were targeted.

Social and Cultural Context

Despite the fact that women's roles had changed dramatically during World War II, when they assumed male roles, including working as land girls, driving buses and ambulances, alongside running the home, once the war was over women returned to a mainly domestic role. As a result, cleaning and other domestic products were largely still targeted at women.

The 1950s was the advertiser's dream decade. Rationing finally ended in 1954, after 14 years, and as a result the post-war economy rebounded, heralding a new age of prosperity. Inflation was low, giving most people more disposable income, which they were encouraged, through advertising, to spend on consumable products, in particular consumable durables such as washing machines and steam irons. The sales of these products increased by 70% in the 1950s and this was aided by advertising. It included the marketing of related products, for example soap powders. The boom in purchasing was also aided by the arrival of commercial television in the 1950s, increasing the platforms by which adverts could reach audiences.

Applying Theory: Gerbner's Cultivation Theory

As has been highlighted, advertising strategies and the audience reach of advertisements developed dramatically during the 1950s. This theory can be useful in considering the ways in which audiences of the time may have been influenced by advertising. Gerbner's idea was that exposure to repeated patterns of representation over long periods of time can shape and influence the way in which people perceive the world around them by cultivating particular views and opinions.

In the *Tide* advert a series of ideas are offered to the female consumer including:

- All women should want their wash to be the 'cleanest' and 'whitest'.
- Everyone else is using the product: *'goes into more American homes than any other washday product'*, so you should be using it too.
- That *Tide* is an innovative product with a unique selling point.
- If you want your wash to be the best you must buy *Tide*.
- That you would be happy (smiling faces of women) and your life complete if you use *Tide*.
- As the values, attitudes and beliefs being sold in these advertisements were also prevalent in other adverts of the time, this would influence the consumers and encourage them to accept the preferred reading of the product's creators (as suggested by Stuart Hall's theory – see page 105).

Quickfire 3.38

How could Stuart Hall's reception theory be applied to this advertisement.

Set Product: *Super. Human.* Tokyo 2020 Paralympic Games Audio-Visual Advertisement (2020)

Some advertising campaigns are not concerned with selling consumable products, but instead aim to promote an event or raise awareness about a particular issue, or, in the case of the Tokyo 2020 Paralympic Games trailer, to do both. The purpose of this advertisement is significantly different from that of *Tide* and other examples of advertisements for consumable products you may have studied and the social and cultural context is also very different. However, they are all examples of advertisements and as such share a repertoire of elements that aim to target, attract, reach and address audiences.

Background Information

The advertisement *Super. Human.* was made by the American, Oscar-nominated cinematographer Bradford Young, known for his work on feature films including *Selma* and the television mini-series *When They See Us*. He was the first African-American cinematographer to be nominated for an award in 2017 for his work on the film *Arrival*.

It was devised and created by Channel 4's in-house creative agency 4Creative and produced by Serial Pictures and Somesuch, a global production company whose aim is to '*give voice to the unexpected, the daring, the authentic, the irreverent, the funny and the sad*' (https://somesuch.co/about). The trailer was part of a bigger campaign including posters and social media.

Tip

Look back at the 'Advertising' topic in Section A of this component where adverts that raise awareness are discussed.

Stretch and Challenge 3.22

Read the article about this and the other Paralympics Games campaigns here: www.campaignlive.co.uk/article/theyve-nailed-again-channel-4-unveils-super-human-campaign-tokyo-paralympics/1722076.

The advertisement explores the sacrifices made and the trials endured by Paralympic athletes in preparation for the 2020 Tokyo Paralympic Games. Channel 4 has become synonymous with the marketing, promotion and broadcasting of the Paralympic Games and this is their third marketing campaign for the event. In creating the 2020 advertisement Channel 4 stated that its aim was to ensure that the Paralympics receives as much promotion as any other global sporting event. Channel 4's Chief Marketing Officer Zaid Al-Qassab said: '*Channel 4 has been instrumental in putting the Paralympics onto the world stage. Our award-winning coverage and epic marketing campaigns have possibly done more to help shift society's perceptions around disability than anything else in the last 20 years*' (www.televisual.com/news/watch-c4s-paralympics-campaign-super-human/).

The advertisement, helped to ensure the success of Channel 4's promotion of the 2020 Paralympics:

- ✓ The coverage was viewed by a third of the UK population (20 million viewers) and a fifth of young people aged 16–34 (22%).
- ✓ The Games attracted 2.6 million on All 4 streams.
- ✓ It accounted for the biggest Channel 4 weekly share of TV viewing since 2016 and the largest daytime share since 2012.
- ✓ There were half a billion global impressions from @C4Paralympics tweets. (Source: www.channel4.com/press/news/channel-4s-coverage-tokyo-2020-paralympic-games-reaches-20-million-viewers)

How Does *Super. Human.*, the advertisement for the Tokyo 2020 Paralympics, Target, Reach and Address its Audience?

- **Personalisation:** the advertisement deals with real, human stories, encouraging the audience to identify with the personalities and their lives. The focus is very specifically on the day to day challenges of being an athlete foremost, reinforced by one of the final shots of the trailer showing the words, '*To be a Paralympian there's got to be something wrong with you*'. Some of the Paralympians will be household names, for example Ellie Simmonds and Kadeena Cox, and audiences will have followed their journey and feel invested in them. '*And our hope is that this powerful and provocative film will once again stir viewers and continue Channel 4's legacy of challenging attitudes and giving a voice to those with disabilities*' (www.televisual.com/news/watch-c4s-paralympics-campaign-super-human/).
- **The audio**: the song is recognisable to audiences as it is taken from *Bugsy Malone*, it is upbeat and fast-paced and encapsulates the athletes' everyday battles. Other audio codes reinforce this struggle and establish realism, for example heavy breathing, grunts and groans. The opening sequence juxtaposes the recognisable sports commentary in the dream sequence 'can she do it again?' and the starting pistol, with the alarm going off and the baby crying, reinforcing everyday life.
- **Technical codes**: the aim of the advert is to grab the attention of the audience through, for example, the pace of the editing, the use of close-ups and the inter-cutting with amusing cartoon clips creating humour to keep them engaged with the advertisement and its message.

Quickfire 3.39

How may using humour in this advertising sub-genre engage audiences?

Quickfire 3.40

How can the uses and gratifications theory be applied to this advert?

- **Unique positive perspective**: there is no voice-over, the narrative is conveyed through the fast-paced editing and the audio codes. There is a clear attempt to create a realistic portrayal of the gruelling training regime. Empathy is encouraged through everyday scenarios relatable to audiences, for example popping the blister, missing the child's birthday party and those scenarios that are less relatable, for example putting on the prosthetic limb.

How May Audiences Interpret this Advert?

Different audiences may interpret the advertisement in different ways:

- In the advertisement, audiences' perceptions of disability are challenged and some audiences may find this uncomfortable. The way in which language is used may cause some audiences to examine their own misconceptions and attitudes of disability, for example the use of the phrase, '*To be a Paralympian there's got to be something wrong with you*', which challenges dated language. Zaid Al-Qasaab of Channel 4 said, '*We've done that to provoke people to think again … the only thing "wrong" with them, is their extraordinary levels of determination and ability*' (https://www.campaignlive.co.uk/article/theyve-nailed-again-channel-4-unveils-super-human-campaign-tokyo-paralympics/1722076).
- Some audiences may be shocked into considering the issues facing disabled people as people just trying to get on with their everyday lives, for example the shot of the rugby player Kylie Grimes, in her daily life who can't get her wheelchair over the step of the café. The shock smashing of the word 'Super' at the end of the advertisement leaving the word 'Human' challenges audiences to consider the message of the advert.
- Channel 4, in producing the advertisement, said they wanted to find a mid-way between representing disabled athletes as to be pitied and putting them on a pedestal, this more realistic approach may resonate with some audiences who feel that they can relate to the everyday scenarios shown in the advertisement.
- *Super. Human.* was clearly a marketing success, received positively by audiences and helping to raise awareness of disability issues, '*Continuing its mission to bring about a fundamental and permanent shift in the UK of perceptions of disability and disability sport Channel 4's acclaimed marketing campaign* Super. Human. *reached 81% of the UK population*' (Channel 4, 'Channel 4's Coverage of the Tokyo 2020 Paralympic Games Reaches 20 Million Viewers', www.channel4.com/press/news/channel-4s-coverage-tokyo-2020-paralympic-games-reaches-20-million-viewers).

Quickfire 3.41

What other ways may an audience interpret the *Super. Human.* advert?

Tip

For more information on the *Super. Human.* advert there is a detailed fact sheet available on the Eduqas website.

Human is more important then Super in this advertisement.

Social and Cultural Context

Advertising campaigns, whether for consumable products, events or charities, reflect the concerns of the society that produces them. The high profile of this campaign reflects the growing success of the event and of audience figures. In creating the trailer, Channel 4 was seeking to address the issue of social groups that are frequently under-represented or misrepresented.

It is arguably the 'Human' rather than the 'Super' element of the campaign's title that reflects the social message that these are real people overcoming obstacles and striving to be their best, just like any other athlete. Campaign film director Bradford Young said of the work: '*It wasn't the super element that spoke to me but the human stories. It's what makes us vulnerable, but stronger too*' (https://www.televisual.com/news/watch-c4s-paralympics-campaign-super-human/).

A criticism of campaigns that include certain social groups is that in order to raise money, or attract an audience, they only offer negative representations, encouraging audiences to pity rather than empathise in order to elicit an emotional response. The advert *Super. Human.* challenges typical representations of disability and includes humour to engage the audience.

Applying Theory: Gerbner

Gerbner's assertion that an audience's perception of the world can be cultivated by the repetition of the same message can be both applied and challenged with regard to the Tokyo Paralympics advert. Audiences will be used to the way in which adverts which raise awareness of a particular social group are constructed and due to the fact that certain codes and conventions are repeated, for example the focus on the specific disability accompanied by a voice-over with serious mode of address, they will accept this view of the world. They may also be exposed to the view that those with disability are not like everyone else and should be put on a pedestal, neither of these giving a realistic viewpoint.

Alternatively, as a result of viewing advertisements like *Super. Human.*, audiences may question how this view of the world is constructed and be more open to the representations in the *Super. Human.* advert as it offers a refreshing and more realistic perception that challenges common preconceptions and mainstream values.

Stretch and Challenge 3.23

Consider how Bandura's media effects theory could be applied to the *Super. Human.* advert.

Investigating Set Forms: Video Games

This form only appears in Component 1 and must be studied in relation to both industries and audience.

Historical Context

The computer games industry is relatively new in comparison with other media industries, but it has seen a rapid growth in recent years. Its profits have rivalled those of major films and sales of consoles are still expanding. Games can be played on a range of different consoles offering diverse gaming experiences including the Xbox 360, PlayStation and PlayStation Vita. These also enable the user to engage in multi-player interactivity that broadens the gaming experience.

In recent years the profile of gamers has changed and it is no longer the case that a gamer is a lone male teenager in their bedroom; gamers are now of all ages and demographics, and of both genders.

The playing of computer games is now also taken more seriously as a media industry, and computer games are accepted as media products valid for study in the same way as films and television programmes. Indeed, some games are very complex in their construction and the demands made on the gamer, compared with other media products.

> *While 20 years ago games were a niche entertainment medium, today they are a strong engine for innovation across sectors. Our industry plays a significant role throughout society.* (www.theesa.com)

Tip

While using the set theories in order to help to analyse the set products, it may be appropriate to consider how relevant the theory is to the product under discussion.

Industry: Regulation

The regulation of video games is a sensitive issue and there are regular reports regarding the suitability of the content of video games and the easy accessibility to this content by young people. The wider media usually waste no time apportioning blame for the violent behaviour and lack of sociability of young people to the gaming industry. Certain games, for example *Grand Theft Auto* and *Call of Duty*, have caused concern over their content and its potential effect on the gamer. This, combined with research showing that children much younger than the age restriction are playing games, has caused concern with parents and the government.

Until 2012 the classification of video games was carried out by both PEGI and the BBFC. This is now the role of the Video Standards Council (VSC), although the BBFC is still responsible for the classification of all non-game linear content on a game disc, such as trailers and featurettes. The role of the VSC is to regulate and classify games using the **PEGI** system to give a game a rating and additional information about the content of the game that will help consumers, particularly parents, to decide upon the suitability of the game. The system is supported by the major console manufacturers, including Sony, Microsoft and Nintendo, as well as by publishers and developers of interactive games throughout Europe. Consumers can contact PEGI if they want to complain about the rating of a game. In July 2012 PEGI became the single video games age rating system, under which it was made illegal for a retailer to sell a game with a PEGI age rating of 12, 16 or 18 to someone below that age.

Key Term

PEGI
The Pan-European Game Information (PEGI) age rating system was established to help European parents make informed decisions on buying computer games. It was launched in spring 2003 and replaced a number of national age rating systems with one single system.

Key Terms

MMORPG
Massively multi-player online role-playing game.

Persistent worlds
A feature of MMORPG games, meaning that the game world continues even when the gamer is not part of it. In this way the virtual world replicates real life.

CRPG
Computer role-playing game.

Augmented reality
Computer-generated content overlaid on a real-world environment commonly used in video games. Augmented reality hardware comes in many forms, including devices that you can carry, such as hand-held displays, and devices you wear, such as headsets and glasses.

Avatar
The player's representation of themselves within the game.

The Audience Appeal of Video Games

As said previously, video games differ from other media products in a range of ways:

- They give the user experiences not available in other products. Many games offer a multi-playing online experience not replicated in any other media platform. In the **MMORPG** format a large number of players can be involved in the virtual world of the game at one time.
- These huge multi-player games are also unique in that they have **persistent worlds**, which add to the realism of the experience.
- Smaller versions are online multi-player games, where there are usually fewer players and a non-persistent world. This interactive experience crosses genres, for example *FIFA 22* and *Dark Souls III* are examples of **CRPGs**, but clearly the roles for the gamers are different.
- The gaming phenomenon of 2016 was *Pokémon Go*, a game incorporating **augmented reality** and location-based technology targeted at the whole family.
- Video games are role-playing games and the aim is usually for the players together to complete a mission. Along the way they will need to work together to overcome challenges in order to reach a common goal.
- Within the game the player may have to succeed at certain tasks in order to proceed to the next level. The tasks generally become more complex and challenging as the player advances through the game. Certain challenges may have to be repeated several times before success.
- Computer games are also different because they are intertextual; that is, they use the codes and conventions of other texts within their structure. For example, they may be derived from a novel, comic or existing audio-visual text, this clearly also helps in the marketing of the product. They may incorporate graphics, cinematic filming or recognisable audio codes from other texts within their structure.
- Different games position the players in different ways, for example single player, multi-player, distanced controller or specific character role-play. The play can be first person or third person.
- One of the main distinguishing features of the MMORPG is the use of the **avatar**. This is a key element of this type of game and allows gamers choices about how they will represent themselves in the game.
- Computer games are available on a range of different platforms which, in turn, will affect the user experience. The Xbox Series X and the PlayStation 5 allow the gamer to speak directly to the other gamers, thus enhancing the credibility of the virtual world experience.

The MMORPG offers a range of game-playing experiences.

Set Product: Assassin's Creed Franchise

You should have knowledge and understanding of the Assassin's Creed franchise in terms of the relevant video games industry and audience issues it illustrates. It is not expected that you will study all the games in the franchise, you must study one game in detail chosen by your centre. In order to develop your awareness of the franchise, and the audience and industry issues related to it, you should consider at least one extract from the chosen game, which may be accessed online.

Production, Distribution and Circulation

- Assassin's Creed is a very successful video game franchise developed by **Ubisoft**. The first game was released in 2007, the games are open-world action-adventure games following linked narratives of assassins operating in different historical periods. The most recent release is *Assassin's Creed Valhalla*, launched in 2021.
- The franchise model has enabled Ubisoft to remain competitive within the industry. There have been several successes in the franchise and Ubisoft has responded to developments in technology to appeal to audiences. For example, *Assassin's Creed 111* was launched in 2012 and was the best-selling game in the UK in the week of its release on PlayStation 3, with the best sales of the series to date. Ubisoft followed this with a successful marketing ploy of releasing *Assassin's Creed: Liberation* alongside it to ride on its success. This game was unique to the franchise in that it was released on the Sony hand-held device **PlayStation Vita**, a new advance in gaming technology.
- The video games industry has had to continually adapt to new developments. One of these was the release, in November 2020, of a new generation of consoles – PlayStation 5 and Xbox Series X which were in direct competition with each other. Ubisoft strategically launched the release of *Assassin's Creed Valhalla*, the latest in the franchise, to coincide with the launch of these new consoles.
- A range of marketing strategies accompanied the launch and distribution of the games in the franchise, including trailers. Continued marketing devices include game-playing videos on YouTube and free content updates, for example in April 2022 the 'Mastery Challenge Pack 2: The Reckoning', was released for *Assassin's Creed Valhalla* with the promise: '*Unlock unique rewards, including the Valkyrie Armor set, all-new weapons, a tattoo set, and new settlement cosmetics*' (www.ubisoft.com/en-gb/game/assassins-creed/news-updates/1hBBcnRVUeGTnz5V2XiMJ5/assassins-creed-valhalla-title-update-151).

Economic Context

The video games industry is a competitive one across all platforms and games producers. It is vital that the production and distribution models for the game ensure financial success, some of which is secured by the games being part of a large, well-known producer in Ubisoft and a successful franchise with a secure fan base.

Revenue is raised in a variety of ways, including the purchase of the game and related physical and digital merchandise. In addition, money is also made not only at point-of-sale, but also in the games producer regularly launching additional elements designed to enhance the game-playing experience, for example digital costuming, props and additional content. Merchandise is often part of a crossover collaboration, for example UNO Valhalla combines Mattel's UNO game with *Assassin's Creed Valhalla*, adding a unique board game element to the traditional UNO format.

Key Figure

Ubisoft
Ubisoft is a French global computer game publisher and developer, with headquarters in France. It is currently the third largest independent game publisher in both Europe and the USA. The company's aim, according to its website, is to '*enrich players' lives by creating memorable and meaningful gaming experiences*' (www.ubisoft.com).

Tip

The games in the Assassin's Creed franchise are PEGI rated 18, your teacher will ensure that any extracts studied are age appropriate for your group.

Tip

You can access extracts of game play online.

Key Term

PlayStation Vita
A hand-held game console developed and released by Sony Interactive Entertainment. It is the successor to the PlayStation Portable as part of the PlayStation brand of gaming devices.

Stretch and Challenge 3.24

Watch the trailer for the game that you are studying and consider its importance in the marketing.

Audience

- Video games offer a range of appeals to audiences. Game playing is a collaborative and interactive experience involving the gamer as part of an online community. Players can directly influence the outcome of a narrative, giving them a sense of ownership and allowing them to be creative in the decisions made. The involvement in the game, often through an avatar, can engender a sense of identification both within the world of the game and of the gaming community.
- The fan base for the franchise is significant in the game's success. There is a diverse range of fan sites available, highlighting audience engagement with the games. The fans are also important in the distribution and marketing of the games, producing in-depth reviews, tips and game-playing videos. The games producer is aware of the importance of fans, Ubisoft hosts a discussion forum on its website with news, player support and community generated content. Some research suggests that playing games develops certain technical and social skills. Fan sites also offer opportunities to audiences from diverse social and cultural backgrounds and experiences to be involved in the game-playing community.
- Some of the games target a new audience, broadening reach and appeal, for example *Assassin's Creed: Liberation*, as well as having the unique selling point of creating the game for the hand-held device PS Vita which offered an immersive experience for the 'on the go' gamer unconstrained by a console, also included a female, mixed race protagonist in the form of Aveline de Grandperé, an assassin. This was an unusual decision for the franchise but highlighted its awareness of the need to broaden its audience base to include female gamers who may want a female role-playing experience.
- The creation and development of new games is a complex process and there may be long gaps between the launch of new games in the franchise. To maintain audience interest in the existing games, the producer introduces new elements including crossover stories available free to gamers, for example the crossover narratives between *Assassin's Creed Odyssey* and *Valhalla*. Another strategy is expansion packs for existing games, offering additional, unique content.

Quickfire 3.42

Why do you think the creators of the game decided to include the character of Aveline de Grandpré?

Social and Cultural Contexts

Video games, like other media forms, reflect the society that produces them and the games may change over the life of the franchise in order to reflect changes in society. Gender issues continue to be debated within the gaming industry, as most of the main protagonists in the best-selling games tend to be male, as a result females have tended to be under-represented or misrepresented in video games. There is an assumption within the industry, that girls and women do not play video games, but this is increasingly being shown as a myth and the female gaming community is growing, reflecting social change. In 2021 data showed that women accounted for 45% of gamers in the US (www.statista.com/statistics/232383/gender-split-of-us-computer-and-video-gamers/).

Audiences may choose games that reflect and reinforce aspects of their culture and identity by choosing, for example, a female avatar. The introduction of Aveline in *Assassin's Creed 111: Liberation* and Kassandra in *Assassin's Creed Odyssey* reflect Ubisoft's awareness that they must broaden their audience reach to appeal to female gamers.

Stretch and Challenge 3.25

Research other responses to the game on, for example, gaming websites. How do they compare to the ones included here?

In your study of the extracts from your chosen game, consider how society is reflected in the game and if there has been a cultural shift in the way in which certain social groups have been represented.

Video games are one such media that is regularly criticised for the assumed effect that over-exposure may have upon young people's behaviour. Some of this criticism stems from the problem of regulating the industry and ensuring that gamers are only playing games that are suitable for their age.

The fact that, with regard to video games, the player is much more actively involved and immersed in the game play, is a subject for debate as this may make it harder for gamers to distance themselves from violent action, albeit fictional.

Applying Theory and Theoretical Perspectives: Media Effects: Albert Bandura

He suggested the idea that:

- The media can implant ideas in the mind of the audience directly.
- That audiences acquire attitudes and emotional responses and new styles of conduct through modelling.
- That media representations of **transgressive behaviour**, such as violence or physical aggression, can lead audience members to imitate those forms of behaviour.

Key Term

Transgressive behaviour
Behaviour that goes beyond the norms of social acceptability.

Quickfire 3.43

Consider how this theory can be applied to the game you have studied from the franchise.

Component 1: Section B Summary

- In Component 1: Section B you have been introduced to the theoretical framework focusing on audiences and media industries.
- The forms to be studied in Section B are: advertising, film (a cross-media study including film marketing), radio, newspapers and video games.
- Advertising is only studied in relation to audiences, and film is only studied in relation to media industries.
- You will analyse set products using this theoretical framework.
- The set products will be studied in breadth.
- These will be supported by examples of contemporary and emerging media related to the set product.
- You will also study how the media products relate to key contexts.
- You will develop your ability to use relevant theoretical approaches, theories and subject-specific terminology.

4 Component 1: Investigating the Media Assessment

How Will I Be Assessed?

The Component 1 examination assesses media language, representation, media industries, audiences and media contexts. It consists of two sections:

Section A: Investigating Media Language and Representation (35 marks)

This section assesses media language and representation in relation to two of the following media forms: advertising and marketing, music video or newspapers. There are two questions in this section:

- One question assesses media language in relation to an unseen audio-visual or print resource.
- One question assesses representation and requires the comparison of one set product and an unseen source. Reference to relevant media contexts will be required.

Tip

You will be given time to watch and study the unseen resources in Section A. The audio-visual unseen resource will always be related to the first question.

Section B: Investigating Media Industries and Audiences (25 marks)

Section B assesses media industries and audiences in relation to the following forms: advertising, film cross-media study, newspapers, radio and video games.

There will be two questions:

- Question 3 will be a stepped question assessing knowledge and understanding of media industries in relation to at least one form studied.
- Question 4 will be a stepped question assessing knowledge and understanding of audiences in relation to at least one different media form from that assessed in question 3.

The examination is 1 hour 45 minutes.

It counts for 35% of the qualification.

Component 1: Section A: What Changes at A Level?

The products set for AS will be carried through into A level and you will be required to study the following additional products for assessment from 2024.

	Advertising and marketing	Music video	Newspapers
AS and A level	*Tide* (1950s) print advertisement *Super. Human.* Tokyo Paralympic Games advertisement and *Kiss of the Vampire* (1963) film poster	*Formation*, Beyoncé * or *Underdog*, Alicia Keys (2020)	The *Daily Mirror* 1 February 2022 Front page and article on 'Partygate'
A level only		One option from Group 1 and one option from Group 2 must be studied: **Group 1** *Formation*, Beyoncé (2016) or *Turntables*, Janelle Monae (2020) or *Underdog*, Alicia Keys (2020) **Group 2** *Riptide*, Vance Joy (2013) OR *Seventeen Going Under*, Sam Fender (2021) or *Little Bit of Love*, Tom Grennan (2021)	*The Times* 1 February 2022 Front page

* This music video has a parental advisory warning.

You will also be required to use more complex and challenging theories, which will include:

- **Media language**: structuralism, including Lévi-Strauss; postmodernism, including Baudrillard
- **Representation**: feminist theories, including van Zoonen and bell hooks
- Theories of ethnicity and post-colonial theory, including Gilroy

Tip

Depending on how this course is delivered in your centre and whether you are being assessed at AS level or A level, you may either study the AS products and then the A level products or both together.

Tip

A quick guide to the key aspects of the theories and theoretical perspectives you are required to study is included in Chapter 10.

Tip

Engaging in a detailed study of the set theories will allow you to develop a better understanding of them and you will therefore be able to use them in relation to the set products.

Component 1: Section B: What Changes at A Level?

The products set for AS will be carried through into A level and you will be required to study the following additional products for assessment from 2024 onwards.

	Advertising	Film (Cross-media study including film marketing)	Newspapers
AS and A level	*Tide* print advertisement (1950s) and *Super. Human.* Tokyo 2020 Paralympic Games audio-visual advertisement (2020)	*Black Panther* (2018)	*Daily Mirror*
A level only		*I, Daniel Blake* (2015)	*The Times*

	Radio	Video games
AS and A level	*Woman's Hour* or *Have You Heard George's Podcast?*	Assassin's Creed franchise

Tip

You will need to have a detailed knowledge and understanding of the theories and theoretical perspectives you studied at AS and the more advanced approaches that have been introduced at A level. You will be expected to use these to inform and support your analysis of the set products.

Tip

You must study the set theories and theoretical perspectives, but you can also refer to other examples in your examination responses.

You will also be required to use more complex and challenging theories, which will include:

- **Media industries**: regulation, including Livingstone and Lunt
- **Cultural industries**: including Hesmondhalgh
- **Audiences**: fandom including Jenkins
- **'End of audience'**: including Shirky.

At A level you will study the role of fans in the construction and circulation of meanings.

Component 2: Investigating Media Forms and Products

5

Section A: Television

The Specification

If you are following the linear Eduqas specification, television is one of the media forms that you are required to study in depth. At AS level, you will be required to study one set television product while at A level you will be required to study two set television products, including one that has been produced for a non-English-speaking audience.

This section provides an introduction to some of the key approaches that can be used to study television products. Further guidance regarding the television products that are only studied at A level can be found in the *WJEC/Eduqas Media Studies for A Level Year 2* book.

WJEC

If you are following the modular WJEC specification you are not required to study television at AS level. However, as part of the A2 module 'Media in the Global Age', you will study three television crime dramas – the Welsh crime drama *Y Gwyll/Hinterland*, one European crime drama, and one UK crime drama from the 1990s. While the *WJEC/Eduqas Media Studies for A Level Year 2* book features some material that is particularly relevant to the study of *Y Gwyll/Hinterland* and the European crime dramas, we would recommend that you read this section first as it provides a useful overview of key issues and debates regarding the study of television as a media form, and also offers an introduction to the codes, conventions and historical development of the crime drama genre.

Television Options

In Component 2, you are required to study one of the following television products:

Option 1: *Peaky Blinders* (UK, 2013). Series 1, Episode 1

- *Peaky Blinders* is a British crime drama that was created by Steven Knight and which stars Cillian Murphy. It was produced for the BBC by Caryn Mandabach Productions and Tiger Aspect Productions. It was first broadcast on BBC Two on 12 September 2013.

Option 2: *Black Mirror* (UK, 2016). Series 3, Episode 4: 'San Junipero'

- *Black Mirror* is a British science fiction **anthology series**, created by Charlie Brooker. The fourth episode of Series 3, 'San Junipero', which stars Mackenzie Davis and Gugu Mbatha-Raw, was produced by House of Tomorrow for Netflix. It was released on Netflix on 21 October 2016.

Option 3: *Killing Eve* (UK, 2018). Series 1, Episode 1

- *Killing Eve* is a British spy thriller, starring Jodie Comer and Sandra Oh. It was produced for BBC America and BBC Three by Sid Gentle Films. It was first broadcast on BBC America on 8 April 2018 and on BBC Three on 15 September 2018.

Key Term

Anthology series
A series that is comprised of entirely separate, self-contained stories. The individual episodes may be connected by a common, over-arching theme but they generally feature different characters.

A Level Television Options

If you are taking the A level course, you will also study a television product that has been produced for a non-English-speaking audience.

- If you study *Peaky Blinders*, the non-English language product you study will be *The Bridge*.
- If you study *Black Mirror*, the non-English language product you study will be *The Returned*.
- If you study *Killing Eve*, the non-English language product you study will be *Tehran*.

Using the Theoretical Framework

In exploring your set television product, you will need to consider all four areas of the theoretical framework. Therefore, in this section we will look at:

- **the media language of television**: how television products communicate meanings through their forms, codes, conventions and techniques
- **representation**: how television products portray individuals, issues and social groups
- **the television industry**: how ownership, production, distribution and regulation affect television products
- **audiences**: how television products target, attract, reach and address audiences, and how audiences interpret and respond to television products.

Media Language

Codes and Conventions of the Media Form

Quickfire 5.1

What is the difference between a tracking shot and a panning shot?

Quickfire 5.2

What is the difference between diegetic and non-diegetic sound?

Media language, as we have already discussed, refers to the codes, conventions and techniques through which media products communicate their meanings.

As an audio-visual media form, television has a particular set of codes and conventions – a particular media language – that it uses to convey messages and meanings. The main codes and conventions that you need to consider when analysing audio-visual products were outlined in Chapter 1. These include:

- **camera shots** or **shot distances** such as close-ups or long shots
- **camera angles** such as high-angle or low-angle shots
- **camera movements** such as tracking, panning or tilting
- **editing** and the use of transitions such as wipes, fades, dissolves or cuts
- **audio codes** such as diegetic and non-diegetic sound
- **mise-en-scène**, which is everything that appears within the frame, including settings, costumes and props, as well as the way in which actors are positioned.

When you analyse your set television product, you need to do more than simply identify the codes and conventions that it uses – you must consider the function or purpose of those codes and conventions, exploring how they contribute to the meaning of the text.

For example, **point-of-view shots** can be used to align the viewer with the perspective of particular characters within the text, while canted angles are often used to signify instability, disorder, disorientation or unease, conveying the idea that something is not quite right. The shot on the right from ITV spy thriller *Our Kind of Traitor* uses a **canted angle** to convey a sense of danger, doubt and uncertainty, effectively establishing the paranoid world in which the spy thriller conventionally takes place.

An example of a canted angle in *Our Kind of Traitor*

Analysing Visual and Technical Codes

Visual codes such as mise-en-scène often work in combination with technical codes such as camera angles and editing to convey meanings in television products. For example, in the two shots below, which are taken from the opening episode of the British crime drama, *No Offence*, the mise-en-scène works with the camera angles and shot composition to signify a shift in power relations.

Key Terms

Point-of-view shot
A shot that is filmed from the perspective of a particular person or character within the text.

Canted angle
A shot filmed from an oblique or slanted angle.

***No Offence* (Series 1, Episode 1)**

The shot on the left shows Detective Superintendent Darren McLaren reprimanding two of his officers for their handling of a case. While he is positioned in the foreground of the shot and dominates most of the space within the frame, Detective Inspector Viv Deering and Detective Sergeant Joy Freers are confined to the lower part of the frame and appear much smaller. The way in which the shot has been composed therefore helps to convey a sense of McLaren's power and authority, as the female officers are shown to be subordinate to him.

However, in the shot on the right, taken from the very next scene, we see a reversal of these power relations. Here it is Deering who dominates the centre of the frame while McLaren is marginalised, occupying the far right corner of the shot. The fact that this scene takes place in the men's toilets is also significant. By intruding on this exclusively male domain, Deering demonstrates her transgression of traditional gender roles and her refusal to defer to male authority.

Framing and shot composition in HBO's *Succession* helps to establish a sense of the power dynamics between different characters.

Symmetrical framing is another technique that can be particularly meaningful. For example, this shot, from HBO drama *Succession*, shows media mogul, Logan Roy, with his daughter, Siobhan, in the offices of Waystar RoyCo. Significantly, the two characters are positioned on either side of the frame, placing them in binary opposition to one another. This, combined with the formality of the mise-en-scène and the stiffness of their gestural codes, suggests an adversarial relationship, while the ornamental arrowheads on the cabinet table hint at the primal conflict and familial power struggle that lie at the heart of the programme.

Television Genres

Genre is an important factor in the production, distribution and reception of television products. It affects the way in which television programmes are **commissioned**, marketed and scheduled, and is commonly used to target, attract and maintain audiences.

While broadcasters such as the BBC, ITV and Channel 4 carry a mix of different genres in order to appeal to a wide range of audiences, **narrowcasting** has become increasingly common in today's **multi-channel era**. This means that there is a growing number of channels dedicated to particular genres. For example:

- Alibi is a channel dedicated to crime drama
- Sky Crime is a channel dedicated to true crime documentaries
- Sky Sci-Fi is a channel dedicated to science fiction.

Video-on-demand (VoD) services such as Netflix, Amazon Prime Video, BBC iPlayer, All 4, and Sky On Demand typically include the facility to search for programmes by genre. Viewers may also be directed towards programmes in certain genres as they are offered recommendations based on their viewing history. This is the result of digital technologies that enable companies to build a more accurate profile of individual viewing preferences.

Key Terms

Commissioning
To give a programme the go-ahead for production – to 'greenlight' it. At the BBC, for example, there are Directors of Programming for different genres. Producers pitch their ideas to the relevant controller who then decides whether or not to commission the programme.

Narrowcasting
Unlike broadcasting, which addresses the needs of a mass audience, narrowcasting targets more specialised audiences.

Multi-channel era
The idea that following the introduction of satellite and cable television in the 1990s and the rise of digital technologies, viewers now have a much wider range of channels to choose from.

Video-on-demand
A form of distribution that enables users to access video content when they choose rather than watching content as it is broadcast. Subscription video-on-demand (SVOD) refers to streaming services such as Netflix and Disney+ that users have to subscribe to in order to access.

Neale's Genre Theory

One of the theorists whose work you will need to consider when analysing the genre of your set television product is **Steve Neale**. His theory of genre is particularly useful as it highlights the dynamic and historically relative nature of genre (the idea that genres change and evolve over time) as well as the importance of the economic and institutional contexts in which genres are produced.

Key Theory: Steve Neale's Theory of Genre

- the idea that genres may be dominated by repetition, but are also marked by difference, variation and change
- the idea that genres change, develop and vary as they borrow from and overlap with one another
- the idea that genres exist within specific economic, institutional and industrial contexts.

One of the main points Neale makes is that while products in the same genre share a common set of conventions and therefore involve a significant degree of repetition, they also show some element of difference, variation and change. This is one of the ways in which genres maintain audience interest and cultural relevance.

Neale also argues that mass-produced, popular genres have to be understood in relation to their economic and institutional contexts. For example, the need to maintain audiences and generate revenue, either by attracting advertisers or by developing products and formats that can be sold internationally, may affect the types of programme that are commissioned or produced. The terms of a broadcaster's licence or remit can also have a bearing on this. For example, public service broadcasters such as the BBC and ITV are required to devote a certain amount of time in their schedules to news and current affairs.

As well as considering genre from an industry perspective, it is also important to consider the functions that genres perform for audiences. For example, Neale points out that the classification of texts *'is a fundamental aspect of the way texts of all kinds are understood'* ('Studying Genre', in G. Creeber (ed.), *The Television Genre Book*, 2015, page 3). In other words, the way in which we decode or make sense of a television product is likely to be informed by our understanding of the codes and conventions that programmes of a similar type generally use. This shows how genres convey meaning through intertextuality.

Named Theorist

Steve Neale
Steve Neale's theory of genre is outlined in the essay 'Questions of Genre', which was first published in the academic journal *Screen* in 1990. While Neale's primary focus was on film, the basic principles that he outlined can be applied to a range of media forms and products. He has also contributed an introductory essay to *The Television Genre Book* edited by Glen Creeber.

***Line of Duty* is one of the BBC's flagship crime dramas.**

Key Terms

Flagship show
A programme that has particular importance for a channel or broadcaster – one that attracts particularly high ratings, for example, or that is strongly identified with the channel.

Police procedural
A crime drama subgenre that places particular emphasis on the processes and procedures involved in investigating crime. Examples of police procedurals include *Line of Duty*, *CSI: Vegas* and *Silent Witness*.

Detective series
A crime drama subgenre that focuses on the attempts of investigators to solve crimes. Closely related to the police procedural, the detective series is generally broader in scope as it encompasses the work of amateur sleuths and private investigators as well as the police. Examples include *Sherlock*, *True Detective*, *Inspector Morse* and *Only Murders in the Building*.

Gangster dramas
A crime drama subgenre that focuses on the criminal activities of gangsters and the world of organised crime. Examples include *The Sopranos*, *Boardwalk Empire* and *Gangs of London*.

Diegetic world
The world in which the story takes place. For example, when we talk about diegetic sound, we are talking about sound that appears to come from within the scene itself.

Quickfire 5.3

Make a list of all the different television crime dramas that you can think of.

Option 1: The Crime Drama Genre

Crime drama is one of the most popular and commonly produced television genres. The fact that crime dramas tend to perform well in the ratings makes them particularly attractive to commercial broadcasters, whose ability to generate advertising revenue largely depends on the size of the audience they can deliver. Crime dramas have also proved to be a valuable asset for the BBC, helping the corporation consolidate its reputation as a global broadcaster of high-quality television through **flagship shows** such as *Line of Duty*, *Sherlock*, *Luther* and *Peaky Blinders*.

Crime dramas can be divided into two broad categories – those that focus primarily on the investigation of crime and those that focus on the perpetration of crime. Within these broad categories there is a variety of subgenres, from **police procedurals** and **detective series** to **gangster dramas**.

Detective series commonly invite the audience to play the role of 'armchair detective', as viewers attempt to solve the case alongside the investigators within the **diegetic world** of the programme. The investigators within these programmes may be law enforcement officers, private detectives or amateur sleuths. They may work alone, or they may be part of a team.

In many crime dramas, there is a partnership between two investigators. These partnerships are often constructed in terms of binary oppositions as the two partners may have contrasting attitudes, values or personalities, or they may differ in terms of gender, ethnicity, age or social class. In some programmes, the two partners will be of equal rank or status while in others there is some form of hierarchy – a veteran cop may be paired with a rookie, for example, or the main investigative figure may have a sidekick.

In **Vladimir Propp**'s terms, the sidekick generally adopts the role of the helper as they assist the detective-hero with their investigations. In some cases, the sidekick also functions as an **audience surrogate**, offering the viewer a **point of identification** within the world of the text. In *Sherlock*, for example, John Watson often asks the questions that the audience would ask. Through him, the audience is able to gain an understanding of Sherlock's deductive reasoning.

The Gangster Drama

Unlike police procedurals and detective series, which focus on the *investigation* of crime, gangster dramas such as *Peaky Blinders* explore the world of organised crime from the perspective of the criminal, focusing on the activities of criminal gangs. The gangster genre is largely recognisable through its stock characters, iconography and narrative themes.

Stock Characters

- **The gangster protagonist**: films and television programmes in the gangster genre conventionally revolve around the criminal activities of a protagonist (usually male) who is either the leader of a criminal organisation or an ambitious, up-and-coming gangster. In some cases, he is an 'heir apparent' – the person next in line to become leader of the criminal gang.

The gangster protagonist is a classic example of an **anti-hero**. Although he operates outside of the law and is typically ruthless and violent, he is the character that the audience is primarily encouraged to identify with.
As **Robert Warshow** argued in his landmark essay, 'The Gangster as Tragic Hero', the gangster performs an important function for the audience as an imaginary figure on whom they project their own fantasies and fears:

> *The real city, one might say, produces only criminals; the imaginary city produces the gangster: he is what we want to be and what we are afraid we may become.*
>
> *Thrown into the crowd without background or advantages, with only those ambiguous skills which the rest of us – the real people of the real city – can only pretend to have, the gangster is required to make his way, to make his life and impose it on others.* (*The Partisan Review*, February 1948)

Although he is, in some ways, a product of his social environment, the gangster can be seen as a self-made man. While his law-breaking and violence may be linked to a past trauma or the world into which he is born, he is able to achieve wealth and status through his own resourcefulness and determination. In this way, the gangster provides an interesting commentary on dominant ideological values such as capitalism, individualism or the American Dream.

- **The rival gangster**: the gangster protagonist is often set in binary opposition to another gangster. This may be the leader of a rival gang or someone within the protagonist's own organisation. The binary opposition between these characters is an important source of narrative conflict, producing a series of power struggles played out over territory ('turf'), trade or influence.

Key figure

Robert Warshow
A New York intellectual whose work largely focused on film and popular culture. His essay 'The Gangster as Tragic Hero', first published in 1948, was highly influential, providing a valuable critical framework for exploring the cultural significance of the gangster genre and its central protagonist.

Key Figure

Vladimir Propp
Propp was a Russian theorist who was particularly interested in narrative structure. He suggested that there were certain character roles or narrative functions common to most narratives – the role of the hero, the villain and the helper, for example.

Key Terms

Audience surrogate
A character within the text that stands in for the audience. They may think as we do, or act as we ourselves might act in the same situation.

Point of identification
A character within the text that the audience can identify with or relate to.

Anti-hero
A protagonist or central character that lacks the conventional traits of a hero and is fundamentally flawed. Anti-heroes typically exhibit some form of moral complexity or ambiguity. They may be criminals who operate outside of the law but follow their own code of honour and administer their own form of justice, for example.

In *Peaky Blinders*, the main law enforcement agent is Major Chester Campbell, a Chief Inspector within the Royal Irish Constabulary.

Stretch and Challenge 5.1

How is Tommy Shelby constructed as the archetypal gangster protagonist in *Peaky Blinders*? In what ways can he be seen as an anti-hero? Does the narrative provide any explanation or justification for his law-breaking and violence?

- **Law enforcement agents**: another important source of narrative conflict in the gangster genre comes from the law enforcement agents who seek to apprehend, contain or eliminate the gangster. These are usually police officers or government agents. In contrast to police procedurals and detective series, the law enforcement agents in gangster dramas are often represented more negatively in order to align the audience with the gangster protagonist. Commonly depicted as humourless, excessively violent or unnecessarily cruel, they may also lack the charisma that makes the gangster such a compelling figure.
- **The undercover agent**: some gangster dramas feature an undercover agent. This is someone who infiltrates the criminal organisation and reports back to the police on the gangsters' plans and activities. The prospect of the undercover agent's true identity being discovered is often used to create narrative suspense. In cases where the undercover agent's true identity is initially withheld from the audience, its revelation can also create a powerful narrative twist.
- **The 'mad dog'**: a further stock character from the gangster genre is the 'mad dog.' This is a gangster whose aggressive, volatile and wildly unpredictable nature threatens to derail the criminal operation. Typically short-tempered and prone to extreme violence, the 'mad dog' is a loose cannon in the criminal enterprise. A notable example is the character of Tommy DeVito, played by Joe Pesci, in Martin Scorcese's gangster film *Goodfellas*.

Iconography

Costumes, settings, and props are important elements of the gangster genre's **iconography**.

- **Settings**: the city streets and urban landscape that are such a pivotal part of the gangster drama not only provide a visual backdrop for the shootouts and turf wars that conventionally feature in the genre, they are also fundamental to the gangster's identity. As Robert Warshow points out, the gangster is '*the man of the city, with the city's language and knowledge*'; he not only inhabits the city, he personifies it.

  Within the broader urban **milieu** of the gangster genre, there are also more specific spaces and settings that are frequently used. One of the most common of these is the gangsters' lair – a hangout or meeting-place where the criminals gather. This may be a nightclub, casino, bar, or mansion.

  Another common setting is the office from which the leader of the gang directs criminal operations. As this space is typically used to hold meetings, conduct business and cut deals, it shows how the criminal enterprise is run like a corporate enterprise. It also provides a visual representation of the gang leader's power, status and authority.

- **Costumes and props**: the gangster's upward progression through the echelons of the criminal underworld is often represented through visual codes. For example, his acquisition of wealth and social status is commonly signified through the sharply tailored suits that he wears. A specific gang may also have its own codified look or style that serves to differentiate it from rival gangs as well as the wider society, conveying a sense of group belonging and subcultural identity.

  Guns and fast cars are also an important part of the gangster genre's iconography. Again, these elements of mise-en-scène commonly function as visual signifiers of the gangster's power and wealth. They are also indexical of action, which is a vital part of the gangster genre.

Key Terms

Iconography
The visual elements of a media product such as the props, costumes and settings that are used.

Milieu
The world or social context that someone inhabits or in which a story or narrative is set. This can refer to both physical surroundings (the urban milieu of the gangster genre, for example) and the social world that someone moves within.

Gangster Narratives and Themes

The classical gangster narrative conventionally follows the rise and fall of the central protagonist. It charts the gangster's journey from humble beginnings as he rises to a position of power and prosperity before suffering a final downfall.

Although the gangster is typically punished at the end of the narrative, the nature of his demise can vary. In some cases, the gangster may lose his wealth, while in others he may lose his life or his liberty. Therefore, the resolution of the classical gangster narrative traditionally conveys the ideological message that crime doesn't pay.

However, some gangster narratives feature more ambivalent endings. *Goodfellas*, for example, ends with its main protagonist in a witness protection programme, having 'ratted' on his friends and broken the gangster's code of silence. His punishment is to live the rest of his life in suburban anonymity as 'an average nobody' as he describes it. The regret here, then, is not for the crimes that he has committed but for the fact that he has lost the status and respect that being a gangster had previously accorded him; he is no longer a 'somebody'.

Gangster narratives may also explore the ideological contradictions that arise within capitalist societies that promote social aspiration and the idea of material success and yet deny the working classes a legitimate means of climbing the social ladder. The gangster is, in many ways, the embodiment of this ideological contradiction, as he turns to crime in order to achieve the dream of material wealth.

Stretch and Challenge 5.2

Consider how Steve Neale's theory of genre could be applied to *Peaky Blinders*. In what ways can the programme be seen to illustrate Neale's suggestion that genres are instances of repetition and difference? What does it have in common with other crime dramas or gangster shows and what makes it different? Think about Neale's suggestion that genres borrow from and overlap with one another too. In what ways could *Peaky Blinders* be seen to borrow from or overlap with the western, for instance?

Themes of loyalty, betrayal and revenge also feature prominently in gangster narratives. As many gangster dramas feature a crime *family* at the heart of the narrative, or at least a group that functions *like* a family, these themes are often given added resonance. For example, the betrayal of one gangster by another can have even greater significance when the gangsters are members of the same family. Similarly, if a member of the gangster's family is killed by a rival gang, this provides an even stronger motive for revenge.

The Crime Drama in Context

In order to develop an understanding of the dynamic and historically relative nature of the gangster genre, it is important to consider how its codes and conventions have evolved and adapted over time.

The way in which the gangster genre has developed reflects the changing nature of organised crime as well as various social and institutional changes. For example, the shift from silent cinema to the age of sound in the late 1920s had a profound impact on the development of the genre, as the diegetic sound of gunshots and screeching car tyres could be added to heists, shoot-outs and chase scenes, giving greater realism and dynamism to the gangster film.

It was during the 1930s that the gangster film entered a golden age. This reflected the rise of organised crime during the Prohibition era in America, as well as a growing public fascination with real-life gangsters such as Al Capone. However, regulatory constraints that were in place during the 1930s affected how these stories were told, as films were not permitted to glamourise or glorify crime. The gangster's inevitable demise in the gangster films of the 1930s was therefore determined, at least in part, by the institutional contexts in which the films were made.

Significantly, as regulatory constraints have loosened in recent decades, representations of the gangster have become more ambiguous and morally complex. More recent gangster series, such as *Gangs of London* and *ZeroZeroZero*, also reflect the changing nature of organised crime in a globalised age.

Contemporary gangster dramas that are set in earlier periods are also shaped and influenced by the historical and cultural contexts in which they are produced. For example, *Boardwalk Empire* and *Peaky Blinders* both look back at the interwar period through a contemporary lens. This is not only apparent in the style and aesthetic of the programmes, but also in the way in which they represent issues such as post-traumatic stress disorder (PTSD) – a condition that is much better understood today than it was in the period immediately following World War I – when each of the shows is set.

Option 2: The Science-Fiction Genre

Science-Fiction Narratives and Themes

Science fiction has a long cultural history that extends across television, film and literature. While the genre has a recognisable repertoire of elements, science-fiction narratives can take a number of different forms. These include:

- **Narratives concerned with space travel and the exploration of new worlds**: the American science-fiction series *Star Trek*, which ran from 1966 until 1969, is a good example of this type of narrative. Each episode would open with the same monologue, reiterating the purpose of the crew's five-year mission – '*to explore strange new worlds, to seek out new life and new civilisations, to boldly go where no man has gone before*'.
- **Alien invasion narratives**: while shows such as *Star Trek* revolve around the idea of humans going out into the universe in search of new worlds and new civilisations, alien invasion narratives focus on the idea of aliens coming to Earth. The aliens in these narratives are typically constructed as hostile and threatening figures, intent on taking over the world.
- **Narratives concerned with time travel**: this is where characters have the ability to travel backwards or forwards in time. For example, in *Doctor Who* the central character is a Time Lord from the fictional planet Gallifrey, who travels across time and space in a time-machine called the TARDIS.
- **Narratives set in the future or an alternative present**: these narratives often explore issues concerning scientific or technological progress. Some celebrate the prospect of technological advancement and the different opportunities and possibilities that such advances might bring, while others warn of the dangers associated with technology and scientific experimentation. The latter type of narrative tends to offer a more **dystopian** view of the world.

Iconography

The science-fiction genre, like the crime drama, is often recognisable through its iconography. The iconography of science fiction includes:

- futuristic weapons, gadgets or technologies
- futuristic costumes
- futuristic modes of transport
- futuristic or alien landscapes: many science-fiction narratives are set in dystopian, post-apocalyptic worlds although some may be set in **utopian** worlds
- the iconography of outer space: stars, planets, spacecraft, etc.
- futuristic worlds that feature high-tech, computerised environments
- science labs
- robots or **androids**
- aliens.

Key Terms

Dystopia
A world or society that is as bad or dysfunctional as can be imagined – a world full of crime, violence or oppression, for example.

Utopia
An ideal or perfect world.

Android
A robot that looks like a human.

Quickfire 5.4

Does the 'San Junipero' episode of *Black Mirror* offer a utopian or dystopian view of the world? Does it celebrate the possibilities and opportunities that technological advancement can bring, or does it warn of the dangers of scientific experimentation?

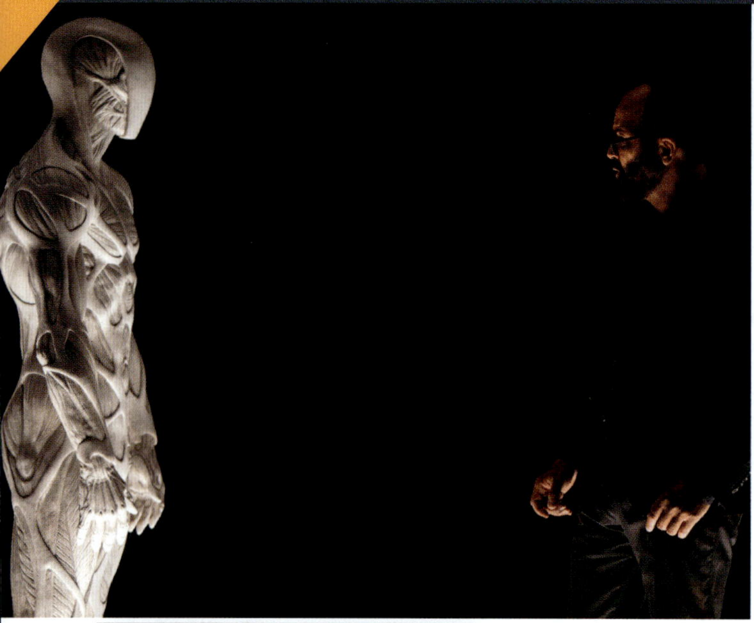

HBO's *Westworld*

As well as conveying a sense of time and place, iconography can also have particular thematic significance. For example, many science-fiction narratives revolve around questions of human identity and what it means to be human in an age of **artificial intelligence**. This is often signified through the iconography that is used. The imagery that features in HBO's *Westworld* helps to establish this theme by exploring the relationship between the organic and the synthetic, and between reality and simulation, for instance.

Key Term

Artificial intelligence
The branch of computer science that is concerned with the capacity of machines to simulate human behaviour by carrying out tasks and actions that normally require human decision-making.

Adaptation, Regeneration and Renewal

Many science-fiction films and television programmes have their roots in the work of literary figures such as Arthur C. Clarke, Philip K. Dick and **Isaac Asimov**. For example, the science-fiction anthology series, *Electric Dreams*, which was broadcast on Channel 4 in 2017, was based on the short stories of Philip K. Dick – the author whose work also inspired *Blade Runner*.

Key Figure

Isaac Asimov
Isaac Asimov was a highly influential writer of science fiction whose work has had a profound influence on the genre. His 'Three Rules of Robotics' were outlined in the story 'Runaround', which was first published in 1942 and later featured in the short story collection *I, Robot* (1950).

These 'rules' have provided the basis and inspiration for many subsequent sci-fi films and television shows, including *Bicentennial Man* (1999) starring Robin Williams and the film adaptation of *I, Robot* (2004), starring Will Smith.

Philip K. Dick's *Electric Dreams* covers similar thematic ground to *Black Mirror*.

Adaptations of existing stories generally have the advantage of a ready-made audience. HBO's *Westworld*, for instance, which is set in a series of themed amusement parks populated by androids, is based on a 1973 Michael Crichton film of the same name. This meant that it was able to generate significant hype and interest among fans of the original movie ahead of its broadcast.

Spin-offs are popular with broadcasters for much the same reason as they too can be **pre-sold**. For example, the BBC has been able to capitalise on the popularity of *Doctor Who* with spin-offs such as *The Sarah Jane Adventures*, *Torchwood* and *Class* as well as the *Doctor Who: Redacted* podcast. These shows offer audiences a pleasing sense of repetition and difference by providing variations on a familiar format.

This pattern of repetition and difference is also apparent in *Doctor Who* itself. By recasting the role of the Doctor every few seasons, the programme is able to renew and replenish itself. This is cleverly worked into the plot as the Doctor undergoes a process of 'regeneration' whenever he or she is mortally injured, taking on a new physical form and personality. Each new actor who plays the Doctor brings something different to the role.

Science Fiction in Context

Even though science-fiction products are often set in another time or another place, they commonly address the concerns and anxieties of the time in which they are produced. Therefore, rather than just functioning as escapist fantasy, science-fiction narratives frequently explore contemporary social and cultural issues. This is one of the reasons why the genre resonates so strongly with audiences. For example:

- Science-fiction products of the 1950s and 1960s could be seen to reflect particular cultural anxieties regarding the effects of nuclear radiation. Narratives often showed characters being exposed to radiation and then undergoing some form of human mutation.
- Alien invasion narratives were also prevalent during this era. These narratives would often show aliens infiltrating unsuspecting American communities by assuming human form. Many critics have read this as a reflection of Cold War paranoia and fears regarding 'the enemy within', as there was a widespread moral panic about Communist spies living within American society at this time.

Recent science-fiction programmes have also addressed a range of contemporary social and cultural issues. *Orphan Black* explores the issue of human cloning, for instance, while *Black Mirror* looks at the cultural impact of technology on society and humanity in an age increasingly dominated by social media and artificial intelligence. As its creator and co-**showrunner**, Charlie Brooker, said in an interview with the *Guardian*, the black mirror that the title of the programme refers to is

> *'the one that you'll find on every wall, on every desk, in the palm of every hand: [it is] the cold, shiny screen of a TV, a monitor, a smartphone.'*

Key Term

Pre-sold
When a product has a ready-made audience, thereby minimising financial risk. A product may be pre-sold based on the previous success of similar types of product or it may be pre-sold through the inclusion of popular and well-known figures.

Stretch and Challenge 5.3

Consider how Steve Neale's theory of genre could be applied to *Black Mirror*. In what ways can the programme be seen to illustrate Neale's suggestion that genres are instances of repetition and difference? What does it have in common with other science-fiction shows and what makes it different? What other genres does it borrow from?

Key Term

Showrunner
The person who has ultimate creative control over a television series and oversees all aspects of production. They are often a writer on the show and in some cases may be the creator of the show.

Quickfire 5.5

What connotations does the title '*Black Mirror*' have?

Key figure

John Le Carré
A popular and critically acclaimed novelist whose work has had a significant influence on the spy thriller genre. Many of his best-known works, including *Tinker, Tailor, Soldier, Spy*, *The Little Drummer Girl*, *The Night Manager*, *The Tailor of Panama* and *The Constant Gardener*, have been adapted for film and television. Before he became a successful novelist, Le Carré spent time in the intelligence services, working in both MI5 and MI6.

Option 3: The Spy Thriller Genre

Like crime drama and science fiction, the spy thriller is a popular genre that has long-established roots in film, literature and television. Spy thrillers generally feature exciting, action-packed or suspenseful narratives that involve espionage (the act of spying) or counterespionage (efforts to thwart or disrupt the espionage operations of the enemy).

The work of novelists such as **John Le Carré**, Len Deighton, Tom Clancy and Ian Fleming has provided the source material for a huge number of spy films and television series. The James Bond films are based on the work of Ian Fleming, for example, while several novels by John Le Carré, including *The Night Manager* and *Tinker, Tailor, Soldier, Spy*, have been adapted for film and television to significant critical acclaim.

Stock Characters

- **The main spy or intelligence operative**: the central protagonist in the spy thriller is conventionally a spy, secret agent or intelligence operative. While some spies operate independently, others are employed by intelligence services and government agencies. These intelligence services may be real organisations, such as the CIA, MI5 or MI6, or they may be fictional.

  The missions that spies and intelligence operatives undertake are usually of national or international importance, and often involve issues of national security. Some missions are concerned with espionage while others are counterespionage operations.

  Spies are generally shown to have a particular set of skills. This may include the ability to elicit information from an asset using persuasion, coercion or even seduction, as well as the ability to maintain cover when working under an alias or assumed identity. Agents may also be trained in combat, martial arts and the use of firearms.
- **The handler**: if the spy or intelligence operative is working for a larger agency or organisation, they may have a handler. This is the officer that they report back to and to whom they pass any intelligence that they gather. Clandestine meetings between agents and handlers are a common convention of the spy genre, as are dead drops, which is where a spy leaves information in a secret location for a handler or fellow agent to collect. The handler may also provide the agent with their cover identity.

  Agents working for the enemy are also likely to have handlers. An assassin may be given their orders or instructions by a handler, for example as she/he send the hero off on their quest.
- **The boss or spymaster**: a spymaster is a character who is in charge of either the intelligence agency or a particular spy ring within it. They direct and oversee espionage or counterespionage operations. A notable example of a spymaster is the character codenamed 'M', who appears in the James Bond films and Ian Fleming's novels on which the films are based. It is 'M' who sends Bond on his missions. Therefore, in Vladimir Propp's terms, the spymaster often performs the narrative function of the dispatcher – the character who initiates the hero's quest.
- **The assassin**: an assassin is someone who is paid to eliminate an enemy target. Usually highly trained and very skilled, assassins are capable of carrying out a 'hit' with ruthless efficiency. Like spies and secret agents, they often work undercover and may adopt a disguise in order to blend in or gain access to their targets.

- **Moles and double agents**: a mole is someone working within the intelligence agency who secretly passes information to the enemy. Similarly, a double agent is someone who appears to be working for one side but is secretly working for another. In spy thrillers, moles and double agents commonly perform a comparable narrative function to the undercover agent in the gangster genre – they are often used to create suspense or a narrative twist. Speculation regarding who the mole or double agent might be can help to facilitate audience engagement with the narrative.
- **Defectors**: another stock character commonly found within the spy thriller is the defector. This is someone who changes sides, switching allegiance from one country or cause to another, either through choice or coercion. They often have information or skills that make them a valuable asset. They may have access to military secrets, for example, or they may be a scientist working on a government-sponsored programme. In some spy thrillers, the main protagonist is tasked with facilitating the defection of someone working for the enemy, while in others they may be ordered to prevent the defection of someone from their own side, keeping them out of enemy hands.

In *Killing Eve*, Villanelle adopts various disguises in order to gain access to her targets.

Iconography

- **Settings**: spy thrillers are often set across a range of international locations, with agents sent on missions that take them around the world. The international scope of the plot gives the agent's mission a sense of importance, emphasising the idea that there are issues of national and international significance at stake. The spectacular nature of many of these locations also creates visual or aesthetic pleasure as well as providing audiences with escapism, taking them out of their own day-to-day worlds.

  In some cases, the spy's mission requires them to mix with the rich and the powerful. This is reflected in the mise-en-scéne, with scenes often set on private islands or estates and in exclusive clubs, restaurants or casinos.

  Another common setting in the spy thriller is the intelligence agency or station itself – the building in which intelligence operatives work. In some spy thrillers, the intelligence agency is represented as a very traditional space. This, again, may be signified through the mise-en-scéne. There may be wood panelling and oil paintings on the walls, for instance. In other spy thrillers, the intelligence agency is represented as a more modern, hi-tech environment – a world of computer screens and surveillance systems.
- **Costumes and props**: while the archetypal image of the trench coat-wearing spy was established by iconic characters such as Harry Palmer in *The Ipcress File* and George Smiley in *Tinker, Tailor, Soldier, Spy* and *Smiley's People*, secret agents in spy thrillers today are seen in a range of costumes. As the need to blend in is an important aspect of spycraft, agents generally tailor their appearance according to the environments in which they operate. In some cases, they will adopt a disguise.

  In some spy thrillers, agents are issued with gadgets to help them go about their work. In the James Bond films, for example, 007 is supplied with an array of gadgets by his Quartermaster, 'Q'. Other props that commonly feature in spy thrillers include surveillance equipment such as bugs and listening devices as well as cameras with telephoto lenses.

Quickfire 5.6

What is the name of the author of the 'Villanelle' novellas on which *Killing Eve* is based?

Spy Thriller Narratives and Themes

Spy thriller narratives often involve games of 'cat and mouse' in which one character, such as an assassin or a secret agent, stalks, hunts or pursues another. While this often provides opportunities for thrilling, action-based sequences, it is common for the cat and mouse games to have a psychological dimension, with a battle of wits played out between protagonist and antagonist. There may also be a series of close escapes over the course of the narrative.

Stretch and Challenge 5.4

Consider how Steve Neale's theory of genre could be applied to *Killing Eve*. In what ways can the programme be seen to illustrate Neale's suggestion that genres are instances of repetition and difference? What does it have in common with other spy thrillers and what makes it different? What other genres does it borrow from?

In many cases, the narrative will involve a race against time, as the agent or intelligence operative has to complete their mission before the enemy achieves their goal. The agent may have to locate and neutralise a bomb before it detonates, for instance, or they may have to track down an assassin before they carry out a 'hit'. This helps to create a sense of narrative urgency and suspense.

Themes of loyalty and betrayal tend to feature prominently in the spy thriller, just as they do in the gangster genre. However, while these themes are played out in relation to the criminal organisation or the crime family in the gangster drama, it is loyalty to one's nation that is typically at stake in the spy thriller. Intelligence operatives are often given the task of identifying and rooting out a traitor either in their own organisation or another area of the state. They may be asked to establish whether a character has been 'turned' (in other words, whether they have been persuaded to work for the other side). A notable example of this can be found in the first series of *Homeland*, which follows CIA officer, Carrie Mathison, as she seeks to establish whether an American Marine is working for al-Qaeda as part of a terrorist cell.

The *Homeland* logo, as seen here on one of the promotional posters for the series, visually alludes to the idea of characters being 'turned' as the letter 'E' has been turned to face the other way.

The Spy Thriller in Context

While spy thrillers may offer a sense of escapism, transporting audiences to an exciting 'other' world, they can also address real-world issues and concerns, reflecting the wider historical, cultural and socio-political contexts in which they are produced.

For example, many spy thrillers made during the Cold War addressed the geopolitical tensions that existed between the Soviet Union and the West throughout this period. Allusions to the Cold War were relatively common in American shows such as *I Spy* (1965–1968) and *Mission: Impossible* (1966–1973) in the 1960s, as these programmes would often pit American agents against hostile characters from Eastern Bloc countries.

More recently, the Cold War has been revisited in *The Americans* (2013–2018), a spy thriller that focuses on the activities of two Soviet KGB agents operating undercover as a married American couple in Washington during the 1980s. The programme has been widely praised for providing a more nuanced exploration of Cold War hostilities, looking at the conflict from both sides as it uses the marital relationship between the two main characters as a vehicle for exploring questions of loyalty, fidelity and cultural identity in the Cold War era.

Contemporary spy thrillers have also evolved to reflect the emergence of different types of threat in the post 9/11 era. Over the past two decades, issues relating to the 'war on terror' have been explored in a wide variety of shows, including British shows such as *Spooks*, as well as American series such as *24* and *Homeland*.

The spy genre has also adapted in response to changing social and cultural values. For example, the appointment of Stella Rimington as the first female Director General of MI5 in 1992 was followed three years later by the first female 'M' in the James Bond films, as Judi Dench became the first female actor to be cast in the role. These more progressive attitudes towards gender roles are apparent in *Killing Eve* too. Significantly, as well as including a female spymaster – Carolyn Martens, who is head of the Russian desk at MI6 – the programme features female characters in the two leading roles.

Stretch and Challenge 5.5

In what ways could the representations of gender and ethnicity in *Killing Eve* be seen to reflect social and cultural changes?

Narratology

Narratology is a term that is used to describe the study of narrative. This is another aspect of media language that you will need to explore when analysing your set television product.

Narratives play an important role in the construction of meanings as they enable us to explain and make sense of the world around us. This is what Chris Barker means when he says that narratives offer us *'frameworks of understanding'* (2008).

To construct a narrative is to impose meaning on events by placing them in a particular order and organising them in a certain way. This is how they are made to signify. For example, in order to explain or make sense of events, television products often use a cause and effect narrative structure. This is the idea that actions or events have particular consequences or effects – they cause other things to happen.

Key Term

Enigma codes
Enigma codes are the questions or mysteries that a narrative sets up in order to make the audience continue watching. Roland Barthes refers to this as the hermeneutic code.

Enigma Codes

Narrative also plays a key role in creating audience interest and appeal. One of the ways in which this is done is through the use of **enigma codes**. Enigma codes create suspense by withholding or delaying the answers to particular questions that the narrative sets up. This is a means of sustaining audience interest. For example, in whodunnits the revelation of the killer's identity is conventionally delayed until the end of the narrative in order to keep the viewer guessing.

Example of a television series: *Endeavour*

Key Terms

Serial
A narrative form in which the story unfolds episode by episode, unlike a series, in which each individual episode constitutes a self-contained narrative.

Self-contained narrative
When a complete story is told within a single episode. Viewers do not have to have seen any previous episodes in order to follow the story.

Cliff-hanger
A narrative device that creates suspense. It is typically used at the end of an episode or, in some cases, before an advert break, as its main function is to persuade the viewer to watch the following instalment of the programme in order to find out what happens next.

Narrative Forms: The Serial and the Series

Different television products use different narrative forms. Some may take the form of a series, for example, while others are presented as **serials**. In order to analyse the narrative structure of your set television product, it is important that you understand the difference between these two narrative forms.

In a television series, each episode generally comprises a separate, **self-contained narrative**. For example, *Endeavour* is a crime drama series, as each instalment features a different mystery that is solved over the course of that particular episode. Similarly, in the original *Star Trek* series, each episode would generally feature a separate adventure.

In contrast, a television serial features a story arc that runs over and across all the individual episodes. *Broadchurch* is therefore an example of a crime drama serial, as the mystery of who killed Danny Latimer runs across the whole of the first season and is only resolved in the final episode. Similarly, the third season of *Star Trek: Enterprise*, a spin-off from the original series, took the form of a serial as there was a single narrative that spanned all the episodes. In order to build interest and encourage audiences to watch the next instalment, serials often use **cliff-hangers** at the end of each episode.

Flexi-narratives

In the television industry, it has become increasingly common for programmes to use a combination of narrative forms. Robin Nelson, for example, argues that the majority of television drama today uses what he refers to as **flexi-narratives**. According to Nelson, flexi-narratives are *'mixtures of the series and the serial form, involving the closure of one story arc within an episode* [like a series] *but with other, ongoing story arcs involving the characters* [like a serial]*'* ('Studying Television Drama', in Glen Creeber (ed.), *Tele-visions*, 2006, page 82).

Sherlock, for example, features a self-contained mystery in every episode, while at the same time there is generally an over-arching narrative that runs across all the episodes in a season.

Restricted and Unrestricted Narratives

When you are analysing the narrative structure of your set television product you should also consider whether it uses an **unrestricted narrative** or a **restricted narrative**. These terms refer to how much the viewer is allowed to see or know.

- In the case of an unrestricted narrative, the viewer is privy to certain knowledge or information that is denied to characters within the text.
- With a restricted narrative, the amount of information that the audience is given is more limited as the viewer only knows as much as the characters within the diegetic world of the programme.

The American crime drama *Dexter*, produced by Showtime, is a good example of a programme that uses an unrestricted narrative. While the audience is aware of Dexter's secret identity as a serial killer, most of the characters within the diegetic world of the text are not.

Dexter's double life is cleverly alluded to in the opening title sequence of the original series, which shows his morning routine. Ordinary, everyday activities are invested with additional meaning here as they appear to reference various means of committing murder. The way in which Dexter's t-shirt clings to his face as he puts it on hints at suffocation, for example, while the close-ups of him pulling his shoelaces tight or stretching out a piece of dental floss suggest the idea of a victim being bound and strangled. The use of extreme close-ups and the amplification of diegetic sound add to this effect as they give uncanny emphasis to these familiar, everyday rituals, encouraging the audience to reconsider their symbolic significance.

Todorov's Theory of Narratology

One of the key narrative theories that you will need to consider when analysing your set television product is that of **Tzvetan Todorov**.

Key Theory: Tzvetan Todorov's Theory of Narratology

- the idea that all narratives share a basic structure that involves a movement from one state of **equilibrium** to another
- the idea that these two states of equilibrium are separated by a period of imbalance or disequilibrium
- the idea that the way in which narratives are resolved can have particular ideological significance.

Key Terms

Flexi-narrative
A narrative structure that combines aspects of the series and the serial. For example, while each episode may feature a self-contained narrative, character relationships may develop over the course of several episodes forming a broader story arc.

Unrestricted narrative
When the audience knows more than the characters within the world of the text, assuming a privileged spectator position.

Restricted narrative
When the audience only sees the narrative from the point of view of a character so only knows as much as they do.

Equilibrium
A state of balance, stability or order. In Todorov's narrative theory, it refers to the status quo – a normal state of affairs. For example, the initial state of equilibrium in a television programme might involve people going about their normal, day-to-day business.

Named Theorist

Tzvetan Todorov
Tzvetan Todorov was a Bulgarian theorist. His work was wide-ranging but he is particularly well-known for his contributions in the field of narratology.

Tip

When applying Todorov's theory, you will need to consider whether the set episode you are studying is part of a broader narrative arc or whether it is self-contained. For example, in the case of a television serial, restoration of equilibrium is unlikely to be achieved until the final episode.

Stretch and Challenge 5.6

Analyse the narrative structure of the programme you are studying. Does the set episode appear to follow the basic narrative structure outlined by Todorov? Which of the stages in Todorov's model can you identify?

According to Todorov's theory, a narrative has to feature some sort of transformation or change. This is what he means when he suggests that all narratives involve a movement from one state of equilibrium to another.

Building on this idea, Todorov's narrative model is often broken down into five key stages:

1. the initial state of equilibrium at the beginning of a narrative
2. a breakdown or disruption of equilibrium
3. a recognition that the equilibrium has been disrupted
4. an attempt to restore or re-establish equilibrium
5. the restoration of equilibrium at the end of the narrative.

While narratives are conventionally resolved with equilibrium restored, it is important to bear in mind that the equilibrium at the end of the narrative is unlikely to be identical to the initial state of equilibrium, as things cannot be exactly the same as they were before.

Todorov also acknowledges that narratives may sometimes begin with a realisation that the equilibrium has been disrupted. However, even if they are not actually shown, the first two stages of the narrative model can still be inferred. In other words, if there is a recognition that the equilibrium has been disrupted, this presupposes that there was some form of equilibrium beforehand and that something has subsequently happened to disrupt it. The decision to omit either the first narrative stage or the first two stages is a common strategy for engaging television viewers as it sets up a series of questions or enigma codes that grip the audience from the very start of the narrative.

Representation

Representation is another of the four areas of the theoretical framework that you are required to study in Component 2.

Named Theorist

Stuart Hall
Stuart Hall was a highly influential cultural theorist whose work covered a wide range of topics from reception theory (see the discussion of audience later in this chapter) to representations of race and ethnicity.

Hall's Theory of Representation

A particular theorist whose work you will need to consider when exploring the representations in your set television product is **Stuart Hall**. His theory provides a useful starting point for thinking about how representation works and what it involves.

Key Theory: Stuart Hall's Theory of Representation

- the idea that representation is the production of meaning through language, with language defined in its broadest sense as a system of signs
- the idea that the relationship between concepts and signs is governed by codes
- the idea that stereotyping, as a form of representation, reduces people to a few simple characteristics or traits
- the idea that stereotyping tends to occur where there are inequalities of power, as subordinate or excluded groups are constructed as different or 'other' (e.g. through **ethnocentrism**).

The basis of Hall's theory is the idea that *'Representation is the production of meaning through language'* (Stuart Hall (ed.), *Representation: Cultural Representations and Signifying Practices*, 2001, page 28). Language is used here in the broader sense of a system of signs. Media language, for example, is the system of signs through which media products convey their meanings.

Therefore, when we analyse representations in television products we need to explore the way in which those representations are constructed through particular aspects of media language. For example, the various codes, conventions and techniques that were outlined in Chapter 1, and which we discussed earlier in this chapter, all play an important role in constructing representations of issues, events, individuals and social groups. A character may be represented as powerful through the use of a low camera angle, for instance, while the costume that they wear may also contribute to their representation.

Another concept that you will need to consider is stereotyping. According to Hall, stereotyping is a representational practice that reduces people to a few simple characteristics or traits rather than dealing with people's complexity as unique individuals. Those simple traits are then exaggerated and presented as if they are part of a person's nature through a process called **essentialisation**.

Hall further argues that stereotyping tends to occur where there are inequalities of power. For example, in a patriarchal society (a society in which men are dominant), gender stereotypes may be used to subordinate women and maintain male power.

Key Term

Essentialisation
A process that involves ascribing certain traits or characteristics to someone by nature. As those traits are seen to be a part of that person's nature or essence, this means that they are fixed and cannot be changed.

Gender Stereotypes

Therefore, when looking at representations of men and women on television, it is useful to consider whether those representations challenge or reinforce gender stereotypes as this can reveal underlying values, attitudes and beliefs.

Stereotypical representations of gender are often constructed in terms of simple binary oppositions:

Men	**Women**
Active	Passive
Rational	Emotional
Powerful	Vulnerable
Strong	Weak
Dominant	Submissive
Aggressive	Timid
Independent/self-reliant	Dependent/reliant on others
Work/career-oriented	Family-oriented

What is noticeable here is the way in which this stereotypical division of traits reinforces male dominance, illustrating Stuart Hall's point that stereotyping tends to occur where there are inequalities of power.

Tip

When analysing representations of gender it is important to consider how the audience is positioned in relation to the views that particular people or characters in the programme embody or express. For example, while a particular character or individual may be sexist, this does not necessarily mean that those ideas are endorsed by the programme itself.

Key Term

Hypermasculinity
Where stereotypically masculine traits such as power, toughness or physical strength are presented in exaggerated form. In many cases this is conveyed symbolically through particular aspects of the iconography or mise-en-scène – cars and guns often function as symbols of masculine power, for example.

Named Theorist

David Gauntlett
A more detailed discussion of Gauntlett's theory of identity can be found in the following section of Chapter 5 where we discuss magazines.

However, it is important to bear in mind that, as social and cultural values change, traditional gender stereotypes can come to seem old-fashioned or obsolete. For example, while stereotypically masculine traits such as aggression, dominance and physical strength are still emphasised in some contemporary television products, they are not as widely idealised as they once were. Images of **hypermasculinity** are less commonplace today, partly because contemporary audiences are more likely to view such representations as comically excessive rather than as an aspirational ideal. As **David Gauntlett** points out: *'Representations of gender today are more complex, and less stereotyped, than in the past'* (*Media, Gender and Identity: An Introduction*, 2008, page 90).

The stereotypical representation of women as weak, submissive or timid has also been widely challenged in contemporary television dramas, as characters such as Polly Gray (below) in *Peaky Blinders* and Villanelle in *Killing Eve* convey a sense of female empowerment through their subversion of patriarchal gender norms.

Gender Roles and Narrative Functions

Social and cultural contexts have a significant influence on representations of gender. This is particularly apparent in the roles that men and women are seen to occupy in television programmes and the narrative functions that they perform.

For example, the way in which women have been represented in the BBC's long-running science-fiction series *Doctor Who* has changed quite considerably over time, reflecting wider changes in social and cultural attitudes.

In the early years of the programme, female characters were typically seen in the role of the **Proppian princess**. Repeatedly placed in situations of peril, they would passively wait to be rescued by the male hero. However, the introduction of Sarah Jane Smith as the Doctor's new assistant or 'companion' during the 1970s marked a significant change in the programme's representations of gender, as she was constructed as a much more independent figure. This has been widely read as a conscious response to the changes that were brought about by the second wave feminist movement during this era.

Key Term

Proppian princess
The princess or 'sought-for person' is one of the character roles or narrative functions identified in Vladimir Propp's narrative theory. The princess is often the object of the hero's quest. Another term commonly used for this type of role is the damsel in distress.

The more recent representation of female characters such as Rose Tyler and Bill Potts has continued this movement away from traditional gender stereotypes. Furthermore, as the first openly gay companion to feature in *Doctor Who*, Bill Potts reflects the way in which the BBC has attempted to increase diversity in its programmes.

It is also noticeable that roles that have traditionally been coded as male have started to be rewritten for women. For example, in recent series the Doctor's arch-enemy, The Master, has taken on a new female form, regenerating as 'Missy'. This demonstrates a significant shift in the programme's **sexual politics**. The introduction of Jodie Whittaker as the first ever female Doctor in 2018, and the casting of Ncuti Gatwa as the first black Doctor in 2022, further reflect the way in which the programme has adapted to wider social and cultural changes.

Issues of Under-Representation

The extent to which women are under-represented both on- and off-screen is an important issue to consider when looking at representations of gender on television. A common way of assessing on-screen representation is through **content analysis**. This typically involves looking at a sample of television programming and measuring the frequency with which men and women appear. Some studies also consider the relative prominence that men and women are given. A researcher may look at the number of men and women who appear in leading roles, for example, or they may look at the allocation of speaking and non-speaking roles to see if there are any signs of gender bias.

Studies have found that, historically, women tended to appear on television less frequently than men and were generally given less prominence. Writing in the late 1970s, **Gaye Tuchman** referred to this as the '**symbolic annihilation** of women', suggesting that in denying women a significant or meaningful presence on screen, television conveyed the message that they 'don't count for much'.

While recent studies suggest that there is now a much more even balance in terms of how frequently men and women appear on screen, there is still evidence of gender inequality in terms of how men and women are represented and the roles in which they are shown. Women are still more likely to be objectified in television programmes than men, for instance.

Many critics have argued that this is due to a lack of female writers, producers and directors working in the television industry. For example, a study published in 2022 by Diamond, a data collection system used to monitor diversity in UK television production, found that only 26% of directors, 33% of writers, 39% of producer directors and 41% of executive producers were women.

In an effort to address the under-representation of women in senior off-screen roles, broadcasters such as the BBC, ITV, Channel 4 and Sky, as well as streaming services such as Netflix, have introduced a number of diversity strategies in recent years, setting targets for gender equality and launching mentoring and leadership development programmes to provide a clear progression path for women working in the industry.

Although there is still a significant way to go before gender parity is achieved, the emergence of a new generation of award-winning female writers, producers and directors, including Michaela Coel, the writer, producer and director of *I May Destroy You*; Phoebe Waller-Bridge, the lead writer, showrunner and executive producer of *Killing Eve*; Issa Rae, the writer, executive producer and star of *Insecure*; and Mindy Kaling, the writer and producer of *The Mindy Project* and *The Sex Lives of College Girls*, suggests that progress is starting to be made.

Key Terms

Sexual politics
Refers to the power relations between men and women.

Content analysis
A research method that provides quantitative data. It generally involves counting the number of times a particular feature appears in a given context – counting the number of women who have speaking roles in prime-time television programmes, for example.

Symbolic annihilation
The idea that the under-representation of particular social groups works to maintain social inequalities by denying those groups any meaningful presence, thereby rendering them silent or invisible. As Gerbner and Gross put it: *'representation [...] signifies social existence; absence means symbolic annihilation'* ('Living with Television: The Violence Profile', *Journal of Communication*, 1976, 26(2)).

Key Figure

Gaye Tuchman
Tuchman's landmark essay 'The Symbolic Annihilation of Women by the Mass Media' was originally published in 1978. It forms the introduction to the edited volume, *Hearth and Home: Images of Women in the Mass Media* (1978).

Quickfire 5.7

What are the limitations of content analysis as a method for exploring representations in the media?

Stretch and Challenge 5.7

Look at the credits of the set television product you are studying. What is the ratio of men to women in key off-screen roles such as producer, director and writer?

LGBT Representations on Television

The representation of lesbian, gay, bisexual and transgender people on television has also changed significantly in recent years. While, in the past, LGBT people were generally under-represented on mainstream television, with representations largely confined to minor roles, LGBT representations have increased considerably over the past decade and there is now a growing number of mainstream television programmes featuring LGBT characters in lead roles. Notable examples include Netflix's popular coming-of-age shows, *Sex Education* and *Showstopper*, as well as HBO's critically acclaimed teen drama, *Euphoria*.

This pattern of increased LGBT representation was noted in Diamond's 2022 report on diversity in the UK television industry where, over a five-year reporting period, they observed '*a strong representation by those who collectively identify as lesbian, gay or bisexual both on and off-screen compared to national population estimates*'. Similar findings were reported in relation to US television and streaming services by the LGBTQ media advocacy organisation GLAAD. In their 'Where We Are on TV' report for 2021–2022, they counted a total of 637 LGBTQ series regular characters, a striking increase from the 12 LGBTQ characters that were counted when they published their first report 26 years earlier.

Stretch and Challenge 5.8

To what extent do men and women have equal screen presence in your set product? How far can the set product be seen to address or correct the historical under-representation and misrepresentation of women in television? Does the set product challenge or reinforce gender stereotypes?

There is also much greater diversity in *how* LGBT people are represented on television today. Significantly, when, in 2009/2010, Stonewall conducted a study of the top 20 programmes watched by young people, it found that half of all portrayals of lesbian, gay and bisexual people were stereotypical, with gay people frequently represented as predatory, promiscuous or figures of fun. A third of all portrayals were negative, with lesbian, gay or bisexual people commonly shown as unhappy or in despair. Stonewall also found that gay men were almost always portrayed as stereotypically effeminate. While these stereotypes still circulate, they now sit alongside a much broader range of LGBT representations that can be found in a diverse array of programmes, from *It's a Sin* – Channel 4's award-winning exploration of the impact of the AIDS epidemic in 1980s Britain – to the BBC/HBO co-production *Gentleman Jack*, based on the diaries of Anne Lister, a groundbreaking 19th century lesbian landowner.

Representations of Race and Ethnicity

The representation of race and ethnicity is another important area to explore. Again, it is useful to think about issues of under-representation and misrepresentation here.

While research suggests that on-screen representation of black, Asian and minority ethnic groups has increased in recent years, there are still disparities in terms of the types of role in which black, Asian and minority ethnic people are shown and the prominence that these representations are given. For example, in its report on race and ethnic diversity in the UK television industry, published in October 2020, Diamond found that people who identify as black or East Asian are more likely to be seen on-screen in supporting rather than lead roles. For instance, black people make 10.1% of contributions as actors in supporting roles but only 4.7% of contributions in lead acting roles. While, on the main channels, people who identify as black or mixed ethnicity are not as well-represented on-screen during primetime (6pm–10.30pm) than at other times.

Racial Stereotyping and the Burden of Representation

Although the representation of black, Asian and minority ethnic groups on UK television is proportionally high in relation to UK population figures, there are still far fewer representations of black, Asian and minority ethnic people on television compared with people from white ethnic groups. According to Diamond, in 2020–2021, 79.1% of all on-screen representations were of white people.

One of the consequences of this is that the few representations that we do see on-screen tend to carry greater cultural weight as they end up representing or standing in for whole social groups. This is what Stuart Hall refers to as the **burden of representation**. Furthermore, the fewer representations of a social group there are, the more likely it is that stereotyping will occur.

As Hall points out, stereotyping frequently reflects and reproduces power inequalities that exist in the wider society in which representations are produced. Therefore, it is important to consider issues of power when analysing racial and ethnic stereotypes as the roles in which characters from different ethnic groups are shown and the traits that they are given can set up particular power relations or racial hierarchies.

The popular British crime drama *Death in Paradise*, which is set on a Caribbean island, is an interesting case in this regard. While some have praised the programme as one of the few on prime-time British television to feature a predominantly black cast, others have suggested that the programme ultimately reinforces racial stereotypes and white **hegemony** through its use of the **white saviour trope**, as the local police force are seen to rely on a white British detective to help them sort out the crimes on the island. In this way, the programme could be regarded as **ethnocentric**, as the stereotypical representation of Caribbean culture is constructed from a white British perspective.

Key Terms

Burden of representation
The idea that when representations of particular social groups are limited, those few representations that do find their way into the media have to carry more weight as they end up standing in for entire groups or communities.

Hegemony
The dominance of one group over another. For example, a patriarchal society could be described as an example of male hegemony while a predominantly white institution could be described as hegemonically white.

White saviour trope
Refers to a type of narrative in which a white character is seen to save, help, liberate or rescue a non-white character or a group of non-white characters. The white saviour is typically represented as a leader or a Messiah-like figure. This is often problematic as it can be seen to reinforce racial hierarchies and stereotypes through its representation of non-white people as dependent on the aid and assistance of white people.

Ethnocentric
Roger Brown defines ethnocentrism as *'the application of the norms of one's own culture to that of others'* (*Social Psychology*, 1965, page 183). Stuart Hall refers to this definition in his theory of representation as he suggests that ethnocentrism is an example of the way in which stereotypes reinforce the power of certain groups over others.

Social, Cultural and Institutional Factors

While some programmes, such as the BBC's *Luther* and E4's *Chewing Gum*, have featured black actors in leading roles, until recently these have tended to be relatively isolated examples, leading to accusations of tokenism. This is a point that British actor Riz Ahmed made in a speech to Parliament in March 2017. Arguing that '*prominent successes can mask structural problems*', he suggested that programmes like these are '*often prominent because they are the exceptions that prove the rule*'. Evidence of the structural problems that Riz Ahmed referred to can be seen in the fact that black, Asian and minority ethnic groups are still under-represented in the majority of senior production roles in the television industry, as the Diamond report noted.

There are signs that the television industry is beginning to address these structural problems though. Most broadcasters and streaming services now have diversity strategies that set specific targets for improving the representation of black, Asian and minority ethnic groups in senior off-screen roles.

These changes are also beginning to filter down into the programmes themselves. For example, while period dramas such as *Poldark* and *Downton Abbey* have traditionally included very few roles for black, Asian or minority ethnic actors, this is starting to change. Shows such as Netflix's hugely successful *Bridgerton* have challenged the hegemonically white nature of the period drama genre through what the programme's creator and showrunner, Chris Van Dusen, describes as 'colour-conscious' casting. In a piece written for *The Hollywood Reporter* in August 2021, Van Dusen said that he had wanted to '*turn the period genre on its head and reimagine it in a new and exciting way. One that included characters of different colors and backgrounds. One that explored the topic of race.*'

Downton Abbey

***Bridgerton* has been praised for its casting of mixed race and South Asian actors in leading roles.**

The BBC has also made increasing efforts to address important aspects of black British cultural history that have often been ignored on mainstream television, commissioning programmes such as *Small Axe*, an anthology series directed by Steve McQueen. Described by the BBC as a series of '*love letters to black resilience and triumph in London's West Indian Community*', *Small Axe* chronicles the experiences of black communities dealing with racism in 70s and 80s Britain. In conversation with his friend and mentor, **Paul Gilroy**, at a talk at University College London in 2020, McQueen discussed what the series meant for him, explaining that for him, *Small Axe* was '*about shoring up the foundations of who we are and where we came from and what we contributed to this country on so many levels*'.

Named Theorist

Paul Gilroy
Paul Gilroy is one of theorists studied at A lvevel. His work on race, ethnicity and postcolonial theory is discussed in the Year 2 textbook.

Industry

The UK broadcasting environment has been described as '*a carefully balanced mix of different organisations, with different missions, business models and governance structures*' ('Britain's Creative Greenhouse: A summary of the 2015 Channel 4 Annual Report and other key facts', https://assets-corporate.channel4.com/_flysystem/s3/2017-07/C4_Creative_Greenhouse_2015_0.pdf).

Before thinking about the specific institutional contexts in which your set product was produced, it is important to understand how the television industry works. In particular, it is important to be aware of:

- different forms of ownership in the television industry
- the various ways in which broadcasters and streaming platforms are funded
- the role and function of public service broadcasters in the television industry.

Ownership

In terms of ownership, one of the key areas to look at is whether an organisation is privately or publicly owned.

- Privately owned organisations are designed to make a profit for their shareholders. ITV, Channel 5 and Sky are examples of privately owned organisations. These organisations are owned by larger media **conglomerates**. For example, Channel 5 is owned by the American multinational conglomerate Paramount Global, which also owns a number of other channels including MTV, Comedy Central and Nickelodeon as well as the streaming service Paramount+, while Sky is owned by the American multinational conglomerate Comcast.
- Publicly owned organisations are run on a not-for-profit basis. This means that they are designed to serve the interests of the general public rather than shareholders. Any surplus that they make is reinvested as it goes towards the cost of making new programmes. The BBC is an example of a publicly owned not-for-profit organisation.

Key Term

Conglomerate
A large organisation that owns other companies and has interests spanning across a number of different businesses or industries. For example, the Walt Disney Company is a media and entertainment conglomerate as it has business interests in several different industries, including film, television, music and radio as well as the theme park industry.

Quickfire 5.8

In what ways could private ownership be seen to impact on the kinds of programmes that a broadcaster commissions or shows?

Funding

There are also significant differences in terms of the way in which television companies are funded.

- Some organisations are commercially funded through advertising. This means that they generate revenue by selling **advertising spots** in commercial breaks. The rate that an advertiser is charged for an advertising spot will depend on the length of the advert and the time of day it is shown. Advertising spots in peak-time programmes are generally more expensive than spots in daytime programmes, for example, as they are likely to be seen by more people.
- Some organisations are funded through subscription. This is often referred to as pay-TV, as customers have to pay a subscription fee in order to receive particular channels.
- Another important source of revenue is sponsorship. This is when a company contributes towards production costs in order to promote its brand. The sponsor's name usually appears as a credit at the beginning of programmes and in the **sponsorship bumpers** that lead into and out of advertisement breaks. Companies may choose to sponsor a particular programme, a particular strand of programming or a particular channel.
- Unlike other channels, the BBC is publicly funded through a licence fee rather than by advertising, subscription or sponsorship. The licence fee is charged to all UK households that watch live television on any channel. In addition to the BBC's television, radio and online services, the licence fee also funds the Welsh language channel S4C as well as other local television channels.

Key Terms

Advertising spots
Advertising spots are the spaces in commercial breaks that are sold to advertisers. Most advertising spots are around 30 seconds long, although they can be longer or shorter than this.

Sponsorship bumper
A short clip featuring the name or logo of the sponsor that appears between the programme and the advertisements.

Remit
A remit outlines a broadcaster's particular areas of responsibility. For example, the BBC's duty to provide impartial news coverage is specified in its remit.

Public Service Broadcasting

Some broadcasters have a public service **remit**. This means that they have to fulfil certain public purposes in accordance with their licence to broadcast.

The main public service broadcasters (PSBs) in the UK are the BBC, ITV, Channel 4, Channel 5 and S4C. While each of these organisations has its own individual remit, all public service broadcasters are required to provide high-quality programmes that cover a wide range of subjects, satisfying the needs and interests of as wide a range of audiences as possible.

These requirements, which are set out in the Communications Act 2003, are intended to ensure that audiences who might otherwise be neglected are catered for and that quality and diversity are not compromised by commercial factors such as the desire to maximise profits.

The regulatory body responsible for monitoring the public service broadcasters and making sure that they fulfil their designated public purposes is Ofcom. Building on the definition of public service broadcasting provided in the Communications Act 2003, Ofcom states that the main purposes of public service broadcasters are to:

- inform our understanding of the world through news, information and analysis of current events and ideas
- stimulate knowledge and learning of the arts, science, history and other topics through accessible content
- reflect UK cultural identity through original programming at UK, national and regional level
- represent diversity and alternative viewpoints through programmes that reflect the lives of other people and communities, both within the UK and elsewhere.

It further specifies that public service programming should be original, innovative, challenging, distinctive and of high quality, and that it should be widely available.

Ofcom also sets certain quotas that the public service broadcasters have to meet. As well as quotas for news and current affairs programming, there are also quotas for **original productions**, **independent productions** and regional productions. These are intended to support the UK television industry and the wider economy. Significantly, according to the UK screen sector trade body, Pact, independent production companies were worth over £3 billion to the UK economy in 2021, with '*over 500 independent television producers employing tens of thousands of people across the country*' (Pact, March 2021, 'Submission to Ofcom's Call for Evidence: public service broadcasters and the UK production sector', https://www.ofcom.org.uk/_data/assets/pdf_file/0016/218041/Pact-CFE.pdf).

This is an important part of the industry context in which *Peaky Blinders*, *Killing Eve* and *Black Mirror* were produced, as they were all made by independent production companies based in the UK.

Peaky Blinders was produced for the BBC by Caryn Mandabach Productions. *Black Mirror*, which was originally commissioned by Channel Four before moving to Netflix, was produced by House of Tomorrow, while *Killing Eve* was produced for BBC America and BBC Three by Sid Gentle Films.

Key Terms

Original productions
Productions that are commissioned by broadcasters rather than bought in.

Independent productions
In the broadcasting industry, these are productions that are produced by companies that are independent of the broadcasters.

The British Broadcasting Corporation (BBC)

The BBC's remit as a public service broadcaster is set out in a Royal Charter, which is reviewed and updated every ten or 11 years. Its mission to inform, educate and entertain, which has been a guiding principle since the corporation was founded by **Lord Reith** in the 1920s, is outlined in the Charter along with the public purposes it has to promote.

Key figure

Lord Reith
Lord Reith was the first Director-General of the BBC. He is widely credited with establishing the corporation's governing ethos.

The most recent version of the Royal Charter, which came into effect in January 2017, placed greater emphasis on distinctiveness compared with previous charters, specifying that the BBC's output and services have to be 'substantially different' from those offered by other broadcasters. The Charter states, for example, that the BBC should '*take creative risks, even if not all succeed, in order to develop fresh approaches and innovative content*'.

This appeared to be an attempt to satisfy some of the BBC's commercial rivals who argue that the corporation should not be competing with commercial broadcasters for audience share by producing populist entertainment but should instead be targeting specialised audiences that are not currently catered for. These arguments are part of an ongoing debate about the role and purpose of the BBC in a global age of digital media, and how the corporation should be funded. For example, Conservative ministers have suggested that the licence fee may be abolished and a new funding model may be imposed on the BBC when the current Charter comes to an end in 2027.

Faced with a funding freeze and rising production costs, the BBC announced a range of cost-cutting measures in May 2022. These included closing or merging a number of services and moving others exclusively online in order to build what BBC Director General Tim Davie described as a '*digital-first BBC* [...] *a Reithian organisation for the digital age*'.

As the cost of making high-quality television drama has risen dramatically in recent years, the BBC has also had to forge partnerships with other broadcasters and streaming platforms in order to spread the financial burden. The BBC's adaptation of Philip Pullman's *His Dark Materials* was co-produced with HBO, for example.

Key Terms

Value chain
The different steps or activities involved in making a product and getting it to the consumer or audience. Vertically integrated companies are able to undertake most or all of these activities themselves as they generally have the means to both produce and distribute products.

Vertical integration
A process through which a company develops control over different levels of the value chain. An example of a vertically integrated business would be a production company that is also able to distribute its products or a magazine publisher that owns a printing company.

Publisher-broadcaster
A broadcaster that commissions all of its programmes from other production companies as it does not have its own in-house production division.

Privatisation
When a company is taken out of public ownership and sold to a private bidder.

Quickfire 5.9

What advantages do international co-productions offer broadcasters?

BBC Studios and BBC America

While the BBC is primarily funded by the licence fee, it also has a commercial subsidiary, BBC Studios, which brings in around £200 million of additional revenue each year. This money is reinvested in programmes for BBC audiences in the UK.

Describing itself as '*a one-stop-shop that touches every aspect of the* ***value chain*** *from production to exploitation – whether that's financing or developing a show, producing it or selling it*', BBC Studios is a **vertically integrated** company comprised of two divisions – a production division, which makes programmes for the BBC and competes to produce programmes for other broadcasters, and a sales and distribution division, which builds the BBC's brand around the world, selling programmes and formats to international buyers.

BBC Studios is also a co-owner of BBC America, the American cable channel that commissioned *Killing Eve*. Unlike the BBC's channels in the UK, BBC America is funded by advertising and subscription. This helps to explain the running time of *Killing Eve*, which averages 40–43 minutes per episode. While peak-time dramas produced for BBC One in the UK generally have a running time of just under an hour, programmes on BBC America are broken up by advert breaks and therefore tend to be slightly shorter.

The production context of the programme also had an impact on the casting of *Killing Eve*, as BBC America was keen to have an American actor in one of the leading roles. This resulted in Sandra Oh being offered the role of Eve.

Channel 4

Channel 4 was launched in 1982. As well as its flagship channel, it has a portfolio of other channels and a catch-up and video-on-demand streaming service.

Historically, Channel 4 has operated as a **publisher-broadcaster** as, unlike the BBC, its remit has prevented it from having its own in-house production division. Instead, it has been required to commission all original programming from independent production companies. However, in January 2023, the government announced plans to relax the publisher-broadcaster restriction in Channel 4's remit, thereby opening up new revenue streams by enabling it to produce some content itself. This meant that Channel 4 would have ownership of any programmes or formats produced in-house, and would be able to monetise this content, for example by licensing it to other international broadcasters.

At the same time, the government announced that its previous plans to privatise Channel 4 were to be reversed and the broadcaster would be kept in public ownership. While Channel 4 has consistently sought to defend its status as a publicly owned, commercially funded broadcaster by emphasising the economic and social value that its current business model offers and the role it plays in sustaining the independent production sector, Conservative ministers had argued that **privatisation** would enable it to compete with streaming giants such as Netflix. These plans were shelved, however, following concerns that privatisation would damage the independent production sector in the UK and make Channel 4 more risk-averse, as the need to make profit for shareholders would lead it to focus on programmes with the broadest, mainstream appeal.

The channel has already had to defend itself from accusations that it has become too commercial. For example, some critics have suggested that its acquisition of *The Great British Bake Off* from the BBC does not sit comfortably with its reputation for risk-taking, experimentation and innovation – key elements not only of Channel 4's brand identity but also its public service remit. However, Channel 4 has argued that this approach makes its risk-taking more financially sustainable, as it uses programmes that generate more revenue to cross-subsidise those with lower commercial value.

Black Mirror can be seen to illustrate some of these issues as, having originally been commissioned by Channel 4, which financed and broadcast the first two series, it was picked up by Netflix. The programme's creator and co-showrunner, Charlie Brooker, has suggested that Channel 4 was hesitant in committing to a third season partly because of the significant costs involved, especially as they had just commissioned another sci-fi anthology series, *Electric Dreams*. While Channel 4 initially explored the idea of bringing a production partner such as HBO, AMC or Netflix on board to share the costs, this idea was eventually abandoned and Netflix completed a deal to acquire the show.

Stretch and Challenge 5.9

Why might an anthology series (and, more specifically, a sci-fi anthology series) prove more challenging to fund than a television serial?

Netflix

The past two decades have seen a number of significant developments in the television industry, including the rapid growth and expansion of online platforms and the emergence of subscription video-on-demand (SVOD) services. According to data from IPA TouchPoints, over half of the British public now use SVOD services each week, with particularly high take-up among younger demographics.

Netflix has been at the forefront of many of these changes. It pioneered the subscription video-on-demand model with the launch of its streaming service in 2007, and since then its reach has expanded dramatically around the world. At the time of writing, it is available in all international territories except for China, Crimea, North Korea, Russia and Syria.

Although, initially, Netflix only distributed video content produced by other companies, it has subsequently moved into production and now has production hubs not only in the US, but also in New Mexico, Canada and the UK. This has enabled it to become a vertically integrated business as it is able to both produce and distribute video content. Notable examples of original shows produced by Netflix include *Sex Education*, *Bridgerton*, *Heartstopper* and *Squid Game*.

Although the shows that it produces in-house are branded 'Netflix Originals', Netflix also uses this branding for third party content that it has exclusive distribution rights to. For example, even though *Peaky Blinders* is a BBC production, it is branded a 'Netflix Original' in the US as Netflix acquired the exclusive US distribution rights to the series from The Weinstein Company in 2014.

While Netflix has been the dominant player in the subscription video-on-demand market for some time, competition has increased dramatically in recent years with the launch of several high-profile SVOD services, including Amazon Prime Video, Now TV, Apple TV+ and Disney+. This has had a significant impact on Netflix's profits, forcing the company to adapt its business model. For example, following a considerable decline in subscriber numbers, in November 2022 it launched a cheaper, ad-supported option in partnership with Microsoft to sit alongside its premium, advertising-free subscription service. This was designed to open up new revenue streams while attracting subscribers who were no longer prepared or able to pay for the premium service.

Netflix has also responded to economic challenges by diversifying into the video game market. The company has acquired a number of game studios in recent years, including Boss Fight Entertainment, Next Games and Night School Studio. This has provided it with an opportunity to create synergy by releasing video game spin-offs based around popular shows like *Stranger Things* and *Squid Game*.

Regulation

The UK television industry is currently regulated by Ofcom. Ofcom's main regulatory duty, which is set by Parliament through the Communications Act 2003, is to further the interests of citizens and consumers. In order to do this, Ofcom has to:

- ensure that television services are provided by a range of different organisations
- ensure that a wide range of high-quality programmes are provided, which appeal to a range of tastes and interests
- protect viewers from offensive or harmful material
- protect people from unfair treatment and ensure that their privacy is not invaded.

One of the main ways in which Ofcom seeks to maintain standards in television programming is through the operation of a Broadcasting Code. This sets out a number of principles that broadcasters have to comply with. In setting and applying the Code, Ofcom takes into account factors such as:

- the likely size, composition and expectation of the potential audience
- the degree of harm and offence likely to be caused
- whether the inclusion of offensive material can be justified by the context in which it is shown.

Section One of the Code is to do with protecting people under the age of 18 from unsuitable content. In order to do this, television broadcasters are required to observe the **watershed**. This means that material that is deemed unsuitable for children cannot be broadcast before 9pm or after 5.30am.

Other aspects of the Code deal with issues such as violence and dangerous behaviour, the use of discriminatory language and the portrayal of crime.

Responsibility for regulating the BBC switched to Ofcom from the BBC Trust in April 2017. Prior to this, the BBC had been bound by some aspects of Ofcom's Broadcasting Code but not others. Under the terms of the most recent BBC Charter, Ofcom is required to check the accuracy and impartiality of the BBC's news and current affairs programming. It also has to ensure that the BBC does not use the license fee to gain an unfair competitive advantage over other broadcasters. In April 2022, the government announced that streaming services in the UK such as Netflix, Disney+ and Amazon Prime Video would also be regulated by Ofcom.

Key Term

Watershed
The watershed is the time when it becomes permissible to show programmes that are unsuitable for younger audiences. In the UK, the watershed is at 9pm.

Quickfire 5.10

Why might it be argued that the watershed is less relevant now than it was in the past?

Stretch and Challenge 5.10

Research the Broadcasting Code in more depth by visiting Ofcom's website.

Marketing

As part of your study of the television industry, you will also need to consider the way in which media organisations maintain varieties of audiences both nationally and globally. Marketing plays a particularly important role in this regard.

There are a number of strategies and techniques that media organisations can employ to market their television products. These include:

- **Trailers**: short promotional films that feature clips from the programme. Teaser trailers tend to be shorter in length as their main purpose is to arouse audience interest by providing small pieces of information about the programme without giving too much away. As well as appearing in the gaps between programmes they are generally made available on social media platforms such as YouTube.

- **Poster/billboard campaigns**: this can be a useful way of building public awareness as they are generally seen by large numbers of people.
- **Viral marketing campaigns**: this typically involves the use of social media platforms such as Instagram, Twitter, TikTok or Facebook. Messages or clips are posted on relevant accounts and are then shared more widely by users. The marketing message therefore spreads like a virus.
- **Websites**: these are often used to develop or extend the brand identity of a programme. They can include a range of different features including clips, interviews, articles and behind-the-scenes footage.
- **Preview screenings and Q & A sessions**: appearances at festivals or conventions such as New York Comic Con and industry events such as SeriesFest help to create buzz and publicity as do red-carpet events such as premieres.
- **Press and publicity**: this can include appearances on talk shows, interviews with newspapers and magazines as well as press events such as the TCA Press Tour in America where the networks promote their new shows.

A special screening promoting the third season of *Black Mirror*, attended by Charlie Brooker, Gugu Mbatha-Raw and other members of the Season Three cast, was held as part of the London Film Festival in October 2016.

Scheduling

Another way in which broadcasters try to maintain audiences is through **scheduling**. This is to do with the placement of programmes – deciding the days and times when they are to be shown. There are a number of factors that schedulers have to take into account when making these decisions. For example, they have to consider the programmes that are being shown by rival broadcasters in the same time-slot as well as the need to build and maintain an audience through the schedule. Institutional factors such as the need to observe the watershed and the requirement for public service broadcasters to provide a balance of programming can also have an impact on scheduling decisions.

Certain slots in the television schedule tend to be reserved for certain genres of programme. Entertainment shows that have broad audience appeal such as *Strictly Come Dancing*, *The Masked Singer* and *Britain's Got Talent* are often shown in **prime-time** on Saturday evenings, while soap operas such as *EastEnders*, *Coronation Street* and *Hollyoaks* are generally broadcast in regular early evening slots. Placing popular programmes like these earlier in the schedule can be useful because viewers may stay with the channel and watch the programme that follows, inheriting some of the previous programme's audience. In order to discourage viewers from switching channels, previews of one programme are commonly shown over the closing credits of the one before.

However, while careful consideration is still given to scheduling decisions, this is not as important as it once was, as the way in which audiences view television has changed significantly in recent years. For example, the growth of digital technologies has seen a dramatic increase in **non-linear viewing**. This means that audiences are able to choose when they watch. All the major broadcasters now have their own dedicated 'on-demand' services or platforms. While the main public service broadcasters have traditionally used these platforms as 'catch-up' services, they are now starting to make more content available ahead of broadcast. For example, a whole series may be released online immediately after the broadcast of the first episode, enabling audiences to 'binge-watch' the complete set rather than waiting for the next episode to air.

Key Terms

Scheduling
Making decisions about when to broadcast programmes.

Prime-time
The time when most viewers are likely to be watching television. Broadcasters will generally schedule their most popular programmes in prime-time slots. Prime-time is defined by Ofcom as the period between 6pm and 10.30pm.

Non-linear viewing
When viewers watch programmes at times of their choosing, whether by using video-on-demand services or by streaming, downloading or watching programmes that have been recorded. Linear viewing, on the other hand, is where programmes are viewed at the time of broadcast.

Audience

Audience Targeting and Audience Appeal

As well as considering how the television industry targets and maintains audiences through marketing, you should also explore how it uses the content and appeal of television products to target and attract audiences. For example, you may find it useful to think about some of the following:

- **The appeal of the genre**: what particular pleasures does the genre of your set product offer audiences? How are genre conventions used to target audiences?
- **The appeal of the narrative**: what particular narrative devices does the television product use to attract and appeal to audiences? Consider the use of suspense and enigma codes, for example.
- **Aesthetic appeal**: how might the look, quality or production values of the product be used to target and attract audiences?
- **The appeal of particular representations**: how might the representations in the set television product be used in order to target and attract different audiences? How is the audience encouraged to view the characters that feature in the programme?
- **Intertextuality**: is there a pleasure in recognising references that are made to other media products? How might these intertextual references appeal to particular audiences?

Hall's Reception Theory

In order to explore how audiences may interpret the same television product in different ways, you need to be able to apply **Stuart Hall**'s reception theory to the television programme you are studying.

Named Theorist

Stuart Hall

Stuart Hall's reception theory is outlined in the essay 'Encoding, Decoding', published in *Culture, Media, Language* (1990).

Key Theory: Stuart Hall's Reception Theory

- the idea that communication is a process involving encoding by producers and decoding by audiences
- the idea that there are three hypothetical positions from which messages and meanings may be decoded:
  - **i.** the dominant-hegemonic position: the encoder's intended meaning (the preferred reading) is fully understood and accepted
  - **ii.** the negotiated position: the legitimacy of the encoder's message is acknowledged in general terms, although the message is adapted or negotiated to better fit the decoder's own individual experiences or context
  - **iii.** the oppositional position: the encoder's message is understood, but the decoder disagrees with it, reading it in a contrary or oppositional way.

As we have discussed in earlier chapters, the central premise of Hall's theory is the idea that audiences do not necessarily interpret media products in exactly the same way. While some viewers may make a preferred reading of a television programme, decoding it exactly as the encoder intended, others may make a negotiated reading, acknowledging the broad legitimacy of the messages that it contains but recognising that there are 'exceptions to the rule'.

The third possibility that Hall identifies is that viewers may fundamentally disagree with the messages that a programme conveys, making an oppositional reading of the product. For example, they may view the representations that a programme offers as sexist or racist.

When you analyse your set television product you will therefore need to consider the different ways in which it might be read.

Gerbner's Cultivation Theory and Mean World Syndrome

Another audience theory that you may wish to explore when considering how audiences respond to television products is **George Gerbner**'s cultivation theory. This suggests that heavy viewers (those who watch a lot of television) are more likely to be influenced by television products than light users (those who only watch television occasionally).

Gerbner argues that the '*repetitive pattern of television's mass-produced messages and images*' cultivates certain ways of thinking, shaping the attitudes, values and beliefs of people who consume television on a regular basis.

Gerbner was particularly interested in the representation of crime on television and the potential effects that this might have on viewers. Significantly, through his research he found that *'Crime in prime time* [was] *at least 10 times as rampant as in the real world'* (George Gerbner, Larry Gross, Michael Morgan and Nancy Signorielli, 'Living with Television: The Dynamics of the Cultivation Process', in Jennings Bryant and Dolf Zillman (eds), *Perspectives on Media Effects*, 1986, page 26). Gerbner therefore argued that heavy exposure to television cultivated an unrealistic view of social reality as heavy viewers were likely to have an exaggerated fear of crime, seeing the world as a more dangerous place than it actually is. The term he uses to describe this phenomenon is **mean world syndrome**.

Named Theorist

George Gerbner
Further information about Gerbner's cultivation theory is provided in the following section on Magazines under 'Audience'.

Key Terms

Mean world syndrome
The idea that regular exposure to television can lead to a distorted view of the real world. In particular, the disproportionate representation of crime on television is likely to make viewers think that the world is a 'meaner' or more dangerous place than it actually is.

Tip

When assessing the different ways in which audiences might interpret or respond to a particular media product it is important to consider realistic or plausible responses. It is also important to avoid generalisations. For instance, do not assume that all women or all older people will respond to a product in exactly the same way. Rather than discussing how these audiences *would* respond, discuss how they *might* respond.

Summary

Key Points

Having read this section on television, you should now be familiar with:

- the codes and conventions of television as a media form
- the different narrative forms that television products may take and the function of the narrative codes, conventions and devices that they use
- the dynamic and historically relative nature of television genres
- issues regarding the under-representation and misrepresentation of particular social groups
- the different ownership and funding models that operate in the television industry and the role of public service broadcasting
- the way in which the television industry is regulated
- the way in which the television industry targets and attracts audiences through marketing and through the content and appeal of products
- the different ways in which audiences may read and respond to television products.

You must be able to apply this knowledge and understanding to your set products.

Essential Theories for Television

When discussing your set television product, you must also be able to use the following theories:

- **Genre theory**, including Neale: for example, the idea that genres such as crime drama, science fiction and spy thrillers are characterised by patterns of repetition and difference, and that they are shaped by the institutional and economic contexts in which they are produced.
- **Narratology**, including Todorov: for example, the idea that television narratives share a basic structure that involves a movement from one state of equilibrium to another.
- **Theories of representation**, including Hall: for example, the idea that representations are constructed through aspects of media language and that stereotypical representations can be seen to reflect particular inequalities of power.
- **Reception theory**, including Hall: for example, the idea that viewers may adopt different positions in relation to the television products they watch, interpreting them in different ways.

Guidance for A Level Students

Remember that if you are taking the A level course, you will also need to use the following theories when analysing your set television products:

- **structuralism**, including Lévi-Strauss
- **postmodernism**, including Baudrillard
- **feminist theories**, including bell hooks and van Zoonen
- **theories of gender performativity**, including Butler
- **regulation**, including Livingstone and Lunt
- **cultural industries**, including Hesmondhalgh
- **fandom**, including Jenkins.

Guidance regarding these theories can be found in the *WJEC/Eduqas Media Studies for A Level Year 2* book.

Section B: Magazines

The Specification

Magazines are one of the three media forms that you are required to study in depth on the Eduqas specification. At AS level you are required to study extracts from one set edition of a historical magazine from the 1960s, while at A level you are required to study extracts from one set edition of a historical magazine from the 1960s and one set edition of a contemporary magazine produced outside the commercial mainstream.

This section provides an introduction to some of the key approaches that can be used to study magazines as a media form and sets out a critical framework for analysing the historical magazine products. Guidance regarding the contemporary magazine products that are only studied at A level can be found in the *WJEC/Eduqas Media Studies for A Level Year 2* book.

WJEC

If you are following the modular WJEC specification, you are not required to study magazines at AS level. However, we would strongly recommend that you read this section in preparation for the A2 module 'Media in the Global Age', as the main critical approaches that are outlined here will provide a useful foundation for your in-depth study of magazines in Unit 3. Further guidance on this topic can be found in the *WJEC/Eduqas Media Studies for A Level Year 2* book.

Magazine Options

In Component 2, you are required to study a specified edition of **one** of the following magazines:

Option 1: *Woman* (1937–). Set edition: 29 August 1964

- *Woman* is a weekly women's magazine. It was originally published by Odhams Press before IPC assumed ownership of the magazine in 1963. It is now published by Future plc.

Option 2: *Woman's Realm* (1958–2001). Set edition: 13 February 1965

- *Woman's Realm* was a weekly women's magazine. Launched in 1958, it was originally published by Odhams Press before the International Publishing Corporation (IPC) took over its ownership in 1963. Publication of the magazine ended in 2001 when it was merged with *Woman's Weekly*.

Option 3: *Vogue* (1916–). Set edition: July 1965

- *Vogue* is a monthly women's fashion magazine. The original American magazine was launched by Arthur Turnure in 1892. Since 1909 it has been published by Condé Nast. The British edition of *Vogue* was launched in 1916.

A Level Magazine Options

If you are taking the A level course, you will also study extracts from a contemporary magazine that has been produced outside the commercial mainstream in addition to one of the historical products outlined above. The historical product you study will dictate which of the three contemporary magazines you look at.

- If you study *Woman* magazine, the contemporary product you study will be *Adbusters*.
- If you study *Woman's Realm*, the contemporary product you study will be *Huck*.
- If you study *Vogue*, the contemporary magazine you study will be *The Big Issue*.

Using the Theoretical Framework

In exploring your set magazine product, you will need to consider all four areas of the theoretical framework. Therefore, in this section we will look at:

- **the media language of magazines**: how magazines communicate meanings through their forms, codes, conventions and techniques
- **representation**: how magazines portray social groups and particular aspects of social identity
- **the magazine industry**: how processes of production, distribution and circulation affect magazines
- **audiences**: how magazines target, reach and address audiences, and how audiences interpret and respond to magazine products.

Media Language

Key Term

Periodical
A publication that is issued at regular intervals – weekly, monthly, quarterly, etc.

Defining the Magazine as a Media Form

A magazine is a **periodical** publication containing a collection of articles that are targeted at a particular audience. The key modes through which it communicates its meanings are images and text.

As this suggests, the magazine shares some of its formal characteristics with another print media form – the newspaper. There are, however, a number of ways in which newspapers and magazines differ. For example:

- magazines are usually printed on higher quality paper stock, whereas newspapers tend to use cheaper newsprint
- magazines are usually stapled or bound, whereas the pages in a newspaper will generally be loose
- magazines are not expected to provide readers with up-to-date information about the previous day's news stories in the way that newspapers are, as they are usually published less frequently.

While magazines are traditionally published in print form, there has been a significant growth in online magazines in recent years as the magazine industry has begun to adapt to the different demands of a digital age.

This is not the first time in its history that the magazine has had to adapt in order to survive. The rise of commercial television in the 1950s and 1960s was also seen as a threat to the magazine industry, as publishers had to compete not only for audiences but also for advertisers. One of the ways in which they did this was by targeting particular segments of the audience rather than aiming for mass market appeal.

Although circulation peaked in the late 1950s and early 1960s, magazines still remain a highly visible part of everyday life. We see them on the newsstands of supermarkets, newsagents and convenience stores, in the waiting rooms of dental practices and doctors' surgeries, in airports and train stations, in hotels, hairdressing salons and coffee bars, and, of course, in readers' homes. While the traditional print magazine faces a number of challenges in a digital age, this would seem to suggest that there is still some shelf-life left in it yet.

The Conventions of Magazine Covers

While magazines come in a wide variety of genres and cater for many different audiences, there are certain common elements that most magazine covers share. The conventions that are common to most magazine covers include:

- **A main image**: this is a key signifier of the magazine's **brand identity**. The nature of the image will generally depend on the genre and target audience of the magazine. It may be an illustration or it could be a photographic image. Some magazines may include several images on the front cover. However, there is generally one focal point.
- **A distinctive masthead**: this is an iconic part of the magazine's branding. In the case of established titles, the masthead will be instantly recognisable even if it is partially concealed by the main image.
- **Cover lines**: these are generally placed around the main image. Their principal function is to create audience interest, enticing the reader to buy the magazine. The number of cover lines and the precise way in which they are arranged may vary. Some publications include a number of different cover lines in order to convey the impression that the magazine is packed with content. Others make more minimal use of cover lines, relying instead on the strength of the cover image to sell the magazine and establish the brand.
- **A date line**: this is conventionally displayed in close proximity to the masthead, often with the price.
- Some covers also feature a **tagline**: this typically conveys a sense of the magazine's brand identity, editorial philosophy or intended audience. For example, *Diva*'s tagline '*The leading magazine for LGBTQ+ women and non-binary people*' clearly denotes who the magazine is for.

Key Terms

Brand identity
The image that a brand projects and the associations the audience makes with the brand. This is built up over time.

Masthead
The title of the magazine presented in the form of a logo. Many magazines use a specially designed typeface for the masthead. This is useful for branding and can also help to distinguish the magazine from its competitors.

Cover lines
The written text that features on the cover of the magazine providing a preview of the content that features inside.

Tagline
A short, memorable phrase that sums up the magazine and conveys a sense of its brand identity.

The Main Functions of the Magazine Front Cover

As well as being able to identify the codes and conventions associated with magazine covers, you also need to have an understanding of the different functions that magazine covers perform. As the front cover is generally the first part of the publication that the reader will see, it has to:

- indicate who the magazine is intended for, drawing the attention of the target audience
- indicate the type of magazine it is (the relevant genre or sub-genre should be clearly signalled to the reader)
- help the magazine stand out from its competitors by conveying a clear sense of brand identity
- persuade potential readers to buy the magazine by creating audience interest and appeal.

Each cover has to be sufficiently different from the one before so that readers feel as if they are getting something new every time they buy the magazine. This is important in order to encourage **repeat purchase**. At the same time, there has to be continuity from issue to issue in order to establish a sense of brand identity. This is typically achieved through a recognisable **house style**.

Key Terms

Repeat purchase
When someone buys the same brand or product that they have done previously, as in the case of readers who buy the same magazine every week or every month.

House style
The distinctive 'look', aesthetic or visual style of a magazine, which helps to convey a sense of its brand identity.

Analysing the Front Cover

When you analyse the front cover of your set magazine, you will need to consider the way in which different elements of media language communicate meanings to the reader, paying particular attention to layout and design as well as language and mode of address.

Tip

When analysing magazines, rather than just describing the particular conventions that you can identify, try to discuss *how* those particular conventions have been used, considering their purpose and effect. This will give your work more analytical depth.

Layout and Design

The key aspects of layout and design to consider when analysing the magazine cover include:

- The **typography**: what are the connotations of the font styles that are used? Are they serif or sans serif? Do they seem modern or traditional? Formal or informal? Masculine or feminine?
- **The colour scheme**: again, what does this connote? For example, the cover of the August 2015 UK edition of *Elle* (which can be found at https://hips.hearstapps.com/elleuk.cdnds.net/15/37/2048x2730/2048x2730-7bb5c30-29f7-11e6-9241-4bea1ac0dbe1-assets-elleuk-com-gallery-26328-august-cover-look-kai-z-feng-jpg.jpg) uses a palette of pale pink, grey and white, which works in conjunction with the other visual codes on the cover to connote sophistication, elegance and femininity.

Key Term

Typography
The font styles that are used. Serif fonts such as Times New Roman have short decorative lines, called serifs, added to the letters. They often look more traditional. In contrast, sans serif fonts, which lack the ornamental flourishes, often look more modern or contemporary.

- **The placement or positioning of the different elements on the cover**: for example, *Elle*'s cover star is cleverly integrated within the masthead. Her image therefore becomes a visual extension of the idea of femininity that the title of the magazine denotes.

Language and Mode of Address

Language and mode of address play an important role in engaging or attracting the reader. Some of the most commonly used features are:

- **Alliteration, assonance or rhyme**: this can give particular lines greater impact, helping to create audience appeal. The August 2015 edition of *Elle* uses alliteration in the cover line *'STREET STYLE FROM THE HIGH STREET'*, for example.
- **Imperatives**: these are often used to convey the idea that the reader must do as the magazine suggests. The cover line *'REFRESH YOUR LOOK'* in *Elle* uses an imperative, for instance.
- **A direct mode of address**: for example, the use of the second-person pronoun 'you' in *Elle*'s cover line *'UPDATE THE PIECES YOU ALREADY OWN'* makes it seem as if the magazine is speaking directly to the reader.

It is also important to consider the **lexis** that the magazine uses. As well as conveying a sense of genre, this can reveal a great deal about the underlying values of the magazine.

Barthes' Theory of Semiotics

A key theory that you will need to use when analysing magazines is semiotics. This theory is primarily concerned with signification – the process through which **signs** convey meaning. One of the basic premises of this theory is the idea that signs are composed of two key elements:

- **a signifier**: which is the material or physical form that the sign takes (this could be a written or spoken word, for example, or an image)
- **a signified**: which is the idea or concept that the signifier refers to or makes you think of.

Key Theory: Roland Barthes' Theory of Semiotics

- the idea that texts communicate their meanings through a process of signification
- the idea that signs can function at the level of denotation, which involves the 'literal' or common-sense meaning of the sign, and at the level of connotation, which involves the meanings associated with or suggested by the sign
- the idea that constructed meanings can come to seem self-evident, achieving the status of myth through a process of naturalisation.

In his theory of semiotics, **Roland Barthes** points out that some signs function at the level of denotation, which involves the 'literal' or common-sense meaning of the sign, whereas others function at the level of connotation and myth. This second **order of signification** involves the additional meanings that are associated with or suggested by the sign.

Key Terms

Lexis
The specific type of language or vocabulary that is used. The football magazine *Four Four Two* uses the lexis of sport, for example, while the women's lifestyle magazine *Glamour* uses the lexis of fashion and beauty.

Sign
A sign is something that stands in for or represents something else. A photograph or a drawing of a car, for example, is not the same as the thing itself (we cannot climb in and drive it); it is a sign that stands for the actual object.

Orders of signification
Roland Barthes draws a distinction between two 'orders' or 'levels' of signification. The first order of signification involves denotation. The second order of signification involves connotation and myth.

Named Theorist

Roland Barthes
Roland Barthes was a key semiotic theorist whose ideas you will need to be familiar with. The main principles of his theory of semiotics were outlined in the book *Elements of Semiology*, which was first published in 1964.

Quickfire 5.11

Analyse the font style that *Elle* uses for its masthead. What does this font style connote?

For example, if we look at the cover of the August 2015 UK edition of *Elle*, we can see that the main image of Lily Donaldson is a sign that is comprised of a signifier (the photographic image itself) and a signified (the person that the photographic image represents). This is the first order of signification. In other words, this is how the sign functions at the level of denotation.

However, what is interesting here is that the cover model has an *additional* meaning or significance, as she is also seen to signify beauty and elegance. These are the *connotations* of the image. The sign therefore becomes part of a second order of signification as it contributes to a particular cultural myth of femininity. In other words, it suggests that style, beauty and sensuality are *naturally* associated with femininity whereas this is in fact a cultural construct.

Key Terms

Paradigm
A set of related signs that the encoder can choose from – the set of colours that a magazine designer might choose from, for instance, or the set of font styles that they might select from. In choosing one sign rather than another, the encoder or media producer makes a paradigmatic choice.

Syntagm
A combination of signs that are linked together in particular ways. A sentence, for example, is a syntagm that is comprised of words placed in a particular sequence in order to convey meaning. Syntagmatic relations are the relations between different signs.

Paradigms and Syntagms

In order to convey the desired message, media encoders have to make sure that they choose the right signs – the words, images, colours or fonts that have the most appropriate meanings. The set of options that the encoder has to choose from is called a **paradigm**. One way of assessing the significance of the paradigmatic choices that the encoder makes is through a simple commutation test. This involves substituting one sign for another from the same paradigm in order to see how it might change the meaning of a text.

- If, for example, we were to substitute the pale pink outfit worn by Lily Donaldson on the cover of the August 2015 edition of *Elle* for the black high-tech bodysuit that Simon Pegg is seen wearing on the August 2015 cover of *Wired*, this would significantly alter the representation of gender that the image is seen to offer. This helps us to establish that the model's dress code is a key signifier of femininity.
- Similarly, if the two mastheads were to be swapped, we would get a very different impression of each magazine.

As well as making the right paradigmatic choices, the encoder also has to make sure that the different signs link or combine effectively in order to convey a coherent message. In semiotic theory, this combination of signs is called a **syntagm**. A magazine cover is a good example of this as the typography has to work with the cover image, the colour scheme, the layout and the lexis in order to convey certain meanings.

In the case of the August 2015 front cover of *Elle*, the colour scheme plays a particularly important role in establishing a link or connection between the different signs that are used. The dusky pink shade of the model's lipstick and eye-shadow is not only picked up by the colour of the decorative features that adorn her dress, it is also used for the model's name as well as other key words on the cover such as 'FASHION' and 'BEAUTY'. All of these signs work together syntagmatically to signify femininity.

Stretch and Challenge 5.11

Conduct a semiotic analysis of the front cover of the set magazine you are studying. Explore the connotations of the signs that are used and the significance of the paradigmatic choices that the encoder has made.

Inside the Magazine

When you analyse your set magazine, you will need to look at more than just the front cover. Eduqas/WJEC will tell you which particular extracts from the magazine you need to study.

While you need to be aware of the different ways in which media language might be used in articles and advertisements compared with magazine covers, the same critical approaches that we have outlined here can also be used to analyse the items inside the magazine. For example, when you analyse a magazine article, you still need to consider the language and mode of address that it uses as well as its layout and design.

Articles are generally designed using a grid layout. The grid is an organisational tool that provides the article with a coherent visual structure. It determines the size of the columns, the margins, the **alley** and the **gutter** as well as the placement and positioning of headlines and images.

Numerous variations are possible within this basic grid layout. A 'busy' layout can create a lively or dynamic feel, for example, while **white space** can be used to create a cleaner or more sophisticated look. Layout and design therefore play an important role in establishing the tone of an article.

Key Terms

Alley
The space between the columns of text.

Gutter
The space between two pages of text in a magazine.

White space
The area on the page that is free of text or images.

Anchorage
The way in which a caption or piece of written text holds or fixes the meaning of an image in place, encouraging the reader to make a preferred reading.

What are the Main Components of a Magazine Article?

A magazine article will generally feature some or all of the following elements:

- **a title or headline**: this establishes the subject of the article and is designed to engage the reader's attention
- **a stand-first or strapline**: this typically follows the title or headline and provides more information about the focus of the article or the angle it will take. Also called a **kicker**
- **pull quotes**: these are extracts that are drawn from the main body of the text and presented as a design feature, typically in a larger typeface. As well as breaking up long sections of text, they are also a useful means of highlighting key points and drawing the reader's attention to particular aspects of the article
- **body copy**: this is the main text of the article
- **images**: these generally support or illustrate the article, conveying particular messages and meanings
- **captions**: these provide **anchorage** for the images, encouraging the reader to interpret them in a particular way.

Magazine Genres

The magazine industry contains a huge range of different genres. These can be divided into three broad categories or groups:

- **Organisation magazines or customer magazines**: these publications are aimed at the customers of particular organisations or companies. *Waitrose Food* and *Tesco Magazine* are examples of this type of magazine. These supermarket magazines have some of the highest circulation figures in the UK.
- **Business or trade magazines**: these publications are aimed at people working in particular businesses, trades or professions. For instance, *Marketing Week* is a magazine for people working in the advertising or marketing industry.
- **Consumer magazines**: these publications are aimed at the general public and cover a wide range of interests. Some consumer magazines target relatively broad demographics while others target niche audiences, catering for more specialised interests.

Tip

The vast majority of magazines carry advertisements as these are a vital source of revenue. Don't overlook the advertisements – they are part of the 'flow' of the magazine. You can learn a great deal about a magazine's brand identity, values and target audience from the advertisements it carries.

Key Term

Sub-genre
A smaller category or subdivision within a larger genre.

The Women's Magazine Genre

Women's magazines are primarily defined in terms of their target audience and their content – they are aimed specifically at women and feature topics that are perceived to be of particular interest to a female demographic. The women's magazine genre also encompasses a number of different **sub-genres**. These include:

- lifestyle magazines such as *Glamour* and *Marie Claire*
- fashion magazines such as *Vogue* and *Harper's Bazaar*
- celebrity magazines such as *OK!* and *Hello!*
- real-life magazines such as *Pick Me Up!* and *Chat*.

A further distinction is often drawn between weekly and monthly women's magazines. Monthly magazines, which are sometimes referred to as 'glossies' due to the quality of the paper they are printed on and their luxurious look and feel, are generally seen as more aspirational than the weeklies, which tend to be more downmarket. However, the distinction between monthly magazines and weekly magazines has begun to blur in recent years, particularly with the launch of more 'upmarket' women's weeklies such as *Grazia*.

Woman and *Woman's Realm* are both examples of women's weeklies, whereas *Vogue* is a monthly women's fashion magazine.

Quickfire 5.12

Quickly list as many different magazine genres as you can think of.

The Content of Women's Magazines

The diversity of the women's magazine genre means that it has a very broad repertoire of elements. A women's magazine may, for example, include any of the following:

- health and beauty tips
- fashion spreads
- celebrity features
- sex and relationship advice
- recipes and cookery items
- sewing and knitting patterns
- fictional stories
- real-life stories
- problem pages
- readers' letters
- horoscopes.

The particular combination of elements found in each magazine and the relative weight that they are accorded will depend on a range of factors. For example, a magazine's **editorial philosophy** and the demographic and psychographic profile of its target audience will have a significant bearing on the content that it carries. A publication such as *Cosmopolitan*, which markets itself as a magazine for the modern woman, is less likely to feature knitting patterns and articles on cooking for the family than a more traditional women's magazine such as *Woman's Weekly*, for instance.

It is also important to bear in mind that the repertoire of elements a magazine uses may change over time as magazines have to be able to respond to the changing needs, tastes, interests and values of their readers. In some cases, it may even become necessary to rebrand or re-launch a magazine in order to re-establish its relevance and its market position.

Key Term

Editorial philosophy
Refers to a magazine's underlying values, attitudes and beliefs, and the particular viewpoint that it adopts. The editorial philosophy helps to determine the style and content of the magazine. It influences decisions regarding what should and what should not be included in the magazine, and shapes and informs the magazine's mode of address and the way in which the content is presented to the reader.

Social, Cultural and Historical Contexts

As we have already discussed, genres are not fixed or static, they are dynamic and historically relative – their codes and conventions evolve and adapt in relation to changes in the wider social and cultural context. This is as true of the women's magazine genre as it is of the crime drama, the spy thriller or the science-fiction series. Therefore, when you analyse your set magazine from the 1960s, one of the things that you will need to be aware of is how it relates to the social, cultural and historical context in which it was produced.

These are some of the issues that you may wish to consider when exploring the influence of social, cultural and historical contexts on the magazine you are studying:

- **The rise of consumerism during the 1950s and 1960s**: as wartime austerity gave way to a new era of economic prosperity, women's magazines were seen to enter a new phase. For example, **James Curran** suggests that, having gone through a 'make-do and mend' phase in the 1940s, middle-market women's magazines became part of the 'shop and spend' euphoria of the 1950s and 1960s.
- **The 1960s as a time of sexual revolution**: the 1960s were seen by many to herald a new era of female liberation. One of the most significant factors in this regard was the introduction of the contraceptive pill in the early part of the decade. Legislative changes such as the revision to the Married Women's Property Act that was made in 1964 also enabled women to gain a greater degree of financial independence than had previously been possible.
- **The 1960s as a time of cultural revolution**: the so-called 'swinging sixties' saw the emergence of new trends in music, fashion and films. Britain was very much at the centre of this cultural revolution.

Representation

Representation is one of the main areas of the theoretical framework that you will need to explore when studying your set magazine. As well as considering the way in which social groups and social identity are represented, you will also need to think about the values, attitudes and beliefs that these representations convey.

Gender Representation in Women's Magazines

The representation of gender in women's magazines is a subject of much critical debate. Discussions have largely focused on the messages and values that these representations convey and the influence that they might have on audiences, particularly in terms of gender **socialisation**.

The advice and guidance that women's magazines provide on various aspects of female identity, from fashion and beauty to sex and relationships, can be seen to have a significant effect in this regard. Readers are generally instructed on how to look, think and behave. An obvious example of this can be found in the problem pages that many magazines of this genre feature. The agony aunts who dispense advice are typically constructed as reassuring yet authoritative figures whose opinions readers are positioned to defer to.

Women's magazines convey messages to the reader about who they are expected to be and what it means to be a woman, both through the content they carry and the representations they offer. They are therefore seen to play a key role in shaping cultural understandings of gender identity.

Key figure

James Curran
James Curran is an academic and theorist whose work mainly focuses on media history and the political economy of the media.

Tip

It is important to note that not all magazines will respond to social and cultural changes in exactly the same way. For example, the 'make-do and mend' ethos that was so integral to women's magazines of the 1940s could still be seen in many magazines of the 1950s and 1960s.

Quickfire 5.13

In what ways could the introduction of the contraceptive pill be seen to have a revolutionary impact on women's lives?

Stretch and Challenge 5.12

Develop your understanding of British culture in the 1960s by conducting further research into this era. Who were the most popular or culturally significant music artists of the time? What films were being produced in Britain during the 1960s? What were some of the key fashion trends that emerged during this era? Who were the style icons of the 1960s?

Key Term

Socialisation
The process through which we learn the norms and values of our culture. Gender socialisation, for example, refers to the way in which we learn what is expected of us as men and women. The media are often said to play an important role in this regard, functioning as agents of socialisation.

Tip

When you analyse the representations of gender in your set magazine, try to consider how those representations have been constructed. Think about the way in which particular messages and meanings are encoded through the representations the magazine offers.

Quickfire 5.14

Peggy Makin and Georgette Floyd, the respective agony aunts of *Woman* and *Woman's Realm* during the 1960s, each wrote under pseudonyms – Peggy Makin's pseudonym was Evelyn Home while Georgette Floyd's was Clare Shepherd. Why do you think they chose these names? What connotations do they have?

Key Term

Pick and mix approach
The idea that audiences may pay attention to some media messages but disregard others. For example, Gauntlett refers to the 'pick and mix reader' who actively chooses which bits of the magazine to take notice of and which to ignore.

Gauntlett's Theory of Identity

One theorist who explores the impact of media representations on identity is **David Gauntlett**.

Named Theorist

David Gauntlett
Gauntlett's theory of identity is outlined in his book *Media, Gender and Identity: An Introduction*. You may find it especially useful to look at Chapters 3 and 9 – 'Representations of Gender in the Past' and 'Women's Magazines and Female Identities' – as these sections will be particularly relevant to the magazine you are studying.

Key Theory: David Gauntlett's Theory of Identity

- the idea that the media provide us with 'tools' or resources that we use to construct our identities
- the idea that whilst in the past the media tended to convey singular, straightforward messages about ideal types of male and female identities, the media today offer us a more diverse range of stars, icons and characters from whom we may pick and mix different ideas.

In his theory of identity, Gauntlett argues that the representations of gender that circulate in contemporary media products are more diverse and complex than those of previous generations. He suggests that today *'we no longer get singular, straightforward messages about ideal types of male and female identities'* – instead, the media appear to offer us an '*open realm of possibilities*' (*Media, Gender and Identity: An Introduction*, 2008, page 255).

According to Gauntlett's theory, media products provide us with tools and resources that we draw upon as we set about the task of constructing our identities. Therefore, rather than being manipulated or controlled by the media, Gauntlett suggests that we use the media to suit our own individual needs, taking a **pick and mix approach** as we borrow and combine different ideas from the various media products we consume.

This idea is particularly applicable to magazines as readers are typically presented with an array of images and lifestyles that they can select from as they construct a sense of self.

When you apply Gauntlett's theory to your set magazine, you will need to think about the relationship between representation and identity as well as the significance of the historical and cultural context in which the magazine was produced. In analysing the magazine's representations of gender you should consider the following questions:

- Does the magazine support Gauntlett's claim that in the past media representations offered singular, straightforward messages about ideal types of male and female identities?
- To what extent do the representations in your set magazine differ from those found in women's magazines today?

Domesticity and Gender Stereotypes in Women's Magazines

One of the main stereotypes that Gauntlett identifies with magazines of the past is the idealised figure of the perfect housewife. This stereotype has a long cultural history as traditional women's magazines have often placed particular emphasis on the **domestic sphere**, with women primarily represented as wives, mothers or homemakers.

Key Term

Domestic sphere
The private space of the home, as opposed to the public world of work, for example.

The stereotypical image of the 'happy housewife' who looked after the home and family while her husband went out to work was especially prominent in women's magazines of the 1950s and 1960s, even though around half of all working-age women were in paid employment during this time. By constructing domesticity as a feminine ideal, these magazines could be seen to reassert the importance of traditional gender roles.

This is an idea that **Betty Friedan** discussed in her book, *The Feminine Mystique*, which was published in 1963. She argued that the stereotypical image of the 'happy housewife' supported patriarchal understandings of gender by suggesting that 'true' female fulfilment or happiness could only be found in the domestic sphere. In other words, this type of representation, which conveyed the message that a woman's place was in the home, reinforced gender inequalities by containing women within a very limited set of roles – those associated with marriage, motherhood and homemaking.

The Sunday Cook

For the nicest, most leisurely, day of the week, Susan King chooses dishes with a difference for breakfast, lunch and tea

A cookery article from *Woman's Realm*, 13 February 1965

Key figure

Betty Friedan's *The Feminine Mystique* (1963) had a significant influence on the Second Wave feminist movement. In it, Friedan drew on her experiences writing for women's magazines in the USA.

Quickfire 5.15

How might the representation of the domestic sphere as a female domain reinforce particular cultural myths regarding gender?

Alternative Representations of Gender in the 1960s

One of the reasons why women's magazines of the 1960s are now so interesting to look at is because of the contrasting messages and images that were starting to circulate during this era.

While many magazines continued to reinforce the message that a woman's place was in the home, others offered more progressive representations of gender, reflecting a growing sense of female independence and liberation.

Magazines such as *Nova*, which was launched in 1965, were explicitly framed as an alternative to the more traditional women's magazine. This was clearly signalled by *Nova*'s tagline, '*A NEW KIND OF MAGAZINE FOR THE NEW KIND OF WOMAN*'. According to its editor, the 'new kind of woman' that *Nova* was targeting had '*a wide range of interests, an inquiring mind and an independent outlook*' (Janice Winship, *Inside Women's Magazines*, 1987, page 48).

When you analyse the representations of gender in your set magazine, you will need to explore how they relate to these different ideas and values. Does the magazine reinforce traditional gender stereotypes of the time, for example, or does it offer a sense of female liberation or independence? You may find that the magazine you are studying does both of these things to a certain extent. There may, for example, be some form of negotiation between traditional gender roles and a more progressive understanding of female identity. As David Gauntlett has pointed out, women's magazines often feature contradictory messages and images. It is important not to overlook these contradictions; instead, you should try to explore how and why they arise and what they signify or reveal.

Representations of Female Beauty

Women's magazines are often said to play a significant role in constructing cultural ideals of female beauty. In so doing, they continually impress upon the reader the importance of physical appearance as a defining aspect of female identity.

As **Marjorie Ferguson** has pointed out, women's magazines constantly reiterate the need to 'Be More Beautiful', first telling their readers what they should aspire to look like and then providing them with the necessary tools to achieve the desired 'look'.

Readers are constantly encouraged to scrutinise and evaluate their own physical appearance, measuring themselves against the ideals of beauty that the magazines construct. Therefore, rather than simply promoting self-confidence and helping readers to overcome any insecurities they already have, it is often suggested that women's magazines play an instrumental role in creating and instilling these anxieties.

Key figure

Marjorie Ferguson

Before moving into academia, Marjorie Ferguson was an associate editor of a weekly women's magazine. Her book, *Women's Magazines and the Cult of Femininity* (1983) and her essay 'Imagery and Ideology: The Cover Photographs of Traditional Women's Magazines' (in Barbara Tuchman (ed.), *Hearth and Home: Images of Women in the Mass Media*, 1978) have had a significant influence on the study of women's magazines.

This is generally seen to have a commercial purpose as, in order to measure up to the beauty ideal, readers are invited to buy various products – firstly, of course, the magazine itself, but also the array of hair, fashion and beauty products that are promoted or advertised inside. By turning readers into consumers, the magazines are able to keep their advertisers happy. This is particularly important as women's magazines generally depend on advertising for much of their revenue.

Readers are also invited to prove or demonstrate their femininity by participating in the rituals of beautification. Femininity, like beauty, is therefore seen as something that has to be constantly worked at, as the magazines frequently suggest that should the reader fail to invest the necessary time, money and effort in her physical appearance she runs the risk of losing her femininity.

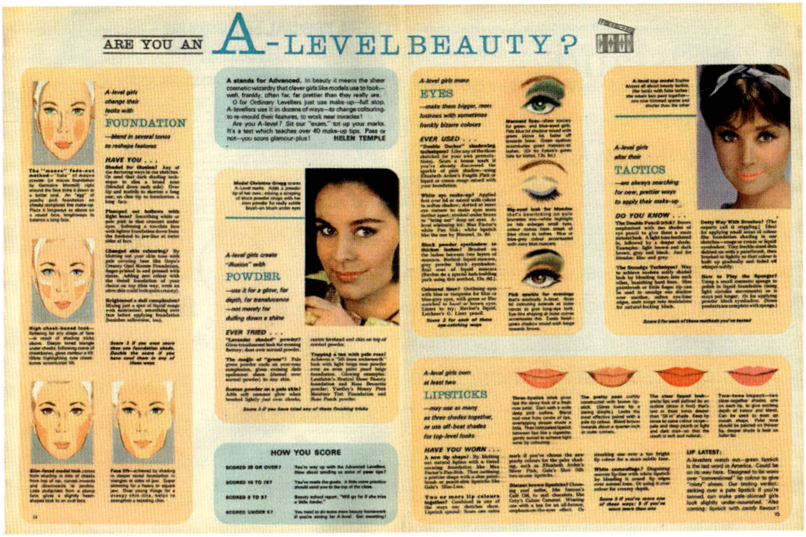
ARE YOU AN A-LEVEL BEAUTY?

A stands for Advanced. In beauty it means the sheer cosmetic wizardry that clever girls like models use to look—well, frankly, often far, far prettier than they really are. O for Ordinary Levellers just use make-up—full stop. A-levellers use it in dozens of ways—to change colouring, to re-mould their features, to work near miracles! Are you A-level? Sit our "exam," tot up your marks. It's a test which teaches over 40 make-up tips. Pass or not—you score glamour-plus! HELEN TEMPLE

A-level girls change their looks with FOUNDATION —blend in several tones to reshape features

HAVE YOU . . .

A-level girls create "illusion" with POWDER —use it for a glow, for depth, for translucence —not merely for dulling down a shine

EVER TRIED . . .

A-level girls make EYES —make them bigger, more lustrous with sometimes frankly bizarre colours

EVER USED . . .

A-level girls alter their TACTICS —are always searching for new, prettier ways to apply their make-up

DO YOU KNOW . . .

A-level girls own at least two LIPSTICKS —may use as many as three shades together, or use off-beat shades for top-level looks

HAVE YOU WORN . . .

LIP LATEST:

HOW YOU SCORE

Feature article from *Woman*, 29 August 1964

A key question that needs to be addressed here is, who is the reader being encouraged to make herself more beautiful for? While the quest for female beauty may be framed in terms of self-improvement, the need to win male approval is often an underlying theme. As Marjorie Ferguson has pointed out, *'getting and keeping a man'* is commonly seen as a primary goal in women's magazines. Making oneself more attractive is therefore presented as a woman's 'duty'.

You may wish to consider some of these issues when you analyse your set magazine. For example:

- What messages does the magazine convey about female beauty?
- How is female beauty defined?
- How is the reader positioned in relation to the representations that the magazine offers? Are the models, stars or celebrities who feature in the magazine constructed as aspirational figures? If so, how?
- To what extent does the magazine define a woman's value in terms of the way that she looks?

Key Terms

Tokenism
Providing a cursory or superficial representation of those groups in society that are often under-represented in order to convey an impression of equality and inclusivity.

Whitewashing
This term can refer to the process through which a person who is not white is made to appear white. It is also used to describe the way in which ethic minorities are written out of the media.

Exotic other
A term used to describe someone or something that is perceived to be different or 'foreign', where that difference or otherness becomes a source of fascination or pleasure.

Stretch and Challenge 5.13

Look at the covers of a few mainstream women's magazines that have been produced during different historical periods. Which particular racial or ethnic groups appear to be under-represented? To what extent do the more recent magazine covers show a greater sense of racial or ethnic diversity?

Key Term

Dual revenue streams
Media products that generate revenue from two different sources (from readers and advertisers, for example) are said to have dual revenue streams.

Quickfire 5.16

In what ways could a recession or an economic downturn impact on a magazine's revenue streams?

Representations of Race, Ethnicity and National Identity

As well as looking at gender representation, you will also need to explore the way in which other aspects of social identity such as race, ethnicity and national identity are represented in your set magazine.

Mainstream women's magazines have often been criticised for a lack of racial and ethnic diversity as it is images of white women that tend to feature most prominently in these publications. While black cultural icons such as Beyoncé, Rihanna, Michelle Obama and Naomie Harris have all appeared on the covers of various women's magazines in recent years, it could be argued that these representations remain largely **tokenistic** as black, Asian and minority ethnic women are still generally under-represented.

Furthermore, the few black celebrities who do feature in mainstream women's magazines are sometimes said to be **whitewashed** as the lighting set-ups or editing techniques that are used often make their skin tone appear lighter. Many critics have therefore argued that these magazines help to cultivate a white beauty myth, as female beauty is defined in relation to a white ideal.

Alternatively, rather than concealing or denying racial and ethnic differences through whitewashing, women's magazines sometimes highlight or fetishise these differences by constructing black, Asian or minority ethnic women as the **exotic other**. In this way, racial or ethnic differences are treated as an object of fascination and visual pleasure. Again, this could be seen to demonstrate the way in which representations of race and ethnicity in mainstream magazines are typically mediated through a controlling white gaze.

Industry

The Economic Context of Magazine Publishing

Magazine publishing, like television production, takes place within an economic context. You will therefore need to consider the influence of economic factors on the set magazine product you are studying.

A key question here is how magazines are funded. While some magazines are financed entirely through the cover price or the cost of subscription, the vast majority have **dual revenue streams** as they rely on advertising for a significant proportion of their revenue. In some cases, over half of a magazine's total revenue will come from advertising alone. It is important to bear this in mind as it means that magazines generally have to attract advertisers as well as readers in order to be commercially successful.

This also explains why publishers sometimes cut the cover price of their titles or give away free copies of the magazine. The boost in circulation that this provides will often make a magazine more appealing to advertisers, as it means that they can broaden their market reach.

For example, when Hearst UK decided to cut *Cosmopolitan*'s cover price from £3.80 to £1 in 2015, the magazine's year-on-year circulation rose by over 50%. While this increase in circulation would not, on its own, be enough to cover the reduction in cover price, it helped to re-establish *Cosmopolitan* as a market leader in the women's lifestyle magazine sector, making it much more attractive to advertisers.

Ownership and Control in the Magazine Industry

As well as exploring how magazines are funded, you also need to consider the significance of patterns of ownership and control in the magazine industry. **Curran and Seaton**'s theory of power and media industries provides a useful critical framework in this regard.

Key Theory: James Curran and Jean Seaton's Theory of Power and Media Industries

- the idea that the media is controlled by a small number of companies primarily driven by the logic of profit and power
- the idea that media concentration generally limits or inhibits variety, creativity and quality
- the idea that more socially diverse patterns of ownership help to create the conditions for more varied and adventurous media productions.

Concentration of ownership is often the result of **horizontal integration**. For example, one of the ways in which the major publishing houses have been able to consolidate their power in the magazine industry is by acquiring or merging with rival publishers. This effectively reduces competition, as power is concentrated in the hands of fewer companies.

There are different critical perspectives regarding the consequences of this concentration of power. Some theorists, such as Curran and Seaton, claim that this has a negative impact on media industries and audiences. They argue that media concentration not only limits or inhibits variety, creativity and quality, but also reduces choice for consumers. This is partly because major companies are **risk averse** and constantly look for ways to minimise costs and maximise profits. For instance, when one publisher buys out another, they may decide to merge or close some of their titles, rationalising their resources in order to produce economies of scale.

However, other critics dispute the idea that concentration of ownership has a detrimental effect on diversity and innovation. They argue that the major publishers are much better equipped to cater for a wide range of audiences as their size and economic power makes it far easier for them to launch new titles as audience tastes change and new markets emerge. Rather than limiting creativity, the financial stability they have gives them the freedom to innovate.

IPC in the 1960s: A Vertically Integrated Media Conglomerate

The mid-20th century is a particularly interesting era to look at in terms of concentration of ownership, as a series of acquisitions and mergers took place in the magazine industry around this time, culminating in the creation of the International Publishing Corporation (IPC) in 1963.

IPC was formed following a merger between the Mirror Group, which owned a large portfolio of national newspapers, and three of the biggest publishers in the magazine industry – Odhams Press, George Newnes and Fleetway.

Named Theorists

James Curran and Jean Seaton
Curran and Seaton's theory of power and media industries is outlined in their book, *Power without Responsibility* (1981), which provides a useful overview of the history of British media.

Quickfire 5.17

Name two key concerns regarding concentration of ownership in the magazine industry.

Key Terms

Horizontal integration
The process through which different companies that produce, sell or distribute similar products join together through a merger or acquisition. This reduces competition and enables companies to increase their market share.

Risk averse
Describes companies that are unwilling to take risks and that avoid them wherever possible. This means that they often adhere to an established formula and avoid doing anything different that might have a negative impact on sales.

Odhams, which was the original publisher of *Woman* and *Woman's Realm*, had already taken over George Newnes and the Hulton Press – two of its main competitors – in 1958. The subsequent merger between Odhams, Newnes, Fleetway and the Mirror Group saw a further concentration of media ownership as IPC established itself as *'the largest newspaper and periodical printing group in the world'* (Howard Cox and Simon Mowatt, *Revolutions from Grub Street: A History of Magazine Publishing in Britain*, 2014, page 91). Its holdings at this time included nine national newspapers, 78 consumer magazines and comics, and 126 trade and technical journals. Book publishing was another area that IPC was involved in.

As this demonstrates, major media companies often attempt to consolidate their power by moving into other sectors of the media rather than concentrating on one particular area of business. This process is called **diversification**. Large organisations such as IPC that are involved in a variety of different businesses are called **conglomerates**.

Another factor that made IPC such a powerful force during the 1960s was its ownership of several large-scale, high-speed printing plants. This meant that it could print its titles in high volume and high quality. *Woman* and *Woman's Realm* were both able to carry a significant number of colour advertisements, for example. Companies, such as IPC, that have control over different stages or levels in the production and distribution process, are said to be **vertically integrated**. Historically, the most powerful magazine publishers have tended to be vertically integrated companies.

Key Terms

Diversification
This involves expanding a company's operations into new or different areas of business.

Conglomerate
A large organisation that owns other companies and has interests spanning across a number of different businesses or industries. For example, the Walt Disney Company is a media and entertainment conglomerate as it has business interests in several different industries, including film, television, music and radio as well as the theme park industry.

Vertical integration
A process through which a company develops control over different levels of the value chain. An example of a vertically integrated business would be a production company that is also able to distribute its products or a magazine publisher that owns a printing company.

Condé Nast and Advance Publications

While IPC established control over the weekly women's magazine market during the 1960s, publishers such as the National Magazine Company, whose titles included *Good Housekeeping* and *Harper's Bazaar*, and Condé Nast, which publishes *Vogue* and *House and Garden*, remained highly competitive in other sectors of the consumer magazine market.

Condé Nast was one of the first publishers to launch international editions of its magazines. While *Vogue* was originally an American publication, a British edition of the magazine was launched in 1916. This was followed by several other international editions including *Vogue Paris* and *Vogue Italia*. These titles were published through Condé Nast International – the international arm of the company.

Unlike IPC, Condé Nast did not own any printing plants in the UK, although it did own a printing company in the USA. However, its long-term contract with the Sun Engraving Company gave it access to some of the highest-quality printing presses in the country. Having the means to produce high-quality colour images was particularly important for *Vogue*, which, as an upmarket fashion magazine aimed at a niche audience, depended on advertising for much of its revenue.

Since 1959, Condé Nast has been owned by the American media company Advance Publications. Originally a newspaper publisher, Advance Publications diversified during the 1950s and 1960s as it moved into other industries such as magazine publishing and broadcasting, acquiring a number of American television stations and magazines to add to its growing roster of newspaper titles. This process of diversification and horizontal integration helped to establish Advance Publications as a powerful media conglomerate.

Audience

When analysing your set magazine product, you will need to consider how audiences are grouped and categorised by the magazine industry, how magazine publishers target, attract, reach, address and potentially construct audiences, and how audiences interpret and respond to magazines in particular ways.

Grouping and Categorising Magazine Audiences

As we have already discussed, most magazines generate a significant amount of their revenue through advertising. The amount that publishers are able to charge for advertising space within a magazine largely depends on the size and nature of their audience. Grouping and categorising audiences is therefore vitally important in the magazine industry, as publishers have to be able to demonstrate their ability to reach particular demographic and psychographic groups in order to persuade advertisers to buy space in their publications.

For this reason, most publishers provide potential advertisers with **readership** and **circulation** figures as well as information about the age and socio-economic grouping of their readers. Together with these demographic details, a psychographic profile of the reader may also be offered. This might include information about the average reader's tastes and spending habits – how much money they typically spend each month on beauty products, for example, or how often they go to the cinema. This is usually included in a media kit or media pack, together with a rate card outlining how much it will cost to advertise in the magazine.

Key Terms

Readership
An estimate of how many readers a publication has. As most publications have more than one reader per copy, the readership estimate is very different from the circulation count. These figures were previously produced by the National Readership Survey (NRS), which operated from 1956 until 2018. They are now provided by the Publishers Audience Measurement Company (PAMCo).

Circulation
A count of how many copies of a particular publication are distributed, including subscriptions. Circulation audits are provided by the Audit Bureau of Circulations (ABC).

Readership and Circulation

PAMCo and the Audit Bureau of Circulations (ABC) play a particularly important role in the magazine industry as they provide publishers and advertisers with vital data on readership and circulation.

PAMCo categorises audiences using demographic variables such as age, sex, ethnicity and marital status as well as socio-economic status or social grade. The social grade method of classifying newspaper and magazine readers was developed by the National Readership Survey (NRS) in 1956 and has been widely used in the publishing industry ever since. In this system, readers are given a grade based on the occupation of the chief income earner (CIE) in their household.

Social grade	Occupation
A	Higher managerial, administrative and professional
B	Intermediate managerial, administrative and professional
C1	Supervisory, clerical and junior managerial, administrative and professional
C2	Skilled manual workers
D	Semi-skilled and unskilled manual workers
E	State pensioners, casual and lowest-grade workers, unemployed with state benefits only

The NRS social grade classification system

Tip

Remember that a magazine's readership may change over time. Those who read *Woman* or *Vogue* today may not belong to the same demographic or psychographic groups as those who read the magazines in the 1960s.

As there is a strong correlation between income and social grade, knowing the proportion of a magazine's readers that fall within each of these demographic categories can be extremely useful both for publishers and for advertisers. For example, magazines that have a high percentage of AB or ABC1 readers often carry advertisements for more expensive brands, as these readers are likely to have higher levels of disposable income. Magazines with a predominantly C2DE readership are more likely to carry advertisements for everyday brands.

PAMCo also gathers valuable information about the tastes, interests and lifestyles of readers. Respondents are typically asked about the topics that they look at when reading a magazine. They are also asked whether they have bought any particular products in the past year as a result of advertisements they have seen in magazines. All of this information enables publishers and advertisers to target audiences more effectively.

Audience Interpretations and Responses

The extent to which magazines influence the behaviour, attitudes and beliefs of their readers is a widely discussed issue. Some critical approaches tend to suggest that magazines simply impose their views and values on a passive audience, and hence have a direct and immediate influence over readers. However, this theory of media effects, which is sometimes referred to as the hypodermic syringe model, is seen by many as a rather crude and outmoded way of thinking about the relationship between media producers and audiences.

Key Theory: George Gerbner's Cultivation Theory

- the idea that exposure to repeated patterns of representation over long periods of time can shape and influence the way in which people perceive the world around them (i.e. cultivating particular views and opinions)
- the idea that cultivation reinforces mainstream values (dominant ideologies).

Named Theorist

George Gerbner
George Gerbner was an academic whose work explored the way in which the media could be seen to influence people's perceptions of reality. While he focused primarily on the cultural influence of television, his cultivation theory can be applied to many different media forms.

Gerbner's Cultivation Theory

An alternative way of thinking about the effects that magazines have on their readers is offered by **George Gerbner**'s cultivation theory.

Gerbner's theory differs from the hypodermic syringe model in two important respects:

- it focuses on the effects of *long-term* exposure rather than suggesting that media products have an *immediate* effect on audiences
- it suggests that audience views are shaped or cultivated by *patterns* of representation rather than by single media products in isolation.

As women's magazines tend to be read on a regular basis, they would seem to lend themselves particularly well to Gerbner's theory. Many critics argue that the patterns of representation that recur across the genre play a key role in constructing and maintaining **gender norms**, shaping the way in which readers perceive men and women and their respective roles and positions in society.

Key Term

Gender norms
Cultural expectations regarding how men and women should act or behave – the patterns of behaviour that a particular society considers to be 'normal' for men or women.

Stretch and Challenge 5.14

Consider how Gerbner's theory might be applied to the set magazine you are studying. In what ways, for example, might the representations that it offers be seen to cultivate particular values, attitudes and beliefs in its readers?

Hall's Reception Theory

Another audience theory that can be used to explore the way in which audiences interpret and respond to magazines is Stuart Hall's reception theory. This provides a particularly useful framework for exploring the different ways in which the messages in women's magazines may be decoded.

Key Theory: Stuart Hall's Reception Theory

- the idea that communication is a process involving encoding by producers and decoding by audiences
- the idea that there are three hypothetical positions from which messages and meanings may be decoded:
  - **i.** the dominant-hegemonic position: the encoder's intended meaning (the preferred reading) is fully understood and accepted
  - **ii.** the negotiated position: the legitimacy of the encoder's message is acknowledged in general terms, although the message is adapted or negotiated to better fit the decoder's own individual experiences or context
  - **iii.** the oppositional position: the encoder's message is understood, but the decoder disagrees with it, reading it in a contrary or oppositional way.

In contrast to the hypodermic syringe model, Hall's theory recognises that readers do not all interpret media products in the same way:

- some readers may adopt what Hall refers to as the **dominant-hegemonic position**, making a preferred reading of the messages that the magazine conveys, interpreting them exactly as the encoder intended
- some readers may assume what Hall refers to as the **negotiated position**, as they broadly accept the magazine's messages in general terms but adapt them in some way to better reflect their own experiences or situations. Readers may, for example, choose to overlook or modify parts of the magazine that are less directly relevant to them. This is similar to Gauntlett's concept of the 'pick and mix reader' who chooses which parts of the magazine to pay attention to and which to ignore
- some readers may disagree with the messages that the magazine conveys, making an **oppositional reading** of the text. They may, for example, disagree with the values that underpin the magazine's representations of gender or ethnicity.

In applying Hall's reception theory to the magazine you are studying it is important to consider how particular aspects of the reader's identity might affect the way in which they read or respond to the product.

- How might their gender, ethnicity, sexuality or social class affect the way in which they read the magazine, for example?
- How might their own attitudes, values and beliefs affect the way in which they interpret the representations that the magazine offers?

Key Terms

Dominant-hegemonic position
The position that the media encoder encourages the decoder to adopt when interpreting a text. If they adopt the dominant-hegemonic position they read or interpret the message in the way that the encoder intended, making a preferred reading.

Negotiated position
The position an audience takes if they acknowledge the broad legitimacy of the messages a media product contains but adapt those messages to better reflect their own experiences.

Oppositional reading
The interpretation an audience member makes of a media product if they disagree with the messages or values it conveys.

Uses and Gratifications Theory

Another audience theory that is particularly useful when considering the relationship between magazines and audiences is Blúmler and Katz's uses and gratifications theory. Again, this differs significantly from media effects theories such as the hypodermic syringe model. Rather than seeing the audience as a passive mass that is manipulated to think and act in certain ways by the media, the uses and gratifications theory suggests that audiences actively seek out media products in order to satisfy particular needs. The four main needs that are identified in the uses and gratifications theory are:

- the need for information (surveillance needs)
- the need for diversion, escapism or entertainment
- the need for personal identity
- the need for social interaction and integration.

Magazines can be seen to meet these particular needs in a number of different ways, as researchers such as Joke Hermes (*Reading Women's Magazines*, 1995) have shown. Hermes conducted extensive interviews with readers of women's magazines in order to find out how they used these products. One of her main findings was that women's magazines are primarily used as a means of relaxation. The fact that they are 'easy to put down' was said to be a particular source of appeal as they could be made to fit within the routines of everyday life.

In order to explore the uses and gratifications your set magazine offers, you may find it helpful to address the following questions:

- What particular information or advice does the magazine offer its readers?
- In what ways could the magazine be seen to distract or divert its readers from the routines of everyday life? What particular pleasures does it offer?
- How might the magazine be used to construct or consolidate a sense of identity?
- In what ways might the magazine be seen to facilitate a sense of belonging? What opportunities does it provide for interaction with others?

The key critical theories that we have outlined here should enable you to explore the various ways in which different audiences might use, interpret and respond to the magazine you have studied.

Summary

Key Points

Having read this section on magazines, you should now be familiar with:

- the codes and conventions of the magazine as a media form
- the significance of layout and design, and language and mode of address
- the dynamic and historically relative nature of the women's magazine genre
- the way in which representations of gender, race and ethnicity convey particular values, attitudes and beliefs.
- the significance of patterns of ownership and control in the magazine industry
- the way in which magazine audiences are grouped and categorised, and the different ways in which readers may interpret and respond to a magazine
- the significance of the social, cultural, historical and economic contexts in which magazines are produced.

You must be able to apply this knowledge and understanding to your set products.

Essential Theories for Magazines

When discussing your set magazine product, you must be able to use the following theories:

- **Semiotics**, including Barthes: for example, the way in which magazines convey messages and meanings through a process of signification.
- **Theories of identity**, including Gauntlett: for example, the idea that in the past magazines offered singular, straightforward messages about ideal types of male and female identities, and the idea that readers may take a 'pick and mix' approach to the magazines they read.
- **Power and media industries**, including Curran and Seaton: for example, the idea that historically the magazine industry has been controlled by a small number of companies driven by the logic of profit and power, and that the general trend has been towards concentration of ownership.
- **Cultivation theory**, including Gerbner: for example, the idea that patterns of representation in women's magazines cultivate particular attitudes and beliefs in their readers.
- **Reception theory**, including Hall: for example, the idea that readers may adopt different positions in relation to the magazines they read.

Guidance for A Level Students

Remember that if you are studying magazines at A level, you will also need to use the following theories when analysing your set magazine products:

- **structuralism**, including Lévi-Strauss
- **feminist theories**, including bell hooks and van Zoonen
- **cultural industries**, including Hesmondhalgh.

Guidance regarding these theories can be found in the *WJEC/Eduqas Media Studies for A Level Year 2* book.

» Section C: Online Media

The Specification

If you are following the linear Eduqas specification, online media is one of the media forms that you are required to study in depth. At AS level, you will be required to study one set online product, while at A level you will be required to study two set online products including one that targets or is produced by a minority audience.

This section introduces some of the key approaches that can be used to study online media products, with a specific focus on blogs and vlogs. Further guidance regarding the online products that are only studied at A level can be found in the *WJEC/Eduqas Media Studies for A Level Year 2* book.

WJEC

If you are following the modular WJEC specification, you are required to study a newspaper and its online version, a news website and an online radio source as well as looking at how a news event is reported across a range of social media sites for the 'News in the Online Age' section of Unit 1. While the focus of this chapter is primarily on lifestyle and entertainment vlogs rather than news-oriented sites, you may find the material covered here useful in terms of providing a general introduction to issues and debates regarding the role of online media in contemporary culture.

Online Media Options

As part of your investigation into online media in Component 2, you are required to study one of the following online products:

Option 1: JJ Olatunji/KSI www.youtube.com/user/KSIOlajidebtHD

- JJ Olatunji, better known as KSI, is a successful YouTuber, music artist and entrepreneur who has built a significant following from his gaming and entertainment vlogs.

Option 2: Zoe Sugg www.youtube.com/channel/UCrUbqTCagwsaP2Fmr0p1TsA https://zoella.co.uk/

- Zoe Sugg is a successful British blogger, YouTuber and entrepreneur. As well as her YouTube channel, where she posts videos about her day-to-day life, she also has a beauty and lifestyle blog that operates under her 'Zoella' brand.

When studying your set online product, you will need to explore the following:

- the codes and conventions of the home page, including aspects of layout and design
- examples of posts, such as specific blogs, vlogs or articles from the online products
- examples of interactivity, including links to and use of social and participatory media.

A Level Online Media Options

If you are taking the A level course, you will also study one of the following online products targeting or produced by a minority group.

- *gal-dem* – an online magazine produced by and for people of colour from marginalised genders
- the website of the gay lifestyle magazine *Attitude*.

Using the Theoretical Framework

In exploring your set online product, you will need to consider all four areas of the theoretical framework. Therefore, in this section we will look at:

- **the media language of online products**: how blogs, vlogs and websites communicate meanings through their codes, conventions and techniques
- **representation**: the way individuals and social groups are represented in blogs, vlogs and websites
- **industry**: the impact of recent technological change on media production, distribution and circulation as well as the significance that economic factors hold for online media forms
- **audiences**: how the producers of blogs and vlogs target, attract, reach, address and potentially construct audiences, and how audiences interact with and respond to online media products.

Media Language

In recent years, digital technologies and the growth of the internet have dramatically altered the media landscape, challenging traditional understandings of the relationship between media producers, products and audiences. The emergence of new online media forms such as blogs and vlogs has played an instrumental role in this regard, reflecting the cultural shift towards user interaction, participation, connection and collaboration that is often said to characterise the **Web 2.0** era.

The growing cultural significance of **content creators** such as KSI and Zoe Sugg is not only evident in the number of subscribers that their YouTube channels attract, it is also apparent in the way their images circulate within the mass media and mainstream culture. For example, KSI has featured as the cover star of *The Sunday Times* magazine supplement, while Zoe Sugg has appeared on the cover of the *Mail on Sunday*'s *You* magazine, as well as featuring on Band Aid 30's re-recording of 'Do They Know It's Christmas?' in 2014, when she became one of the first non-music artists to appear on a Band Aid charity single. Further evidence of YouTubers' status as cultural icons can be found in Madame Tussauds, where a wax figure of Sugg, along with her partner and fellow YouTube star, Alfie Deyes, was unveiled to mark the launch of the museum's new YouTube-themed area in 2015.

KSI and Zoe Sugg can be seen as prime examples of what Jean Burgess and Joshua Green refer to, in their book *YouTube: Online Video and Participatory Culture* as YouTube stars – figures who, *'despite their carefully cultivated "homegrown" brand identities, seem to be making a living via advertising revenue, reaching large audiences with content produced within and for YouTube, often with their own external websites as well'* (2009, page 24).

The Zoe Sugg and Alfie Deyes waxworks in London's Madame Tussauds

Key Terms

Web 2.0
A new phase in the Internet's development, characterised by interactivity, user participation, connection and collaboration.

Content creators
Those who are involved in creating and sharing content online – bloggers and YouTubers for example.

Quickfire 5.18

Why do you think Zoe Sugg was invited to participate in the Band Aid 30 charity single? How might her participation in the project be seen as beneficial?

Conventions of the Blog as a Media Form

A blog is a regularly updated website that features a series of entries posted in reverse-chronological order. This means that the most recent entries or 'posts' appear first.

Blogs tend to be far more interactive than more traditional media forms. As well as including **hyperlinks** that enable users to navigate between different parts of the website, most blogs allow readers to respond to posts by adding their own comments at the bottom of the blog page. Significantly, this not only enables users to interact with the **blogger**, it also enables them to interact with one another.

Types of Blog

Blogs come in many different forms and have a wide range of purposes or functions. They can be political or personal, instructional or journalistic. Some are created by amateurs while others are produced by professionals. They may be commercial or non-commercial. They also cover a wide range of topics. There are food blogs, health blogs, film blogs, travel blogs, research blogs and news blogs to name just a few.

One of the most popular types of blog is the fashion, beauty and lifestyle blog. These blogs may be journalistic in tone, reporting on the latest developments in the fashion and beauty world, or they may be more personal, offering an insight into the everyday life and interests of the blogger. For example, the blogger may share their personal beauty routines or discuss the places they have recently been to. This can be an important source of audience appeal as the blogger is able to build a more intimate relationship with their readers. While Zoella was originally more of a *personal* fashion, beauty and lifestyle blog, as Zoe Sugg would write it all herself from her bedroom in Wiltshire, it has since evolved into a magazine-style blog and is now produced by a team of editorial staff working out of an office in Brighton, with Sugg in the role of Editor-in-Chief.

Types of Vlog

The term **vlog** is used to describe a blog in video form. Again, it is possible to identify many different types of vlog. These include:

- **Personal vlogs**. Videos in which the vlogger shares their thoughts, experiences or feelings with viewers. The vlogger generally uses a direct mode of address, speaking straight into the camera in the style of a video diary. The predominant use of close-ups combined with minimal editing helps to foster a sense of intimacy and authenticity. The illusion of face-to-face conversation that this creates is commonly described as **para-social interaction**.
- **Fashion and beauty vlogs**. These may include:
  - Demonstration or tutorial videos in which the vlogger shows viewers how to achieve a specific look or how to use a particular technique. Hairstyle and makeup tutorials are common examples of this type of video.
  - Haul videos in which the vlogger displays and discusses the shopping purchases they have made (their 'haul').
  - Reviews – videos in which the vlogger reviews or comments on specific fashion or beauty products.

Key Terms

Hyperlink
A word, phrase or image in an electronic document or web page that the reader can click on to navigate to a different part of the document or a different page.

Blogger
Someone who engages in blogging, which is the practice of updating or adding material to a blog. The term blog is short for weblog.

Stretch and Challenge 5.15

Compare the homepage of Zoe Sugg's website (www.zoella.co.uk) with that of another fashion, beauty and lifestyle blog. What similarities can you identify in terms of content, layout and design? What codes and conventions do they both use?

Key Terms

Vlog
A blog in video form. Short for video blog.

Para-social interaction
The illusion of face-to-face conversation constructed through techniques such as a direct mode of address. The term was originally coined by Horton and Wohl in their article 'Mass Communication and Para-social Interaction: Observations on Intimacy at a Distance', which was first published in *Psychiatry* 19 in 1956. While Horton and Wohl's concept of para-social interaction was initially applied to mass media forms such as television, it has subsequently been applied to online media forms such as blogs and vlogs.

- **Entertainment vlogs**. This is a broad category that encompasses comedy sketches and pranks as well as challenges and competitions.
- **Gaming vlogs**. These may include:
  - **Walkthroughs**: videos in which a gamer demonstrates how to complete certain stages or levels in a video game, providing viewers with gaming tips and strategies.
  - **'Let's play' videos**: videos in which a gamer records themselves playing a video game, usually accompanied by their own personal commentary. 'Let's play' videos tend to be less instructional than walkthroughs as their primary purpose is to entertain. One of the most popular producers of this type of video is Felix Kjellberg, otherwise known as PewDiePie. PewDiePie's YouTube channel currently has over 110 million subscribers. KSI is also a notable exponent of the 'Let's play' genre.

Key Terms

Walkthrough
A demonstration of how to play a video game in which the vlogger 'walks' the viewer through the necessary stages or levels.

'Let's play' video
A recording of someone playing a video game, usually accompanied by some form of commentary.

Analysing Blogs and Vlogs Using Semiotic Theory

When you analyse your set online product you will need to use semiotic theory. As we discussed in the previous section, semiotics is primarily concerned with the processes through which signs convey meaning.

Key Theory: Roland Barthes' Theory of Semiotics

- the idea that texts communicate their meanings through a process of signification
- the idea that signs can function at the level of denotation, which involves the 'literal' or common-sense meaning of the sign, and at the level of connotation, which involves the meanings associated with or suggested by the sign
- the idea that constructed meanings can come to seem self-evident, achieving the status of myth through a process of naturalisation.

In applying semiotic theory to the online product you are studying, you should consider the significance of the paradigmatic choices that have been made as well as the connotations of the various signs that are used.

For example, when analysing the homepage of a blog or vlog it is important to think about the significance of its design. Although homepages often follow a similar format and have the same basic layout, there may be certain design features that contribute to the visual branding of the product. For instance, one of the ways in which YouTubers create a brand identity for their channel is through the customised banner that appears at the top of their homepage. This often includes a symbolic sign in the form of a logo. The images, colours and typography that are used can also help to convey messages and meanings about the product, establishing a particular mode of address.

Quickfire 5.19

What is the difference between denotation and connotation?

Semiotics can also be used to analyse the images or videos that feature on a blogger or vlogger's website or YouTube channel. Consider the significance of the setting, for example. What connotations does this have? What can you see in the shot? How does the mise-en-scène convey messages and meanings?

You should also analyse the vlogger or blogger's **non-verbal communication**. What does their facial expression or posture connote? Think about the significance of the gestural codes they use. Analyse their dress codes. How do these aspects of non-verbal communication help to construct a sense of their identity or persona?

Representation

Gauntlett's Theory of Identity

In exploring the representations that your set online product offers, you will need to consider **David Gauntlett**'s theory of identity.

Key Theory: David Gauntlett's Theory of Identity

- the idea that the media provide us with 'tools' or resources that we use to construct our identities
- the idea that whilst in the past the media tended to convey singular, straightforward messages about ideal types of male and female identities, the media today offer us a more diverse range of stars, icons and characters from whom we may pick and mix different ideas.

As we discussed in the previous section on magazines, a key element of this theory is the idea that the media provide us with some of the tools that we use to carry out identity work. In other words, we draw on the representations that we find in the media as we set about the task of constructing our sense of self.

What is particularly significant about the new age of online media is that it offers us a much greater variety of resources to draw on as we undertake this task. As images and messages multiply online in seemingly limitless ways, this contributes to *'the perception of an open realm of possibilities'* (Gauntlett, page 287). In other words, the plurality and diversity of online media representations gives us much more choice in terms of how we create and communicate a sense of who we are.

An important part of Gauntlett's theory of identity is the idea that the media provide us with resources in the form of stories. He suggests that *'we use these narratives to frame our experiences and to bring order to the stream of "stuff" that goes on in our lives'* (page 288). In this way, the stories that circulate in the media *'provide an opportunity for individuals to think about the kind of person they want to be'* (*Media, Gender and Identity: An Introduction*, 2008, page 272).

Key Term

Non-verbal communication
Communication that doesn't involve words. The way in which we communicate messages and meanings through our facial expressions, our body language and our tone of voice for example.

Named Theorist

David Gauntlett
Gauntlett's theory of identity is outlined in *Media, Gender and Identity: An Introduction* (2008). Chapter 11, 'Exploring Identity Stories,' provides a particularly useful framework for thinking about identity construction in relation to online media. Gauntlett's later book *Making is Connecting* develops these ideas further as it explores debates regarding the role and uses of online media in everyday life.

Stretch and Challenge 5.16

Look at the comments that have been posted by users of the online media product you are studying. What evidence can you find to support Gauntlett's suggestion that we use media products such as these to *'frame our experiences and to bring order to the stream of "stuff" that goes on in our lives'*?

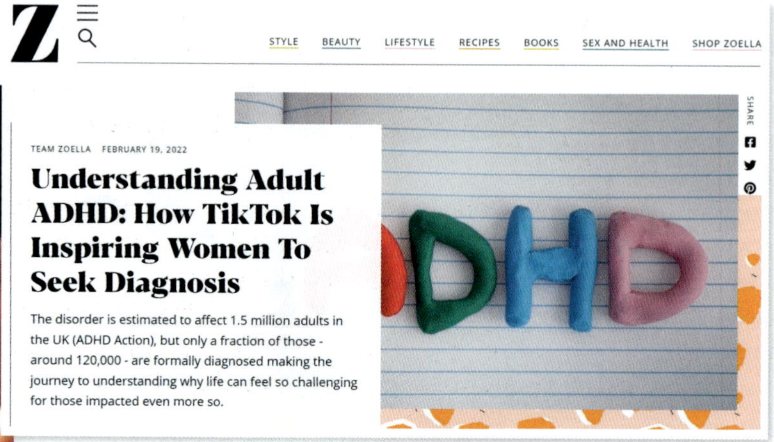

Zoe Sugg and KSI have both used social media to highlight a range of issues relating to mental health.

This is a particularly useful way of thinking about the function and appeal of blogs and vlogs. For example, by sharing their personal stories and experiences online, bloggers and vloggers such as Zoe Sugg and KSI provide fans with a means of imposing order and meaning on the 'stuff' that they experience in their own day-to-day lives.

Hall's Theory of Representation

Another theorist whose work you will need to consider when analysing representation in your set online product is Stuart Hall.

Key Theory: Stuart Hall's Theory of Representation

- the idea that representation is the production of meaning through language, with language defined in its broadest sense as a system of signs
- the idea that the relationship between concepts and signs is governed by codes
- the idea that stereotyping, as a form of representation, reduces people to a few simple characteristics or traits
- the idea that stereotyping tends to occur where there are inequalities of power, as subordinate or excluded groups are constructed as different or 'other' (e.g. through ethnocentrism).

As we discussed in the earlier section on television, the basis of Hall's theory is the idea that *'representation is the production of meaning through language'* (Stuart Hall, *Representation*, 2013, page 2). Language in this broader sense is a representational system or a system of signs. As Hall points out:

> *In language, we use signs and symbols … to represent to other people our concepts, ideas and feelings. […] Representation through language is therefore central to the processes by which meaning is produced.* (page xvii)

In applying this theory to your set online product, you may find it useful to consider how the content creator represents their concepts, ideas and feelings through the signs and symbols that Hall refers to. For example, if you are analysing a blog, you could explore how written words combine with photographic images to produce particular meanings. Similarly, in the case of a vlog, you may find it instructive to analyse the way in which sounds, images or objects contribute to the representations that the set product offers.

Self-representation

Self-representation is a key area that you will need to explore when studying your set online product. Significantly, online media forms such as blogs and vlogs enable content creators to create and disseminate representations of themselves without the need for intermediaries. This is one of the main ways in which they differ from more traditional mass media forms.

While the seemingly unmediated nature of these representations helps to create a greater sense of authenticity, it is important to remember that these representations are constructed through processes of selection and combination. For example, in choosing what to disclose or share with their viewers and what to withhold, bloggers and vloggers are able to represent themselves in particular ways. The **gatekeeping** function they perform therefore has a significant influence in terms of the persona they construct.

Tip

Further discussion of Hall's theory of representation can be found in the earlier section on television.

Stretch and Challenge 5.17

As a way of exploring the concept of self-representation you may find it useful to consider your own social media use. For example, if you use social media platforms such as Facebook and Instagram, think about the way in which you represent yourself online and the processes of selection and construction that this involves.

Key Terms

Gatekeeper
A person or organisation that is involved in filtering content in some way. For example, in the newspaper industry, editors generally perform this gatekeeping function as they determine which stories make it into the paper (through the gate) and which do not.

Tip

While lifestyle magazines and beauty blogs and vlogs share certain similarities in terms of the kind of content they include and the functions they perform, it is important not to ignore the differences between these media forms.

Key figure

Germaine Greer
Germaine Greer is an academic and theorist whose works such as *The Female Eunuch* (1970) and *The Whole Woman* (1999) have made a significant contribution to the second-wave feminist movement and the development of feminist theory.

Tip

Although Germaine Greer is clearly critical of the emphasis placed on beautification in cultural products aimed at young girls, you should also consider alternative viewpoints. Is there a more positive way of reading the functions that beauty blogs and vlogs perform?

Representations of Gender

As well as looking at self-representation, you will also need to look at how aspects of social identity are represented in your set online product. Think about the representations of masculinity or femininity that your set product offers, for example, considering the following questions:

- To what extent does it reinforce or challenge gender stereotypes?
- Does it use a gender-specific mode of address?
- What topics and interests does it cover or explore? Are these gendered in any particular way?

For example, the emphasis on fashion and beauty that is commonly found in blogs and vlogs aimed at women and girls could be seen to reinforce stereotypical understandings of gender. In many ways, the function that these products perform, particularly in terms of gender socialisation, is similar to the role that has traditionally been performed by women's lifestyle magazines.

Look, for instance, at the following quote from **Germaine Greer**'s book *The Whole Woman* (1999, page 28) where she discusses the messages that circulate in magazines aimed at young girls:

> *Magazines financed by the beauty industry teach little girls that they need make-up and teach them to use it, so establishing their lifelong reliance on beauty products.*

The makeup tutorials and demonstrations that feature prominently on the YouTube channels of beauty bloggers such as Zoe Sugg could be said to perform a similar function. Significantly, these channels are also financed by the beauty industry through sponsorship and advertising deals.

'Get Ready With Me (On The Hottest Day Ever!)' – an example of a sponsored beauty tutorial on Zoe Sugg's YouTube channel

Industry

Online Media and the Impact of Recent Technological Change

The impact of the internet on media industries is a widely discussed issue. Some theorists argue that the rise of online media has disrupted the power structures that traditionally operate within media industries to a significant extent. However, others claim that this has simply reinforced the dominance of major corporations, as they have been able to consolidate their cultural and economic power by exploiting the commercial potential that these new platforms offer. What lies at the heart of this debate is the extent to which recent technological change has democratised the media by enabling 'ordinary' users to create and distribute their own content without the need for professional intermediaries.

Traditionally, decisions regarding what does and does not get produced, published, distributed or broadcast have been made by media professionals working within particular organisations. For example, in the television industry it is generally the channel controllers or Directors of Programming who determine whether a programme is commissioned or broadcast. Similarly, in the magazine industry, it is the editors who decide whether an article should be published. These media professionals function as gatekeepers as they control the audience's access to the media. The decisions they make are influenced by the institutional contexts in which they work.

However, recent technological change has made it easier for individual content creators to bypass these gatekeepers. For instance, all a vlogger needs to produce and distribute video content to audiences around the world is a digital camera or a webcam and access to the internet. This has led to a huge growth in **user-generated content** over the past decade, demonstrating that media production and distribution are no longer the preserve of a professional media elite.

Key Terms

User-generated content
Material created by everyday users of media platforms rather than by professionals working for media organisations.

Tip

The relationship between recent technological change and media production, distribution and circulation is a specific aspect of the theoretical framework that you are required to explore when studying your set online product.

The Economic Context of the Online Media Industry

While the rise of new online media platforms can be seen to mark a democratisation of the media by placing more power in the hands of amateur content creators, it is important to remember that these platforms are not entirely free of commercial interests. Major corporations and businesses operate within these online spaces too.

A number of YouTube Spaces, providing content creators with access to professional workshops and studio facilities, were set up in cities around the world between 2012 and 2018. Although several of these spaces, including those in London, Los Angeles and New York, were permanently closed following the Covid pandemic, facilities in Sao Paolo, Mumbai and Dubai continue to operate.

Key Term

Web traffic
The number of people who visit a particular page or website.

Multi-channel networks
Organisations that curate a large number of channels, offering creators support in areas such as video production as well as marketing and promotion.

Monetisation
The process through which a product or service – a blog or vlog for example – is converted into a source of commercial revenue.

Algorithm
A set of steps or rules that are followed in order to make a calculation, solve a problem or complete a task – the steps involved in determining which advertisements are most suitable for a particular website, for example.

Digital influencer
Someone with a significant online following who has the ability to shape and influence the opinions or behaviour of their followers. Also known as an online influencer.

Stretch and Challenge 5.18

Trackalytics provides information regarding how much advertising revenue YouTube channels generate, along with other quantitative data about subscribers, views and comments. Use the website trackalytics.com to find out more information about the set product you are studying.

Channels or vlogs with large numbers of subscribers can be highly lucrative due to the amount of **web traffic** they generate. This has led to the rise of **multi-channel networks** (MCNs) – organisations that curate hundreds or thousands of different channels. MCNs typically offer content creators assistance with marketing, promoting and **monetising** their channels in return for a percentage of their advertising revenue. Some MCNs also produce content themselves.

KSI signed to Polaris, a gaming subnetwork of the large MCN, Maker Studios, in 2013. Maker Studios was then purchased by the Walt Disney Company for $500 million two years later, becoming part of the Digital Disney Network. This shows how major corporations have sought to capitalise on the commercial potential that new online media forms offer.

Significantly, YouTube is itself owned by a multinational technology company, having been bought by Google for $1.65 billion in 2006, a year after it was first launched.

Advertising

One of the main ways in which content creators generate revenue is through advertising. For example, the YouTube Partner Programme enables creators who have achieved a certain number of channel views to monetise the content they produce by running advertisements alongside their videos. The advertising revenue that this generates is then shared between YouTube and the content creators.

The advertisements that feature on a YouTuber's channel can take various forms. These include:

- Display ads or banners which generally appear beside or below the video that is being played.
- Overlay ads which are placed over the top of the video content in the lower portion of the video.
- Video ads which appear before, during or after the video. Those that appear before the video are called pre-roll ads. Video ads may be skippable or non-skippable. Skippable ads provide viewers with the option to skip the advert after a certain number of seconds, whereas non-skippable ads have to be watched in their entirety. Shorter, non-skippable ads that are up to six seconds long are called bumper ads.

A significant advantage that online media has over traditional mass media forms is that advertising can be targeted to match the tastes and interests of individual users based on their personal browsing histories and the information that is gathered about them whenever they go online. For example, Google's AdSense program uses **algorithms** to place carefully targeted advertisements on the websites of those who sign up to use the service.

Sponsorship

Sponsorship is another important source of revenue. This is where content creators are paid to review, endorse or promote particular brands or products. Beauty bloggers may be paid to demonstrate certain cosmetic products for example, while gamers may be paid to feature particular video games in their 'let's play' videos or walkthroughs.

The endorsement of **digital influencers** can have a significant effect on sales. Therefore, companies are often willing to pay bloggers and vloggers substantial sums of money to promote their products. While in some cases the content creator is paid a set fee, in others they are paid according to the number of views their page generates or the number of people who click through to the promoted product from their web page.

Merchandising and Diversification

Many vloggers, bloggers and YouTubers also have their own branded merchandise. This is usually available for purchase via an online store on the creator's website. The type of merchandise that each creator sells varies but it may include:

- clothing such as branded t-shirts, hoodies, caps and beanies
- accessories such as branded phone cases, PopSockets, wristbands, keyrings and jewellery
- stationery such as branded notebooks, pens and pencils
- branded mugs, water bottles and backpacks.

As well as generating revenue, merchandising also helps to build **brand recognition**. It is common, for example, for merchandise to feature a logo, slogan or catchphrase that is closely associated with the content creator. PewDiePie's merchandise often features his distinctive 'BroFist' logo for instance.

As this demonstrates, content creators often look to diversify as they move beyond the online world into other commercial sectors, extending their brand across a range of different platforms and products. Zoe Sugg previously had her own range of Zoella-branded beauty products, for example, and has since worked with the sexual wellness brand, SheSpot, to curate a subscription box of sexual wellness and intimate care products, while KSI has worked with Adidas to launch a limited edition sneaker. Sugg has also helped to produce a video editing app and an Instagram template app – products that are likely to be of particular interest to other prospective content creators.

Book publishing is another area that content creators often move into. This helps to create **synergy** as books can be used to push readers towards a creator's blog or vlog while the blog or vlog can be used to promote the book. Downloadable apps may also be included with the book, encouraging readers to interact via social media.

This is also an example of **convergence** – a process that **Henry Jenkins** defines as *'a move from medium-specific content toward content that flows across multiple media channels, toward the increased interdependence of communications systems* [and] *toward multiple ways of accessing media content'* (*Convergence Culture: Where Old and New Media Collide*, 2006, page 254). Jenkins uses the term **transmedia storytelling** to refer to the way in which story fragments can be dispersed across different media platforms, with each platform making a unique contribution to the storytelling process.

Regulating Online Media

A specific issue that you will need to explore when looking at online media is the impact that new digital technologies have had on media regulation. In many ways, online media is more difficult to regulate than traditional mass media forms such as television, radio, newspapers and magazines. Monitoring the millions of new blog posts that are created every week or the thousands of hours of new footage that are uploaded to YouTube every day presents a far greater challenge than monitoring the output of licensed television broadcasters, for example. This is partly because of the quantity of media content being produced and distributed online and partly because this content comes from so many different sources.

Key Terms

Brand recognition
The extent to which a brand can be quickly and easily identified. Brand recognition is often facilitated by visual codes such as logos.

Synergy
A term used to describe the cross-promotion of products – the theme song for a Bond movie such as *Spectre* will help to promote the film for instance, while the film will also help to promote the theme song. Synergy is therefore about different products and processes working together.

Convergence
The process through which different media industries and forms merge with one another or move closer together. This process is often facilitated by digital technologies. For example, smartphones bring together many different functions in a single device – as well as making phone calls, users can browse the internet, play games, watch video content and listen to music.

Transmedia storytelling
Defined by Henry Jenkins as *'a process where integral elements of a fiction get dispersed systematically across multiple delivery channels for the purpose of creating a unified and coordinated entertainment experience'* ('Transmedia Storytelling 101', 2007, available online).

Key Figure

Henry Jenkins
Henry Jenkins is an American academic who has published widely on a range of topics. Much of his work focuses on media convergence, participatory culture, fandom and the changing nature of the audience in the digital era. If you are taking the A level course, Jenkins' theory of fandom is one of the specific theories that you are required to study. This is discussed in the *Media Studies for A Level Year 2* book.

Quickfire 5.20

What is the name of the organisation that provides age ratings for music videos uploaded to Vevo and YouTube by UK record companies?

Key Terms

CAP Code
This is the Advertising Code that covers non-broadcast media. The Code is written by the Committee of Advertising Practice (CAP) and administered by the ASA. Its full title is the 'UK Code of Non-broadcast Advertising and Direct and Promotional Advertising'.

Advertorial
An advertisement that is presented in the style of the media product in which it features. An advertorial vlog, for instance, is an advertisement that is presented by the vlogger in their usual editorial style.

Metadata
The additional or contextual information that accompanies an online video, such as the title and description of the video as well as tags and thumbnails.

Stretch and Challenge 5.19

Research YouTube's 'Community Guidelines' in more detail, looking at the kind of content that can and cannot be shown. These guidelines can be found in the 'Policy and Safety' section of the website.

There are also questions regarding who should be responsible for regulating online content – whether this should be the responsibility of internet service providers (ISPs), the companies who own social media platforms such as Twitter and Facebook, or whether there is a need for wider regulation by independent bodies or national governments.

The convergent nature of online media platforms such as YouTube is a further complicating factor here. For example, the fact that YouTube hosts many different media forms from film trailers to music videos to advertisements means that there are several different stakeholders involved in regulating the content it carries.

The Regulation of Advertising in Blogs and Vlogs

Bloggers and vloggers are also subject to regulation by the Advertising Standards Authority (ASA). For example, the **CAP Code** stipulates that paid-for content in blogs and vlogs, whether in the form of advertisements, **advertorials** or sponsored content, must be clearly signposted to users in order to ensure that audiences are not misled.

Further to this, bloggers and vloggers are required to comply with consumer protection laws. In the UK, these laws are enforced by the Office of Fair Trading (OFT) while in the US a similar role is performed by the Federal Trade Commission (FTC). Again, one of the key elements of these laws is the need to declare promotions and sponsorships so as not to mislead consumers. Failure to comply with these laws can lead the OFT or FTC to impose sanctions on offending bloggers and the organisations that sponsor them. For example, Warner Bros. were censured for contravening FTC regulations in 2014 as several digital influencers including PewDiePie failed to disclose that they had been paid thousands of dollars to produce gameplay videos featuring the Warner Bros. game *Middle Earth: Shadow of Mordor*.

YouTube 'Community Guidelines'

In addition to these regulations, YouTube has its own 'Community Guidelines', which cover issues such as:

- nudity or sexual content
- violent or graphic content
- hate speech or hateful content
- spam, misleading **metadata** and scams
- harmful or dangerous content
- copyright
- threats.

These guidelines are intended to make YouTube not only a user-friendly environment but also an advertiser-friendly environment. For example, as part of its Partner Programme policies, YouTube encourages creators to produce content that is appropriate for all audiences and therefore 'advertiser-friendly', warning that videos that do not comply with these policies may not be eligible for monetisation. This shows the way in which commercial or economic factors can shape and influence media content.

YouTube can also impose age restrictions in order to protect younger audiences from unsuitable content. Like many other social media platforms, it also provides users with the facility to flag content that they believe to be inappropriate. Once a video has been flagged, it is reviewed by a member of YouTube staff. Videos that violate the 'Community Guidelines' are then removed. In more serious cases, users' accounts may also be terminated.

Audience

Targeting and Attracting Audiences

The way in which media producers target, attract, reach, address and potentially construct audiences is something that you will need to consider when exploring your set online product.

In terms of audience targeting, you will need to look at two key areas:

- How audiences are targeted through the content and appeal of online media products.
- How audiences are targeted through the ways in which online media products are marketed, distributed and circulated.

You will find that some of the ideas we discussed in the earlier sections on 'Media Language' (pages 181–184) and 'Representation' (pages 184–187) are also relevant here. For example, we have already explored the way in which the mode of address that bloggers and vloggers use can facilitate para-social interaction. This is an important source of audience appeal.

Collaboration Videos

Another way in which content creators target, attract and reach audiences is through **collaboration videos**. This can help to broaden a vlogger's fan-base, as appearing in a video alongside another creator enables them to reach a wider audience.

A commonly used strategy is to create two separate collaboration videos or to divide the video into two parts. One video can then be uploaded to the channel of one creator and one to the channel of the other. This means that viewers have to visit both channels in order to see the two videos.

Collaboration videos will often end with a **call to action** as viewers are encouraged to subscribe to the channel of each creator. A link in the description box on the video page is conventionally used to facilitate navigation between channels.

Collaboration videos such as 'Mark felt the baby kicking and things we don't share online', with Zoe Sugg and Mark Ferris can help to expand a YouTuber's audience.

Festivals, Conferences and Conventions

Audiences can also be targeted through festivals, conferences and conventions. Events such as these play an important role in the marketing of online media products. VidCon, for example, is described as a convention *'for people who love online video'* (vidcon.com). Staged annually in the United States, it attracts thousands of visitors every year. As well as providing those who work in the online video industry with a chance to network and exchange ideas, the convention offers fans an opportunity to see their idols in person. Featured creators participate in a range of events from talks, interviews and **Q & A sessions** to signings and **meet-and-greets**.

Key Terms

Collaboration video
A video that features two or more content creators working together in collaboration.

Call to action
An instruction that is issued to the audience with the aim of prompting an immediate response – the instruction to 'subscribe now' or to click on a link, for example. This technique is widely used in advertising and marketing.

Quickfire 5.21

What is para-social interaction?

Quickfire 5.22

In what way could collaboration videos be seen as an example of synergy?

Stretch and Challenge 5.20

Consider how the persona that the content creator constructs or projects can be used to target and attract audiences by creating audience appeal.

Key Terms

Q & A session
An abbreviation for question and answer session. At a public event such as a convention, the questions may be supplied by interviewers or journalists or by members of the audience. Many vloggers and bloggers also hold Q & A sessions online.

Meet-and-greet
An event at which a celebrity or public figure meets and interacts with their fans.

In addition to the original American convention, which has been running since 2010, a number of international versions have been launched in recent years, reflecting VidCon's growing global reach. For example, there is now VidCon Australia, VidCon Asia, Vidcon Mexico and VidCon Abu Dhabi, as well as VidCon London. These conventions attract some of the most successful figures working in the online video industry. Felix Kjellberg (PewDiePie), Jimmy Donaldson (Mr Beast), Charli D'Amelio, Khaby Lame and Tana Mongeau have all appeared at VidCon events, as have KSI and Zoe Sugg.

There have also been similar events in the UK. The most popular and long-running of these is Summer in the City, *'the UK's largest YouTube and online video festival'* (sitc-event.co.uk). Like VidCon, Summer in the City is an annual event that caters for industry professionals and fans, featuring seminars and discussion panels as well as live performances and meet-and-greet sessions with creators.

Public Appearances

Public appearances at awards ceremonies and film premieres are also useful in marketing terms as these red carpet events are often covered in the mass media. This can help online creators gain greater exposure and reach a broader audience, as their images circulate in television, newspaper and magazine reports of the event.

These events also provide an opportunity for creators to interact directly with their audiences. For example, as they walk down the red carpet, they will often pose for selfies with fans. This has an additional benefit as fans will often share the photographs they take via social media. In this way, they become active participants in the marketing and promotion of the content creator.

Stretch and Challenge 5.21

Try to find out more about the festivals and conferences that KSI or Zoe Sugg have appeared at. What appeal do events like these have for audiences?

KSI posing for photographers at the Brit Awards in London in February 2022.

Content creators such as Zoe Sugg and KSI have also embraced more traditional media forms, appearing in various magazines as well as featuring on different television programmes and radio shows. This is a useful means of extending their brand identity and star image while reaching different audiences. Sugg and KSI have both appeared on the celebrity edition of *The Great British Bake Off* in aid of charity, for instance.

KSI has taken part in a number of well-publicised boxing bouts against other YouTubers, including Logan Paul. He has also established himself as a successful music artist.

Audience Interaction and Participation

Online media is a particularly interesting area to explore in terms of how audiences interact with the media and how they can be actively involved in media production. These are specific aspects of the theoretical framework that you are required to consider when studying your set online product.

However, the extent to which audiences can now be regarded as media creators is the subject of some debate. As **David Buckingham** points out, there is a problem in defining what the difference between participation and 'creating content' is. For example, *'There's a big difference between posting an occasional comment on an online forum or a social networking profile, and filming, editing and posting a video'* (David Buckingham, 'In the Age of Media 2.0', *MediaMagazine 39*, February 2012, page 8).

While the degree to which audiences actively create their own media content may be open to question, there is no doubt that online platforms enable users to interact with content creators, media products and other users in a variety of different ways. As David Gauntlett argues, YouTube is *'not just a site where videos are hosted, it's a place where conversations and connections are developed'* ('Creativity and Digital Innovation', in Gillian Youngs (ed.), *Digital World: Connectivity, Creativity and Rights*, 2013, page 81).

Stretch and Challenge 5.22

What do you notice about the public events that the online creator you are studying has appeared at? What do they tell you about their target audience?

Stretch and Challenge 5.23

Try to find out which television programmes, radio shows, video games or magazines Zoe Sugg or KSI have appeared in. What audiences were they able to target through these appearances?

Key Figure

David Buckingham
David Buckingham is an academic and theorist whose work focuses on youth, media and education. His essay, 'In the Age of Media 2.0', which is published in *MediaMagazine 39*, provides a useful introduction to key issues and debates relating to media participation in the online age.

Tip

These debates about the extent to which audiences have become active producers who are part of a participatory culture will be explored more fully in the *WJEC/Eduqas Media Studies for A Level Year 2* book where we look in more depth at the work of theorists such as Henry Jenkins and Clay Shirky. These are two of the named theorists for A level. Although you do not have to look at Jenkins' and Shirky's theories at AS level, you may find it useful to do so.

Named Theorist

George Gerbner
See the 'Magazines' section of this chapter for further discussion of Gerbner's cultivation theory (page 176).

What is significant about these conversations and connections is that they become part of the online products themselves. For example, content creators often solicit audience interaction and participation by asking those who read their blogs or watch their videos to provide feedback in the form of 'likes' or comments. This feedback is typically displayed on the blog or video page where other users can respond or join in the conversation. Creators may also ask their fans or subscribers what they would like to see in future blogs or videos. In this way, audiences can be seen to have a direct influence on online media products.

This not only demonstrates how audiences interact with online media and how they can be actively involved in media production, it also demonstrates the interrelationship between media technologies and patterns of consumption and response. Again, these are key aspects of the theoretical framework that you need to be familiar with when analysing your set online product.

Gerbner's Cultivation Theory

As well as looking at how audiences interact with online media forms such as vlogs and blogs, it is also important to consider the extent to which their values, attitudes and beliefs might be shaped by the products they engage with online.

Key Theory: George Gerbner's Cultivation Theory

- the idea that exposure to repeated patterns of representation over long periods of time can shape and influence the way in which people perceive the world around them (i.e. cultivating particular views and opinions)
- the idea that cultivation reinforces mainstream values (dominant ideologies).

George Gerbner's cultivation theory is particularly relevant in this regard. This is one of the specified theories that you are required to explore when studying your set online product.

Although Gerbner was primarily concerned with the effects of *television* viewing on audiences, the fact that many people, particularly in younger demographic groups, now spend more time engaging with online media than they do with traditional media forms suggests that their views of social reality are more likely to be cultivated by online content creators such as KSI and Zoe Sugg than by television programmes. Significantly, Ofcom's 2022 'Online Nation' report found that '*For most people in the UK, being online is a major part of daily life*', with UK adult internet users spending an average of 3 hours 59 minutes a day online. This figure rises to an average of 5 hours 6 minutes a day for young adults aged 18–24.

One of the concepts that Gerbner refers to in his theory is resonance. This is the idea that the effects of cultivation are likely to be more pronounced when the media messages that a viewer encounters resonate with their own day-to-day experiences. In other words, the more a media text matches the everyday reality of the individual's own life the more likely it is to shape their view of the world.

This is something that you may wish to consider when exploring your set online product. How might the topics it addresses and the representations it offers resonate with the experiences of the target audience? Look at the comments that users have posted on the blog or video page, for example. Is there any evidence to suggest that the online product you are studying has shaped or cultivated the attitudes, values and beliefs of its users?

Summary

Key Points

Having read this section on online media, you should now be familiar with:

- the way in which digital technologies and the internet have changed the relationship between media producers, products and audiences in the Web 2.0 era
- the conventions of online media products such as blogs and vlogs
- issues regarding self-representation and the representation of social identity in blogs and vlogs
- the way in which online media products can be monetised through sponsorship and advertising
- the way in which bloggers and YouTubers target and attract audiences through the content and appeal of their products and through the marketing strategies they employ
- the way in which users interact with online media products.

You must be able to apply this knowledge and understanding to your set products.

Essential Theories for Online Media

When discussing your set online product, you must be able to use the following theories:

- **Semiotic theory**, including Barthes: for example, the idea that blogs and vlogs convey their meanings through a process of signification.
- **Theories of identity**, including Gauntlett: for example, the idea that online media products provide users with an array of resources with which to construct their identities.
- **Theories of representation**, including Hall: for example, the idea that online representations are constructed through media language.
- **Cultivation theory**, including Gerbner: for example, the idea that over time blogs and vlogs may come to shape and influence the way in which users see the world around them.

Guidance for A Level Students

Remember that if you are studying online media at A level, you will also need to use the following theories when analysing your set online products:

- **structuralism**, including Lévi-Strauss
- **postmodernism**, including Baudrillard
- **theories of gender performativity**, including Butler
- **theories around ethnicity and postcolonial theory**, including Gilroy
- **regulation**, including Livingstone and Lunt
- **cultural industries**, including Hesmondhalgh
- **fandom**, including Jenkins
- **'end of audience' theories**, including Shirky.

Guidance regarding these theories can be found in the *WJEC/Eduqas Media Studies for A Level Year 2* book.

6 Component 2: Investigating Media Forms and Products Assessment

How Will I Be Assessed?

The Component 2 examination assesses your knowledge and understanding of media language, representation, media industries, audiences and media contexts in relation to the three media forms that you have studied in depth: television, magazines and online media.

The examination is 2 hours long. It counts for 35% of the qualification.

The paper consists of three sections:

- **Section A: Television**
- **Section B: Magazines**
- **Section C: Online media.**

In each section, there will be one two-part question or one extended response question based on the set product you have studied for that particular media form. The question may be on any area of the theoretical framework.

Some questions may ask you to apply or discuss a particular theory. The table below shows which theories you need to have studied for each of the three media forms.

	Television	Magazines	Online media
Semiotics, including Barthes		✓	✓
Narratology, including Todorov	✓		
Genre, including Neale	✓		
Theories of representation, including Hall	✓		✓
Theories of identity, including Gauntlett		✓	✓
Power and media industries, including Curran and Seaton		✓	
Cultivation theory, including Gerbner		✓	✓
Reception theory, including Hall	✓	✓	

Tip

Each section carries the same number of marks. However, if the question is in two parts you should check to see how many marks are available for each part of the question as this will give you an indication of how much you are expected to write.

Tip

The table shows the key theories that you must be able to use when studying each media form. This does not mean that you have to limit yourself to just these theories though. For example, although you are not specifically required to use Gerbner's cultivation theory when studying your set television product you may find it useful to do so.

Tip

A short summary of the key ideas of each of the named theorists you are required to study is included at the end of this book.

Component 2: What Changes at A Level?

At A level, you are required to study an additional set product for each of the three media forms studied in depth.

	Television	Magazines	Online media
AS level	*Peaky Blinders* or *Black Mirror* or *Killing Eve*	*Woman* or *Woman's Realm* or *Vogue*	JJ Olatunji/KSI or Zoe Sugg
A level	*Peaky Blinders* and *The Bridge* or *Black Mirror* and *The Returned* or *Killing Eve* and *Tehran*	*Woman* and *Adbusters* or *Woman's Realm* and *Huck* or *Vogue* and *The Big Issue*	JJ Olatunji/KSI or Zoe Sugg and *gal-dem* or the *Attitude* website

At A level, you will also be required to study more complex and challenging theories in addition to those studied at AS level. The additional theories studied at A level are:

Media Language

- Structuralism, including Lévi-Strauss
- Postmodernism, including Baudrillard

Representation

- Feminist theories, including van Zoonen and bell hooks
- Theories around ethnicity and postcolonial theory, including Gilroy
- Theories of gender performativity, including Butler

Media Industries

- Regulation, including Livingstone and Lunt
- Cultural industries, including Hesmondhalgh

Audiences

- Fandom, including Jenkins
- 'End of audience' theories, including Shirky

At A level, you will also be expected to evaluate and reflect critically on the theories you study.

Tip

Remember that the theories that are specific to the A level course are additional to those that are studied at AS level.

Tip

Specific guidance regarding the set products and advanced theories to be studied at A level can be found in the *WJEC/Eduqas Media Studies for A Level Year 2* book.

7 Component 3: Media Production

OVERVIEW

The aim of this component is to:

- allow you to demonstrate your knowledge and understanding of media products
- illustrate your skills in research, planning and production
- bring together elements you have learned during the course
- allow you to show your knowledge and understanding in a practical way
- allow you to apply your knowledge and understanding of the theoretical framework:
  - media language
  - representation
  - media industries
  - audiences.

Tip

A brief will be set for you by WJEC/Eduqas. A brief outlines what you need to do for your internally assessed work and what is expected of you. It may also incorporate deadlines set by your teachers to ensure you manage your time effectively.

Key Terms

Industry context
This includes aspects of production, including the media organisation, production processes, distribution and marketing, and regulatory issues.

Tip

In order to ensure that you do not spend an undue amount of time on your production work, it should all be completed in no longer than eight weeks.

Non-Exam Assessment

Component 3 is the non-exam assessment unit of the AS course that you will complete in your centre and is then assessed by your teachers. A sample of the work from your centre is then sent to an external moderator whose job it is to ensure that the standard of marking in your centre is the same as it is in other parts of the country.

Component 3 is worth 30% of AS.

WJEC/Eduqas will release the production briefs and you will be given time to work on your production. There will be choices and these will reflect and develop from topics you have studied in class. The briefs will also allow you to explore your own interests. You will be required to create an individual production for an intended audience based on one media form. The production briefs will always specify the intended target audience and **industry context** as well as other key requirements.

WJEC

Unit 2

Below is an overview of the non-assessment unit for the WJEC specification. Overlaps with the Eduqas specification in terms of research and planning and the production briefs are indicated in the Tip on page 200.

Non-Exam Assessment: Creating a Media Production

This unit is worth 80 marks. It is internally assessed by your teachers and externally moderated. As the WJEC specification is modular, not linear, the marks for this unit can be carried forward if you continue onto A level.

You must demonstrate your ability to:

- research, develop and create media products for an intended audience
- apply knowledge and understanding of the key concepts of media studies.

The Production Brief

There will be a choice of production briefs set by WJEC. They will be in the following media forms:

- music video, advertising and marketing
- online news
- film.

Key Points to Remember

- The production briefs will specify the context, genre and intended target audience but will provide a choice of options in terms of the form and medium of production.
- For audio-visual productions you may work in pairs but you must have clearly identified roles – one person will be responsible for the camera work and another person will be responsible for editing, including sound.
- It is recommended that you complete the production within 32–40 hours.
- You must create original images for the production, although found material can be used for planning. In cases where it may be impossible to create original images some found images may be used but these cannot be assessed.

Tip

The set briefs are available on the WJEC website.

Tip

You can only work in pairs for the audio-visual brief. You must work individually for the print and online briefs.

Tip

You will need to check the specification for the details regarding non-original material.

If you work in pairs each person must have a clearly defined role.

Research

Your research is assessed and is worth 10 marks. If you are working as part of a pair you must produce individual research. It must include:

- Analysis of three contrasting products comparable with your chosen production. This should focus on how media language is used to establish genre conventions, construct representations and target specific audiences.
- Analysis can include annotations and notes or in the case of audio-visual products, suitable illustrations from the products.
- The annotations and notes should be 600–750 words in length.

Tip

The following sections of the Eduqas Component 3 can help for Unit 2 of the WJEC specification:

- The television brief:
  - analysing – audio-visual technical codes using specific terminology
  - creating a storyboard
- Film advertising and marketing brief:
  - the analysis of *Submarine* gives ideas for how to analyse a film product
  - there is also information about analysing and producing DVD covers and film posters
- Music marketing brief:
  - analysis of existing music videos
  - planning and creating a music video.

Planning

This is assessed and is worth 10 marks. You should use your research findings to create a plan for your production task. If you are working in a pair you must produce individual planning. This should take one of the following forms:

- A storyboard for the audio-visual options.
- A draft design for each page of the print or online options. This should demonstrate how media language is used to establish genre conventions and representations.
- Original images are not required for planning; found images may be used for illustrative purposes.

Reflective Analysis

You must analyse and evaluate your production in relation to the three products you chose for your research. You should focus on:

- how you have used genre conventions in your production
- the representation issues raised in your production
- how you attracted your target audience through the use of media language.

Also:

- You must produce 650–850 words. This can be presented as an illustrated report.
- If you worked collaboratively you must link the product to your individual research.

A storyboard is an appropriate audio-visual planning task.

WJEC

What Do I Need to Submit?

- Research into three products comparable with the production [10 marks]
- Planning for the production [10 marks]
- A production [50 marks]
- A reflective analysis [10 marks]

The Eduqas Production Briefs

The following forms will always be set. The audience and industry context will change from year to year. You will be asked to create one of the following:

- A sequence from a new television programme or a website to promote a new television programme.
- A print marketing campaign or a website to promote a new film. For this brief the campaign or website must not include a complete short film, film sequence or trailer.
- A music video or a website to promote a new artist or band.
- A new print or online magazine.

Your teacher or centre may decide to offer all of these briefs, one of the forms, for example print, or they may select a menu of briefs for you to choose from. This may be dictated by the facilities you have available at your centre. For the creation of websites it is acceptable for you to use web design software or templates but you must be responsible for the design and the content must be original, for example the images and any audio-visual material.

What Do I Need to Submit for Component 3?

- A compulsory Statement of Aims and Intentions
- A media production
- A completed cover sheet containing relevant information linked to your production work. This will be available on the WJEC/Eduqas website.

Key Points to Remember

- You must create an individual production piece. However, you may use unassessed students and others, for example members of your family, in your work. These can be used as actors or models or can crew for you by operating lighting or sound recording equipment. These people must operate under your direction to ensure it is your own work.
- You must create original material for your production. You will need to consider this when you make decisions about what you want to create. For example, if the production brief requires you to create a lifestyle magazine you cannot use an image of an existing celebrity as this is not your image, but you can make your friends into new celebrities who can then appear on the front cover with images taken by you!
- Your teacher will monitor you throughout the production process in order to ensure that your work is authentic and has been created by you.
- You must list the software packages that have been used in the creation of your production on the cover sheet. You must also give a brief explanation of how you have used them in your work.
- Your production must show your ability to apply your knowledge and understanding of the theoretical framework in your production work.
- You must produce a Statement of Aims and Intentions.

Tip

A Statement of Aims and Intentions is an assessed element of Component 3. It must be completed after your research and planning and before you create your production, and in it you will outline your aims and intentions for your production, including how you will demonstrate your knowledge and understanding of the theoretical framework.

Tip

Whatever form you choose or are directed to work in, what you produce must be your own work (original material). The images must be taken by you and not downloaded from the internet, for example. This is the case even if you have engaged in substantial manipulation of the found image. You must bear this in mind in the planning stages of your work.

Tip

Primary research is information you gain first-hand from looking at actual examples of existing media products, for example television drama opening sequences. Primary research allows you to formulate your own opinions.

Secondary research is found in books and on websites, for example, and is written by someone else about the media product you may want to create. It will contain the ideas and opinions of the writer.

Quantitative research is measurable in numbers and is usually obtained through questionnaires. This type of research will tell you, for example, how many of the people questioned preferred *The Masked Singer* to *Strictly Come Dancing*. However, it will not give you the reasons for their decision. Quantitative data are linked to statistics.

The qualitative method of research gives more information and is more concerned with the 'quality' of the responses rather than the 'quantity'. This type of research is usually obtained through interviews and focus groups.

Key Term

Focus group
A form of qualitative research in which a group of people are asked about their perceptions, opinions, beliefs and attitudes about a product. The aim is to help the producers of the product ascertain the needs of their target audience.

Tip

Your research will be guided by which brief you choose from the options set by WJEC/Eduqas. Make sure that all your research is relevant and focuses on the theoretical framework: media language, representations, industry and audience.

Research and Planning

Before you create your production you will need to undertake a substantial amount of research and planning. This will not be assessed but the use of this research and planning will be evident in the standard of the production you create.

Why Do I Need to Conduct Research?

You cannot produce a professional and valid piece of production work without first researching the form in which you are working. This is particularly true as you do not actually work in the industry, therefore you need to find out as much as you can about the product you want to create. It is also essential that you research the audience who may consume your particular product in order to discover their opinions. Thorough and useful research will help you to create a better media production. You need to employ the most appropriate research for the product you intend to create. It is also important that you are clear about what specifically you want to find out and how it will help you to create your product. Both primary and secondary research will be useful.

What Types of Research are Appropriate?

- **Product analysis**: analysing the way media language is used to construct meanings in media products similar to the one you want to produce. This may focus on layout and design, mode of address, and the use of technical and audio codes. You should also consider how media language constructs representations of events, issues, individuals and social groups depending on the product. It may also be appropriate to research characters, narrative and specific genre conventions.
- **Industry context**: this will involve research into the organisations that produce the type of product you want to create, how the product may be produced, distributed and marketed, and how your chosen industry is regulated. You must consider how this impacts upon a production.
- **Audience research**: this will focus on how particular industries and organisations appeal to, engage and position audiences, the different and complex ways in which audiences interact with media products and how audiences may respond to media products.
- **Primary audience research**: this may be appropriate. In the industry a media product would not be created without first conducting research into the audience who will buy it. The industry employs market research companies to conduct their research for them – you will need to consider ways to find out the opinions of your target audience. However, audience research must be relevant and useful.
- **Audience research**: can be quantitative or qualitative. An example of quantitative research is designing a questionnaire. If you choose this method of audience research you need to spend some time constructing a questionnaire that will give you the information you require.
- A **focus group**: an example of a method of qualitative research. Conducting research with a focus group allows you to:
  - gather more detailed information
  - have more control over the situation
  - direct the questions and feedback so that you have the information you need.
- **Secondary audience research**: for example, relevant academic theories may help to develop your understanding and support your analysis.

Tips for Using Focus Groups for Research

- Decide how you want your focus group to be made up. Do you want a group of random people or are you going to be more selective? For example, if the production brief asks you to create a lifestyle magazine for young men it may be more useful to research the opinions of the specific target audience of the magazine rather than a random group.
- Make sure that members of your group are cohesive and will gel well together so that you are sure that everyone will have a chance to give their ideas and opinions.
- Have a plan. This may be a list of questions you want to cover or discussion topics you want the group to cover. Letting the group discuss freely may not be a good idea.
- It may be helpful to have some stimulus material for the group to look at. For example, you could have some pages of existing fashion magazines for them to look at and comment on.
- Consider how you are going to keep a record of what is said. It may be difficult to make notes and steer the discussion – you could actually record what is said or you could ask a friend to make notes for you. Make sure that they know what you want to find out so that the notes they make are useful. Alternatively, the group members could make notes on a grid you have constructed in advance.
- Finally, you need to analyse your findings and consider how you are going to use the research in production and how it fits into the theoretical framework.

A focus group may be a good way to learn the opinions of your target audience.

Tip

It is important that the focus group research is the right research method for your product as it is time consuming. Think carefully about how to demonstrate the way you have used your findings in your production.

Planning

Once your research has been completed you will be ready to plan your production piece. Planning is another essential element of the production process and good planning will help to ensure that your final product is successful. If you have done your research well you will have developed your knowledge and understanding of the product you are about to create. For example, if you intend to create a sequence for a television programme from a specific genre for a particular audience, your research into similar examples will have given you a good understanding of the codes and conventions of the form that you can use in your own production work.

The planning work you may choose to engage in could include:

- a **pitch** or **treatment** for your production
- a project plan, including a timeline or **Gantt chart**, and planned use of, for example, resources. This will be particularly important if you will have to share resources with other learners.
- Planning documents appropriate to the form or product you intend to create. These may include:
  - a shot list
  - a storyboard
  - a script
  - draft designs
  - **mock-ups** of compositions
  - recce photographs.

Photographs of possible settings for your production will help you to plan your storyboard.

Key Terms

Pitch
A presentation of ideas for a new media product to a selected audience, with the aim of persuading them of the viability of the project.

Treatment
A brief synopsis of ideas for a media project. It serves two purposes: to summarise elements of the idea, for example the plot and main characters, as well as to sell your idea to a producer. A treatment should communicate your idea in a concise but compelling manner, similar to a marketing pitch.

Gantt chart
A time-tool; it is a chart in which a series of horizontal lines shows the amount of time allocated to a project and then maps the work done or production completed at various stages.

Mock-up
Used to describe the planning ideas that a professional designer may engage in before the final product is created.

Stretch and Challenge 7.1

You can find out more about how to construct a Gantt chart at www.gantt.com.

Examples of Research into Specific Forms

As has been stated earlier, the briefs will always cover the following forms:

- magazine (print or online)
- television (audio-visual or online)
- film marketing (print or online)
- music video or a website.

The additional specific details regarding, for example, target audience and industry elements will change each year. Here we will explore the different types of generic research you could use to prepare for creating your production.

Magazines

Example brief:
Create a front cover, contents page and double-page spread article for a new **lifestyle magazine** in a genre (or sub-genre) of your choice. You should create a product for a **mainstream publisher** aimed at an audience of 25- to 44-year-old affluent 'aspirers'.

In all the set forms, the specific detail of the production brief will change each year, for example the publisher and the target audience, but you will always be required to create a new print or online magazine. You will also always be given some element of choice, as well as be given other minimum requirements for what you must create. For example, for this brief these may be:

A front cover plus double-page spread article, four pages including a contents page and at least eight original images in total.

Front cover:

- original title and masthead for the magazine
- strapline
- cover price and barcode
- main cover image plus at least three smaller/minor images (all original)
- at least five cover lines.

Contents page:

- full list of contents for the whole magazine
- at least three images related to different articles (all original and different from the images used on the cover and double-page spread).

Double-page spread:

- headline and **stand-first**, sub-headings
- one main image and at least two smaller/minor images (all original and different from the images on the cover and contents page)
- representations of at least one specific social group
- feature article (approximately 400 words) relating to one of the cover lines on the front cover
- pull quotes and/or sidebar.

Key Terms

Lifestyle magazine
An umbrella term for men's and women's magazines that are concerned with aspects of modern living, such as fashion, beauty, health and fitness, culture, the home, etc. The ideology of these magazines tends to focus on consumerism and aspiration.

Mainstream publisher
Applied to media producers who create products, for example magazines, that appeal to and are therefore read by a broad number of people.

Stand-first
The sentence after a headline and before an article begins that 'sells' a feature to a reader.

Researching Magazines

Product Analysis

Analyse products that are similar to the one you are required to create considering media language, representation, audience and industry. Study the *GQ* magazine front cover featuring James Cordon found here: www.thefashionisto.com/photo-shoot/james-corden-2016-cover-british-gq/.

Media Language

- The genre of *GQ* is men's lifestyle.
- The magazine uses visual codes, including a sophisticated colour scheme to attract a more mature audience and to establish a brand identity.
- The layout and design is formal and sophisticated and establishes a **house style**.
- The masthead is iconic and recognisable and 'GENTLEMAN'S QUARTERLY' has connotations of sophistication and tradition.
- James Corden is a popular, successful celebrity. Other celebrities included will be recognisable to the target audience and reflect their interests, for example Channing Tatum and Mo Salah.
- Cover lines reflect **discourse**: political stories, economics, how to be successful and current affairs.
- The use of lexis: 'style' rather than 'fashion' suggests appeal to a more discerning target audience.
- The direct mode of address engages the audience; James Corden is almost leaning out of the page towards the readers, inviting them into the magazine.
- The visual codes of gesture and expression suggest this is a successful, confident man with style, hence reflecting the magazine's genre and appealing to the aspirer.

Representation

- Representations are constructed through the selection of elements contained on the front cover. This will influence the meaning.
- *GQ* offers a representation of masculinity that is defined by style. The representations tend to be more traditional to appeal to the older, more serious-minded individual. This is reflected in their cover images, which usually show men dressed formally, often in suits and with a serious mode of address.
- The front page featuring Mo Salah creates a different representation of the sportsman as a fashion icon to reflect the magazine's genre. The football boots around his neck are a reminder of why he is famous.

Tip

Remember that when you create your own production you will need to demonstrate that you have addressed all elements of the theoretical framework.

Key Terms

House style
The distinctive 'look', aesthetic or visual style of a magazine, which helps to convey a sense of its brand identity.

Discourse
The topics and language used by a media product and the way they are used. There are certain topics that would never appear in the discourse of a magazine such as *Glamour*. The discourse for *Glamour* tends to centre on image and how to look good.

Tip

Many magazines produce a media pack aimed at potential advertisers. This gives very useful information about the industry context of the magazine, including circulation, advertising rates and audience profiles.

Stretch and Challenge 7.2

Research online the media pack of a magazine similar to the one you want to produce.

- It claims to be *'a community where people gather to be inspired and exchange ideas around style, creativity and culture'* (GQ Media Pack), so establishing a brand image.
- The representation of men is aspirational, shown by the fact that they tend to use high-profile, successful men as their cover celebrities, including Eddie Redmayne, Leonardo Di Caprio and Benedict Cumberbatch.
- The representation of masculinity in this genre of magazine tends to be defined by consumerism and what you own. The products featured are at the elite end of the style market.
- The men in *GQ* are constructed as powerful and in control of their lives. *'How Carpool Karaoke made James Corden TV's most powerful man'* and *'The King Claims His Throne'* (Mo Salah). They are defined by their success.

Audience

The production brief may ask you to create a product for a target audience with which you may not be familiar, therefore target audience research is very important.

- The average age of the *GQ* reader is 33.
- This is reflected in the discourse and cover lines, for example *'ALASTAIR CAMPBELL ON THE CHILCOT INQUIRY'* suggests that the audience is more mature and politically aware, and will understand this reference.
- The choice of the celebrity image of James Corden demonstrates selection of an 'of the moment' man who may be aspirational for the target audience.
- The readership of *GQ UK* is 212,000 and 61% of these are from the ABC1 demographic (2022).
- The brand identity and the cover lines construct the idea of a man who has a high consumable income and is concerned about lifestyle and appearance.

Quickfire 7.1

How will you reflect the industry context of your magazine in the pages you construct?

Industry

- *GQ* is produced and distributed by Condé Nast, a publishing company with other high-profile titles including *Vogue*, *Glamour*, *House and Garden* and *Tatler*. It produces magazines in a similar genre, which enables cross-marketing to similar target audiences.
- It is a successful magazine with a cross-platform presence.
- *GQ* was one of the first magazines to introduce a **mobile first strategy**. It also has a *GQ* video channel showing short films, series and documentaries.

The magazine production brief will also require you to produce other pages for your magazine, for example a double-page feature spread or a contents page. You will therefore need to research similar examples of those pages in preparation for creating your own product applying the theoretical framework.

Tip

Ensure that in your research you focus on how specific techniques, for example layout and composition, are used to create meaning in the product.

Key Term

Mobile first strategy
The practice of companies that design their products for mobile phones before making designs for traditional laptops and computers. This is particularly the case with smartphones that are linked to a large network coverage area. The strategy enables the producers to capture this market early.

Online Magazines

The production brief will also offer the option of producing pages of an online magazine, it is therefore important that, as part of your research, you explore the conventions of online magazines similar to the one you want to produce.

Example brief:
Create a working homepage and two other linked pages for a new online lifestyle magazine in a genre (or sub-genre) of your choice. You should create a product for a mainstream publisher aimed at an audience of 25- to 44-year-old affluent 'aspirers'.

Length: three pages, including 45 seconds of audio or audio-visual material related to the topic.

Stretch and Challenge 7.3

Become an expert on the genre of magazine you want to produce. Engage in research that allows you to become familiar with magazines similar to the one you want to create and their audience.

Tip

During the research process consider how you will reflect the key elements of the media theoretical framework in your production.

Key Features of an Online Magazine

- **Navigational features**: these are displayed clearly on the web page in order to help the user to move easily around the site. They are the key areas that the web designers want the audience to focus on. They allow the audience to select the elements of the magazine that are relevant to them.
- **Title/banner headlines**: these work in the same way as headlines in magazines and newspapers do – they draw in the audience. The font style of the magazine homepage will suggest the magazine's genre.
- **Brand identity**: there will usually be clear links between the style of the print product and the online version to make it recognisable and familiar to an audience.
- **Flash elements**: these are the animations and moving elements of the site, including roll-overs. They encourage the audience to interact with the content.
- **Banner advertisements**: these, along with **pop-ups** are the most common form of internet advertising and appear at the top of web pages. These will sometimes be examples of **contextual advertising**, which are more likely to be successful. The user will click on the banner and a full version of the advert will appear.
- **Multimedia features**: websites will use a mixture of text, images and sound.
- **External web links**: an image or a key word that will take the user to another page or website.
- **Interactive features**: these are the elements of the website that allow the user to become involved with the site through blogs, forums, surveys, email opportunities, etc. This feature may encourage the user to return regularly to the site as their involvement develops.

Quickfire 7.2

How important are the digital copies of a magazine?

Above is the 'Home' page from the *GQ* online magazine.

- The navigation bar allows the audience to select from a range of options. The lexis used reinforces the genre of the magazine and the sophisticated target audience, for example 'Grooming' and 'Culture'.
- The multimedia features include *GQ* video, which reflect the interests of the target audience including sport and upmarket cocktails.

- The layout and design of the page is sophisticated and uncluttered, the topics included echo the representation of masculinity as defined by style that was apparent on the front cover.
- Interactive features allow the audience to 'Follow' the magazine on a range of social media platforms and through a newsletter.
- The magazine's discourse suggests that it is at the forefront of fashion and has the style answers for its audience.

Planning Print and Online Magazines

Once you have conducted your research into print or online magazines similar to the one you want to create, you are ready to engage in some planning tasks to prepare you for creating your magazine pages. For this form planning tasks may include:

A pitch or treatment setting out your ideas. This type of planning will help to ensure that you are applying the theoretical framework and that you have considered:

- media language including the codes and conventions of your chosen product
- representations and how they are constructed to communicate meaning
- how to appeal to, engage and position your target audience
- how your product will be produced, distributed and marketed.

Draft designs of your ideas. Look back at your research and consider what you may replicate and what you may decide to do differently. Even the simplest draft designs help you to visualise what your pages will look like and how you will establish and maintain the brand identity of your publication.

Mock-ups of your pages. This will be the template you will use when you begin to produce your pages. The composition will be guided by the findings of your research. Mock ups can be produced digitally and adapted as you add the actual elements you want to include, for example your central image.

Photographs. Practice taking a range of photographs for your pages and then select those that best fit the production brief, the style of your magazine and will appeal to your target audience.

Quickfire 7.3

How can the theoretical framework be applied to the online page of *GQ* magazine?

Tip

You will need to be organised in your planning and you will need to show your planning documents to your teacher at some stage in the process to demonstrate that it is your own work.

Choosing the right photographs for your production is an important part of the planning process.

Production Project Treatment
Example production brief: **Create a product for a mainstream publisher targeting an audience of 25- to 40-year-old affluent 'aspirers'.**
Name and genre of magazine: The genre will be men's lifestyle similar to GQ. It will be called Homme, this has connotations of a high-end lifestyle and the use of French suggests sophistication.
Pages to be produced: A front cover, contents page and feature page. The front page will feature a fictional celebrity. The feature page will be a fashion review for a specific season, e.g. spring, which will allow creativity in design and the use of original images.
Target audience: Men aged 25–40 with a high disposable income or who aspire to the lifestyle constructed by the magazine.
Application of media language: My research into similar products suggested that the genre conventions of this style of magazine establish a clear brand identity through, for example a sophisticated colour palette. This will communicate the sophistication of the magazine. Visual codes will include the more formal dress worn by the 'celebrity' on the front cover and this will be reinforced throughout the chosen pages produced. The layout and design will be formal and sophisticated and the lexis used will demonstrate the discourse of the magazine and the interests of the target audience, for example current affairs, money matters and tips on how to achieve success in a particular field.
Representations and how they will be constructed: The main representation will be of modern masculinity. This will be constructed through the clothing, gesture and mode of address of the men featured in the pages I am constructing. This representation will also be reflected through the pages by focusing on the interests of the reader and their aspirations. My fashion page will contain examples of high-end fashion but will also show where similar products may be bought for a lower price to appeal to the aspirers in the readership. The front cover will also mention powerful men adding to the representation of masculinity linked to power and success, for example Barack Obama.
Industry: production, distribution and marketing: In my research I found that products similar to mine were published by Condé Nast, so this would be my publisher of choice. This would allow for marketing of the new magazine within similar existing titles. As part of the initial marketing campaign I would appeal to readers by an introductory subscription offer which would allow them to purchase the magazines more cheaply if they commit to a year's subscription. Other marketing possibilities include billboards and adverts in magazines targeting a similar audience.

Tip

Ensure that your planning addresses the theoretical framework and demonstrates how you will reflect it in your production.

Tip

Remember that what you produce can reflect your research but can also be a bit different in some way to offer a new experience for the reader and to make it easier to market. You can apply what you know of Neale's theory here – 'repetition with difference'.

Tip

It is useful to present your ideas to members of your target audience to get their opinion of your idea.

Stretch and Challenge 7.4

Consider how you can be creative and innovative in the way in which you construct representations in your print and digital magazine pages.

Producing Print and Online Magazine Pages

Now that you have finished your research and planning you are ready to produce the print or online pages of your magazine. You should now have a very clear understanding of what to produce and how you will reflect the theoretical framework in your product.

Tips for Success

- Ensure that what you produce responds to the requirements of the production brief and that you have planned to allow you to complete all of the tasks set out in the brief.
- Be clear about the codes and conventions of your chosen form. It is important that you employ the relevant features to ensure that your work looks as professional as you can make it. Bear in mind what you found out in your research into similar products.
- Use your own images. You do not need to have a high specification camera, many mobile phones can take adequate photographs for the purpose. You cannot be given credit for photographs you have not taken, even if you have manipulated them digitally. Similarly, you should not appear in the photograph yourself as that would raise doubts as to if you had taken it!
- Give some thought to what you want your photographs/images to look like before you take them. Do a **recce** of possible locations, select appropriate subjects and consider the framing of your photograph. You will also need to consider how to construct the photograph in order to reflect the representations contained within the product. You will need to direct your models/actors carefully with regard to clothing, props, expression and gesture.
- If you take a good quality photograph to start with, you will have less editing to do afterwards.
- Consider carefully the style of your piece. Your research, if done well, will have given you ideas for how your production pages should look. Think about all the aspects of media language including the font styles you will use, the layout and design that reflects the genre, the use of colour and other generic codes and conventions.
- Don't forget the small details that will make your text look professional, for example the bar code, publication date and price.
- Whether you are producing a print or online magazine you need to ensure that there is a sense of the house style of the publication. Each of the pages must link together stylistically in some way so that it is clear they are from the same magazine.
- Consider the genre of your print production and ensure that this is reflected in the design choices you make. For example, the font styles, colour and central images should illustrate the conventions of the magazine's genre.

Key Term

Recce
An informal term derived from the word reconnoitre. In a media context this is a pre-production visit to a location to work out its suitability for photographing or filming. This may take into consideration possible technical issues, for example sound and lighting.

Tip

Remember you are not required to create websites through programming languages such as HTML. It is acceptable to use web design software but the design of the website and all content must be original.

Creating Print Productions: Examples

As explained earlier in this section, the production brief will change each year and whilst there will always be a print and online magazine option, the industry elements and target audience will be different each year. On the following page are examples from the work of a student who produced magazine pages in the music genre, which he called *Catch 22*. However, the key points related to this work are relevant regardless of the genre focus.

Work courtesy of Simba Makuvatsine, Heaton Manor School

Key Points

There is clear evidence in the magazine pages above of the research undertaken by the student into media language, including the conventions of the specific music genre. This is reflected in the layout and composition, the choice and use of original images, and the selection of iconography.

- Attention has been paid to the construction of the representation of the music genre and the performers within the genre. This is achieved through attention to visual codes including clothing and expression. The central image also creates a narrative enigma in its construction.
- The representation is also constructed through the use of subject-specific lexis, creating a community who understand the references contained within the cover lines. In this way the target audience is clearly addressed.
- The niche audience is also positioned through the rhetorical questioning on the front cover, the promise of 'exclusive' content and the direct mode of address of the model on the contents page.
- The inclusion of social media links would have established a way for the audience to interact with the product.
- The photographs taken are original and there is evidence that thought has gone into the framing. The subject has been well instructed in terms of gesture, expression and clothing.
- The industry elements, including the clear brand identity, will aid in the marketing of the product

Key Terms

Pre-title sequence
Refers to the section of the television programme shown before the opening credits. Its purpose is to hook the audience.

Title sequence
Often termed a credit sequence. It is the section in which the television programme presents aspects of its production, for example the main characters, the actors, the setting and the genre. Its construction is often a montage of images with a recognisable soundtrack.

Television

Example brief:
Create a **pre-title** and **title sequence** for a new television programme in a factual or fictional genre of your choice. You may choose to produce a programme in a sub-genre or create a hybrid product. You should create a product for a mainstream broadcaster (such as BBC One or ITV) targeting a mainstream audience of 16- to 34-year-olds who have an interest in your genre/topic.

Length: 2 minutes 30 seconds–3 minutes

As with the other forms, the specific detail of the production brief will change each year, for example the channel and the target audience, but you will always be required to create a sequence from a new television programme or a website to promote a new television programme. You will also always be given some element of choice. Also, you will be given other minimum requirements for what you must create. For example, for the example brief on page 210 these may be:

- Two or more filming locations.
- At least three different characters or contributors representing at least two social groups.
- Exposition of narrative/topic or issue, including conflict and equilibrium.
- A wide range of camera shots, angles and movement, to establish the locations, narrative/topic or issue/and representations.
- Diegetic sound (including dialogue and/or narration as appropriate) and non-diegetic sound (including soundtrack).
- Editing of footage, dialogue and soundtrack. Continuity editing in the pre-title sequence; montage of footage for the title sequence.
- Graphics/titles to include the title of the programme, episode title, names of key personnel.

Researching Television

Product Analysis

Analyse products that are similar to the one you are required to create considering media language, representations, audience and industry.

Watch the pre-title and title sequence of the first episode of the BBC crime drama Luther, https://www.bbc.co.uk/iplayer/episode/b00sbjbv/luther-series-1-episode-1. Luther, the detective, is chasing the suspected killer to find out where he has hidden his latest victim.

Media Language

- The narrative cuts between the chase and the crime scene. The audience is placed in a privileged spectator position as we can see what is about to happen and Luther's colleagues cannot.
- The setting moves from the domestic to the disused factory, establishing an urban milieu.
- The use of real locations enhances the realism of the sequence.

- The genre is established through the iconography and the hierarchical character roles.
- The characters are introduced. As this is the first episode in the series the audience will be working out character roles, and in *Luther* their expectations may be challenged. It is not clear initially that Luther is a detective or that he is in control. The serial killer also challenges expectations in his formal code of clothing and accent.
- A range of technical codes are used including tracking shots in the chase, long shots to establish the setting, close-ups and extreme close-ups to enhance the emotional involvement of the audience. There is evidence of **continuity editing** so that the audience can keep track of the narrative despite the fast pace.
- The audio codes include non-diegetic dramatic music and diegetic sounds – heavy breathing and shouted dialogue.
- The fact that the sequence is filmed at night makes it seem more sinister and claustrophobic.
- Fast-paced editing disorientates the audience and builds tension.
- The final scene of the pre-title sequence is shocking and unexpected.

Key Term

Continuity editing
To combine a series of shots into a sequence, to create a clear and continuous narrative that can be understood by the audience.

Quickfire 7.4

What key elements of an effective pre-title sequence can be seen in *Luther*?

Representation

- There are different representations of gender evident in the sequence. In terms of masculinity, Luther is represented as powerful and determined. This representation is constructed through the camera angles, which are often low angled to make him appear dominant and intimidating. However, the close-ups also represent him as emotional and not entirely in control. The use of low-key lighting reflects the dark and brooding nature of this character. The audience will be aware that his final action in this scene, of letting the killer fall, will have consequences.
- As a representation of ethnicity Luther is interesting as at times he appears 'dangerous', conforming to a racial stereotype. He is not a typical representation of a detective. More typical in terms of clothing and behaviour is the male detective at the crime scene.
- There is a positive representation of a woman detective who is instrumental in saving the life of the child, thus demonstrating that she has a key role in the narrative, but she is also represented with maternal characteristics.

Stretch and Challenge 7.5

Watch a range of different pre-title sequences from your chosen sub-genre to gain information about the different techniques used.

Quickfire 7.5

What techniques could you use to construct a particular representation in your television programme?

Audience

- This is a BBC crime drama therefore an audience will have expectations of high production values and a quality programme.
- The casting of Idris Elba will appeal to his fanbase, he previously appeared in *The Wire* and will attract those who are curious to see him in this role.
- The high-octane opening episode will serve to hook the audience. The introduction of the maverick protagonist working within a more conventional team will create enigmas.
- The programme is post-watershed suggesting to the audience that it will be grittier and hard hitting, which is reinforced by the opening sequence.

Industry

- *Luther* is made by the BBC and distributed globally by BBC Worldwide. It is typical of the quality expected of a BBC drama.
- It was pre-sold to Sweden and Belgium before it premiered on BBC One.
- The BBC logo appears during the pre-title sequence, establishing the brand.
- The marketing techniques included pre-season and inter-episode trailers.

The example brief also requires you to produce a title sequence for the television programme. This will usually remain the same across the whole series, whereas the pre-title sequence will obviously be different. While this allows you to be creative and to create a montage of images relating to your programme rather than adhering to the rules of continuity editing, you will also need to establish the programme's genre, the characters and the setting.
As part of your research you will need to analyse title sequences from your chosen genre.

Tip

Conducting focus group research with people who watch crime dramas may help you to collect ideas and opinions that will influence your own production.

Stretch and Challenge 7.6

When you are engaging in your research try to consider how you can create a product that is original while conforming to the requirements of the brief.

Product Analysis: *Luther*

The title sequence of *Luther* is very stylised and is a montage of images with a soundtrack.

In the title sequence, the main character is established along with the setting. Luther is presented in silhouette throughout the sequence, suggesting the dark enigmatic elements of his character. This reinforces the representation first established in the pre-title sequence. He is always pictured alone, suggesting his isolation. The red colour wash has connotations of blood and danger.

While still keeping the surreal style of the title sequence, there are clear clues to the programme's genre. The iconography of the crime scene tape establishes the programme as a crime drama. Here the London skyline is used, again establishing the urban setting and giving clues to the narrative. The bullet hole in the glass suggests the dramatic narrative. Other iconography includes fingerprints and images related to solving crimes. Often the channel logo appears on screen as part of the programme's branding.

Consider how media language has been used to construct meanings in these images of Luther.

The urban setting is further reinforced in the sequence, the use of red is continued as a theme and the iconography of barbed wire suggests danger. The buildings are less distinctive but clearly this is a city milieu. Another convention of the title sequence is the inclusion of the actors' names. The font style is bold and in capitals, emphasising the realism of the programme.

The low-key lighting combined with the low-angle shots makes the setting appear intimidating. The pre-title sequence will also usually include industry elements, for example the writers, director and production companies.

The final shot of the sequence leaves us with a long shot of Luther and the programme's title establishing an enigma. He is again in silhouette and turned away, the audience are intrigued to know more about the character.

The audio is a slow, evocative song, which contrasts with the fast pace of the pre-title sequence and suggests the complexity of the character. There is no other audio included, which again contrasts with the dramatic dialogue of the pre-title sequence.

Production Brief

The production brief for television also offers you the option to create a working website:

Example brief:
Create a **functioning website**, to include a **working homepage** and **two linked pages**, to promote a new television programme in a factual or fictional genre of your choice. You may choose to produce a website for a programme in a sub-genre or a hybrid product. You should create a product for a mainstream broadcaster (such as BBC One or ITV) targeting a mainstream audience of 16- to 34-year-olds with a specific interest in your genre/topic.

Length: three pages, including 45 seconds of audio or audio-visual material related to the topic

You will also be given other minimum requirements for what you must create. For example, for this brief these may be:

One working homepage and two further, linked, pages.

Homepage:

Original title and logo for the programme.

Menu bar.

Main image plus at least two other images (all original) that establish the locations, characters/social groups and narrative/topic of the programme.

Working links to two further pages from the website:

1. Either an 'Episodes' or 'Further information' page on a topic/issue (factual programme) or 'Characters' page (fictional programme).
2. A blog by the director detailing either the research undertaken for the programme or a production diary.

These pages must include written text that introduces the characters, narrative or topic/issue of the programme (approximately 250 words in total), and 45 seconds of original audio-visual material related to the topic, embedded into one of the pages (such as an interview with the director or 'making of' footage).

Tip

Remember, you are not required to create websites through programming languages such as HTML. It is acceptable for you to use web design software or templates in the online options. However, you must be responsible for the design of the website and all content (such as written text/language, images, audio-visual material) must be original.

Tip

Ensure that you incorporate the main conventions of a title sequence in your product. Making the title seqeunce stylistically different allows you to develop elements of media language and representation in a different way from the pre-title sequence which will tend to be narrative based.

Tip

Decisions such as font style and audio tracks are important in establishing the genre of your programme.

The sections shown here from the homepage and linked pages for the Channel 4 crime drama *No Offence* give examples of some of the requirements of the brief:

- There is a main image that establishes the character in a setting and a navigation bar showing all the options.
- **250 words of written text**: in a separate linked page there are profiles of the actors and the characters they play. There is also a link to a 'Help and Support' page
- **45 seconds of original audio-visual footage**: there is a link to an interview with Paul Abbott the creator of *Shameless* and *No Offence*.

Quickfire 7.6

What elements could be included if this was a non-fiction text?

Quickfire 7.7

How does the overall look of the web page reflect the genre and themes of the television programme?

Planning Television/Online Products

Once you have conducted your research into television programmes and their websites similar to the one you want to produce, you are ready to engage in some planning tasks to prepare for creating your own products. For this media form, planning tasks may include:

A Pitch or Treatment

This sets out your ideas. This type of planning will also help to ensure that you are applying the theoretical framework and that you have considered:

- media language including the generic codes and conventions of your chosen product
- the representations contained in your product and how they are constructed to communicate meaning
- how to appeal to, engage and position your target audience
- how your product will be produced, distributed and marketed.

A Recce

Visit the different locations for a **recce** that you may use in your film and take photographs of them; you can then use these in your storyboard. Consider the best time of day to film in these locations taking account of aspects such as, for example, lighting. Choose locations that reflect the genre of your programme.

A Storyboard

A storyboard is an essential planning device undertaken by most film and television directors. It allows them to think in advance about how they want the narrative to develop and the technical and audio codes they will use to convey this to the audience. Although the storyboard is a print process you must not view it as such – instead think about it as a way of recording a moving image. You must have thought through and be able to see the finished moving image in your head before you commit it to paper. This will help you to think about camera shots, angles and transitions.

Do not worry if you cannot draw, just ensure that if you state that the shot is a close-up, for example, then the visual looks like a close-up. Alternatively, you can take photographs or use a combination of both.

Make sure that you include a range of different shots and **transitions** in order to hold the attention of your audience. It is also important that there is a sense of **continuity** and that the audience will be able to follow the narrative.

Consider the narrative techniques that apply to your chosen genre. For example, crime dramas often employ non-linear narratives in the opening sequence where they show the crime committed and then move back in time to the events leading up to the crime. It is also important to consider how you will introduce the characters and how you will construct their representation. Remember, the job of the technical codes and editing is to 'show' the audience the characters and narrative, and maybe to introduce narrative enigmas, for example a character in the shadows, to intrigue the audience and keep them watching.

A well-constructed and planned storyboard will save you a lot of time when it comes to filming. It is a mistake to rush into filming your sequence without first planning what you want the finished product to look like and the effect you want to have on your audience.

When producing a storyboard for your production work, the expectation is that you will produce about 20–30 frames containing the information suggested in the template below.

Key Term

Recce
An informal term derived from the word reconnoitre. In a media context this is a preproduction visit to a location to work out its suitability for photographing or filming. This may take into consideration possible technical issues, for example sound and lighting.

Tip

Make sure you have addressed all the requirements of the brief in your planning.

Tip

Look at the example of a project treatment on page 210 for a magazine and adapt it to suit your television programme ideas.

Key Terms

Transitions
The way in which the shots move from one into the other, producing a particular effect. Different transitions include cuts that produce a faster-paced sequence. Fades and wipes suggest a more controlled and slower section.

Continuity
When one frame of your storyboard links to the next in a sequence, in order to effectively convey the narrative.

Shot length	Visuals	Technical codes	Audio	Comment
transition				

Tip

The inclusion of the 'Comment' box in the table will help when you need to explain your decisions to your teacher.

Tip

A Gantt chart or a similar organisational device is useful to help your planning. Look back at page 203 for the link to a template.

Key Terms

Mise-en-scène
Everything that appears within the frame in, for example, a television programme. This includes characters, iconography and graphics.

Inter-weaving plot strands
Some television dramas include three or more narratives in their opening sequences and then move the action between these narratives to keep the audience's attention.

BBC Writers Room
It is good practice to format your script correctly according to the type of text you are creating. For example, the format of a situation comedy is different from that of a television drama. There is a range of different places to help you with this. One of the most useful is the BBC Writers Room: www.bbc.co.uk/writersroom/scripts.

Stretch and Challenge 7.7

The **BBC Writers Room** is a very useful resource to help with script writing. It allows you to look at scripts that have been written for BBC programmes as well as those from other genres. It also features writers discussing their ideas and inspirations, and allows you to download a template specific to a particular format to help you write your script. If you are very pleased with your script then you can submit it to the BBC!

The template is used for the following information:

- **Shot length**: this information suggests how long you want the shot to remain on the screen. This should take into account what actually happens in the shot and the overall pace of the extract. For example, if it is a pre-title sequence the pace may be faster than if it is a title sequence in order to hook the audience.
- **Visuals**: in the boxes, draw a sketch or place a photograph as an indication of what you want to film. The quality of your drawing is not important – the purpose of the storyboard is to help you when you are filming. Think about the framing of the shot and what you will include in the **mise-en-scène**.
- **Technical codes**: this refers to camera shots, angles and editing. Make sure that the technical code you describe in this column matches the drawing in the 'visuals'. Try to make your shots varied and interesting. You will also need to explain any movement of the camera, for example a zoom to a close-up shot, as this is easier than drawing it.
- **Audio**: here you need to clearly indicate any sound you want to include, diegetic or non-diegetic, including music, dialogue, narration and sound effects.
- **Comment**: this is useful as it allows you to explain your decisions at the time of planning, including the purpose of the action in the storyboard cell. It also helps to highlight the desired effect upon the audience. It may also allow you to demonstrate your use of media language including the codes and conventions of your chosen genre.

A script

Another planning option is a script. Use your research to familiarise yourself with the codes and conventions of your selected genre so that you can replicate some of them in your script. Obviously, you will also need to pay particular attention to the dialogue and sound in the examples you research.

Tips for Writing a Script

- Consider the narrative format you intend to use and the codes and conventions of your chosen genre. The narrative conventions of, for example, a regular soap opera will be different from a one-off BBC drama.
- Remember that your aim is to attract and maintain the attention of the audience. Open your story with an exciting plot situation or narrative. If it is a pre-title sequence or a trailer, choose some dramatic scenes to illustrate the programme's narrative.
- Ensure that your characters are believable so that the audience will want to know what happens to them and therefore stick with your programme. This does not mean that they have to be in believable situations. The television crime drama *Life On Mars* asked us to believe that the policeman travelled back in time to the 1970s, but the character of Sam Tyler was such that it caught the imagination of the audience who empathised with his plight. Consider how you will create your characters through the script dialogue and brief descriptions. You may want to create character profiles as part of your planning, which will allow you to develop your character ideas more fully.
- Just like with the storyboard, you need to visualise your script and imagine how it would work when filmed and the lines and actions are carried out by real people. It should not be a paper exercise.
- Consider how you will demonstrate other elements of media language, for example the narrative structure you will employ. Will it be linear? Will you concentrate on one narrative or introduce a series of **inter-weaving plot strands**?
- Include the recognisable genre conventions you discovered in your research to help you to attract your audience.

Creating a Script: An Example

WHICKHAM AND BOYD (1)

"The First Death"

ACT ONE

FADE IN: (2)

INT.#1 PUB – NIGHT (3)

[THE PUB IS BUSTLING AND THERE IS LOUD NOISE, LAUGHTER, ETC. A GROUP OF GIRLS IS SITTING IN THE CORNER SINGING 'HAPPY BIRTHDAY' TO ONE PARTICULAR GIRL. ANOTHER GIRL, LAURA, GETS UP AND PUTS ON HER COAT.] (4)

LAURA (5)
Hey, guys, I will have to go now or I will miss my bus. It's been great to meet up with you all again. Enjoy the rest of your night Sarah. Happy Birthday! (6)

SARAH
Shame you can't stay. Thanks for coming.

Laura walks out of the pub.

EXT.#2 ROAD OUTSIDE PUB – SAME NIGHT

[IT IS RAINING HEAVILY. CARS ARE PASSING QUICKLY WITH HEADLIGHTS GLARING. THE BUS PULLS AWAY FROM THE STOP JUST AS LAURA GETS THERE.]

LAURA
Damn!

[LAURA LOOKS AT HER WATCH THEN TAKES HER PHONE OUT OF HER POCKET. CU OF PHONE SHOWS IT IS OUT OF BATTERY. (7) **SHE LOOKS AROUND. THERE IS NO-ONE ABOUT. THE RAIN CONTINUES. HEADLIGHTS APPROACH AND A CAR STOPS AT THE BUS STOP, THE WINDOW WINDS DOWN. THE DRIVER IS NOT VISIBLE. LAURA GETS INTO THE CAR.]**

1. Even though you are only writing the script for a section of a television programme, the example is a crime drama, you need to give your programme and this particular episode a title. This may give a clue to the genre. The font style used for the BBC scripts is Courier 12 point.
2. Usually scripts for dramas start with a 'fade in' to the action.
3. Next you set out where the action will take place: INT (inside) EXT (outside) and specifically. Adding a number is helpful if you intend to return the action to this location.
4. Information about the scene action is in bold upper case and double-spaced below the heading.
5. Character names appear in capitals indented around the middle of the page but not centred. This can be the character's name, their role or both.
6. Dialogue appears under the name of the character, indented and in upper and lower case.
7. As this is not a shooting script, in the industry you would not include camera shots. However, it is sometimes useful to suggest the camera actions to enhance the visuals.

8 Divide your script into acts to suggest changes in the narrative. Here, the location has changed and new characters have been introduced.

9 The new characters are briefly described along with the action. This gives a clear indication of the genre through inclusion of iconography. Character profiles can be developed separately.

10 Indications of character's actions are placed in parentheses underneath the character's name.

11 Remember to indicate when the phone conversation ends.

12 The dialogue here reflects understanding of media language through the codes and conventions of the genre.

13 You can make your narrative more interesting by including a movement in time such as a flashback. The use of black and white indicates to the audience that the narrative has changed.

14 O.S. indicates that the character is present but 'out of shot'.

ACT TWO 8

EXT. WOODS CLOSE TO PUB. NEXT DAY, EARLY MORNING

[DETECTIVE INSPECTOR WHICKHAM AND HER SERGEANT BOYD ARE LOOKING AT A CRIME SCENE. WHICKHAM IS A 40 YEAR OLD, TOUGH POLICE OFFICER WHO HAS WORKED HARD TO GET WHERE SHE IS. SHE IS FORTHRIGHT AND SPEAKS WITH A STRONG NORTHERN ACCENT. BOYD IS A WELL-SPOKEN GRADUATE ENTRY YOUNG POLICEMAN WHO KNOWS HIS STUFF BUT IS NEW TO THIS PATCH. THERE ARE UNIFORMED POLICE SEARCHING THE IMMEDIATE AREA, CRIME SCENE TAPE AND TWO POLICE CARS. IT IS STILL RAINING.] 9

D.I. WHICKHAM
(into phone) 10
We need forensics over here as soon as possible before the rain washes all the evidence away!
(hangs up) 11
What have we got?

BOYD 12
Young girl about 20. Dressed for a night out, looks like. A lot of blood but can't say cause of death until the doc gets here. Looks like she was dragged here from the road.

FLASHBACK: 13 EXT. MAIN ROAD BY WOODS. PREVIOUS EVENING. BLACK AND WHITE

[A CAR STOPS AND LAURA IS SEEN JUMPING OUT. SHE STUMBLES AND FALLS. A MAN GETS OUT OF THE DRIVER'S SIDE AND RUNS AFTER HER. A SCREAM IS HEARD.]

EXT. WOODS. EARLY MORNING

[BOYD AND WHICKHAM ARE LEANING OVER THE BODY. ONLY THE SHOES ARE VISIBLE AND THEY ARE RECOGNISABLE AS THOSE OF LAURA.]

POLICE OFFICER (O.S.) 14
Over here, ma'am. Looks like we've got something.

Additional Planning for a Website

- Draft designs of your ideas. Look back at your research and consider what you may replicate and what you may decide to do differently. Even the simplest draft designs help you to visualise what your pages will look like and how you will establish the key conventions of your programme and demonstrate your understanding of the theoretical framework.
- Adapt an existing template to suit the ideas for your programme and to reflect the genre.

Producing a Television Sequence

Now that you have finished your research and planning you are ready to produce your television sequence or promotional website pages. You should now have a very clear understanding of what you want to produce and how you will reflect the theoretical framework in your product.

Tips for Success

- Check the equipment at your disposal. Make sure that you know how to use it if it is new to you. You may also need to check that it is compatible with your editing software otherwise this will cause problems later.
- Sort out sound in advance. It is invariably the case that students do not give adequate attention to sound, yet nothing can reduce the effectiveness of your programme more than poor quality sound. If you are filming outside you will need to use a suitable microphone, particularly if you want to pick up dialogue. It is often better to add sound **post-production**.
- Be organised – create a filming schedule and try to stick to it. It will help, if you are using actors, to choose other students who are reliable and can fit in with your requirements. There is nothing worse than casting a lead character who is always late or who doesn't turn up when you need them.
- Use your storyboard – that is what it is for! This will give a structure to your filming. However, it is also a working document and can be tweaked and amended should new ideas appear.
- Just as for a still photo shoot, as part of your planning you should have conducted a recce of the locations you want to use before you start filming. Check the logistics – for example, if you want to film in school in the evening, do you need to ask permission? If you want to film around school it is also important to get the permission of people you film, particularly if they are younger members of the school – this may involve contacting parents. You also usually need permission to film in certain locations, for example inside shopping centres.
- Concentrate when you are filming. Always film more footage than you need and for longer – this gives you flexibility when editing. Avoid zooming in and out or panning quickly unless you want to create that effect. Be clear about what you want your actors to do and they should know exactly when filming starts and stops.
- Pay attention to the continuity. If you break in filming a scene and then return to film the next day, make sure your actors are dressed the same, the weather hasn't changed dramatically and the locations are similar. This will avoid confusing your audience!

Key Term

Post-production
The term for any production work that takes place on moving or still images after the initial filming or photography shoot has taken place.

Tip

If you are producing online pages for your television programme the planning tasks will be similar to those for the television extract, as your website pages will also include original audio-visual footage.

Tip

If you are adding post-production sound, make sure the sound quality matches the location. For example, if your sequence is filmed outside and you record the dialogue separately inside it will not sound realistic.

Tip

Managing your time effectively is the key to a successful production piece.

Tip

Be organised! If you are working with a group of people work out in advance what you want them to do.

Tip

It may work better to shoot short scenes at different times rather than trying to do a lot all at once.

Creating Audio-Visual Productions: Examples

As explained earlier in this section, the production brief will change each year and while there will always be a television option, the industry elements and target audience will be different each year. The shots on this page are from the work of a student who has produced the opening sequence for a gangster/crime television programme. However, the key points related to this work are relevant regardless of the genre focus.

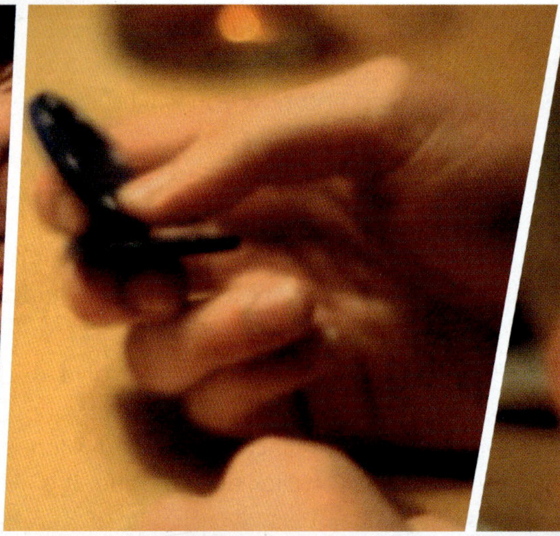

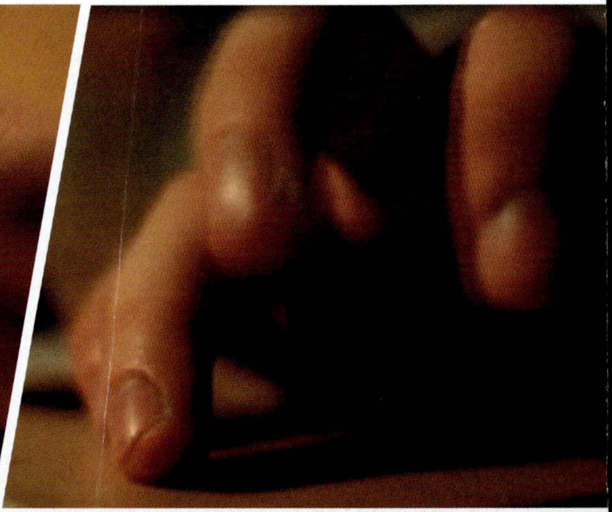

Courtesy of Joe Lunec

Quickfire 7.8

What else would be required in the rest of the sequence to fulfil the production brief?

Key Points

This student has addressed some of the requirements of the brief and shown their understanding of the media framework:

- Different characters have been established. Their representation has been constructed through visual codes including clothing, gesture and expression.
- There is a wide range of shots that have been well framed, filmed and edited together. This holds the attention of the audience and allows them to accept and become involved in the action.
- Attention has been also paid to the lighting, which is low key and thus reflects the generic codes and conventions.
- A narrative is established involving character interaction and conflict.
- There is no dialogue in this section of the pre-title sequence but attention has been paid to sound. This was added post-production and includes mood music and heightened sound effects, for example the drumming of fingers on the table and the clicking of the roulette chips – all audio codes conventional of the genre.

Advertising and Marketing: Film Including Film Posters

Example brief:

Create a DVD front and back cover, a 'teaser' poster and a main theatrical release poster for a new film in a genre of your choice. You may choose to produce marketing materials for a hybrid or sub-genre of film. You should create a product for an **independent UK film company** (such as Warp or DNA) targeting an audience of 16- to 34-year-old fans of your chosen film genre.

Length: four pages. (Note: the front and back cover count as one page each.)

The media production must not include a complete short film, film sequence or trailer.

Key Term

Independent film company
A company that operates outside of the main film companies.

As with the other forms, the specific detail of the production brief will change each year, for example the industry context and the target audience, but you will always be required to create a print marketing campaign or a website to promote a new film. You will also always be given some element of choice. You will be given other minimum requirements for what you must create. For example, for this brief these may be:

DVD cover, **teaser poster** and main theatrical poster release poster to include:

- A minimum of ten original images in total.
- At least three different locations for photography.
- At least three different characters representing at least two different social groups.

DVD front cover:

- At least one main image.
- Original title for the film.
- Age rating; names of director and actors.
- Spine: title, production company logo, age rating.

Key Term

Teaser poster
When a film poster appears before the release of the main marketing campaign. The aim is to use enigmas, for example a tagline or a single image, to catch the interest of the audience.

Key Terms

Billing block
A block of text that contains the industry information, including actors, directors, producers, crew members, and production and distribution companies.

Production values
The features of a media product that illustrate how much it cost to make. A high-budget film is recognisable by its settings, use of stars and more complex editing, for example. The reverse is true of low-budget films.

Tip

Ensure that you look closely at all aspects of the brief, e.g. the film company and the target audience.

Tip

Make sure that you do not replicate images on your production pages.

Key Term

Star billing
The positioning of the names of the stars on the poster; where the names are placed and how large they are suggest the importance of the particular star to the film and its marketing.

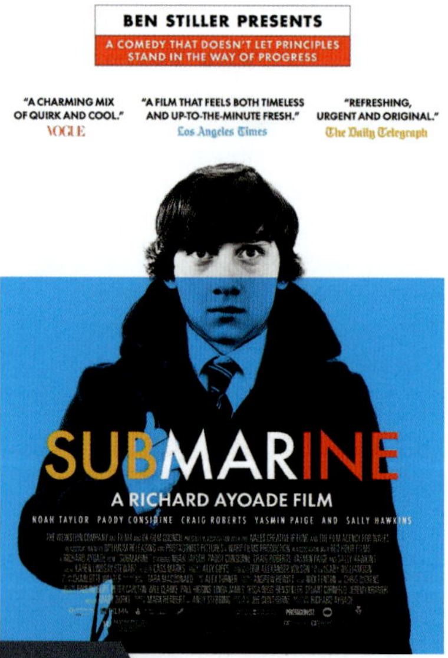

DVD back cover: background image and main image

- Four thumbnail images depicting different scenes from the film.
- Promotional 'blurb' for the film (approximately 200 words), including reference to narrative conflict/equilibrium.
- **Billing block**.
- Production company logo, age rating and technical information.
- 'Teaser poster' (portrait format):
  - At least one main image (different from the images on the DVD cover). Written text: tagline/title/release date as appropriate.
  - Narrative enigma.
  - Main theatrical release poster.
  - (landscape format): Original title for the film and tagline. At least one main image (different from images on DVD and teaser poster). Release date, billing block and production company logo. Details of awards/quotes from critics.

Researching Film Marketing

Product analysis

Analyse products that are similar to the one you are required to create considering media language, representations, audience and industry.

Researching Film Posters: *Submarine*

- The central image draws the eye and demonstrates the genre conventions of a 'coming of age' film with the use of a young male.
- The name of the film is enigmatic; the fact that the young boy seems to be just peering over the surface of the water, like a submarine gives clues to the possible narrative.
- The omission of settings on the poster suggests the narrative focus will be his story and also suggests the low **production values** of the film.
- The visual code of expression, coupled with the indirect mode of address, suggests his confusion.
- The code of clothing of the school uniform further reinforces the film's sub-genre, suggesting that the narrative will focus on issues surrounding the young man featured. The clothing also suggests that this is not set in the present.
- The layout and design is simple, demonstrating the conventions of a low-budget independent film; this is reinforced by the lack of high-profile **star billing** and the fact that the quotes are in a larger font than the actor's names.
- The use of star rating suggests the quality of the film as do the **expert witnesses** used in the quotes to suggest the film is a 'must see'.
- The **marks of quality** – the director's name and the independent film festival logos further reinforce the independent film credentials.

Researching DVD Covers

DVD covers are another important device used to market a film. Study the DVD cover for the film *Submarine* found here: https://cover.box3.net/index.php?pid=cove2&p=v&rid=117013&&por=1&mod=front.

- The front cover of the DVD shows an image of the central character and replicates the colour scheme of the poster, suggesting they are from the same marketing campaign.
- The tagline gives clues to the narrative and, although it is enigmatic, suggests there may also be some comedy in the film.
- This is further reinforced in the promotional blurb on the back cover, which refers to the narrative and suggests the areas of conflict and possible resolution provided by the love interest within the film. It also highlights some of the comedic potential of the film through the characters' introductions, for example '*Jordana, a self-professed pyromaniac*'.
- An image of Jordana also features on the back cover along with Oliver Tate. They both have an indirect mode of address and are also not looking at each other, suggesting their quirky relationship. In some of the international versions of the DVD cover, other **thumbnails** are included on the back cover giving clues to plot situations from the film.
- As this is a low-budget, independent film, the focus of the marketing will usually be the sub-genre, the characters and the narrative, as there are no high-profile stars to draw the attention of the audience.
- The DVD also includes a range of other conventional features, including industry information, the production company logo and the age certification.

Thumbnails communicate further information about the film's narrative.

Quickfire 7.9

What elements of this product could be used in a teaser trailer?

Key Terms

Expert witnesses
Quotes from experts who the audience will trust.

Mark of quality
In the case of film, usually the film logo, the director's name or references to other successful films made by this director. These are included to convince the audience that this new film is a quality product.

Thumbnail
On DVD covers these are small images used to convey aspects of the film's narrative.

Tip

Consider how the images you include on your DVD cover will reflect the characters and the sub-genre of your film.

Tip

Always be aware of the specified requirements of the brief. For this example you are required to include four thumbnails on the back cover and a background and main image.

Representation

- The DVD cover and the film poster construct representations of 'troubled' young people as the sub-genre is 'coming of age'.
- The visual codes of clothing, gesture and expression combined with the narrative blurb reinforce the idea that these are more realistic representations of youth than in other more mainstream films.
- There is also the social and cultural representation of 1980s Britain.
- The blurb suggests that issues related to the young people of the time will be represented in the film. This is also suggested by the film's tagline. These issues are transferable to young people today, the target audience of the film.

Key Terms

Hyperbole
Exaggerated language used to create a dramatic effect.

Promises of pleasure
Phrases that tell the audience what they will experience through the film, for example fear, laughter. The audience will then have expectations of the film.

Horizontal integration
The process through which different companies that produce, sell or distribute similar products join together through a merger or acquisition. This reduces competition and enables companies to increase their market share.

Audience

- The language included on the film poster employs **hyperbole** to persuade an audience to go and see the film by offering **promises of pleasure**, for example 'hilarious and touching', suggesting emotional engagement.
- The idea for the film came from an existing book, therefore there was already an audience with knowledge of the narrative and characters who would be interested in the film.
- Setting the film in the 1980s may attract a nostalgic audience who remember their own adolescence at that time.
- This DVD is a 'collector's edition' suggesting its exclusivity to the audience and attracting the fan base for this genre of film.
- The 'Special Features' may also attract an audience to buy this particular edition of the DVD.
- The music for the film was created by Alex Turner from the Arctic Monkeys; this information is on the poster to suggest quality and to attract fans of the band. This is reinforced on the DVD cover and suggests the credibility of the director.

Stretch and Challenge 7.8

Research a range of products similar to the one you want to create to familiarise yourself with a range of conventions used.

Industry

- *Submarine* was made by the independent film company Warp Films, known for making innovative films including *This Is England* (2006), *Yardie* (2018) and *Everybody's Talking About Jamie* (2021).

> *Sorry we'd like to help you but that's not what we do. We're better at distinctive, amusing and thought-provoking content … When our audience is being intelligently entertained then we're happy.* (www.warpfilms.com)

- Warp also has an independent record label as part of its extended company and there is evidence of **horizontal integration** as Alex Turner wrote the soundtrack for *Submarine*.
- Below-the-line advertising was used in the marketing of this film. This is a strategy in which a product is promoted on platforms other than radio, television, billboards, print and film.
- Funding is often a problem for independent film companies, whose aim is to foster new talent and innovative ideas. Other smaller companies joined together to ensure the success of the film, including Film 4 Productions, Film Agency for Wales and Red Hour Films.
- *Submarine* was directed by Richard Ayoade and produced by Red Hour Films.

Quickfire 7.10

Give another example of how you could suggest the target audience of your product in what you create.

- *Submarine* has won many awards worldwide, including the Best Screenplay award at the 2011 British Independent Film Awards. Richard Ayoade was nominated for a BAFTA for Outstanding Debut by a British Writer, Director or Producer at the 65th British Academy Film Awards.
- Much of the film's success came from **below the line** and word of mouth advertising, and from its success at independent film festivals.
- Success was ensured when the Weinstein Company, a mini-major New York film studio, became involved and promotion was also aided by Hollywood actor Ben Stiller. The American version of the posters and DVD included 'Ben Stiller Presents', thus broadening the audience through celebrity endorsement.
- 'Optimum Releasing' distributed the film in the UK; they have a lot of experience in releasing smaller, independent films.

Production Brief

The production brief for Film Marketing (below) will also offer you the option to create a working website. Much of the research explored already for the print task will be relevant for an online product. Look back at the 'Key Features of an Online Magazine', page 208, as many of these can be replicated for a film website.

Example brief:
Create a functioning website, including a working homepage and two linked pages, to promote a new film in the genre of your choice. You may choose to produce a website for a hybrid or sub-genre of film.

You should create a product for an independent film company (such as Warp or DNA) targeting an audience of 16- to 34-year-old fans of your chosen film genre.

Length: three pages including 45 seconds of audio or audio-visual material related to the topic.

You will also be given other minimum requirements for what you must create. For example, for this brief these may be:

One working homepage and two further, linked, pages.

Homepage:

Menu bar.

Main image plus at least two other images (all original) to establish the locations, characters/social groups and narrative of the film.

Original title and logo for the film.

Synopsis of film, including reference to narrative conflict/equilibrium.

Working links to two further pages from the website.

1. Either a 'Characters' or 'Locations' page featuring at least three further original images.

2. A production diary blog by an actor or the director.

These pages must include written text promoting the film (approximately 250 words in total), 45 seconds of original audio or audio-visual material related to the topic embedded into one of the pages (e.g. an interview with the director).

The media production must not include a complete short film, film sequence or trailer.

Key Term

Below the line advertising
An advertising strategy in which a product is promoted on platforms other than radio, television, billboards, print and film.

Quickfire 7.11

How can you show evidence of understanding of the film industry on your DVD and film posters?

Tip

To avoid overlap with the Film Studies specification you must not produce a short film, film sequence or trailer but, as indicated, you can produce other audio-visual material, for example an interview with a fictional film director.

Stretch and Challenge 7.9

These are minimum requirements. Including more original images will allow you to demonstrate a more sophisticated understanding of the theoretical framework.

Stretch and Challenge 7.10

To prepare for your 45 seconds of audio/audio-visual material it will be useful to research how interviews with actors and directors are conducted and the types of questions asked.

The screenshots below, from the homepage and linked pages for the independent film *'71*, give an example of some of the requirements of the brief:

- On the homepage there is a **main image** that establishes the character through visual codes of clothing and a **navigation/menu bar** showing all the options. The homepage has a synopsis of the story suggesting narrative conflict and possible resolution.
- **250 words of written text promoting the film**: in a separate linked page there are profiles of the actors and the characters they play.

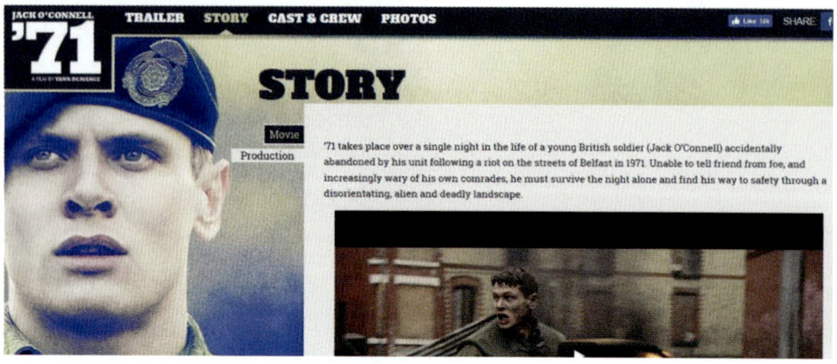

Quickfire 7.12

How could 45 seconds of audio/audio-visual be added to this type of website?

Tip

Although the website for *'71* replicates an image across the two pages, you will be required to ensure that your images are original and different.

Planning a Print Film Marketing Campaign or a Website

Once you have conducted your research into DVD covers and film websites similar to the one you want to create, you are ready to engage in some planning tasks to prepare you for creating your products. With this particular brief you will need to think of an idea for a film that reflects the demands of the brief and then consider how that will then be marketed through the film posters, DVDs and website pages. Consider what will be the main selling points of your film.

For this form planning tasks may include:

A pitch or treatment setting out your ideas. This type of planning will help to ensure that you are applying the theoretical framework and that you have considered:

- media language including the codes and conventions of your chosen product
- representations and how they are constructed to communicate meaning
- how to appeal to, engage and position your target audience
- how the products you produce will help in the distribution and marketing of the film.

Draft designs of your ideas. Look back at your research and consider what you may replicate and what you may decide to do differently. Even the simplest draft designs help you to visualise what your pages will look like and how you will introduce an audience to your film.

Mock-ups of your pages. This will be the template you will use when you begin to produce your pages. The composition will be guided by the findings of your research. Mock-ups can be produced digitally and adapted as you add the actual elements you want to include, for example your central image.

Photographs. Practise taking a range of photographs for your pages and then select those that best fit the production brief, the sub-genre of your film and will appeal to your target audience. You will need a strong central image for your poster and DVD cover and these must be different. You will also need thumbnails for the back of the cover.

A script for the 45 seconds of audio/audio-visual material. If you decide that this will be an interview with the director/actor then you will need to consider how you want the fictional director/actor to be represented.

Production Project Treatment

Example production brief:

Create a DVD front and back cover, a 'teaser' poster and a main theatrical release poster for a new film in a genre of your choice OR pages of a functioning website targeting a 16- to 34-year-old audience.

Name, sub-genre and brief synopsis of the film:

The sub-genre will be 'coming of age'. It is based on a girl who wants to succeed in women's football. Her parents, who are in the middle of an acrimonious divorce, want her to go to university and have an academic career.

Pages to be produced:

A DVD back and front cover featuring the main character in a split image showing her in her football strip and her school uniform. The back cover will include a narrative blurb and thumbnails depicting key events in the story. I will also produce a teaser and theatrical poster with a distinctive branding and tagline. 'Her goals weren't theirs.'

Target audience:

Young people aged 16–34 with an interest in this sub-genre and up and coming new stars. They will be attracted by the young actors and the accessible narrative. I will also include other hooks, for example 'From the director of ...' and logos from independent film festivals as marks of quality.

Application of media language:

My research into similar products suggested that the genre conventions of this film sub-genre focus more on the narrative due to the lack of stars as a selling tool. The main characters will be featured and their visual codes, including clothing, gesture and expression, will give clues to their characters, their role in the narrative and their interaction. These characters will appear in different situations on the film posters. The thumbnails on the DVD cover will show other aspects of the narrative and construct enigmas for the audience.

Representations and how they will be constructed:

The main representation will be of young women. This will be constructed through the clothing, gesture and mode of address of the women featured in the pages I am constructing. The blurb on my DVD cover will suggest how my character reinforces the representation of a modern woman. The DVD cover and theatrical poster will also feature representations of older people in positions of authority, as I found this to be a convention of this sub-genre. The issue of the pressures faced by young people at school and home will also be represented.

Industry: production, distribution and marketing:

In my research I found that products similar to mine were produced by independent film companies, for example Warp Films, so I will use their logo on my pages. This would allow for marketing of the new film along with similar films. As I am targeting a young audience, I will make use of social media in my marketing campaign. On my DVD and poster I will also show any other companies that may have contributed to the film as this is usual with independent films.

Tip

Remember the focus of this brief must be **film marketing**. You must not make extracts from the film or a trailer.

Tip

Your teacher is required to check the progress of your work at key stages in its development. A treatment, like the one on the left, is useful to show your ideas.

Tip

The ideas set out in the treatment for DVD covers and posters are transferable for websites. Here you will also need to consider the audio-visual features of your product.

Tip

Ensure that your planning addresses the theoretical framework and demonstrates how you will reflect it in your production.

Stretch and Challenge 7.11

Consider how you can be creative and innovative in the way in which you construct representations in your print and online products for your new film.

Additional Planning for a Website

- Draft designs of your ideas. Look back at your research and consider what you may replicate and what you may decide to do differently. Even the simplest draft designs help you to visualise the look of your pages and how you will establish the key conventions of your film and demonstrate your understanding of the theoretical framework.
- Adaptation of an existing template to suit the ideas for your programme and to reflect the genre.
- Consideration of aspects of a website, for example interactivity. You may want to include a blog or another way in which the audience can be involved in the website and so contribute to the marketing of the film.

Tip

Look back at the 'Tips for Success' for Magazines (page 211) and for Television (page 223), as most of these are applicable to the Film Marketing brief.

Creating Print Productions: Examples

As explained earlier in this section, the production brief will change each year and whilst there will always be a print and online 'Film Marketing' option, aspects like the production information and target audience will be different each year. Below is an example of the work of a student who produced a DVD cover for a new film in the crime genre. However, the key points related to this work are relevant regardless of the sub-genre.

Tips for Success

Key Points

- There is clear evidence in the DVD cover for *Odious* (below) of the research undertaken into media language, including the conventions of the specific film sub-genre. This is reflected in the layout and composition, the choice and use of original images and the selection of iconography.
- Attention has been paid to the construction of the representation of the film sub-genre and the characters within this genre. This is achieved through attention to visual codes, including clothing and expression. The central image also creates a narrative enigma in its construction.

Crime drama DVD cover by Olivia Cullen

- The cover incorporates industry information, including the age certification.
- The main image establishes the central characters and their positioning on the page creates an enigma regarding their relationship within the film. The images are original and there is evidence that instruction has been given to the models about gesture, expression and clothing in order to establish the representation.
- The promotional blurb on the back cover gives a clear synopsis of the narrative, creates enigmas and suggests a conflict and possible equilibrium.
- The name of the film and the tagline give a clear indication of the film's sub-genre and therefore appeals to a specific audience.
- The absence of star names suggests that the actors are relatively unknown; a convention of an independent film and the focus is therefore on the narrative.
- The expert criticism 'Truly Thrilling' is a marketing device and will persuade an audience to go and see the film.

Tip

Consider carefully how you construct your central image as this will allow you to demonstrate your understanding of representation and the conventions of the sub-genre.

Quickfire 7.13

What else should be included in this DVD cover to fulfil the requirements of the production brief?

Music Marketing

Example brief:
Create an original music video to promote a new artist or band in a genre of your choice. You may choose to work in a sub-genre or hybrid genre of music. You should create a product for an **independent record label** (such as Warp or Rough Trade), targeting a **niche audience** of 25- to 44-year-olds who have a specific interest in your chosen genre of music.

Length: 3 minutes to 3 minutes 30 seconds

Key Terms

Independent record label
A record label that is not necessarily linked to a major record label.

Niche audience
A relatively small audience with specialised interests, tastes and backgrounds.

As with the other forms, the specific detail of the production brief will change each year, for example the record company and the target audience, but you will always be required to create a music video or a website to promote a new artist or band. You will also always be given some element of choice. There will always be other minimum requirements for what you must create. For example, for this brief these may be:

Promotional music video in the chosen genre, which interprets the music and lyrics of the song

- At least three locations (e.g. studio, rehearsal or live venue, or other locations).
- Wide range of camera shots, angles and movement to interpret/amplify the music and lyrics.
- Shots of the artist or band to establish a clear identity.
- Performance footage (rehearsal and/or live).
- Clear structure and an element of narrative conflict and equilibrium.
- Representations of at least one social group.
- Editing of original footage to the music track.
- Original name of artist or band, title of the track.

Tip

You may use an existing song for your music video (this does not need to be copyright-free), but the song must not have an existing official music video.

Stretch and Challenge 7.12

The more examples of music videos you watch the more you will be prepared to produce your own.

Researching Music Videos

Product Analysis

Analyse products that are similar to the one you are required to create, considering media language, representations, audience and industry. The stills featured here are from the music video *Proud Family* from the British grime MC, rapper and songwriter Ghetts. The music video was directed by Nathan James Tettey.

Media Language

Music videos made by independent record labels tend to be lower budget and elements of this style are evident in this music, including the easily accessed locations. The mise-en-scène and the visual codes of clothing immediately establish a realistic aesthetic for the production, reinforcing the musical style.

The main narrative of this music video and others like it revolves around the life of the artist and he is often filmed in 'ordinary' situations. In this music video the narrative takes the audience through the struggles of the artist's life and features Ghetts himself vand some of his actual family, further creating a credible representation of reality.

The narrative journey and the social commentary are further reinforced through the use of the split screen contrasting the 'then' and 'now' and the changes that have occurred in the artist's life. The editing of the music video with the use of close-ups and point-of-view shots makes the audience feel part of the artist's story and encourages empathy. The entire production with the bleached-out colour palette on one side and the warm, ambient lighting on the other, is constructed to appear naturalistic: a common convention of indie music videos.

The choices of the different locations also exemplify key elements of the artist's journey.

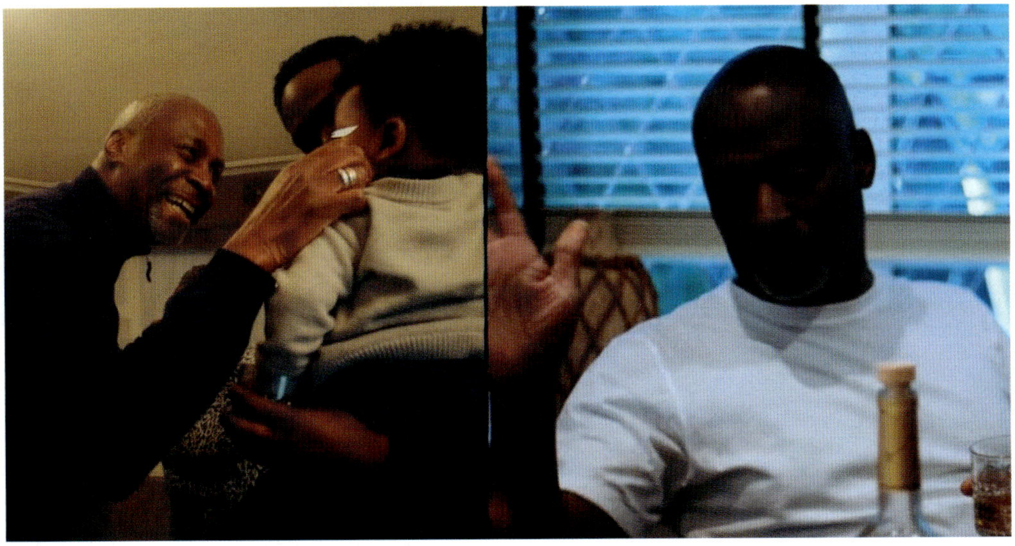

Tip

Consider how the existing products you analyse as part of your research fulfil the requirements of the production brief. For example, the music video for *Proud Family* includes:

- at least three locations, the domestic setting at Christmas, the prison and the live performance venue
- the shots of the artist Ghetts clearly establishe his identity as a young man and an adult
- live performance footage
- evidence of a clear structure and an element of narrative conflict and equilibrium
- editing of footage to match the music track
- the name of the band and the track are included.

Audience

- The audience will be fans of this music genre and the related bands and artists. They may already know the artist from previous releases and/or public appearances. e.g. at music festivals.
- The artist's original record label was Disrupt. A record label which, as well as signing established artists, showcases unreleased and unexposed music artists – this may attract fans.
- The filming and editing of the music video have lower production values resulting in a more social realistic style, positioning the viewer to feel more involved with the artist and the subject matter. This is further emphasised by the use of close-ups of the participants. The audience feel as if they are getting exclusive access to the artist and his life story.

Representation

- Consider how the artist and the director have made choices about how to construct different representations in this music video and how this also represents the music genre.
- Visual codes are important, including the iconography of the prison contrasting with that of the house at Christmas and the clothing establishing the young man as part of an institution with a 'uniform'.

Consider how media language communicates meaning and constructs representations in this music video.

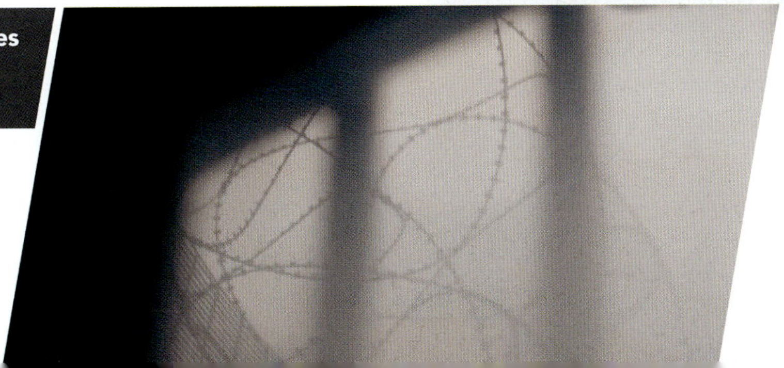

- The contrasting settings in the different time frames, e.g. the warm, welcoming house at Christmas and the cold, lonely prison cell construct representations of the young man who has made mistakes and the adult who has turned around his life.
- The use of gestures and expressions, in particular those of the mothers and the young man, contribute to the realism of the story and establishes its credibility.

Industry

- Ghetts is a grime artist who at the start of his music career was signed to Disrupt Records.
- The style and aesthetic of *Proud Family* reflects the music genre and the industry context.
- Artists such as Ghetts are often known for their support of up and coming artists and elements of the industry established to support them, for example the Suede Music Studio in London created to support emerging artists.
- Artists such as Ghetts use music festivals, social media and appearances at smaller, more intimate venues to raise their profile and connect with their audiences.

Music Marketing Brief

The music marketing production brief will give you the option of creating a website.

Example brief:
Create a functioning website, to include a working homepage and two linked pages, to promote a new artist or band in a genre of your choice.

You may choose to produce a website for an artist or band within a sub-genre or hybrid genre of music.

You should create a product for an independent record label (such as Warp or Rough Trade) targeting a niche audience of 25- to 44-year -who have a specific interest in your chosen genre of music.

Length: three pages, including 45 seconds of audio or audio-visual material related to the topic.

Tip

Watch the full music video Proud Family here: www.youtube.com/watch?v=pggyuY6Z3eY.

Explore how the director Nathan James Tettey has used real locations and people to construct representations and communicate messages. Consider how you could replicate some of his techniques using your surroundings and people you know to construct a narrative music video.

Tip

Consider how you will use the knowledge and understanding gained from the study of your music video set products in Component 1 to help you to produce your own music video.

Tip

Consider how you want to represent the band/artist you create. How can you use visual codes to construct this representation? For example, how you decide to dress the band members and where you decide to film.

Quickfire 7.14

If the brief asked you to produce a more mainstream music video, what codes and conventions would be different?

Tip

Look back at the 'Key Features of an Online Magazine' on page 208. Many of these general features can be transferred to a promotional website for a new band or artist.

You will also be given other minimum requirements for what you must create. For example, for this brief these may be:

One working homepage and two further, linked, pages:

Homepage:

Menu bar

Main image plus at least two other images (all original) to establish the identity of the new artist or band and promote the music.

Original logo for the artist or band name.

Working links to two further pages from the website.

1. Either a 'News' or 'Biography' page, or
2. a 'Blog' by a band member detailing either the making of a new album or the making of a music video.

These pages must include written text promoting the band or artist and their music (approximately 250 words in total).

45 seconds of original audio or audio-visual material related to the topic embedded into one of the pages (e.g. an interview with the artist or band, or live performance/rehearsal footage).

Planning Music Marketing Products

Once you have conducted your research into music videos and the promotional websites for bands and artists similar to the one you want to produce, you are ready to engage in some planning tasks to prepare you for creating your own products. For this media form planning tasks may include the following.

A Pitch or Treatment

This sets out your ideas. This type of planning will also help to ensure that you are applying the theoretical framework and that you have considered:

- media language including the generic codes and conventions of your chosen product
- the representations contained in your product and how they are constructed to communicate meaning
- how to appeal to, engage and position your niche target audience
- how your product will be produced, distributed and marketed.

Tip

It is important to research websites for artists and bands similar to the one you are marketing. Consider how the website's layout and design, images and content help to promote the artist/band and establish their identity.

Tip

Your choice of locations for your music video and still images for your website can allow you to be creative while also demonstrating aspects of the theoretical framework, for example media language, representations and industries.

Tip

Look at the storyboard template on page 219, this will help you with your planning of shots.

Locations can reflect the music sub-genre.

A Recce

Visit the different locations you may use in your music video and take photographs of them; you can then use these in your storyboard. Consider the best time of day to film in these locations, taking account of aspects such as, for example, lighting. Pick locations that reflect the music sub-genre you have chosen and demonstrate your understanding of the conventions of low-budget, independent music videos. Remember, you will be told in the brief how many locations must feature in your video and how many images should appear on your web pages.

Quickfire 7.15

Give an example of how locations can reflect a music sub-genre.

Quickfire 7.16

How would the locations change if this was a mainstream band targeting a broad audience?

A Storyboard

A storyboard is an essential planning device undertaken by most music video directors. It allows them to think in advance about the different elements of a music video they may want to include in order to promote the band or artist, for example studio rehearsals and live performance intercut with a narrative about the band. Although the storyboard is a print process you must not view it as such – instead, think about it as a way of recording a moving image. You must have thought this through and see the finished moving image in your head before committing it to paper. This will help you to think about camera shots, angles and transitions.

Make sure that you include a range of different shots and transitions in order to hold the attention of your audience. Think about how the lyrics of your chosen track will be interpreted in your narrative.

Consider how you want to represent your performer.

Give some thought to how you will film your band/artist in performance, for example using close-ups of the lead singer and cutting between different band members to establish their different personalities and musical skills.

Consider the narrative techniques that apply to your chosen genre. For example, music videos will often intercut a narrative strand with shots of rehearsals or live performance. Flashbacks can manipulate time and space in a music video. It is also important to consider how you will introduce the characters/performers and how you will construct their representation. Remember the job of the technical codes and editing is to 'show' the audience the characters and narrative and introduce some enigmas to keep them interested.

Producing a Music Video

Now that you have finished your research and planning you are ready to produce your music video or promotional website pages. You should now have a very clear understanding of what you want to produce and how you will reflect the theoretical framework in your product.

Tips for Success

- **Equipment**: consider what you need to produce your music video. You may need to film with more than one camera in order to show your performer in a more interesting way.
- In your music video you may want to distinguish between the external and internal settings you have chosen by experimenting with the lighting to achieve a more naturalistic feeling for the outside shots. The three stills here are from one student's music video. She has represented her artist differently in various locations.
- **Sound**: lip-synching is important and very obvious if it is not executed correctly. It needs careful consideration. If you are going to dub the sound on **post-production** then it is important that your artist sings along to the track, playing while you are filming and does not try to mime, this will make the post-production process much easier. It is also important that they have learned the words of the song!

Music video stills courtesy of Lucy-Alice Williams

Quickfire 7.17

How does the music video made by the student reflect the research?

Key Term

Post-production
The term for any production work that takes place on moving or still images after the initial filming or photography shoot has taken place.

Tip

Always have a backup copy of your footage and your edit, just in case!

- Your artist/band should sing the entire song in each of the locations you choose to give you plenty of potential for editing.
- Remember that you can use an existing song but you need to choose a track that does not have an existing official music video. This will allow you to be more creative and original. Making the right choice about the song you choose is important and must suit the sub-genre of music and the representation of your band/artist.
- Consider what iconography you can include in your music video to reflect the style of it and to reinforce the representation of the artist/band. For example, filming against a wall of graffiti immediately gives an edgier feel and enhances the style of the music represented.
- Make sure that you film in enough time – editing always takes longer than you think! Build in 'disaster time' in case you lose footage and have to re-shoot a scene.

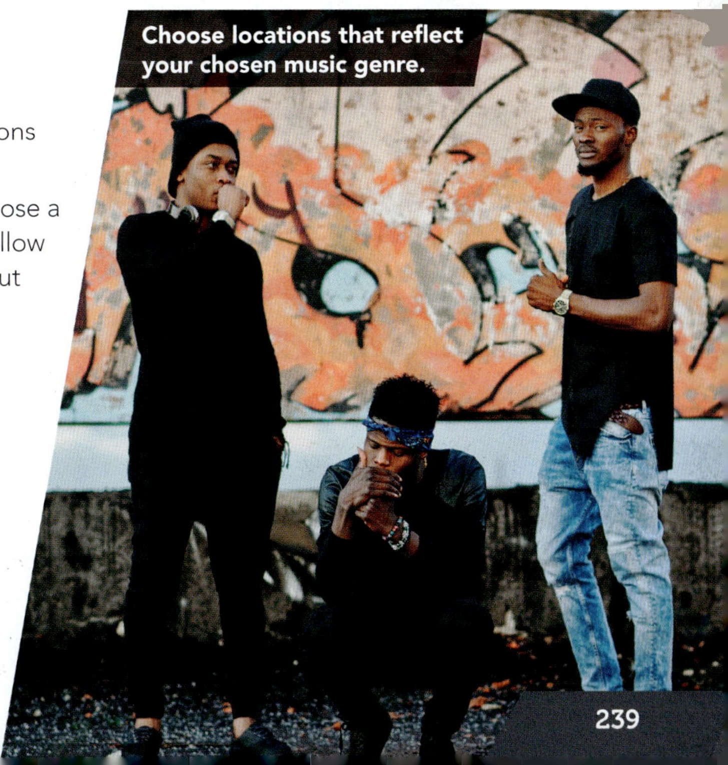

Choose locations that reflect your chosen music genre.

Creating Music Videos: Examples

As explained earlier in this section, the production brief will change each year and while there will always be an audio-visual and online music marketing option, the industry elements and target audience may be different each year. On this page are examples of a music video produced for an independent band. However, the key points related to this work are relevant regardless of the specific focus.

Key Points

This student has addressed some of the requirements of the brief and shown their understanding of the media framework, while also incorporating their knowledge and understanding of the key codes and conventions of music videos produced by independent record labels.

The different characters and band members are established. Their representation has been constructed through visual codes including clothing, gesture and expression. This also reflects the style of music.

Music video stills courtesy of Hannah Phipps and Azura Alwi from Heaton Manor School

- The music video is clearly low budget, featuring easily accessed locations, including the roof top, school classroom and other urban settings.
- The main iconography is the setting, an inner city roof top, the instruments played by the band members, and the microphone and stand used as the prop for the lead singer.
- A wide range of camera shots, angles and movements are used to convey the style of music and the supplementary narrative.
- The technical codes are conventional for this sub-genre of music video, for example the close-up of the hand playing the guitar; this also establishes the credibility of the performers.
- The band members are represented as 'rebellious youth', both in their performance style and their behaviour in the classroom.
- The structure of the music video cuts between live performance, the band members at school and the relationship narrative, which involves conflict and reflects the lyrics.

Summary

This component is internally assessed and externally moderated by Eduqas.

This component allows you to apply the knowledge and understanding of the theoretical framework you have learned during the course to a practical production task.

There will be a set of production briefs released at a set time each year. The briefs will change but options will always be available. You will be required to create a production for a different intended audience and/or industry context each time.

The following media forms will always be set:

- **Television**: a sequence from a new television programme or a website to promote a new television programme.
- **Music marketing**: a music video or a website to promote a new artist or band.
- **Film marketing**: a print marketing campaign or a website to promote a new film.
- **Magazines**: a new print or online magazine.

You are not required to create websites through programming languages such as HTML. It is acceptable to use web design software and templates but all content must be original.

In your production you must apply and demonstrate your knowledge and understanding of media language, representation, audience and media industries. This is the focus of the assessment.

All still images and audio-visual footage must be your own.

You must complete an **individual** media production but you can use unassessed people to help you.

You must complete a **Statement of Aims and Intentions**; this should briefly outline your aims and intentions for the media production. It will be assessed and is a means to allow you to explain the ways in which you have applied the theoretical framework.

You must also complete a cover sheet giving additional information.

You should not spend more than eight weeks on this component.

8 Component 3: Statement of Aims and Intentions

The Statement of Aims and Intentions is a requirement of the non-exam assessment and is worth 10 marks. It allows you to outline the ways in which you will apply the theoretical framework in response to the production brief and how you will target the intended audience.

This should be completed after you have decided how to interpret the production brief and **after** the research and planning stages but **before** the production stage.

The Statement of Aims and Intentions must be approximately 250 words in length. Its purpose is to enable you to outline your plans for meeting the requirements of the brief and to demonstrate the ways in which you will apply your knowledge and understanding of the theoretical framework.

The Statement of Aims and Intentions must be submitted to your teacher before production work commences. You will use the template on the cover sheet provided by Eduqas to guide you and you will be required to explain:

- Your response to the brief, including how you will reflect the industry context and target the intended audience. This may include reference to:
  - The production processes, distribution and marketing, scheduling or regulatory issues.
  - How the product reflects the values of the organisation, for example if it is a television sequence for the BBC as a public service broadcaster or a music video for an artist signed to an independent record company.
  - The demographics and psychographics of your target audience.
- The methods you intend to use to position/appeal to target audience, for example:
  - the codes and conventions of media language
  - the mode of address that will suit your audience – formal/informal.

Tip

The Statement of Aims and Intentions must be closely linked to the form you have chosen for your production brief.

Tip

The Statement of Aims and Intentions is not reflective or an evaluation, it must be completed before you embark upon the chosen production.

Quickfire 8.1

What is the purpose of completing a Statement of Aims and Intentions?

The Statement of Aims and Intentions helps you to formalise your planning.

How you intend to use appropriate conventions and representations.
This may include:

- The choices you made about the selection and combination of elements of media language you intend to use in your product.
- Any intertextual references or genre hybridity.
- How you intend to use the codes and conventions to communicate meaning.
- The message you intend to communicate in your product. This may show your understanding of semiotics and the values, attitudes and beliefs contained in your product.

The specific techniques you intend to use to construct representations including:

- visual codes, technical codes, language
- the inclusion of under-represented or misrepresented groups or individuals
- how the way in which you construct the representations communicates meaning
- the reinforcing or challenging/subverting of stereotypes
- how the representations you have constructed will relate to context, for example social, cultural, historical or political.

You should use subject-specific terminology to demonstrate your knowledge and understanding of the chosen form.

Your teachers will check your research and planning work and the Statement of Aims and Intentions, and then sign the relevant authentication statement on the cover sheet.

The Cover Sheet

The Statement of Aims and Intentions is completed as part of a cover sheet that will be submitted with your production.

One part of the cover sheet will be completed by you and it should give details of key aspects of your production work including:

- details of the planning undertaken and the production process. These stages will have been signed off by you and your teacher at key points
- the software used in constructing your production
- information about any non-original music you have used
- details of any non-assessed participants you have used in your production.

You and your teacher are required to sign the cover sheet to authenticate your work at three key stages during the process. Your teacher will also complete a section with their comments and marks.

Tip

It is very important that you reflect the aims and intentions you have written in your statement in what you create for your production. Your teacher will assess your production in the light of what you say in your statement.

Tip

Guidance for completing your cover sheet can be found here: www.eduqas.co.uk/umbraco/surface/blobstorage/download?nodeId=34574.

Tip

It is also important that you complete your cover sheet in as much detail as possible, as this will help the moderator who may look at your work.

9 Examination Preparation and Tips

Component 1: Investigating the Media

> **Tip**
> As you are expected to be able to structure an extended examination response, it is important that you practice these types of examination questions.

> **Tip**
> You will be expected to refer to the theories you have learned in your response and be able to apply them to both the set product and the unseen resource.

> **Tip**
> In class you will have studied a range of extended examples from the set forms to prepare you for responding to the unseen response.

> **Tip**
> The unseen resource will be taken from one of the following set forms: advertising and marketing, music videos or newspapers. You will need to apply the skills you have learned in class when analysing the unseen resource.

In this assessment you are expected to:

- Analyse critically and compare how media products construct and communicate meanings.
- Use theories appropriate to each level and subject-specific terminology.
- Debate key questions relating to the social, cultural, political and economic role of the media.
- Construct and develop a sustained line of reasoning in an extended response.

Section A: Investigating Media Language and Representation

This section assesses your knowledge and understanding of media language and representation in relation to: advertising and marketing, music video or newspapers.

There will be two questions in Section A.

- One question will assess your knowledge and understanding of media language in relation to an unseen resource.
- One extended question will assess knowledge and understanding of representation by asking you to compare one set product with a second unseen resource. Reference to relevant media contexts will be required in this question.

For a Media Language or Representation question where you are required to view an audio-visual unseen resource, you will see this resource three times.

You will be given one minute to read the question.

- First viewing: watch the extract
- Second viewing: watch the extract and make notes. You will then have five minutes to make further notes.
- Third viewing: watch the extract and make final notes.

Once the third viewing has finished, you should answer Question 1.

This section is assessing Assessment Objective 2:

Apply knowledge and understanding of the theoretical framework to:

- analyse media products, including in relation to their contexts and through the use of academic theories
- make judgements and draw conclusions.

Taking Notes

Note-taking is a skill that needs to be practised before it is perfected. In the examination, if the stimulus is audio-visual, you will be guided to make notes during and between the second and third viewings. As you will not have access to the audio-visual material after the third screening, it is vitally important that you make effective notes, as you will need to look back at these when writing your answer.

Tips

- You are given time at the beginning of the exam to read the question; this will help you to prepare what the focus of your note-taking should be.
- Use any bullet points you may be given to guide your note-taking. You must respond to each bullet point in your answer to the question.
- Consider how you will make notes that will be useful in answering the question. Grids are very useful for this task. A well-designed grid will help you to focus on the most important and relevant aspects of the unseen product.
- Avoid merely writing a description of what you see on the screen. Instead, focus on how meanings are conveyed through, for example, particular camera shots, angles and editing techniques.
- Listen as well as watch when you are analysing the stimulus material. Consider the role of audio codes in communicating messages; audio is often analysed less well or even ignored.

Tip

Practise a method of taking notes that works for you and allows you to select the required information to help you answer the question, for example using a grid.

Tip

Remember to avoid descriptions. Consider the purpose and effect of techniques that are used by the product.

Tip

Remember to consider all aspects of the theoretical framework when you are viewing the unseen resource, including context and theoretical perspectives.

Taking the right notes is important.

Sample Questions

Question 1

1. How does media language communicate meaning in the audio-visual unseen resource? [10 marks]

If the focus of the question is media language the following points may be mentioned. This is not an exhaustive list; the points you will need to make will relate specifically to the form of the unseen product, but may include:

- The use of technical codes, for example camera shots, movement, angles and use of lighting. Consider their purpose and effect.
- For an audio-visual unseen resource you will need to consider audio codes including diegetic and non-diegetic sound, for example sound effects, music and dialogue.
- The use of editing, mentioning key aspects, for example pace and transitions and how these create meaning. The editing also contributes to the narrative in terms of the manipulation of time and space.
- How the technical and audio codes may appeal to and position the audience.
- The use of visual codes, demonstrating an awareness of semiotics. These may include iconography, clothing, expression and gesture.
- The use of codes and conventions related to the genre of the product. Consider how these codes and conventions may have been subverted.
- The use of language and mode of address. Consider how this reflects the codes and conventions of the genre.
- The narrative structure of the product and how narrative conventions are used to appeal to the target audience.

To be awarded a mark in the Upper Band you need to:

- Show excellent knowledge and understanding of the theoretical framework when analysing the unseen product, applying that knowledge and understanding in a consistent and accurate manner.
- Offer a perceptive and detailed analysis of the unseen product. This may be informed by relevant theories.

Question 2

If the focus of the question is on representation you will be required to compare one of the set products you have studied in class with an unseen product from one of the forms you have studied for this component – advertising and marketing, music videos and newspapers.

In this sample question the focus is on representation. In this example Question 2 is **an extended response question** worth 25 marks.

Question 2 in this sample question is based on both of the following:

- Resource A, the film poster for *Hidden Figures* (2016).
- The set music video you have studied – either *Formation* by Beyoncé, or *Dream* by Dizzee Rascal.

Dream is the set product until 2023 and is then replaced by *Underdog*, Alicia Keys. However, the approach to the examination question is transferable to the new set product.

Tip

An introductory paragraph helps you to create a more sophisticated response. It also allows you to define any terminology and to show your understanding of the focus of the question and the form of the set product. Practising writing opening paragraphs for a range of possible questions is good exam preparation.

Tip

Semiotics is one of the media language theories that may support and inform your analysis of the unseen product.

Tip

Try to avoid a descriptive response. Analyse how media language communicates meaning considering the purpose and effect of the examples you give from the product. For example, if you give an example of a close-up shot as a technical code, explore how and why it has been used.

2. Compare the choices that have been made in the representation of ethnicity in the film poster and the music video.

In your answer you must consider:

- How ethnicity is represented through processes of selection and combination.
- The reasons for the choices made in the representation of ethnicity.
- The similarities and differences in the representations of ethnicity.
- How far the representations relate to relevant media contexts.

In an extended question like this it is important to unpick the question so that you are sure of what is being asked. The bullet points help you to do this.

In this question you need to consider these key terms and phrases:

- **Compare**: this means that you need to analyse both products, considering the similarities and differences in the way in which they have made choices about how to construct the representations contained within the products.
- **The choices that have been made**: this suggests that you will need to show your awareness that all representations are constructed and informed by a process of selection. This may differ according to the form of the product and its purpose and effect
- **Representations of ethnicity**: here the expectation is that you have an understanding of how ethnicity is represented in different media forms. You may also be able to apply a theoretical perspective linked to representation generally or the representation of ethnicity specifically.

Tip

An extended response is one that is an essay-style response that needs thought. It is a response in which you demonstrate your ability to analyse in detail, showing your understanding of the question. It should be well structured and coherent, including an introduction and a conclusion.

Tip

The extended examples of film posters you have considered in class will prepare you for analysing the unseen product in this question.

Tip

If the unseen product is print, as it is in this example, it is important that you spend some time studying and annotating it in relation to the exam question before you begin your response.

Tip

The extended response question may include bullet points. You must use these to help you to construct your response. However, it is not expected that you address all of the bullet points equally. Some may be more relevant than others to the products you are analysing.

Addressing the Bullet Points

How ethnicity is represented through processes of selection and combination

You should show your knowledge and understanding of representation. As this is the first bullet point it serves as an introduction, enabling you to demonstrate your understanding of the key terms.

Your response should demonstrate:

- Your knowledge and understanding of the fact that all representations are constructed and that what we see in media products is not reality but a representation of reality.
- Your knowledge and understanding of how social groups are represented through the way in which products are encoded.
- Your awareness of the processes that lead media producers to make choices about how to construct representations.

Tip

Look back at Chapter 1 where there is an introduction to representation.

Tip

If the focus of the question is on representation, then it is important to include terminology related to this concept. For example, construction, selection, mediation, stereotypes.

Quickfire 9.1

How could the image on the previous page support a point you may make about context?

Quickfire 9.2

How does the choice of the tagline in *Hidden Figures* help to construct the representation of ethnicity?

The reasons for the choices made in the representation of ethnicity

You should analyse both media products and your response may include:

- How the selection and combination of media language, for example technical, audio and visual codes, constructs representations.
- How the purpose of the product may influence the decisions made by media producers with regard to how they represent ethnicity.
- How the product is edited in order to attract an audience
- The choices made regarding language and mode of address and how this constructs the representations of ethnicity.

Similarities and Differences in the Representations of Ethnicity

The expectation is that you will compare the two products and how they represent ethnicity. These particular products use selection and combination to challenge stereotypical representations of ethnicity.

The Key Similarities

You may refer to some of the following points for the different products:

Hidden Figures:

- Positive visual representations of black women – strong, intelligent and attractive.
- The construction of the poster on page 247 creates a hierarchy that features the black women as powerful and important. The representation of characters from white ethnic groups features lower down the poster. This different focus will appeal to a wider audience.
- The use of visual codes – the women are dressed as professionals and there are clues to the time in which it is set through choice of clothing.
- Visual codes combined with the graphics of formulae/equations/blackboards creating a narrative enigma related to the role of the women in the film. Maths and science careers would not be typically associated with women, particularly black women, at this time.
- This is reinforced by the tagline '*Genius has no race. Strength has no gender. Courage has no limit.*'

Formation also subverts stereotypes through:

- The range of different representations of Beyoncé, for example sitting on the police car, dressed in historical costume and as a performer, reflecting the complexity of identity related to her culture and race, and the resistance to reducing her persona to a simple stereotype.
- Placing the black woman in the typical role of a white woman of the time challenges the audience expectations.
- The celebration of her ethnic identity through lyrics that make references to specific racial characteristics.
- The sense of 'sisterhood' in the dance numbers creating a positive representation.

Dream subverts stereotypes through:

- The positive story of a rapper who triumphs over adversity, gets a record deal and becomes a success, encouraging young people to 'go far'. This representation may appeal to an audience as a refreshing change from more stereotypically negative representations.
- The marketing of the performer as a positive role model from a minority ethnic group.
- The inclusion of a moral, sending a positive message to the target audience.
- The relationship between the rapper and the 1950s TV presenter, challenging preconceived ideas and appealing to a wider audience.

The Key Differences in Representations of Ethnicity

You may refer to some of the following points for the different products:

- *Hidden Figures* appeals to the audience by constructing predominantly positive representations of black women and their 'untold' true story.
- This is combined with more stereotypical representations of white ethnicity: white male astronauts and scientists. The inclusion of the intertextual reference of Jim Parsons who plays Sheldon the sociopathic science 'geek' in *The Big Bang Theory* will appeal to an audience of young men.
- In *Formation* the focus is very much a historical one based on notions of race and history. The substitution of black characters in place of white colonials constructs a message about the history of black people. However, it is important to bear in mind that Beyoncé's music video functions primarily as a marketing device.
- The focus in *Dream* is on modern stereotypical representations and uses the intertextuality of the song and the children's presenter to construct a message that reinforces dominant values, for example 'keep school in your plans', which challenges more typical representations of ethnicity, particularity with regard to young people, seen in this music genre. This music video has a moral and a message.

Tip

These are just some of the points you may make in response to this sample question.

Tip

It is important to select specific examples from both the unseen resource and your set product to support the points you want to make.

How Far Representations Relate to Relevant Media Contexts

All of the products relate to social and cultural contexts. You may mention some of the following points in your response:

Hidden Figures:

- The film poster constructs positive representations of ethnicity and gender. It challenges negative and preconceived ideas of representation offering a more diverse view of ethnicity in contemporary society.

- In terms of social context, the fact that this story was 'hidden' at the time and has only just come to light offers an interesting perspective on contemporary views of ethnicity and redressing the balance.
- The representations constructed in the product also relate to wider cultural debates regarding the representation of race and ethnicity in the film industry, such as the lack of racial diversity in Oscar-nominated films: #OscarsSoWhite.

Formation:

- This music video includes direct references to contemporary American culture and social issues. There are references to Hurricane Katrina and the floods in New Orleans.
- There are repeated references to modern and historical contexts related to ethnicity in America. References to the 'stop shooting us' campaign are included in the video, reflecting the social context of the time.
- There are also direct references in the video to Beyoncé's cultural identity within contemporary American society.

Dream:

- This music video reflects aspects of contemporary British society in relation to ethnic and social groups. There is the use of binary opposites reflecting tensions within society, for example police and young people.
- However, the social and cultural context is seen in a more positive way as Dizzee Rascal's 'dream' becomes a reality, showing that contemporary society can offer opportunities to under-represented cultural groups.
- The juxtaposition of the young peoples' cultural context with the nostalgia of the 1950s provides a wider social, cultural and historical context.

Stretch and Challenge 9.1

Using the information here about how to structure a response, come up with a set of bullet points you could use to answer the question comparing *Hidden Figures* and *Underdog*.

Section B: Media Industries and Audiences

This section includes stepped questions that allow you to demonstrate your knowledge and understanding of the theoretical framework. There are no unseen products in this section of the examination paper.

Sample Questions

Question 3

The focus of this question is Media Industries.

3. (a) Give one example of a public service radio station. [1 mark]

This question has only one mark but a variety of answers including:

- BBC radio stations, for example Radio 1
- Asian Network
- local stations, for example Radio Newcastle.

Tip

Look at the mark allocations for the questions and respond accordingly. Question 3 (a) is 1 mark so only needs a very brief answer. Question 3 (b) is worth 4 marks so needs more detail but is not an extended response. The clue here is the word 'briefly'.

3 (b) Briefly explain two key features of public service broadcasting. [4 marks]

You may include two of the following features in your answer:

- Public service broadcasting channels do not show adverts and are a not-for profit service.
- Public service broadcasting is funded by the licence fee.

Tip

In Question 3 (b) another command word is 'explain'. It is not enough to just name a feature, for example the licence fee; you must also show your knowledge and understanding by giving a more detailed explanation.

- Public service broadcasting is required to fulfil certain criteria as part of its remit. With regard to the BBC, this will be set out in its charter.
- Public service broadcasters are publically accountable and will produce annual reports on their service.

3 (c) Explain how social and cultural contexts influence radio production. Refer to *Late Night Woman's Hour* to support your points. [10 marks]

This question provides you with the opportunity to draw together knowledge and understanding from across the full course of study. You will be rewarded for including knowledge and understanding of the radio industry but also for other areas of the theoretical framework including audience, representations and media contexts.

Your response will demonstrate knowledge and understanding of how social and cultural contexts influence radio production, for example:

- the cultural context of public service broadcasting
- the social and cultural context of gender issues
- the cultural context of popular culture
- the contemporary social and cultural context of the set product
- the need for the industry to appeal to and address contemporary audiences.

You may include some of the following in your response.

Points that show you can draw together knowledge and understanding of the theoretical framework:

- The remit of Radio 4 is to appeal to listeners who want '*intelligent programmes in many genres which inform, educate and entertain*'. The industry context of the BBC as a public service broadcaster influences programmes such as *Late Night Woman's Hour.*
- As BBC radio is funded by the licence fee it has some freedom to produce programmes that may target a less mainstream audience.
- The guests on *Late Night Woman's Hour* often represent social and cultural diversity. In one episode, 'Home', these included: Susie Orbach, a psychotherapist, Rachel Hurdley a research fellow at Cardiff University, Helen Zaltzman a podcaster and crafter, and Trine Hahnemann a chef and author. The inclusion of this diverse group of successful women reflects greater gender equality in society. The presenter Lauren Laverne is also a successful radio broadcaster.
- The range of representations of strong women that regularly feature on this programme is influenced by the place of women in contemporary society. *Late Night Woman's Hour* provides a platform to discuss social and cultural issues related to women.

Tip

Consider the stems of the question. In question 3 (c) the broader stem at the beginning of the question encourages you to demonstrate your understanding of context in relation to the radio industry generally. The second stem asks that you then apply this understanding to your set product.

Tip

Late Night Woman's Hour is the set radio product until 2023 and then is replaced by either *Woman's Hour* or *Have You Heard George's Podcast?* As the focus of this question is Industry, the relevant industry bullet points can be applied to the new set products.

Tip

Remember you are not engaging in a textual analysis of your set product, you are using it to support the points you make about the radio industry in terms of a social and cultural context.

Examples of how social and cultural contexts influence *Late Night Woman's Hour*, for example:

- Radio 4 is a talk-based radio format and its remit suggests that in its news and current affairs programmes it will discuss pertinent issues in the world today, and so comment on social and cultural changes.
- The creation of the programme by BBC Radio 4, as a spin-off from the long-running *Woman's Hour*, suggests recognition of the need to reflect cultural changes and address a younger female audience.
- The title of the programme, *Late Night Woman's Hour*, suggests that there is a need to reflect these cultural changes through what is now deemed acceptable to be discussed by women. The scheduling time suggests that the audience is niche and the subject matter may be controversial at times.
- The programme includes gender issues regularly as part of its discourse. The subject matter discussed in the programme 'Home' reflects the change in popular culture regarding the place of the woman in the home and the choices women have regarding domesticity. The discussion of past ideas of domesticity shows changes in the social and cultural context of women and their relationship with the home.
- The programme has received some criticism in the press and on social media with regard to its subject matter and use of language not deemed appropriate for the BBC, but this in itself demonstrates how radio can push the boundaries and is influenced by society and culture.

This section assesses Assessment Objective 1:

- Demonstrate knowledge and understanding of the theoretical framework of media.
- Demonstrate knowledge and understanding of contexts of media and their influence on media products and processes.

To be awarded a mark in the Upper Band of the mark scheme you need to be able to:

- demonstrate excellent, detailed and accurate knowledge and understanding of social and cultural contexts and their influence on radio production
- make detailed reference to the set radio programme to support points.

Stretch and Challenge 9.2

Create a set of bullet points that answer this question referring to either *Woman's Hour* or *Have You Heard George's Podcast?* (set products for assessment from 2024).

Question 4

The focus of this question is Audience and it will usually be stepped.

4. (a) Identify two ways in which media organisations categorise audiences. [2 marks]

This question has two marks, one for each organisation identified. Possible answers include:

- demographics, e.g. age, gender, social class, ethnicity/race, income/socio-economic group
- psychographics, e.g. lifestyle, taste, values, attitude.

4. (b) Explain how producers of video games target audiences. Refer to *Assassin's Creed 111: Liberation* to support your points. [8 marks]

The mark here suggests that this response demands more detail. Responses are expected to demonstrate knowledge and understanding of how producers of video games target audiences. You may include some of the following points in your response:

- use of familiar elements of a franchise to appeal to existing users and fans of the franchise, for example in *Assassin's Creed*:
  - historical setting
  - narrative situation of the Assassins v. the Templars
  - open world gameplay
- use of new narrative elements and characters to target a new and/or wider audience
  - for example, in *Assassin's Creed*, the use of a strong female African-French protagonist, Aveline, a freedom fighter, with whom the gamers are positioned through the front cover of the game and the gameplay
  - *Assassin's Creed 111: Liberation* includes elements such as gamers collecting supplies, not merely killing each other, suggesting that a broader audience is being targeted
- use of technology to target its audience
  - for example, *Assassin's Creed 111: Liberation* was designed specifically for the PlayStation Vita, with '*dual touchpads, motion detection and built-in camera*' to enhance the experience for gaming fans
  - use of technology to create a realistic, life-like world to create an immersive experience for the target audience
  - use of websites and social media campaigns to reach the target audience and create a sense of community
  - distribution strategies, such as release of the *Assassin's Creed 111: Liberation* game on the same day as the *Assassin's Creed 111* film, to which it can be linked, which targets the avid fans of the franchise as well as a new audience.

To be awarded a mark in the Upper Band of the mark scheme you must demonstrate:

- Excellent, detailed and accurate knowledge and understanding of how producers of video games target audiences.
- Detailed reference to the set video game to support points.

Tip

The current requirement is to study a game from the *Assassin's Creed* franchise. However, many of the bullet points here related to Audience can be adapted to apply to whichever game you have studied.

Quickfire 9.3

What specific terminology is related to the concept of representation?

Quickfire 9.4

What is the purpose of a connective?

Quickfire 9.5

Think of two more complex synonyms for 'shows'.

Structuring a Response

For the questions with higher marks it is important that you show that you can:

- make informed arguments, reach substantiated judgements and draw conclusions about media issues
- analyse critically and compare how media products construct and communicate meanings
- use appropriate theories and specialist subject-specific terminology appropriately
- construct and develop a sustained line of reasoning in an extended response.

You also need to be able to express yourself in a coherent, articulate way and be able to structure a response to a question. This means:

- Using subject-specific terminology, including vocabulary related to specific media forms such as newspapers, as well as that related to particular concepts such as representation.
- Structuring paragraphs to create a sustained argument. For example, the final sentence of one paragraph should link to its opening sentence of the next paragraph. The reader should be able to anticipate the content of each paragraph from their introductory sentence.
- Using connectives to construct longer, more complex sentences.
- Avoiding generalisations. Support your points with specific examples to illustrate what you want to say.
- Using the PEE structure – point, evidence, explanation. This will help to ensure that you avoid description.
- Using synonyms to make your writing more sophisticated and less repetitive.

Component 2: Investigating Media Forms and Products

In this assessment, you are expected to:

- Analyse how media products construct and communicate meanings.
- Use relevant theories of media studies and specialist subject-specific terminology.
- Debate key questions relating to the social, cultural and economic role of the media.
- Construct and develop a sustained line of reasoning in an extended response.

The examination assesses your knowledge and understanding of media language, representation, media industries, audiences and media contexts in relation to television, magazines and online media.

As we discussed in Chapter 6, the exam paper is divided into three sections – one for each of the media forms that you have studied in depth.

- **Section A** is on Television
- **Section B** is on Magazines
- **Section C** is on Online Media.

In each section, there will be **either** one two-part question **or** one extended response question on the set product you have studied for that particular media form.

Tip

The total number of marks available in each section of the exam is exactly the same. Therefore, you should divide your time evenly across the three sections of the paper, spending about 40 minutes on each.

Tip

In the exam, rather than starting to write your answer straightaway, spend a few minutes planning your response. The plan doesn't have to be extensive or detailed – it may just consist of four or five bullet points. The main purpose of this is to help you identify the key points you want to make. This will also help you structure your answer, as you should try to write a separate paragraph for each of the points in your plan.

Preparing for the Exam

In order to prepare for the Component 2 exam, you will need to go back over the set products you have studied for each of these three media forms. While your revision of each set product should cover all four areas of the theoretical framework, the specific aspects of media language, representation, media industries and audiences that you need to revise for each media form and product will vary.

For example, while you are required to explore the dynamic and historically relative nature of genre in relation to television and magazines, this is not required for online media. Similarly, while you must be able to apply Gauntlett's theory of identity to your set magazine and online media product, you do not have to apply this theory to your set television product.

Information regarding the specific aspects of the theoretical framework that need to be covered for each of the set products can be found in the specification. There are separate grids for each media form. You can use these grids as a check-list when you are revising. Not only will this ensure that you have covered all the relevant topics, it will also give your revision more of a focus.

Tip

Make sure you leave yourself some time at the end of the exam to go back over your answers. Check that you have answered the question and that you have used relevant theories and subject-specific terminology where appropriate. You should also make sure that you have expressed your ideas as clearly as possible.

Sample Questions

Section A: Television

There are three options in this section. The questions are all exactly the same; it is only the set television product that differs. Therefore, which question you answer will simply depend on the set product you have studied.

Option 1: *Peaky Blinders*

To what extent does the set episode of *Peaky Blinders* conform to Todorov's theory of narrative equilibrium?

[20 marks]

Option 2: *Black Mirror*

To what extent does the set episode of *Black Mirror* conform to Todorov's theory of narrative equilibrium?

[20 marks]

Option 3: *Killing Eve*

To what extent does the set episode of *Killing Eve* conform to Todorov's theory of narrative equilibrium?

[20 marks]

Assessment Objective

This question is addressing Assessment Objective 2:

AO2: Apply knowledge and understanding of the theoretical framework of media to:

- analyse media products, including in relation to their contexts and through the use of academic theories
- make judgements and draw conclusions.

Therefore, what you are being assessed on here is your ability to apply Todorov's narrative theory to the set television product you have studied and your ability to make judgements and draw conclusions about the extent to which your set product conforms to Todorov's narrative model.

To be awarded a mark in the Upper Band:

- Your analysis of the set episode must be perceptive and informed by a detailed knowledge and understanding of specific aspects of Todorov's narrative theory.
- The judgements and conclusions you make must be fully supported with detailed reference to specific aspects of the set episode.

As this is an extended response question, you are also required to construct and develop a sustained line of reasoning. Your argument must be logical, coherent and relevant and you need to make sure that the points you make are fully **substantiated**.

Tip

To substantiate something is to provide evidence to support or illustrate a point, idea or argument – for example, supporting the idea that a television product does or does not conform to Todorov's theory by referring to a specific aspect of its narrative construction.

Note

These Sample Assessment Materials questions have been changed to reflect the new set products.

Tip

Remember that you only have to answer one question in each section of the exam paper.

Tip

When you are revising, check which theories you need to be able to apply to each of the products you have studied. This information is provided in the summary at the end of each section in Chapter 5. You can also cross-reference this by looking at the AS Media Studies specification in the Eduqas section of the WJEC website.

Tip

Although the sample question included here is addressing Assessment Objective 2, there is no fixed pattern in terms of how the sections of the paper relate to the different assessment objectives. A question in Section A could address either AO1 or AO2, for instance.

Making judgements and drawing conclusions

Questions such as this that require you to make judgements and draw conclusions often use phrases like 'To what extent …?' or 'How far can …?' It's important not to ignore this part of the question. In other words, you need to make sure that your analysis or discussion leads to some form of judgement or conclusion.

For example, with this particular question there are a number of possible conclusions that you could draw. Having analysed the narrative structure of your set television product in relation to Todorov's narrative theory, you might conclude that:

- the set product conforms fully to Todorov's theory, or
- the set product conforms to Todorov's theory to a certain extent, or
- the set product does not conform to Todorov's theory at all.

As this demonstrates, there is a range of legitimate responses to this question, all of which are perfectly acceptable. What is important, therefore, is that you are able to substantiate your answer by making detailed reference to specific aspects of the product you have studied.

Analysing media products using academic theories

What you would also need to do here is demonstrate your ability to analyse your set television product using Todorov's narrative theory. For example:

If your set television product is *Peaky Blinders*, you could discuss:

- the way in which the opening scenes establish an initial state of equilibrium by focusing on the everyday life of working-class families such as the Shelbys in Birmingham in 1919
- the way in which the initial equilibrium is disrupted when the crate of guns goes missing, providing Tommy Shelby with a new business opportunity.

If your set television product is *Black Mirror*, you could discuss:

- the way in which Yorkie's quest to find Kelly could be regarded as an attempt to restore equilibrium
- the way in which the the final scene establishes a new equilibrium with Kelly and Yorkie reunited in the virtual reality of San Junipero.

If your set television product is *Killing Eve*, you could discuss:

- the way in which the opening scenes establish an initial state of equilibrium by showing the nature of Eve and Villanelle's everyday working lives (e.g. conveying a sense of Eve's boredom and restlessness)
- the way in which the initial equilibrium is disrupted when Eve's and Villanelle's paths cross after Eve is given the task of protecting the only witness to a Russian politician's murder.

You could also demonstrate your ability to apply narrative theory by referring to narrative structures such as flexi-narratives or narrative devices such as flashbacks and enigma codes.

Tip

A mistake that is commonly made with questions on narrative is to simply describe what happens in the product, outlining particular aspects of the story. In order to give your answer more analytical depth, you need to consider the significance of the narrative's construction. How and why has the narrative been constructed in the way that it has? What is the purpose or effect of this?

Quickfire 9.6

What are the five key stages in Todorov's theory of narrative equilibrium?

Section B: Magazines

As with Section A, there are three options in this section. Again, the questions are all the same except for the set magazine product that they refer to.

Option 1: *Woman*

(a) With reference to the front cover of the set edition of *Woman*, explain the difference between denotation and connotation.

[5 marks]

(b) How far do the representations in the set edition of *Woman* (1964) reflect social and cultural contexts?

[15 marks]

Option 2: *Woman's Realm*

(a) With reference to the front cover of the set edition of *Woman's Realm*, explain the difference between denotation and connotation.

[5 marks]

(b) How far do the representations in the set edition of *Woman's Realm* (1965) reflect social and cultural contexts?

[15 marks]

Option 3: *Vogue*

(a) With reference to the front cover of the set edition of *Vogue*, explain the difference between denotation and connotation.

[5 marks]

(b) How far do the representations in the set edition of *Vogue* (1965) reflect social and cultural contexts?

[15 marks]

These are examples of two-part questions. You need to make sure that you answer both parts of the question. Remember that two-part questions could feature in any of the three sections of the Component 2 exam paper.

Tip

Look carefully at the number of marks available for each part of the question. They may not be equally weighted. In this example, for instance, the first part of the question is worth 5 marks while the second part is worth 15. This means that you should spend more time on the second part of the question compared with the first.

Tip

While you may be given an extract from the set magazine to analyse in Section B, this will not always be the case. Therefore, you need to make sure that you have a detailed knowledge of your set magazine and that you are able to refer to specific features, articles, adverts, cover lines and images to support the points you make. Remember that it is not the entire magazine that you have to be familiar with – it is only specified extracts. You can access these extracts via the WJEC Eduqas secure website.

Assessment Objectives: Part a

The first part of this question is addressing Assessment Objective 1:

AO1: Demonstrate knowledge and understanding of the theoretical framework of media.

In particular, what you are being assessed on here is your knowledge and understanding of a specific aspect of media language – semiotics.

To be awarded a mark in the Upper Band you need to:

- Demonstrate excellent, accurate knowledge and understanding of semiotic terms.
- Define and exemplify the difference between denotation and connotation clearly and precisely by referring to specific aspects of the magazine cover.

Demonstrating knowledge and understanding

To demonstrate your knowledge and understanding of these semiotic terms you need to explain how the front cover of the set magazine functions at the level of denotation by identifying relevant signs such as:

- the type of camera shot or angle that is used
- the type of words that are used
- the typographical devices that are used
- the colours that are used
- the iconography that is used (e.g. costumes, props, etc.)
- the facial expressions, postures or gestures that are adopted or used.

You also need to explain how the magazine cover functions at the level of connotation by discussing the meanings associated with or suggested by relevant signs – discussing what a particular camera shot, word, colour or facial expression suggests, for instance.

In order to explain the difference between denotation and connotation, you might point out that:

- The cover of *Woman* denotes a woman wearing a floral dress who is smiling as she turns towards the camera. Her facial expression connotes happiness and contentment while her floral dress has connotations of femininity.
- The cover of *Woman's Realm* denotes a woman wearing a hat, coat and gloves, who is raising her hand to her face as she looks towards the camera, smiling. Her gestural codes have connotations of female modesty.
- The cover of *Vogue* denotes a woman wearing a turquoise turban that is covered in jewels. The jewels can be seen to connote wealth and opulence.

As this question requires you to *explain* the difference between denotation and connotation rather than just identify the denotative and connotative meanings of the magazine cover, you would need to briefly add that what this demonstrates is that denotation refers to the 'literal' or common-sense meaning of the sign, whereas connotation refers to the meanings associated with or suggested by the sign.

Tip

Look back at the Magazines section of Chapter 5 for a reminder of how to use semiotic concepts to analyse a magazine.

Tip

Although you are not specifically required to refer to particular theories in this question, doing so may give your work more analytical depth. Gauntlett's theory of identity and Hall's theory of representation could be usefully applied here for example.

Tip

This is another example of a question that requires you to make judgements and draw conclusions. If a question uses the phrase 'How far ...?' or 'To what extent ...?' you know that this is something you need to include in your answer.

Tip

Remember that you need to support the points you make by referring to specific aspects of the set magazine you have studied.

Assessment Objectives: Part b

The second part of the question is addressing Assessment Objective 2:

AO2: Apply knowledge and understanding of the theoretical framework of media to:

- analyse media products, including in relation to their contexts and through the use of academic theories
- make judgements and draw conclusions.

In particular, this question is assessing your ability to analyse the set magazine product in relation to the social and cultural contexts in which it was produced. It is also assessing your ability to make judgements and draw conclusions about the extent to which its representations reflect those social and cultural contexts.

To be awarded a mark in the Upper Band:

- Your analysis of the set magazine and the links you make between the magazine and the social and cultural context in which it was produced must be perceptive and insightful.
- The judgements and conclusions you make must be fully supported with detailed reference to specific aspects of the set magazine.

Analysing media products in relation to their contexts

In analysing your set magazine product in relation to its social and cultural contexts, you could consider the way in which it relates to particular:

- social and cultural norms
- social and cultural ideals
- social and cultural attitudes, values and beliefs
- social and cultural anxieties and issues.

Making judgements and drawing conclusions

In making judgements and drawing conclusions about how far the representations reflect social and cultural contexts, you could discuss:

- How far the representations in your set magazine can be seen to reflect specifically British cultural concerns, interests or issues.
- How far the representations of gender in your set magazine can be seen to reflect dominant social and cultural ideals of femininity.
- How far the representations of gender roles in your set magazine can be seen to reflect patriarchal norms and values.
- How far the representations in your set magazine can be seen to reflect particular cultural attitudes regarding race, ethnicity or nationality.

Section C: Online Media

There are two options in this section. These Sample Assessment Materials questions have been changed to reflect the new set products.

Option 1: JJ Olatunji/KSI

Explain the strategies that the producers of blogs and vlogs use to attract their audiences. Refer to JJ Olatunji/KSI in your response.

[20 marks]

Option 2: Zoe Sugg

Explain the strategies that the producers of blogs and vlogs use to attract their audiences. Refer to Zoe Sugg in your response.

[20 marks]

Assessment Objective

This question is addressing Assessment Objective 1:

AO1: Demonstrate knowledge and understanding of the theoretical framework of media.

In particular, it requires you to demonstrate knowledge and understanding of the strategies that the producers or creators of blogs and vlogs use to attract their audiences.

To be awarded a mark in the Upper Band you need to:

- Demonstrate excellent knowledge and understanding of how media producers attract audiences.
- Make detailed reference to the set product, demonstrating thorough knowledge and understanding of how and why strategies have been used by producers of blogs and vlogs to attract audiences.

Demonstrating knowledge and understanding

In discussing the strategies that producers of blogs and vlogs use to attract audiences, you could refer to some of the following:

- opportunities for audience interaction/participation such as the 'ONE QUESTION GO' feature on JJ Olatunji's YouTube channel
- content and subject matter – the emphasis placed on issues of particular interest and relevance to Zoe Sugg's target audience on her blog and YouTube channel, such as mental health and sexual wellness, for example
- the use of different modes of address – friendly, instructional, etc.
- collaborations and synergies such as the 'Mark Felt The Baby Kicking and Things We Don't Share Online' collaboration video with Mark Ferris on Zoe Sugg's YouTube channel
- marketing and promotion (appearances at online conventions such as VidCon, for example)
- the branding of blogs and vlogs through design features
- links to social and participatory media such as Twitter, Instagram and Facebook.

Tip

Like the sample question in Section A, this is an extended response question. Therefore, you will need to construct and develop a sustained line of reasoning. Your argument must be logical, coherent, relevant and fully substantiated. For tips on how to structure an extended response, look at page 254 of this chapter.

Tip

There is a danger with this type of question that you may end up just listing strategies that the producers of blogs and vlogs use. As the question requires you to *explain* those strategies, you need to say more about how and why they might be used rather than just describing them.

Tip

Make sure you support the points you make by referring to specific aspects of the set product you have studied.

10 Quick Guide to Theoretical Approaches

Media Language

Semiotics: Roland Barthes

Semiotics is the study of signs and meaning. Roland Barthes is a key semiotic theorist whose ideas you will need to be familiar with. The main principles of his theory of semiotics, which are outlined in the book *Elements of Semiology* (1964), include:

- The idea that texts communicate their meanings through a process of signification.
- The idea that signs can function at the level of denotation, which involves the 'literal' or common-sense meaning of the sign, and at the level of connotation, which involves the meanings associated with or suggested by the sign.
- The idea that constructed meanings can come to seem self-evident, achieving the status of myth through a process of naturalisation.

Narratology: Tzvetan Todorov

Narratology is the study of narrative. A particularly influential narrative theorist is Tzvetan Todorov. The main principles of his theory of narrative include:

- The idea that all narratives share a basic structure that involves a movement from one state of equilibrium to another.
- The idea that these two states of equilibrium are separated by a period of imbalance or disequilibrium.
- The idea that the way in which narratives are resolved can have particular ideological significance.

Genre Theory: Steve Neale

Genre theory is concerned with the way in which media products are classified and categorised. Steve Neale is a theorist who has written extensively on genre. Although his work focuses primarily on film, his ideas can also be applied to other media forms. The main principles of Neale's genre theory include:

- The idea that genres may be dominated by repetition, but are also marked by difference, variation, and change.
- The idea that genres change, develop and vary, as they borrow from and overlap with one another.
- The idea that genres exist within specific economic, institutional and industrial contexts.

Representation

Theories of Representation: Stuart Hall

Stuart Hall is a cultural theorist whose work encompasses a wide range of topics, including how representations are constructed and the ways in which audiences may respond to these constructions. The main principles of Hall's theory of representation include:

- The idea that representation is the production of meaning through language, with language defined in its broadest sense as a system of signs.
- The idea that the relationship between concepts and signs is governed by codes.
- The idea that stereotyping, as a form of representation, reduces people to a few simple characteristics or traits.
- The idea that stereotyping tends to occur where there are inequalities of power, as subordinate or excluded groups are constructed as different or 'other' (e.g. through ethnocentrism).

Theories of Identity: David Gauntlett

David Gauntlett is a theorist who has published widely on a range of topics including media and identity, everyday creativity and the use of digital media. The main principles of his theory of identity include:

- The idea that the media provide us with 'tools' or resources that we use to construct our identities.
- The idea that while in the past the media tended to convey singular, straightforward messages about ideal types of male and female identities, the media today offer us a more diverse range of stars, icons and characters from whom we may pick and mix different ideas.

Industry

Power and Media Industries: Curran and Seaton

James Curran and Jean Seaton are academics whose work focuses mainly on media history and the political economy of the media. Their theory of power and media industries is outlined in the book *Power without Responsibility*, which provides a broad overview of the history of British media. The main principles of this theory include:

- The idea that the media are controlled by a small number of companies primarily driven by the logic of profit and power.
- The idea that media concentration generally limits or inhibits variety, creativity and quality.
- The idea that more socially diverse patterns of ownership help to create the conditions for more varied and adventurous media productions.

Audiences

Media Effects: Albert Bandura

Media effects theories are concerned with the effects that the media may have on audiences. Albert Bandura is a psychologist whose research explores the way in which the media can influence social behaviour. The main principles of his 'social learning theory' include:

- The idea that the media can implant ideas in the mind of the audience directly.
- The idea that audiences acquire attitudes, emotional responses and new styles of conduct through modelling.
- The idea that media representations of transgressive behaviour, such as violence or physical aggression, can lead audience members to imitate those forms of behaviour.

Cultivation Theory: George Gerbner

George Gerbner is another theorist whose research is concerned with the effect that the media can have on audiences. His work explores the way in which the media can influence people's perceptions of social reality. The main principles of his cultivation theory include:

- The idea that exposure to repeated patterns of representation over long periods of time can shape and influence the way in which people perceive the world around them (i.e. cultivating particular views and opinions).
- The idea that cultivation reinforces mainstream values (dominant ideologies).

Reception Theory: Stuart Hall

Stuart Hall's reception theory is outlined in the essay 'Encoding, Decoding', which features in the book *Culture, Media, Language* (1990). The main principles of this theory include:

- The idea that communication is a process involving encoding by producers and decoding by audiences.
- The idea that there are three hypothetical positions from which messages and meanings may be decoded:
  - the dominant-hegemonic position: the encoder's intended meaning (the preferred reading) is fully understood and accepted
  - the negotiated position: the legitimacy of the encoder's message is acknowledged in general terms, although the message is adapted or negotiated to better fit the decoder's own individual experiences or context
  - the oppositional position: the encoder's message is understood, but the decoder disagrees with it, reading it in a contrary or oppositional way.

Glossary of Key Terms

ABC figures The Audit Bureau of Circulations is responsible for measuring the reach of different media across a range of platforms.

Active audience This describes an audience who responds to and interprets the media products in different ways and who actively engages with the messages encoded in the products.

Actively purchased circulation A term used by the industry to describe the copies of a magazine purchased by an individual. This includes single copy purchases, retail sales and subscriptions.

Advertising campaign Run by an advertising agency, a campaign incorporates all of the ways in which a product, event or service is promoted to the audience, for example the packaging, television, print and online adverts.

Advertising spots Advertising spots are the spaces in commercial breaks that are sold to advertisers. Most advertising spots are around 30 seconds long, although they can be longer or shorter than this.

Advertorial An advertisement that is presented in the style of the media product in which it features. An advertorial vlog, for instance, is an advertisement that is presented by the vlogger in their usual editorial style.

Afrofuturism A movement in the arts including film featuring futuristic or science fiction themes and narratives incorporating elements of black culture and history. The aim is to connect audiences from black diaspora with their African heritage.

Algorithm A set of steps or rules that are followed in order to make a calculation, solve a problem or complete a task – the steps involved in determining which advertisements are most suitable for a particular website, for example.

Alley The space between the columns of text.

American Dream The idea that every American can have equal chances to achieve their aspirations.

Anchorage The way in which a caption or piece of written text holds or fixes the meaning of an image in place, encouraging the reader to make a preferred reading.

Android A robot that looks like a human.

Anthology series A series that is comprised of entirely separate, self-contained stories. The individual episodes may be connected by a common, over-arching theme but they generally feature different characters.

Anti-hero A protagonist or central character that lacks the conventional traits of a hero and is fundamentally flawed. Anti-heroes typically exhibit some form of moral complexity or ambiguity. They may be criminals who operate outside of the law but follow their own code of honour and administer their own form of justice, for example.

Artificial intelligence The branch of computer science that is concerned with the capacity of machines to simulate human behaviour by carrying out tasks and actions that normally require human decision-making.

Aspirational Aimed at or appealing to people who want to improve how they look, attain a higher social position or have a better standard of living.

Audience surrogate A character within the text that stands in for the audience. They may think as we do, or act as we ourselves might act in the same situation.

Audio streaming Where listeners can click on a link to play the radio programme instantly. This has increased the global reach of BBC radio, as listeners abroad can tune in to hear the live programme.

Augmented reality Computer-generated content overlaid on a real-world environment commonly used in video games. Augmented reality hardware comes in many forms, including devices that you can carry, such as handheld displays, and devices you wear, such as headsets and glasses.

Avatar The player's representation of themselves within the game.

BBC Writers Room It is good practice to format your script correctly according to the type of text you are creating. For example, the format of a situation comedy is different from that of a television drama. There is a range of different places to help you with this. One of the most useful is the BBC Writers Room: www.bbc.co.uk/writers room.

Below the line advertising An advertising strategy in which a product is promoted on platforms other than radio, television, billboards, print and film.

Billing block A block of text that contains the industry information, including actors, directors, producers, crew members, and production and distribution companies.

Binary opposites When products incorporate examples of opposite values, for example poverty and wealth.

Binary opposition Occurs when two people, ideas, concepts or values are set up in conflict with one another. In a crime drama there is conventionally a binary opposition between the investigator and the criminal, for example.

Binge watching Watching multiple episodes of a television programme in succession. On its website, Netflix has a section entitled 'Binge-worthy TV Programmes', which in January 2022 included, *Squid Game*, *The Witcher* and *Emily in Paris*. Netflix states: 'When it comes to great TV, portion control is for suckers. Here are the best programmes – from sitcoms to dramas to reality – to devour all at once' (www.netfl ix.com/gb/browse/genre/1191605), tapping into the new ways in which audiences access programmes.

Blog A regularly updated website or web page, usually posted by an individual or small group, written in an informal or conversational style.

Blogger Someone who engages in blogging, which is the practice of updating or adding material to a blog. The term blog is short for weblog.

Brand That which identifies one company's products from those of another. The branding may be clearly identifiable by a name, logo or some other trademark, for example the font style used by Kellogg's or the Nike swoosh.

Brand ambassador A person, often a celebrity, who is paid to endorse or promote a particular company's products or services. They become the face of the brand and are associated with the product.

Brand identity The image that a brand projects and the associations the audience makes with the brand. This is built up over time.

Brand recognition The extent to which a brand can be quickly and easily identified. Brand recognition is often facilitated by visual codes such as logos.

Broadsheet Describes a quality newspaper that publishes more serious news, for example the *Daily Telegraph*.

Burden of representation The idea that when representations of particular social groups are limited, those few representations that do find their way into the media have to carry more weight as they end up standing in for entire groups or communities.

Buzz marketing Can also be simply termed 'buzz' and refers to word-of-mouth advertising whereby the interaction of consumers creates a positive association, excitement and anticipation about a new product.

Call to action An instruction that is issued to the audience with the aim of prompting an immediate response – the instruction to 'subscribe now' or to click on a link, for example. This technique is widely used in advertising and marketing.

Canted angle A shot filmed from an oblique or slanted angle.

CAP Code This is the Advertising Code that covers non-broadcast media. The Code is written by the Committee of Advertising Practice (CAP) and administered by the ASA. Its full title is the 'UK Code of Non-broadcast Advertising and Direct and Promotional Advertising'.

Circular narrative Where the narrative starts at the end and then explores the action up to that point. It is sometimes only at the very end of the film or television programme that the narrative makes sense.

Circulation A count of how many copies of a particular publication are distributed, including subscriptions. Circulation audits are provided by the Audit Bureau of Circulations (ABC).

Classification A rating given to a film, informing the audience of its suitability according to criteria that include levels of violence, sexual content and use of inappropriate language.

Cliff-hanger A narrative device that creates suspense. It is typically used at the end of an episode or, in some cases, before an advert break, as its main function is to persuade the viewer to watch the following instalment of the programme in order to find out what happens next.

Codes These are signs contained within a media product that give clues to the product's meaning.

Collaboration video A video that features two or more content creators working together in collaboration.

Colloquialism An informal expression that is often used in casual conversation rather than in writing. However, it is used in some media products to establish an informal communication with the audience.

Commissioning To give a programme the go-ahead for production – to 'greenlight' it. At the BBC, for example, there are Directors of Programming for different genres. Producers pitch their ideas to the relevant controller who then decides whether or not to commission the programme.

Conglomerate A large organisation that owns other companies and has interests spanning across a number of different businesses or industries. For example, the Walt Disney Company is a media and entertainment conglomerate as it has business interests in several different industries, including film, television, music and radio as well as the theme park industry.

Connotation Refers to the meanings we associate with the sign, for example a red rose may connote love or the hoot of an owl may connote night-time.

Consumable products These are the products that we use regularly and that need to be replaced. Some audiences are loyal to a particular brand, whereas others may be persuaded to change as a result of successful marketing devices.

Consume Another way of saying how an audience uses a media product. We consume media products for different reasons.

Content analysis A research method that provides quantitative data. It generally involves counting the number of times a particular feature appears in a given context – counting the number of women who have speaking roles in prime-time television programmes, for example.

Content creators Those who are involved in creating and sharing content online – bloggers and YouTubers for example.

Contexts The aspects of the environment that surround a product at the time of its creation, distribution, circulation or reception and that may affect its meaning.

Continuity When one frame of your storyboard links to the next in a sequence, in order to effectively convey the narrative.

Continuity editing To combine a series of shots into a sequence to create a clear and continuous narrative that can be understood by the audience.

Contrapuntal Sound that does not match what is happening on screen. For example, the introduction of ominous music in a seemingly peaceful scene.

Convergence The process through which different media industries and forms merge with one another or move closer together. This process is often facilitated by digital technologies. For example, smartphones bring together many different functions in a single device – as well as making phone calls, users can browse the internet, play games, watch video content and listen to music.

Copy This is the writing on the media product.

Cover lines The written text that features on the cover of the magazine providing a preview of the content that features inside.

Cross-platform marketing When one form is advertised on another media platform. For example, BBC One will broadcast promotional advertisements for its radio stations; these will also be on the BBC website.

CRPG Computer role-playing game.

Cultural competences Within a media context, this concept suggests that the cultural competence of an audience is the shared knowledge, related to their cultural understanding, of that audience, which means that they will take a particular pleasure from a media product. For example, the audience who understand and engage with the rules of *Call of Duty*, and have a certain computer literacy, will enjoy the control aspect of the game and the online sharing of techniques.

Decode The process through which an audience interprets a message.

Demographic profiling A way of categorising audiences by dividing consumers into groups based on age, sex, income, education, occupation, household size, marital status, home ownership or other factors. This information is of use to some media industries, for example it can help advertisers determine their target audience for particular products and develop adverts that focus on a specific demographic.

Denotation The literal or common-sense meaning of a sign rather than the associated meaning of the sign.

Desensitisation This is a psychological process which suggests that audiences who are exposed regularly to acts of violence through films and video games, for example, are increasingly less likely to feel empathy or concern when exposed to violence, bad language or other forms of aggressive behaviour.

Detective series A crime drama subgenre that focuses on the attempts of investigators to solve crimes. Closely related to the police procedural, the detective series is generally broader in scope as it encompasses the work of amateur sleuths and private investigators as well as the police. Examples include *Sherlock*, *True Detective*, *Inspector Morse* and *Only Murders in the Building*.

Diegetic sound Sound that is part of the mise-en-scène and can be heard by characters in the scene. For example, a gunshot as we see it being fired in a crime drama.

Diegetic world The world in which the story takes place. For example, when we talk about diegetic sound we are talking about sound that appears to come from within the scene itself.

Digital influencer Someone with a significant online following who has the ability to shape and influence the opinions or behaviour of their followers. Also known as an online influencer.

Discourse The topics and language used by a media text and the way they are used. There are certain topics that would never appear in the discourse of a magazine such as *Glamour*. The discourse for this magazine tends to centre on image and how to look good.

Disposable income The money left when bills, etc. have been paid that can be spent on items such as luxury goods and non-essentials. The people with high disposable incomes can be targeted by advertisers.

Distribution The link between the producer and the audience; refers to all the strategies used in the release, marketing and promotion of the product.

Diversification This involves expanding a company's operations into new or different areas of business.

Domestic sphere The private space of the home, as opposed to the public world of work, for example.

Dominant-hegemonic position The position that the media encoder encourages the decoder to adopt when interpreting a text. If they adopt the dominant-hegemonic position they read or interpret the message in the way that the encoder intended, making a preferred reading.

Dominant ideology A set of values and beliefs that have broader social or cultural currency. This may be implicit or explicit as is evident in texts such as tabloid newspapers.

Dual revenue streams Media products that generate revenue from two different sources (from readers and advertisers, for example) are said to have dual revenue streams.

Dynamic Constantly changing, evolving and progressing.

Dystopia A world or society that is as bad or dysfunctional as can be imagined – a world full of crime, violence or oppression, for example.

Editing The way in which the shots are put together to create a particular effect. Editing can be described in terms of pace and the transitions that are employed.

Editorial The part of the newspaper written, supposedly, by the editor who comments on the day's stories. It offers an opportunity for the paper to express its views and to demonstrate its values, attitudes and beliefs.

Editorial philosophy Refers to a magazine's underlying values, attitudes and beliefs, and the particular viewpoint that it adopts. The editorial philosophy helps to determine the style and content of the magazine. It influences decisions regarding what should and what should not be included in the magazine, and shapes and informs the magazine's mode of address and the way in which the content is presented to the reader.

Effect The impact a code may have upon the audience.

Ellipsis Where sentences are incomplete and instead are finished with a set of three dots; the words need to be filled in by the reader.

Emerging media Refers to communication through digital technology and new platforms with interactive elements, for example podcasts, social media, etc.

Encode Communicate ideas and messages through a system of signs.

Enigma codes Enigma codes are the questions or mysteries that a narrative sets up in order to make the audience continue watching. Roland Barthes refers to this as the hermeneutic code.

Equilibrium A state of balance, stability or order. In Todorov's narrative theory, it refers to the status quo – a normal state of affairs. For example, the initial state of equilibrium in a television programme might involve people going about their normal, day-to-day business.

Essentialisation A process that involves ascribing certain traits or characteristics to someone by nature. As those traits are seen to be a part of that person's nature or essence, this means that they are fixed and cannot be changed.

Ethnicity Many people confuse ethnicity and race. Your ethnicity is defined by your cultural identity, which may demonstrate itself through customs, dress or food, for example. Ethnicity suggests an identity that is based on a sense of place, ideology or religion. You can be British but of Jewish ethnicity, for instance.

Ethnocentric Roger Brown defines ethnocentrism as *'the application of the norms of one's own culture to that of others'* (*Social Psychology*, 1965, page 183). Stuart Hall refers to this definition in his theory of representation as he suggests that ethnocentrism is an example of the way in which stereotypes reinforce the power of certain groups over others.

Event Something that occurs or is about to occur and is of interest to an audience. Events come in a range of shapes and forms and can be local, national or international, for example a royal wedding or birth, the Olympic Games or a pop festival. International events may include wars and global recession. A local event may be the local football team being promoted.

Event television Describes programmes such as, for example, the final of *The Great British Bake Off* that attract a large, live audience and as such become an 'event'.

Exhibition All the opportunities available to an audience to view a film, including at multiplex and independent art house cinemas, at film festivals and online.

Exotic other A term used to describe someone or something that is perceived to be different or 'foreign', where that difference or otherness becomes a source of fascination or pleasure.

Expert witnesses Quotes from experts who the audience will trust.

Facial action coding system A technique whereby computer technology is used to capture a plethora of high-resolution skin textures and different facial expressions. This helped the animators to replicate the computer-generated (CG) Audrey Hepburn and make her look real in the Galaxy chocolate advert.

First-run A first-run programme is one that is available for public viewing for the first time.

Flagship show A programme that has particular importance for a channel or broadcaster – one that attracts particularly high ratings, for example, or one that is strongly identified with the channel.

Flexi-narrative A narrative structure that combines aspects of the series and the serial. For example, while each episode may feature a self-contained narrative, character relationships may develop over the course of several episodes forming a broader story arc.

Fly-on-the-wall A form of documentary filmmaking in which the camera is an invisible presence, positioning the viewer voyeuristically as an unseen observer – hence the term 'fly-on-the-wall'.

Focus group A form of qualitative research in which a group of people are asked about their perceptions, opinions, beliefs and attitudes about a product. The aim is to help the producers of the product to ascertain the needs of their target audience.

Forms Different types of media, for example music, newspapers and radio.

Formulaic structure Where the text has a clear structure that is recognisable and rarely changes. For example, the front cover of a lifestyle magazine has key conventions and the audience has expectations of what will appear throughout the publication.

Franchise A series of related media products, for example films, that are recognisable by their common elements, such as the same fictional universe or characters. Franchises are lucrative for film producers as audiences know what to expect and may be fans of the previous films in the franchise.

Gangster dramas A crime drama subgenre that focuses on the criminal activities of gangsters and the world of organised crime. Examples include *The Sopranos*, *Boardwalk Empire* and *Gangs of London*.

Gantt chart A time-tool; it is a chart in which a series of horizontal lines shows the amount of time allocated to a project and then maps the work done or production completed at various stages.

Gatekeeper A person or organisation that is involved in filtering content in some way. For example, in the newspaper industry, editors generally perform this gatekeeping function as they determine which stories make it into the paper (through the gate) and which do not.

Gender norms Cultural expectations regarding how men and women should act or behave – the patterns of behaviour that a particular society considers to be 'normal' for men or women.

Global implications The importance of a product in a worldwide context.

Graphics A precise type of design. For example, in media terms, the titles and credits in a film or for a television programme, or the seemingly hand-drawn but usually computer-generated images in a video game.

Gutter The space between two pages of text in a magazine.

Hand-held camera A style of filming whereby a decision has been made not to use the steadicam on the camera or a tripod but to allow the camera to move freely during filming. This gives a jerky style of filming that suggests realism and makes the audience feel involved in the action.

Hard sell This is 'in your face' advertising. These adverts are usually short, loud and employ a direct mode of address. They give clear information about the product, for example the price and where you can get it.

Hegemony The dominance of one group over another. For example, a patriarchal society could be described as an example of male hegemony while a predominantly white institution could be described as hegemonically white.

High-concept film This is a film that can be summed up in a sentence or two. It is recognisable to audiences, easily marketable and high budget.

Hook The element of a media product that catches the attention of the audience and draws them in. On a film poster it may be the image, the tagline or the copy.

Horizontal integration The process through which different companies that produce or distribute similar products join together through a merger or acquisition. This reduces competition and enables companies to increase their market share.

House style The distinctive 'look', aesthetic or visual style of a magazine, which helps to convey a sense of its brand identity.

Hybrid genres These are media texts that incorporate features of more than one genre. *Strictly Come Dancing* includes features of reality television, game shows and entertainment programmes, for example.

Hyperbole Exaggerated language used to create a dramatic effect.

Hyperlink A word, phrase or image in an electronic document or web page that the reader can click on to navigate to a different part of the document or a different page.

Hypermasculinity Where stereotypically masculine traits such as power, toughness or physical strength are presented in exaggerated form. In many cases this is conveyed symbolically through particular aspects of the iconography or mise-en-scène – cars and guns often function as symbols of masculine power, for example.

Hypodermic syringe model Also known as the hypodermic needle model. Now largely viewed as an outdated effects theory, which suggests that the audience are a mass that behave the same way in response to a media product. The media product injects ideas into the minds of the assumed passive audience who will respond as one.

Iconic representation The actual image of the product.

Iconography The visual elements of a media product such as the props, costumes and settings that are used.

Ident A graphic that conveys a sense of a channel's identity. It plays an important role in the visual branding of the channel.

Independent film company A company that operates outside of the main film companies.

Independent productions In the broadcasting industry, these are productions that are produced by companies that are independent of the broadcasters.

Independent record label A record label that is not necessarily linked to a major record label.

Industry context This includes aspects of production, including the media organisation, production processes, distribution and marketing, and regulatory issues.

Intertextuality When one text is used or referenced within another. For example, the use of memorable scenes from an iconic film in an advert. A good example of intertextuality is the use of Yoda from *Star Wars* in the Vodafone advert.

Inter-weaving plot strands Some television dramas include three or more narratives in their opening sequences and then move the action between these narratives to keep the audience's attention.

Issue An important matter or topic that is of public concern.

Jump line Used at the end of a cover line. Usually tells the audience which page to turn to in order to read the full story.

Juxtaposition Involves placing two or more items next to one another to meaningful effect.

Left wing A term that refers to people whose views are left of the centre of politics. They believe that existing social inequalities must be addressed and they have more liberal political views.

Left-wing newspapers Those that tend to support political parties such as the Labour party and socialist policies that advocate social equality.

'Let's play' video A recording of someone playing a video game, usually accompanied by some form of commentary.

Lexis The specific type of language or vocabulary that is used. The football magazine *Four Four Two* uses the lexis of sport, for example, while the women's lifestyle magazine *Glamour* uses the lexis of fashion and beauty.

Lifestyle magazine An umbrella term for men's and women's magazines that are concerned with aspects of modern living such as fashion, beauty, health and fitness, culture, the home, etc. The ideology of these magazines tends to focus on consumerism and aspiration.

Mainstream publisher The term applied to media producers who create products, for example magazines, that appeal to and are therefore read by a broad number of people.

Mark of quality In the case of films, usually the film logo, the director's name or references to other successful films made by this director. These are included to convince the audience that this new film is a quality product.

Masculinity The state of 'being a man', which can change as society changes. It is essentially what being a man means to a particular generation. This is then reflected in media texts.

Masthead The title of the magazine presented in the form of a logo. Many magazines use a specially designed typeface for the masthead. This is useful for branding and can also help to distinguish the magazine from its competitors.

Mean world syndrome The idea that regular exposure to television can lead to a distorted view of the real world. In particular, the disproportionate representation of crime on television is likely to make viewers think that the world is a 'meaner' or more dangerous place than it actually is.

Media language The way in which the meaning of a media product is conveyed to the audience through a range of techniques.

Media/press pack Put together by the owners of products, for example magazines and newspapers, and is intended to give information to advertisers. It informs them about the details of the assumed target audience, including income, marital status and age. It usually gives a pen portrait of the audience. The pack also includes the rates to place an advertisement in the print publication. However, they are also a useful resource for media students and can be downloaded or requested from the magazine.

Meet-and-greet An event at which a celebrity or public figure meets and interacts with their fans.

Metadata The additional or contextual information that accompanies an online video, such as the title and description of the video as well as tags and thumbnails.

Milieu The world or social context that someone inhabits or in which a story or narrative is set. This can refer to both physical surroundings (the urban milieu of the gangster genre, for example) and the social world that someone moves within.

Mise-en-scène Everything that appears within the frame in, for example, a television programme. This includes characters, iconography and graphics.

MMORPG Massively multi-player online role-playing game.

Mobile first strategy The practice of companies that design their products for mobile phones before making designs for traditional laptops and computers. This is particularly the case with smartphones that are linked to a large network coverage area. The strategy enables the producers to capture this market early.

Mock-up Used to describe the planning ideas that a professional designer may engage in before the final product is created.

Monetisation The process through which a product or service – a blog or vlog for example – is converted into a source of commercial revenue.

Motif A recurrent thematic element used by an artist and recognised by fans of that artist. It is usually established by the iconography surrounding the artist, including props, costumes and settings.

Multi-channel era The idea that following the introduction of satellite and cable television in the 1990s and the rise of digital technologies, viewers now have a much wider range of channels to choose from.

Multi-channel networks Organisations that curate a large number of channels, offering creators support in areas such as video production as well as marketing and promotion.

Narratology Refers to the study of narrative structure and how this communicates meaning through, for example, common conventions and signs.

Narrowcasting Unlike broadcasting, which addresses the needs of a mass audience, narrowcasting targets more specialised audiences.

Negotiated position The position an audience takes if they acknowledge the broad legitimacy of the messages a media product contains but adapt those messages to better reflect their own experiences.

New man A term that was introduced to describe a new era of masculinity. These men rejected sexist attitudes; they were in touch with their feminine side and were therefore not afraid to be sensitive and caring, and could sometimes be seen in a domestic role.

News agenda The list of stories that may be in a particular paper. The items on the news agenda will reflect the style and ethos of the paper.

Niche audience A relatively small audience with specialised interests, tastes and backgrounds.

Non-diegetic sound Essentially, sound the characters within the frame cannot hear. It is sound that may have been added post-production or has been used to suggest mood and atmosphere.

Non-linear viewing When viewers watch programmes at times of their choosing, whether by using video-on-demand services or by streaming, downloading or watching programmes that have been recorded. Linear viewing, on the other hand, is where programmes are viewed at the time of broadcast.

Non-verbal communication Communication that doesn't involve words. The way in which we communicate messages and meanings through our facial expressions, our body language and our tone of voice, for example.

Objective truth The idea that there is a single definitive version of events that is not subject to personal interpretation.

Opinion leaders Those in positions of power who aim to persuade an audience of their point of view. Within the media these may be newspaper editors, programme producers or bloggers.

Oppositional reading The interpretation an audience member makes of a media product if they disagree with the messages or values it conveys.

Orders of signification Roland Barthes draws a distinction between two 'orders' or 'levels' of signification. The first order of signification involves denotation. The second order of signification involves connotation and myth.

Original productions Productions that are commissioned by broadcasters rather than bought in.

Paparazzi photographer A freelance photographer who aggressively pursues celebrities and royalty to take pictures to sell to magazines and newspapers for the highest price.

Paradigm A set of related signs that the encoder can choose from – the set of colours that a magazine designer might choose from, for instance, or the set of font styles that they might select from. In choosing one sign rather than another, the encoder or media producer makes a paradigmatic choice.

Para-social interaction The illusion of face-to-face conversation constructed through techniques such as a direct mode of address. The term was originally coined by Horton and Wohl in their article 'Mass Communication and Parasocial Interaction: Observations on Intimacy at a Distance', which was first published in *Psychiatry*, 19, in 1956. While Horton and Wohl's concept of para-social interaction was initially applied to mass media forms such as television, it has subsequently been applied to online media forms such as blogs and vlogs.

Participatory culture A culture where individuals are not only the consumers of media products but also contribute to existing products or produce their own.

Participatory media This term explains the way in which audiences today are increasingly seen to play an active role in finding, reporting, creating and disseminating media content. This has been made easier by the rise of social media and online platforms.

Passive audience This describes an audience that does not engage actively with the product. They are more likely to accept the preferred meaning of the text without challenge. This also suggests that passive audiences are more likely to be directly affected by the messages contained within the product.

PEGI The Pan-European Game Information (PEGI) age rating system was established to help European parents make informed decisions on buying computer games. It was launched in spring 2003 and replaced a number of national age rating systems with one single system.

Periodical A publication that is issued at regular intervals – weekly, monthly, quarterly, etc.

Persistent worlds A feature of MMORPG games, meaning that the game world continues even when the gamer is not part of it. In this way the virtual world replicates real life.

Pick and mix approach The idea that audiences may pay attention to some media messages but disregard others. For example, Gauntlett refers to the 'pick and mix reader' who actively chooses which bits of the magazine to take notice of and which to ignore.

Pitch A presentation of ideas for a new media product to a selected audience with the aim of persuading them of the viability of the project.

Platforms A range of different ways of communicating to an audience, for example television, social media, etc.

PlayStation Vita A hand-held game console developed and released by Sony Interactive Entertainment. It is the successor to the PlayStation Portable as part of the PlayStation brand of gaming devices.

Point of identification A character within the text that the audience can identify with or relate to.

Point-of-view shot A shot that is filmed from the perspective of a particular person or character within the text.

Police procedural A crime drama subgenre that places particular emphasis on the processes and procedures involved in investigating crime. Examples of police procedurals include *Line of Duty*, *CSI: Vegas* and *Silent Witness*.

Political bias When a newspaper may show support for a political party through its choice of stories, style of coverage, cartoons, etc. It may be subtle and implicit or explicit as in the case of the tabloids on Election Day.

Polysemic A sign that has more than one meaning.

Positioning When audio, visual, technical or narrative codes place the audience in a particular position. This may be emotionally to empathise more clearly with a character, or to have expectations of how the narrative will develop.

Post-production The term for any production work that takes place on moving or still images after the initial filming or photography shoot has taken place.

Pre-sold When a product has a ready-made audience, thereby minimising financial risk. A product may be pre-sold based on the previous success of similar types of product or it may be pre-sold through the inclusion of popular and well-known figures.

Pre-title sequence Refers to the section of the television programme shown before the opening credits. Its purpose is to hook the audience.

Primary research Information you gain first-hand from looking at actual examples of existing media products, for example television drama opening sequences. Primary research allows you to formulate your own opinions.

Prime-time The time when most viewers are likely to be watching television. Broadcasters will generally schedule their most popular programmes in prime-time slots. Prime-time is defined by Ofcom as the period between 6pm and 10.30pm.

Privatisation When a company is taken out of public ownership and sold to a private bidder.

Production values The features of a media product that illustrate how much it cost to make. A high-budget film is recognisable by its settings, use of stars and more complex editing, for example. The reverse is true of low-budget films.

Products What is produced by media organisations, for example films, video games, television programmes and music videos.

Profile For radio stations this refers to how they are defined to their target audience through their brand identity, which may be defined by, for example, the presenters or programme style. This includes their aims and their ethos.

Promises of pleasure Phrases that tell the audience what they will experience through the film, for example fear, laughter. The audience will then have expectations of the film.

Proppian princess The princess or 'sought-for person' is one of the character roles or narrative functions identified in Vladimir Propp's narrative theory. The princess is often the object of the hero's quest. Another term commonly used for this type of role is the damsel in distress.

Prosumer Derives from a marketing term 'production by consumers' and is used to describe those individuals who comment on, create and adapt existing content, and then distribute it through the internet and social media. These people can be very valuable to the success of a product.

Psychographic profiling A way of categorising audiences based on personality, values, opinions, attitudes and lifestyles.

Public service broadcaster A radio or television broadcaster that is seen to offer a public service by catering for a range of tastes and audiences. The main public service broadcasters in the UK are the BBC, ITV, Channel 4, Channel 5 and S4C.

Publisher-broadcaster A broadcaster that commissions all of its programmes from other production companies as it does not have its own in-house production division.

Q & A session An abbreviation for question and answer session. At a public event such as a convention, the questions may be supplied by interviewers or journalists or by members of the audience. Many vloggers and bloggers also hold Q & A sessions online.

Race Your race is defined by the fact that you descend from a common ancestor giving you a particular set of racial characteristics. These may be related to the colour of your skin and facial features, for example.

Readership An estimate of how many readers a publication has. As most publications have more than one reader per copy, the readership estimate is very different from the circulation count. These figures were previously produced by the National Readership Survey (NRS), which operated from 1956 until 2018. They are now provided by the Publishers Audience Measurement Company (PAMCo).

Recce An informal term derived from the word reconnoitre. In a media context this is a preproduction visit to a location to work out its suitability for photographing or filming. This may take into consideration possible technical issues, for example sound and lighting.

Register The spoken or written register of a media product is the range and variety of language used within the product. This will change according to the purpose and the target audience.

Remit A remit outlines a broadcaster's particular areas of responsibility. For example, the BBC's duty to provide impartial news coverage is specified in its remit.

Repeat purchase When someone buys the same brand or product that they have done previously, as in the case of readers who buy the same magazine every week or every month.

Repertoire of elements Key features or conventions that distinguish one genre or sub-genre from another.

Representation The ways in which the media represents the world and aspects of it, for example social groups, issues and events.

Restricted narrative When the audience only sees the narrative from the point of view of one character so only knows as much as they do.

Right-wing newspapers Those that tend to support political parties such as the Conservative Party and UKIP, believe in the free market and oppose socialism.

Risk averse Describes companies that are unwilling to take risks and that avoid them wherever possible. This means that they often adhere to an established formula and avoid doing anything different that might have a negative impact on sales.

Scheduling Making decisions about when to broadcast programmes.

Selection What is chosen to be included by the creators of the product. This selection may reflect the values, attitudes and beliefs of the product, as decisions have been made about what to include and what to leave out.

Self-contained narrative When a complete story is told within a single episode. Viewers do not have to have seen any previous episodes in order to follow the story.

Self-identification How you see yourself and how you may categorise yourself as belonging to a particular group or class, for example a skater, a member of the Green Party, etc.

Semiotics The language of codes and signs; it deals with the way in which media texts are encoded and the way in which audiences decode them.

Serial A narrative form in which the story unfolds episode by episode, unlike a series, in which each individual episode constitutes a self-contained narrative.

Sexual politics Refers to the power relations between men and women.

Showrunner The person who has ultimate creative control over a television series and oversees all aspects of production. They are often a writer on the show and in some cases may be the creator of the show.

Sign A sign is something that stands in for or represents something else. A photograph or a drawing of a car, for example, is not the same as the thing itself (we cannot climb in and drive it); it is a sign that stands for the actual object.

Silver surfer An older person who is computer literate and uses the net to purchase goods and find out information.

Socialisation The process through which we learn the norms and values of our culture. Gender socialisation, for example, refers to the way in which we learn what is expected of us as men and women. The media are often said to play an important role in this regard, functioning as agents of socialisation.

Sponsorship bumper A short clip featuring the name or logo of the sponsor that appears between the programme and the advertisements.

Stand-first The sentence after a headline and before an article begins that 'sells' a feature to a reader.

Star billing The positioning of the names of the stars on the poster; where the names are placed and how large they are suggest the importance of the particular star to the film and its marketing

Star persona Used to refer to those music stars who have an identity beyond their ability to make music, for example Beyoncé. That persona may be demonstrated through character and personality, and be evident in other media products and platforms, for example magazine interviews and advertising campaigns. Some stars are adept at changing their star persona to keep fans interested; this is true of Madonna and Lady Gaga. The producer of the star may be instrumental in creating their persona.

Statutory regulation A system of regulation that is implemented by law. It is often seen to threaten the principles of self-regulation – a system in which media industries assume responsibility for regulating themselves, limiting the need for outside interference.

Stereotypes This is a construction whereby characters' traits are over-exaggerated to make them easily recognisable. Stereotypes can be positive or negative and are quick ways for the creators of products to convey messages to an audience.

Story arc The way in which the narrative progresses from the beginning to the end of the product. A story arc may also cross episodes.

Stripping This is a technique used in radio and television whereby a certain programme is broadcast at the same time every day. In radio this attracts an audience who associate a particular programme with their daily routine, for example driving home from work.

Sub-genre A smaller category or subdivision within a larger genre.

Subject-specific terminology Media Studies as a subject has a range of specific terminology that you must be able to use when analysing products. This may be vocabulary specific to the form or terminology that enhances your analysis, for example the language of semiotics.

Suspension of disbelief Where the audience are involved in the action and do not question impossible aspects of it; for example the sound of dramatic music in a crime drama confrontation scene.

Symbol A sign that suggests another idea beyond the simple denotation, the meaning of which has been culturally agreed. A woman wearing a red dress in a music video may symbolise that she is passionate or dangerous.

Symbolic annihilation The idea that the underrepresentation of particular social groups works to maintain social inequalities by denying those groups any meaningful presence, thereby rendering them silent or invisible. As Gerbner and Gross put it: '*representation [...] signifies social existence; absence means symbolic annihilation*' (1976, 'Living with Television: The Violence Profile', *Journal of Communication*, 1976, 26(2)).

Syndicated output When radio stations make and sell a programme to other stations, or buy a programme that may be available to other radio stations.

Synergy A term used to describe the cross-promotion of products – the theme song for a Bond movie such as *Spectre* will help to promote the film, for instance, while the film will also help to promote the theme song. Synergy is therefore about different products and processes working together.

Syntagm A combination of signs that are linked together in particular ways. A sentence, for example, is a syntagm that is comprised of words placed in a particular sequence in order to convey meaning. Syntagmatic relations are the relations between different signs.

Tabloid Refers to the dimensions of the newspaper: a tabloid is smaller and more compact in size than a broadsheet. Also refers to a newspaper the content of which focuses on lighter news, for example celebrity gossip, sport and television.

Tagline (film) These are the short slogan-like phrases that sum up a film. They are usually found on film posters and other print promotional material.

Tagline (printed products) A short, memorable phrase that sums up the printed product and conveys a sense of its brand identity.

Target audience The specific group at whom the product is aimed.

Teaser poster When a film poster appears before the release of the main marketing campaign. The aim is to use enigmas, for example a tagline or a single image, to catch the interest of the audience.

Technique In advertising this describes what has been done to the advert to create an effect. For example, using soft focus in a fragrance advert or enlarging nails to promote nail varnish.

Theoretical framework This is discussed in detail in Chapter 1. It provides you with the tools to develop a critical understanding of the media and consists of the following inter-related areas: media language, representation, media industries and audiences.

Thumbnail On DVD covers these are small images used to convey aspects of the film's narrative.

Title sequence Often termed a credit sequence. It is the section in which the television programme presents aspects of its production, for example the main characters, the actors, the setting and the genre. Its construction is often a montage of images with a recognisable soundtrack.

Tokenism Providing a cursory or superficial representation of those groups in society who are often under-represented in order to convey an impression of equality and inclusivity.

Transgressive behaviour Behaviour that goes beyond the norms of social acceptability.

Transitions The way in which the shots move from one into the other, producing a particular effect. Different transitions include cuts that produce a faster-paced sequence. Fades and wipes suggest a more controlled and slower section.

Transmedia storytelling Defined by Henry Jenkins as *'a process where integral elements of a fiction get dispersed systematically across multiple delivery channels for the purpose of creating a unified and coordinated entertainment experience'* ('Transmedia Storytelling 101', 2007).

Treatment A brief synopsis of ideas for a media project. It serves two purposes: to summarise elements of the idea, for example the plot and main characters, as well as to sell your idea to a producer. A treatment should communicate your idea in a concise but compelling manner, similar to a marketing pitch.

Typography The font styles that are used. Serif fonts such as Times New Roman have short decorative lines, called serifs, added to the letters. They often look more traditional. In contrast, sans serif fonts, which lack these ornamental flourishes, often look more modern or contemporary.

Unrestricted narrative When the audience knows more than the characters within the world of the text, assuming a privileged spectator position.

User-generated content Material created by everyday users of media platforms rather than by professionals working for media organisations.

Utopia An ideal or perfect world.

Value chain The different steps or activities involved in making a product and getting it to the consumer or audience. Vertically integrated companies are able to undertake most or all of these activities themselves as they generally have the means to both produce and distribute products.

Vertical integration A process through which a company develops control over different levels of the value chain. An example of a vertically integrated business would be a production company that is also able to distribute its products or a magazine publisher that owns a printing company.

Video-on-demand A form of distribution that enables users to access video content when they choose rather than watching content as it is broadcast. Subscription video-on-demand (SVOD) refers to streaming services such as Netflix and Disney+ that users have to subscribe to in order to access.

Vlog A blog in video form. Short for video blog.

Walkthrough A demonstration of how to play a video game in which the vlogger 'walks' the viewer through the necessary stages or levels.

Walled garden A broadcasting provider that controls access to its services and how content is distributed through, for example, subscription.

Watershed The watershed is the time when it becomes permissible to show programmes that are unsuitable for younger audiences. In the UK, the watershed is at 9pm.

Web 2.0 A new phase in the internet's development, characterised by interactivity, user participation, connection and collaboration.

Web traffic The number of people who visit a particular page or website.

White saviour trope This refers to a type of narrative in which a white character is seen to save, help, liberate or rescue a non-white character or a group of non-white characters. The white saviour is typically represented as a leader or a Messiah-like figure. This is often problematic as it can be seen to reinforce racial hierarchies and stereotypes through its representation of ethnic minorities as dependent on the aid and assistance of white people.

White space The area on the page that is free of text or images.

Whitewashing This term can refer to the process through which a non-white person is made to appear white. It is also used to describe the way in which non-white people are written out of the media.

Answers to Quickfire Questions

1 Introducing the Media Studies Framework

1.1 For example, a bird's-eye view shot shows a scene from directly overhead. This places the audience in an omniscient position, looking down on the action. For example, it can be used in a car chase in an action film. An oblique or canted angle suggests imbalance and is often used in horror films to disorientate the audience.

1.2 A zoom can also be used to quickly change the position of the audience, for example in a tense scene.

1.3 Meanings can be constructed using aspects of layout and design, and technical and visual codes. For example, the choice of colour in a fragrance advert will communicate meanings about the product because of the associations made with the colour codes.

1.4 A red rose on a Valentine's Day card suggests romance and love. It has a different meaning as the emblem of the Labour Party.

1.5 Film posters use colour codes to convey messages about the film genre. Romantic comedies tend to use bright primary colours, whereas horror films may use darker hues.

1.6 Adverts for beauty products will incorporate technical and scientific terminology linked to the ingredients of the product. The aim is to convince the audience of its credibility and efficacy.

1.7 A direct mode of address can make the audience feel involved. For example, the use of personal pronouns in adverts and magazines makes the audience feel they are being spoken to directly and are part of the product's community.

1.8 The clothing, including the style of jackets and the caps, is indicative of the music genre, as is the 'bling' jewellery.

1.9 Whichever genre you choose the repertoire of elements should include reference to: characters, setting and iconography, technical and audio codes, narrative and representations.

1.10 The *WaterAid* charity advert incorporates some of the typical conventions of the sub-genre, but by its upbeat approach and use of positive images it is also different and so subverts generic conventions.

1.11 Some media products include flashbacks to provide additional narrative information for the audience.

1.12 Whatever the event, the techniques used to construct the narrative in different newspapers are similar. For example, popular/tabloid newspapers often use puns, alliteration and single-word headlines to capture the essence of the story. They may also apply punctuation, for example exclamation marks and ellipsis, to increase the drama and create enigmas. Quality, broadsheet newspaper headlines will be more detailed and informative and may be accompanied by straplines giving further information. The selection of images and the anchoring of these with a caption also helps to construct the narrative.

1.13 The narrative is related to the plight of the refugees. The iconography of the barbed wire suggests they are being prevented from moving freely. The direct mode of address and the codes of expression urge the viewer to empathise. The tents in the background reinforce the negative narrative surrounding the people.

1.14 Without any words or anchorage an image is an open product, an audience can put their own interpretation upon it. Once the image is accompanied by words it becomes closed and the audience is more likely to accept the meaning implied by the creator of the product.

1.15 When particular representations are repeated, audiences become used to seeing them and therefore accept them as normal. For example, representations of developing countries in some charity adverts that tend to focus on the negative aspects of the country and its people.

1.16 Through mediation a media product is interpreted for an audience by the use of selection and construction. The creators of the product may therefore encode the product with messages and meanings, which may affect the way in which the audience responds to the text.

1.17 The disadvantage of self-representation is that it does not reflect reality. The creator can construct a representation of themselves that is selective and manipulated.

1.18 The advertisement represents women as weak, defined by domesticity and needing a man. The visual codes of her appearance suggest femininity through her gesture and expression – she is shocked that she can open the bottle. The copy language states: 'without a knife blade, a bottle opener or even a husband!' showing the reliance of women of the time on a man for strength. The copy also suggests it is the role of the woman to do the shopping and reinforces her clumsiness when unable to exert strength.

1.19 For example, in the 2017 *Wonder Woman* film, the representation of women is strong and subverts the expectations of the superhero genre.

1.20 In the Bond films of this time, James Bond would have more than one female 'partner'. This is reflected in the poster through the range of women featured. They are all in the background, sexually objectified and seen as accessories to the main protagonist. In contrast, he is represented as cool, strong and in control, through codes of clothing and expression. At the time, it would be typical for the central characters in films of this genre to be male. The inclusion of the iconography of Russia also reflects the political situation of the time, with Russia as the country to be feared.

1.21 The rap genre represents masculinity as powerful and at times misogynistic. The lyrics and the construction of the music video construct this representation through direct mode of address, iconography and codes of clothing that are typical of the genre. Women, when they feature, tend to be prizes and accessories for the male and are sexually objectified.

1.22 The producers of a documentary may have a particular message that they want to convey about an event, for example the election of Donald Trump. They will therefore select material that supports that particular viewpoint. If this is that the result was a disaster for America, they may select images and sound bites that support this and show Trump in a negative way. The audience may therefore receive a biased view that may affect their perception of the American election.

1.23 Media industries must be aware of their audience in order to target them effectively. Once industries have conducted audience research they will construct their product to appeal to the target group.

1.24 Channel 4's research may be useful to other industries, including advertising, as part of the research focuses on the brands consumed by the audience segment. Finding out how young people spend their time will also provide useful data for industries looking to target that age group across different media platforms.

1.25 For example, *Huck* is a magazine that targets a niche audience, including those who are politically aware, forward thinking and are interested in sub- and counter-cultures.

1.26 Women's lifestyle magazines construct an idea of their reader. For example, the front cover of *Cosmopolitan* constructs a version of femininity that is *Cosmopolitan* woman. This woman does not actually exist; the magazine creates this construction through the choice of central image, cover lines and discourse that suggest the lifestyle of this woman.

1.27 YouGov research is useful as the detailed information helps newspaper producers to attract advertisers as well as consider how the content of their newspaper can more effectively target the readers.

1.28 The mode of address of a vlog will target the specific youth audience. It will be informal and chatty to establish a relationship with them. The lack of scripting creates a conversational style that will appeal to the target audience. Depending on the vlog it may use lexis that establishes the audience as part of the vlogger's community.

1.29 For example, *Underdog*, by Alicia Keys, targets a young, largely female demographic who are fans of the artist and the music genre. However, there will be young people of both genders who share the artist's concerns about how aspects of society are represented. While older people may not be familiar with the artist or understand some of the references contained in the lyrics and the video, they will understand and empathise with the messages contained within the product.

1.30 Bandura's theory can be applied to modern video games, which may encourage the engagement in violent acts. His idea that an audience may acquire attitudes, emotional responses and new ways of behaving through modelling those they observe may also be applied to the ways in which some newspapers reflect their ideology through the way in which they choose to represent people, issues and events.

1.31 Interaction with a media product allows audiences to feel directly involved with the product and with other audiences who share their interest. They may feel that their direct responses are valued. Products that allow audience voting make the audience feel an ownership of the product and what happens as a result of their involvement.

1.32 Bloggers and vloggers usually have a large online following and are opinion leaders. They also have immediate access to their audience, who will be influenced by what they say about a product. This may affect the product's success.

1.33 Vertical integration allows companies such as Viacom to be in control of the production, distribution and exhibition of their product without relying on any other agencies.

1.34 The advert represents women as being very entrenched in their domestic role. Her code of expression, showing she is delighted with her gift of the Kenwood Chef, also reflects the rise in the production of time-saving domestic products at this time. The man is clearly the main earner, shown through the code of clothing of the suit and his dominant gesture, he is also, as was common at the time, the one who would make the purchase but not actually use it. The slogan and the fact that she is wearing the chef's hat, reinforces the domestic role of the wife.

1.35 One advantage of a media conglomerate is that the marketing of the product is facilitated across different platforms.

1.36 Newspapers are part of an industry that still has a very traditional way of distribution. Although they have online versions, they also still have a print presence. The front page tells the audience if it is national or local, the price will reflect its readership and the fact that it is in a competitive market (the price wars mean that some newspapers use this as a marketing device). The font style of the masthead, the main headline and the front-page stories reflect the ideas and messages of the paper.

2 The Media Studies Specification

2.1 Theories and theoretical perspectives will inform and support your analysis. They will allow you access to the ideas of theorists who have conducted detailed exploration into their areas of study. Your knowledge and understanding of this will develop your conceptual understanding, which will enable to engage in a more sophisticated exploration of your products.

2.2 You would never create a product without considering how similar existing examples have been constructed. Studying how existing products and the industries that produce them use media language, construct representations and engage audiences is essential to allow you to reflect your understanding in your own production.

2.3 It is important not to study your set products in isolation, but to develop an understanding of how the products reflect the time in which they were made and the context of the production. This will include, for example with regard to newspapers, how the product reflects the political context in which they were produced, which may be apparent through the front pages you study and the messages they contain.

2.4 The products and forms you will study in breadth for Component 1 will introduce you to the theoretical framework. Breadth means that you will study a range of different media forms and products related to key aspects of the framework. This will then prepare you for the in-depth study undertaken in Component 2, where you will apply the framework to three media forms in more specific detail covering all areas of the framework for each form.

2.5 They are usually the same age as the target audience, which makes them relatable. They are accessible through media platforms used by young audiences and the topics they deal with are relevant to young people. The mode of address they use is informal and conversational, making them easy to engage with for a younger audience. The blogs and vlogs also offer interactive opportunities, allowing the audience to be involved in the world of the blogger/vlogger, so erasing the distance that normally occurs between the product and the audience.

3 Component 1: Investigating the Media

3.1 As the audience cannot actually smell the product through the advert, the colours used serve to tell the audience what to expect from the fragrance. The producers of the advert will rely on the audience's understanding of the meanings attached to certain colours; these have been established over time and across other texts. For example, the pastel colours and iconography of summer in the *Miss Dior* advertisement have connotations of a lighter, floral perfume.

3.2 Hard sell advertising techniques will usually be for products at the lower end of the market, for people with a limited budget. This includes cleaning products, discount furniture stores, double glazing and insurance adverts for smaller companies.

3.3 O2's 2017 campaign 'Follow the Rabbit' makes intertextual references to 'Alice in Wonderland' to encourage audiences to be more dynamic and active.

3.4 The *This Girl Can* campaign uses some typical conventions of advertisements across its different products, for example constructing a recognisable 'look' to the advertisements so raising audience expectations and establishing a brand identity through, for example, the use of colour, the logo and the font style. However, the campaign also subverts conventions of awareness-raising advertisements in that it has a very specific target audience of women. Also, the campaign is positive rather than more negative as is the case with some advertisements in this sub-genre, the upbeat feel is communicated through the inclusion of the strong soundtrack and the use of role models who are aspirational, ordinary women of all shapes, ages, sizes and ethnicity creating a diverse community, all striving for the same attainable goals.

3.5 This *Shelter* advertisement follows the conventions of an awareness-raising campaign in that it introduces the audience to issues of which they may not be aware, in a way that engages their interest. The campaign uses personalisation, a typical convention, challenging the preconceived ideas audiences may have of the homeless so encouraging an audience to empathise. Images of real people appear on actual homes reinforcing their plight and the song lyrics highlight that what they are asking for are what the audience may take for granted, 'a kitchen and a fridge'. The use of the muted colour scheme and the night-time setting reinforce the bleak situation of the homeless. The statistics at the end are used as a shock tactic.

3.6 There is iconic representation of the product, which has been manipulated through post-production techniques to appear more enticing. There is a strong central image which has been digitally enhanced to make claims about the efficacy of the product. The model engages with the audience through direct mode of address. The persuasive language techniques used include hyperbole. The visual codes of colour communicate meanings about the product. The slogan has been established over time and is recognisable as part of the brand identity of the product.

3.7 A teaser poster is released well in advance of the film's release. Its purpose is to generate a buzz around the film and, consequently, teaser campaigns construct enigmas through withholding information. They may just include an image and a tagline, for example, or a logo. In contrast, a theatrical poster is released later in the campaign and provides the audience with more information about the film, including genre conventions, stars and a release date.

3.8 *The Lost Boys* poster has is a tagline that helps to establish the genre but challenges audience expectations. The image of the characters suggests a hierarchy and gives a clue to their roles within the narrative. Their code of clothing and the use of the colours red and black suggest the horror genre. The direct mode of address communicates with the audience and involves them in the narrative.

3.9 We might expect some expert criticism, including quotes from film critics and a star rating. The layout and design would be more sophisticated to appeal to the target audience and there would be a memorable tagline that would be used on all the marketing material.

3.10 It suggests the nostalgia of the time associated with the glamour of Audrey Hepburn and the romance associated with the Italian setting.

3.11 Positive representations make audiences feel more positive about the effect they may have on a situation. Some audiences may feel saturated by negative images associated with charity campaigns and have become desensitised. The use of more upbeat audio codes and images challenges the audience's perceptions and offers them a more refreshing representation.

3.12 The construction of the representation using specific images, visual codes and language serves to communicate specific meanings to an audience. In charity adverts, cracked land, bleached colours, distressed codes of expression and crying children communicate desperation and may shock the audience into action. Alternatively, bright colours, sounds of laughter and images of positive action may also evoke an active response in an audience.

3.13 The *Spicebomb* advert constructs an idea of masculinity, which is one of perfection. It is a representation of a modern metrosexual man who is concerned about his appearance. The representation is unreal as it has been enhanced post-production. However, the suggestion is that this is a representation that men should aspire to emulate and therefore puts men under the same pressure women have been subjected to for some time.

3.14 In a car advert, the colour red may be used to suggest power and speed.

3.15 The narrative is constructed around the lyrics, which focus on the idea of there being 'bad blood' or conflict between the characters. Taylor Swift sings, *'You've got to live with the bad blood now*' when she is betrayed by her friend. The repetition of the lyric *'bandaids don't fix bullet holes*' suggests the depth of the problem and that it cannot easily be solved.

3.16 In the early days of radio, audiences would listen as they would later watch television, by sitting around the radio set as a family. It would be a shared experience. With advances in technology, radio audiences have a range of listening experiences on offer including 'listen again' and podcasts.

3.17 Commercial radio stations advertise within other radio programmes on the same station. Local radio stations use opportunities for local advertising, for example on bus shelters, the sides of buses, the local press and billboards.

3.18 BBC Taster allows audiences to feel involved in the BBC through interaction about the programmes and to see, in advance, planned programmes. For the BBC it provides quick, free and easy feedback about proposed programmes, and allows them to test out ideas on an audience without going to the expense of creating a pilot programme to be aired on television.

3.19 An independent regulator works outside of the industry and is therefore impartial. It can effectively protect audiences and oversee the workings of the industry.

3.20 *Woman's Hour* and *Have You Heard George's Podcast?* fulfil some of the strategic objectives set by the BBC, including to reflect UK culture and represent diverse communities and to broaden audience reach through BBC Sounds.

3.21 This is done through the title of the programme, the themes that are covered, the mode of address of the presenter and the guests that may appear on the programme.

3.22 It could be assumed that as the listener has tuned into or downloaded the programme they are part of the target audience and will therefore accept the preferred reading of the text. However, some audiences may adopt a negotiated response because they do not agree with some of the themes that are covered by the programme.

3.23 A high-concept film has a large budget and thus demonstrates high production values. This includes high-profile stars, which help to appeal to a global audience. These films are usually made by large multinational conglomerates that have the means to produce and distribute the film thus ensuring economic success.

3.24 The trailer is often rated months before the actual film is given a certification. As the trailer is much shorter and the aim will be to ensure the broadest distribution, including before films of a lower classification, the trailer may not include any of the material that may result in a different certification.

3.25 Films that are part of a franchise eliminate risk and consequently are lucrative for film producers as audiences know what to expect, may be fans of the previous films in the franchise and will flock to see the film. For example, the dominance of Marvel in the sci-fi/superhero genre ensures the financial success of its films even when some risks are taken as with the themes in *Black Panther*. There is a built-in awareness of film franchises and that, combined with the expected merchandise, ensures profits for film companies.

3.26 The *Black Panther* trailer has high production values evident in the use of recognisable stars, settings, technical effects (Imax 3D) and special effects. The trailer also establishes the film as part of the Marvel franchise with a recognisable aesthetic but focusing on different characters, ensuring audience interest and so profits. The character of T'Challa and Wakanda were introduced in *Captain America: Civil War*, the comic is over 50 years old, and all previous Marvel films have been hugely successful. The Marvel Studios and Marvel logo appear in the trailer reinforcing the importance of ownership, Marvel is a subsidiary of Disney, a multi-national conglomerate. There are also digital platform links, e.g. #BlackPanther. A further industry link is the collaboration with Kendrick Lamar on the soundtrack.

3.27 Audiences now access their news across different media platforms. As a result, newspaper sales are falling and the press have addressed this change in readership by offering an alternative way of reaching their audience through an online newspaper, which offers a different range of experiences.

3.28 Technological change has affected the way in which newspapers select, produce and distribute news. The advances in digital technology mean that audiences now expect the news to be more immediate and constantly changing. This cannot be achieved through the print press; therefore, the producers of newspapers have created digital versions of newspapers that can address different audience needs.

3.29 The stats show the changing ways in which audiences consume what was a traditional print product. While print readership is falling, audiences are increasingly accessing the newspaper's content on a range of digital platforms.

3.30 As well as the traditional print version, the *Daily Mirror* has an online presence and has also used social media platforms including Twitter and Face book to reach their audience.

3.31 Other factors that may affect how an audience responds to a newspaper may be their ethnicity, age and gender.

3.32 A website is easily accessible and portable. It offers interactivity opportunities and the chance for enhanced viewing through audio-visual clips. Blogs and emails allow the audience to communicate directly and immediately with the newspaper.

3.33 Consider the content, style and mode of address of the edition you are studying and how this may affect audience responses. Also consider how the newspaper represents certain social groups and events and how it communicates its ideas and opinions to the audience.

3.34 As a newspaper with left-wing ideas, how the *Daily Mirror* covers certain stories, particularly those related to the current Conservative government, will influence what the reader thinks. In 2022 the front pages of the *Daily Mirror* condemned Boris Johnson and his government after revelations of their behaviour during the pandemic lockdown.

3.35 The social and cultural context may also be apparent through other elements of the newspaper, for example the extended news articles, the features, the editorial and the cartoons.

3.36 Categorising audiences allows products and services to have a detailed profile of their target audience and their values, attitudes and lifestyles. This will influence how they construct their marketing campaign.

3.37 The historical advert for *Tide* included conventions of modern adverts, including demonstrative action to illustrate the effectiveness of the product, a slogan, persuasive claims for the product, and iconic representation.

3.38 Audiences who accepted the preferred reading for this advertisement will have been persuaded by the claims made in these soap powder advertisements and purchased the products, as having soft, clean clothes for your family was important to women at the time, which was related to their role in society. However, some purchasers may have had a more negotiated reading, they may have been aware that the claims for the product are exaggerated but also aware of the social pressures to be seen to be a good housewife with the added pressure of keeping their family 'safe'.

3.39 The stats show the changing ways in which audiences consume what were traditional print products. Whilst print readership is falling, audiences are increasingly accessing newspaper contents across a range of digital platforms.

3.40 An audience will be educated and informed by the advert.

3.41 A certain audience may have an oppositional reading of the advertisement and feel that they are being manipulated and positioned emotionally by the images used and the construction of the product. Another audience may have an active response and watch the coverage of the Paralympics when they would not have engaged previously.

3.42 The inclusion of a main female protagonist into the game may be to address the rise in female gamers. This would therefore provide them with a strong female representation that they can relate to. This in turn would increase the sales of this game, as the audience would be broader.

3.43 The media effects theory (Bandura) could be applied to this set product in that it does contain violent content. The fact that the gamer is directly involved in this through the game play may encourage them, according to the theory, to behave in a violent manner outside of the confines of the game. However, you must also be prepared to challenge this theory.

5 Component 2: Investigating Media Forms and Products

5.1 In a tracking shot, the whole camera moves from one point to another, whereas in a panning shot the camera remains in the same place but rotates around a fixed axis, pivoting to one side or the other. If you were to stand in a fixed position while turning your head to look to one side, this would produce the same effect as a pan. Panning shots are often used to provide information about setting or context. A slow pan across a desolate landscape might be used to illustrate a character's isolation, for example. Pans can also be used to track the movement of people or objects in the frame. A panning shot might be used to follow a character as they walk across the shot, for instance. Tracking shots are also commonly used for this purpose. For example, in order to film a car as it speeds down a road a tracking shot may be used. This would typically involve mounting the camera on tracks so that it can move alongside the travelling vehicle.

5.2 Diegetic sound appears to come from within the text and is therefore audible to the people or characters we see on screen as well as the audience. For example, the sound of tyres screeching in a scene featuring a car chase would be diegetic as would the sound of characters in the car talking to one another. Non-diegetic sound is only audible to the audience; it cannot be heard by people or characters within the text. This type of sound is generally used to influence our reaction to what we are seeing on the screen. Tense, dramatic music can help to create a sense of suspense, for example.

5.3 As crime drama is one of the most popular and widely produced genres of television programme, there are many examples you could have included. These are just some of the examples you could have listed: *Sherlock, Line of Duty, Luther, River, Happy Valley, The Missing, Top of the Lake, The Fall, Waking the Dead, Silent Witness, Life on Mars, Ashes to Ashes, Broadchurch, Grantchester, Foyle's War, Midsomer Murders, Vera, Marcella, Unforgotten, Lewis, Endeavour, Inspector Morse, No Offence, Dexter, CSI, CSI: Miami, CSI: NY, NCIS, True Detective, Breaking Bad, Criminal Minds, The Mentalist, Hinterland, The Five, The Tunnel, The Bridge, The Killing, Wallander, Arne Dahl, Beck, Spiral, Modus, Inspector Montelbano, Narcos, White Collar, Criminal Minds, Hawaii Five-O, The Blacklist, The Sopranos, Gomorrah, Bones, Elementary, How to Get Away with Murder, Lethal Weapon, Miami Vice, Death in Paradise, Law and Order, Hannibal, Castle, Columbo, Agatha Christie's Poirot, Agatha Christie's Marple, Murder She Wrote, Miss Fisher's Murder Mysteries, Veronica Mars, Diagnosis Murder, New Tricks, Jonathan Creek, Scott & Bailey, Prime Suspect, Prime Suspect 1973* and *A Touch of Frost*.

5.4 Although alternative readings are possible, unlike the majority of episodes in the *Black Mirror* anthology series, the 'San Junipero' episode appears to offer a largely utopian view of the world as it explores the possibility that technological advances might facilitate an idyllic, eternal afterlife. This is anchored by the lyrics of Belinda Carlisle's 'Heaven is a Place on Earth', which closes the narrative.

5.5 The title suggests that we are likely to see ourselves reflected in the technology we use. *Black Mirror* is therefore a programme that holds a mirror up to society, showing us who we really are.

5.6 Luke Jennings

5.7 While content analysis can be used to identify broad representational patterns within the media, it may not be as effective when it comes to analysing the nature of specific representations within particular media products. Counting the number of men or women who feature in a given text is certainly useful, but it is also important to consider *how* those men and women who appear are represented. For example, a music video may feature dozens of women and only one male figure but if the women in the video are consistently objectified and the male figure is glorified or heroised, the fact that the man is outnumbered by women does not necessarily mean that the representation of gender is any less patriarchal.

5.8 The need to make a profit for shareholders might lead privately owned broadcasters to commission or show more populist or commercial programmes that are likely to achieve higher viewing figures. This is particularly important in terms of generating advertising revenue. As publicly owned, not-for-profit organisations such as the BBC and Channel 4 are not subject to the same kind of commercial pressure, it might be argued that they have greater freedom to offer niche programming that caters for minority audiences rather than simply delivering programming that targets mainstream audiences in the quest for higher ratings. Privately owned broadcasters are therefore seen to be more risk averse, as the programmes that they commission or show tend to be safer or more formulaic, replicating established, successful formats.

5.9 International co-productions enable broadcasters to spread the cost of the programmes they make. This gives the programme-makers a bigger budget to work with, leading to higher production values.

5.10 The way in which audiences watch television has changed significantly in recent years. The advent of catch-up and video-on-demand services such as the BBC's iPlayer service and Netflix has led to a decline in linear viewing as, rather than watching programmes when they are broadcast, audiences are now able to stream or download programmes to watch at a time of their choosing. For this reason, it might be argued that the watershed is less relevant in the context of this new era of non-linear viewing.

5.11 The serif font that is used for *Elle*'s masthead has connotations of sophistication and elegance, which fit with the brand image that the magazine seeks to project.

5.12 There are many different genres that you could list. Here are some:

- women's magazines
- men's magazines
- teen magazines
- celebrity gossip magazines
- health and fitness magazines
- fashion magazines
- music magazines
- entertainment magazines
- television listings magazines
- sports magazines
- motoring magazines
- current affairs magazines
- technology magazines
- home and garden magazines
- food and drink magazines
- science and nature magazines
- hobby magazines
- travel magazines.

This is by no means an exhaustive list – there are many other examples you could cite. It is also possible to identify numerous sub-genres of magazine. For example, the broad category of hobby magazines encompasses knitting magazines and angling/fishing magazines as well as many other sub-genres. Similarly, the music magazine genre encompasses several sub-genres relating to particular types of music – rock magazines, pop magazines and hip-hop magazines, for example.

5.13 The introduction of the contraceptive pill gave women greater control over their own bodies and their own fertility. For example, the pill made it easier for women to plan when to have children. This had a positive effect in terms of career progression and education. The pill was also seen to give women a greater degree of sexual freedom, marking an important step towards sexual equality.

5.14 The chosen pseudonyms help to construct the agony aunts as reassuring figures. Significantly, the word 'Home' is often associated with the personal sphere of family. This fits neatly with the function of the agony aunt – someone who assumes the role of an older female relative as they dispense advice to readers. The use of the word 'Shepherd' as part of Georgette Floyd's pseudonym is also significant, as the role of a shepherd is to protect or take care of a flock. The word also has religious connotations. Again, this reflects the traditional role of the agony aunt as someone who provides moral direction and guidance.

5.15 The representation of the domestic sphere as a female domain reinforces the cultural myth that a woman's place is in the home, as it implies that women are *naturally* suited to domesticity. In suggesting that this patriarchal division of gender roles is simply part of the natural order rather than a cultural construct, the representation achieves the status of myth.

5.16 Most magazines rely heavily on advertising for a significant proportion of their revenue. This makes them particularly susceptible to changes in the wider economy. For example, as advertising spend generally tends to fall when there is an economic downturn or a recession, this could lead to a significant decline in magazine revenue. A recession or economic downturn could also impact on sales as this would generally lead to a squeeze on readers' disposable income.

5.17 One concern regarding concentration of ownership is that it leads to large companies becoming too powerful, making the magazine industry less competitive and forcing smaller publishers out of business. Another concern is that this may result in a lack of choice for consumers as publishers rationalise their holdings in order to produce economies of scale.

5.18 Zoe Sugg has a large following on social media. Therefore, her involvement in the Band Aid 30 charity single would have been particularly beneficial in terms of generating publicity.

5.19 Denotation refers to the 'literal', common-sense meaning of a sign, whereas connotation refers to the meanings that are *associated* with or suggested by a sign. For example, at the level of denotation, a photograph of Zoe Sugg attending a film premiere might denote her walking down a red carpet, waving to crowds of fans.

5.20 The British Board of Film Classification (BBFC) is responsible for providing age ratings for music videos that are uploaded to Vevo and YouTube by record companies in the UK. The record companies are required to send the BBFC any video for their artists that they expect to receive an age rating of 12 or higher. The BBFC uses a similar age rating system to the one it uses for films, classifying music videos at 12, 15 or 18. Once the music video has been classified by the BBFC, the age rating is displayed under a 'Partner Rating' label that appears beneath the video on the YouTube page. On Vevo, the rating appears in the top left-hand corner of the video player.

5.21 The term para-social interaction refers to the way in which techniques used in certain media products such as a direct mode of address can facilitate the illusion of personal, face-to-face communication. For example, the way in which YouTubers such as Zoe Sugg speak directly to camera, using a friendly, conversational mode of address when talking to their fans, helps to create a sense of intimacy even though they are actually speaking to millions of subscribers.

5.22 Collaboration videos could be seen as an example of synergy as they help to promote the work of two or more content creators simultaneously. For example, fans of one collaborator may subscribe to the channel of another as a result of watching a collaboration video.

7 Component 3: Media Production

7.1 Your choice of name, masthead and central image will suggest if this is an upmarket magazine or not. This will also be reflected by the price and how often it is produced, for example weekly, monthly or quarterly.

7.2 As print magazine sales are falling, digital versions of the magazine are very important for the publishers. These can be published and distributed across a range of different digital platforms, thus appealing to a wide audience. The digital versions also offer opportunities not available through the print versions of the magazine, for example audio-visual content and interactive opportunities.

7.3 The online image of *GQ* magazine demonstrates some of the generic conventions of the lifestyle magazine form. It also uses the magazine's content to target and appeal to the magazine's audience of men with a high disposable income. It also offers a specific representation of men who are interested in fashion, health and food. The additional content of '*GQ* video' offers different audience pleasures while also showing how the magazine industry has diversified to appeal to a broader audience.

7.4 The pre-title sequence of *Luther* introduces the characters, the setting and a narrative enigma. The narrative is fast paced and tense, to hook the audience and keep them watching. Genre conventions are also established through visual and action codes.

7.5 You will need to consider visual codes, for example clothing, expression and gesture. How you film your character also will be important, for example the use of low-angle shots to suggest vulnerability and close-up shots for emotional scenes. It is also important to consider how to edit the sequence to construct the narrative surrounding your character.

7.6 Elements may include an interview with a director, or location reports depending on the topic area of the documentary. The 'Help and Support' element would still be relevant, as a documentary deals with actual issues.

7.7 The blue code of colour has connotations of the police genre. The iconography of setting is recognisable as related to the genre. The serious codes of expression and formal clothing also give clues to the genre of the programme.

7.8 This would need to include a pre-title sequence, including graphics/titles with the title of the programme, the episode title and the names of key personnel. There would also need to be at least one other location and the inclusion of characters from another social group, for example women.

7.9 A teaser trailer would include the film's name, the tagline and a central image featuring the protagonist. It would also be relevant to include the colour branding used across all the marketing materials.

7.10 You could include a link to an existing film from the film company, for example 'From the makers of ...', or links to a director recognisable to the target audience, 'From the director of ....'.

7.11 References to the film industry may include the film company logo, the distributor's logo, film festival awards, for example Sundance, the director and star billing.

7.12 Forty-five seconds of audio/audio-visual material may include an interview with one of the actors, where they discuss their character's role in the film. Alternatively, this could also be an interview with the director on a film location discussing the conception of the film.

7.13 The front cover of the DVD needs also to include the names of directors and actors. The back of the DVD cover needs to include thumbnails depicting different scenes from the film.

7.14 There would be reference to a more mainstream recording label. The style of the music video would be more obviously produced with more high-profile settings and locations.

7.15 For example, urban locations of streets, rundown areas and graffiti walls reflect a more edgy style of music such as rap.

7.16 The location may be a high-profile recording studio or an arena concert rather than one in a smaller, more intimate venue. The setting itself may be more constructed through props and iconography, suggesting high production values.

7.17 There is use of more than one location. Also, there is a shot of the artist in performance as well as one of her as part of a narrative. The external setting used is natural and uses ambient lighting to create a more realistic representation.

8 Component 3: Statement of Aims and Intentions

8.1 The Statement of Aims and Intentions is part of the planning and as such it is a means to show how you have understood and applied the theoretical framework through your response to the production brief. It also allows you to outline how you intend to appeal to the stated target audience.

9 Examination Preparation and Tips

9.1 The image has interesting points to make about the cultural context as it reflects the specific time and events that have cultural significance. This is evident through the setting, code of clothing and the direct mode of address suggesting there is a story to tell.

9.2 The tagline in *Hidden Figures* implies that there is no difference between genders when it comes to intelligence and strength. This suggests that the products will construct positive, strong representations of black women.

9.3 When discussing representation, the terminology used should include: construction, selection, mediation, ideology and stereotypes.

9.4 Connectives help you to construct more complex sentences. As the word suggests, they connect sentences together making links between parts of sentences. They are also useful ways of connecting paragraphs to demonstrate a sustained line of reasoning.

9.5 Demonstrates and illustrates.

9.6 Todorov's narrative model is often broken down into the following five stages:
1. an initial state of equilibrium at the beginning of a narrative
2. a breakdown or disruption of equilibrium
3. a recognition that the equilibrium has been disrupted
4. an attempt to restore or re-establish equilibrium
5. a restoration of equilibrium at the end of the narrative.

Index

Photo Credits

p1 iStock/dem10; p15 (t) Alexey Rotanov/Shutterstock; p15 (m) Corepics VOF/Shutterstock; p15 (bl) TCD/Prod.DB/Alamy Stock Photo; p15 (br) Michael Dechev/Shutterstock; p16 (t) Courtesy of Channel 4; p16 (b) Chaikorn/Shutterstock; p17 NinaMalyna/Shutterstock; p19 (t) Oliver Huitson/Shutterstock; p19 (b) Couperfield; p20 (l) Dima Asianian/ Shutterstock; p20 (r) Ground Picture/Shutterstock; p21 Ground Picture/ Shutterstock; p22 RTimages/Shutterstock; p26 Allstar Picture Library Limited. / Alamy Stock Photo; p27 Malcolm Chapman/Shutterstock. com; p29 Mirrorpix.com; p30 Peter Bernik; p31 Image courtesy of The Advertising Archives; p32 PA Images/Alamy Stock Photo; p35 smile 23/Shutterstock; p37 (t) RetroClipArt/Shutterstock; p37 (b) Courtesy of *UK Tribes*; p38 Blend Images/Shutterstock; p39 (t) Courtesy of YouGov; p39 (b) DuetPandG/Shutterstock; p42 (t) Marcos Mesa Sam Wordley/Shutterstock; p42 (b) Courtesy Zoe Sugg; p43 (t) gpointstudio/ Shutterstock; p43 (b) 360b/Shutterstock.com; p44 (t) Retro AdArchives/ Alamy Stock Photo; p44 (b) Dragon Images/Shutterstock; p45 Courtesy of bbfc; p46 Monkey Business Images/Shutterstock; p48 PHILIPIMAGE/ Shutterstock; p49 Roman Seliutin/Shutterstock; p50 Claudio Divizia/ Shutterstock; p51 Nejron Photo/Shutterstock; p52 ESB Professional/ Shutterstock; p54 Africa Studio/Shutterstock; p55 sirtravelalot/ Shutterstock; p56 Anna Jurkovska/Shutterstock; p57 Netfalls Remy Musser/Shutterstock; p59 SpeedKingz/Shutterstock; p60 Ground Picture/ Shutterstock; p63 (t) Courtesy of Sport England; p63 (b) Courtesy of Channel 4; p64 Syda Productions/Shutterstock; p65 Retro AdArchives/ Alamy Stock Photo; p66 (t) LMPC/Contributor/Getty Images; p66 (b) BFA/Alamy Stock Photo; p67 steeve-x-art/Alamy Stock Photo; p68 Retro AdArchives/Alamy Stock Photo; p69 Courtesy of Wateraid; p70 Retro AdArchives/Alamy Stock Photo; p71 (both) Courtesy of Oxfam; p72 Kohihuber Media Art/Shutterstock; pp73–74 (all) Nathan James Tettey: www.nathanjamestettey.com; p76 Courtesy of Sport England; p78 (l) Copyright Guardian News & Media Ltd 2017; p78 (r) The Times/News Syndication; p79 (t) Mirrorpix.com; p79 (b) sirtravelalot/Shutterstock; p80 (l) Mirrorpix.com; p80 (r) The Times/News Syndication; p81 Vitalii Vodolazskyi/Shutterstock; p82 (t) fabiodevilla/Shutterstock; p82 (b) Nestor Rizhniak/Shutterstock; p83 Everett Collection/Shutterstock; p84 chrisdorney/Shutterstock.com; p85 Dmitri Ma/Shutterstock; p86 re:publica, https://commons.wikimedia.org/wiki/File:-rpTEN_-_Tag_3_(26811456545)_(cropped).jpg, Creative Commons Attribution 2.0 Generic; p88 Alan Tunnicliff/Shutterstock; p89 Everett Collection/Shutterstock; p91 PA Images/Alamy Stock Photo; p93 Jacob Lund; p94 © British Board of Film Classification 2021. All rights reserved. Terms and conditions; p96 (t) Pictorial Press Ltd/Alamy Stock Photo; p96 (m) PictureLux/ The Hollywood Archive/Alamy Stock Photo; p96 (b) Lifestyle pictures/ Alamy Stock Photo; p100 Courtesy of NRS; p104 (t) Gts/Shutterstock; p105 legenda/Shutterstock; p107 oneinchpunch/Shutterstock; p108 red mango/Shutterstock; p109 Courtesy of The Advertising Archives; p110 Hearst UK; pp113–114 Courtesy of Channel 4; p116 smile23/Shutterstock; p120 Chinnapong/Shutterstock; p121 ESB Professional/Shutterstock; p122 maxsaltana/Shutterstock; p125 (t) Everett Collection Inc/Alamy Stock Photo; p125 (2 b) Courtesy of Abbott Vision; p126 LANDMARK MEDIA/Alamy Stock Photo; p128 BBC DRAMA PRODUCTIONS/ Album/Alamy Stock Photo; p130 ©Netflix/courtesy Everett Collection/ Alamy Stock Photo; p134 (t) Album/Alamy Stock Photo; p134 (b) Parrish Lewis/©Amazon Studios/Channel 4/Courtesy: Everett Collection/Alamy Stock Photo; p137 SID GENTLE FILMS/Album/Alamy Stock Photo; p138 AJ Pics/Alamy Stock Photo; p140 © ITV/Courtesy: Everett Collection/ Alamy Stock Photo; p144 Landmark Media/Alamy Stock Photo; p148 (l) Photo 12/Alamy Stock Photo; p148 (r) Liam Daniel/©Netflix/Courtesy Everett Collection; p155 WENN Rights Ltd/Alamy Stock Photo; p161 (t) Retro AdArchives/Alamy Stock Photo; p161 (b) PackStock/Alamy Stock Photo; p162 (l & m) Courtesy of Future Publishing Ltd; p162 (r) Courtesy of Condé Nast; p165 DayOwl/Shutterstock; p166 (both) Lawrey/Shutterstock; p169 Courtesy of Future Publishing Ltd; p170 Courtesy of Future Publishing Ltd; p171 Courtesy of Future Publishing Ltd; p178 (t) I_B; p178 (bl) ESB Professional/Shutterstock;; p178 (br) Phase4Studios; p181 Anton_ Ivanov/Shutterstock.com; p182 Courtesy of Zoe Sugg; p183 Courtesy of Mark Ferris; p184 (l) Tom Rose/Shutterstock; p184 (r) Courtesy of Zoe Sugg; p186 Courtesy of Zoe Sugg; p187 Barry Paterson/Shutterstock. com; p188 dennizn//Shutterstock; p191 Courtesy of Zoe Sugg; p192 REUTERS/Alamy Stock Photo; p193 REUTERS/Alamy Stock Photo; p198 Antonio Guillem/Shutterstock; p199 aodaodaodaod/Shutterstock; p200 Erdark/Shutterstock; p203 (t) Vgstockstudio/Shutterstock; p203 (b) Sergey Furtaev/Shutterstock; p208 Chris Dorney/Shutterstock.com; p209 wavebreakmedia; p213 BRITISH BROADCASTING CORPORATION (bbc)/ Album/Alamy Stock Photo; p214 PictureLux/The Hollywood Archive/ Alamy Stock Photo; p216 (both) PictureLux/The Hollywood Archive/ Alamy Stock Photo; p218 (all) Courtesy of Abbott Vision; p223 domturner/ Shutterstock; p226 Cinematic Collection/Alamy Stock Photo; p227 AJ Pics/Alamy Stock Photo; p230 Courtesy of Studio Canal; pp234–236 Nathan James Tettey: www.nathanjamestettey.comp; 238 (t) pjs/ Shutterstock; p238 (b) welcomia/Shutterstock; p239 (b) AS photo studio; p242 Roobcio/Shutterstock; p244 bleakstar/Shutterstock; p245 EM Karuna/Shutterstock; p247 Entertainment Pictures/Alamy Stock Photo; p254 ESP Professional/Shutterstock; p255 Aysezgicmeli/Shutterstock